Gender, Work and Industrial Revolution Britain

Joyce Burnette

CAMBRIDGE
UNIVERSITY PRESS

CAMBRIDGE UNIVERSITY PRESS
Cambridge, New York, Melbourne, Madrid, Cape Town,
Singapore, São Paulo, Delhi, Tokyo, Mexico City

Cambridge University Press
The Edinburgh Building, Cambridge CB2 8RU, UK

Published in the United States of America by Cambridge University Press, New York

www.cambridge.org
Information on this title: www.cambridge.org/9780521312288

First published 2008
First paperback edition 2011

A catalogue record for this publication is available from the British Library

Library of Congress Cataloguing in Publication data

Burnette, Joyce.
   Gender, work and wages in industrial revolution Britain / Joyce Burnette.
     p. cm.
   Includes bibliographical references and index.
   ISBN 978-0-521-88063-3 (hardback : alk. paper)
  1. Women employees–Great Britain–History–19th century.
  2. Sex discrimination against women–Great Britain–History–19th century.
  3. Industrial revolution–Great Britain. I. Title.
HD6135.B87 2008
331.40941′09039–dc22
2007051670

ISBN 978-0-521-88063-3 Hardback
ISBN 978-0-521-31228-8 Paperback

Gender, Work and Wages in Industrial Revolution Britain

A major new study of the role of women in the labor market of Industrial Revolution Britain. It is well known that men and women usually worked in different occupations, and that women earned lower wages than men. These differences are usually attributed to custom but Joyce Burnette here demonstrates instead that gender differences in occupations and wages were largely driven by market forces. Her findings reveal that, rather than harming women, competition actually helped them by eroding the power that male workers needed to restrict female employment and by minimizing the gender wage gap by sorting women into the least strength-intensive occupations. Where the strength requirements of an occupation made women less productive than men, occupational segregation maximized both economic efficiency and female incomes. She shows that women's wages were then market rather than customary wages and that the gender wage gap resulted from actual differences in productivity.

JOYCE BURNETTE is Daniel F. Evans Associate Professor of Economics at Wabash College, Indiana.

Cambridge Studies in Economic History

Editorial Board

Paul Johnson
London School of Economics and Political Science

Sheilagh Ogilvie
University of Cambridge

Avner Offer
All Souls College, Oxford

Gianni Toniolo
Università di Roma 'Tor Vergata'

Gavin Wright
Stanford University

Cambridge Studies in Economic History comprises stimulating and accessible economic history which actively builds bridges to other disciplines. Books in the series will illuminate why the issues they address are important and interesting, place their findings in a comparative context, and relate their research to wider debates and controversies. The series will combine innovative and exciting new research by younger researchers with new approaches to major issues by senior scholars. It will publish distinguished work regardless of chronological period or geographical location.

Titles in the series include:

Robert Millward *Private and Public Enterprise in Europe: Energy, Telecommunications and Transport, 1830–1990*

S. D. Smith *Slavery, Family, and Gentry Capitalism in the British Atlantic: The World of the Lascelles, 1648–1834*

Stephen Broadberry *Market Services and the Productivity Race, 1850–2000: British Performance in International Perspective.*

Contents

Figures

Tables

Preface

Once upon a time women were largely missing from economic history. Economic historians somehow managed to make claims about the standard of living without examining women's wages. Happily, that has now changed, thanks to the efforts of pioneering feminists who made the case for the importance of including women in economic history. Since the value of studying women as well as men is now well established, I do not feel a need to justify the existence of this book. The subject matter is contentious, but it is my hope that the book will stimulate, not an all-or-nothing debate about the existence of gender discrimination, but a nuanced discussion of where, when, and how gender discrimination may have operated, and of the relationship between discrimination and markets.

This book began fifteen years ago as a PhD dissertation at Northwestern University. The origin of the project was a paper I wrote for Joel Mokyr's European Economic History class on the correlation between male and female wages in the "Rural Queries" of 1833. This paper got me thinking about how the labor market treated women, a process which eventually led to the ideas expressed here. I am grateful for the input of Joel Mokyr, my dissertation advisor, and Rebecca Blank and Bruce Meyer, the labor economists on my committee. A grant from the Mellon Foundation supported a year of dissertation research, and a Northwestern University Dissertation Year Grant supported the purchase of microfilm from the archives.

After receiving my PhD, I published parts of my research as articles, but otherwise put the dissertation aside while I concentrated on collecting data from farm accounts. I continued to think about the issues raised in this book, but did not begin to revise it until my sabbatical in 2002–3. I spent that academic year as a visitor at the London School of Economics, supported partly by Wabash College and partly by a Sabbatical Fellowship from the American Philosophical Society. Most of the revisions to the manuscript were accomplished in the spring of 2005, during a one-semester leave funded by a grant from the National Science Foundation (Grant no. 0213954). Any opinions, findings, and conclusions or recommendations expressed in this book are those of the author and do not necessarily reflect the views of the National Science Foundation. I thank Dan Newlon for working with someone who didn't understand the grant process very well.

I am thankful for the many comments I have received from colleagues when I have presented portions of the material. Colleagues who have been especially helpful are Greg Clark, Jane Humphries, and Andrew Seltzer, who have commented on my work multiple times over many years. I am especially grateful for critics of my work who have forced me to think more carefully about specific claims. I thank James Henderson for teaching me to love economics as an undergraduate at Valparaiso University. Last but not least, I am thankful for the support of my husband Patrick, both for helping me with my prose, and for running the household when I was doing other things.

Introduction

Early in the morning of Friday, January 28, 1820, a night watchman at the Broomward Cotton Mill in Glasgow discovered a fire in the carding room. He:

gave the alarm, and, on going to the spot, found that some Person or Persons had, by getting up on a tree opposite to, and within three feet of the east side of the Mill, thrown in, through the opening pane of one of the windows, a Paper Bundle or Package, filled with Pitch and Gunpowder, and dipped in Oil, which had exploded, and set Fire to a Basket full of loose Cotton, which communicated to one of the Carding Engines, and which, unless it had instantly and providentially been discovered and got under, must have consumed the whole Building.[1]

James Dunlop, the owner of the mill, was probably not surprised. The motives of the arsonists were no mystery. On January 31 the *Glasgow Herald* reported:

This fire, there is good ground to believe, has been occasioned by a gang of miscreants who, for some time past, have waylaid, and repeatedly assaulted and severely wounded, the persons employed at the Broomward Cotton Mill, who are all women, with the view of putting the mill to a stand, and throwing the workers out of employment.[2]

A few years later twenty-five mill owners from Glasgow petitioned the Home Secretary Robert Peel to extend the anti-union Combination Laws to Scotland. Their petition describes this case in more detail.

Messrs James Dunlop and Sons, some years ago, erected cotton mills in Calton of Glasgow, on which they expended upwards of 27,000l. forming their spinning machines (chiefly with the view of ridding themselves of the combination) of such reduced size as could easily be wrought by women. They employed women alone, as not being parties to the combination, and thus more easily managed, and less insubordinate than male spinners. These they paid at the same rate of wages, as were paid at other works to men. But they were waylaid and attacked, in going to, and returning from their work; the houses in which they resided,

---

[1] *The Glasgow Herald*, Monday, January 31, 1820, p. 3, col. 2. [2] *Ibid.*, p. 2, col. 4.

were broken open in the night. The women themselves were cruelly beaten and abused; and the mother of one of them killed; in fine, the works were set on fire in the night, by combustibles thrown into them from without; and the flames were with difficulty extinguished; only in consequence of the exertions of the body of watchmen, employed by the proprietors, for their protection. And these nefarious attempts were persevered in so systematically, and so long, that Messrs. Dunlop and Sons, found it necessary to dismiss all female spinners from their works, and to employ only male spinners, most probably the very men who had attempted their ruin.[3]

The women spinners employed by Dunlop lost their jobs as a direct result of the male workers' opposition.

The attempt to burn Dunlop's mill was just one battle in a war between the cotton spinners' union and their employers. Other mills were attacked, and one employer was even shot at in the doorway of his father-in-law's house on his wedding night.[4] The dispute included, among other points, an objection to the employment of women. On November 27, 1822, Patrick McNaught, manager of the Anderston Cotton Mill in Glasgow, received the following note from the spinners' union, which emphasized the employment of women:

Sir,
I am authorized to intimate jeoperdy and hazardious prediciment you stand in at the present time, by the operative cotton spinners, and lower class of mankind, in and about Glasgow, by keeping them weomen officiating in mens places as cotton spinners, and plenty of men going idle out of employ, which would I accept of them for the same price omiting the list which you know is triffling. So they present this proposal as the last, in corresponding terms, so from this date they give you a fortnight to consider the alternative, whether to accept the first or the latter, which will be assassination of body; which you may relie upon no other thing after the specified time is run, for you will be watched and dogged by night and by day, till their ends are accomplished; for you well deserve the torturings death that man could invent, being so obstinate, more so than any other master round the town, and seeing poor men going about the street, with familys starving, and keeping a set of whores, as I may call them, spending their money, drinking with young fellows, and keeping them up. So mark this warning well, and do not vaunt over it like you foolish neighbour, Mr. Simpson, in Calton, with his, for he was soon brought to the test, and you will be the same with murder.[5]

The writer of this note, identified only as "Bloodthirst void of fear," draws on gender ideology to create a sense of outrage. He calls the women whores for the offenses of "spending their money" and "drinking with young fellows," activities which do not seem to us worthy of condemnation

---

[3] *Fifth Report from the Select Committee on Artizans and Machinery*, BPP 1824 (51) V, p. 525.
[4] *Ibid.*, p. 527.   [5] *Ibid.*, p. 531.

but clearly fall outside what the writer considers to be proper feminine behavior. One suspects, though, that the real reason for the opposition to female employment is that the women are working "in men's places." If women were employed, men would be unemployed, or at least would have to work for lower wages. Employers were somehow immune to these concerns about proper feminine behavior, and actively sought to hire women because they could benefit economically from doing so. It was the male workers, who would lose economically from their employment, who expressed such concerns about proper female behavior. Thus a man's opinions on whether women should work in the factory seem to have been determined by whether he would win or lose economically from the employment of women. The union's grievances were not directed only at women spinners, but also at other forms of competition; the employment of male workers not approved by the union was also violently opposed. The violence was economic warfare, aimed at protecting the spinners' wages and working conditions. The actions of the Glasgow mule spinners are just one example of barriers to women's employment that were erected because of economic motivations; men excluded women to reduce competition and raise their own wages.

In the late eighteenth and early nineteenth centuries women and men generally did not work at the same jobs, and they did not receive the same wages. These differences are widely known, and the most common explanation is that they resulted from discrimination or gender ideology. This book will argue that economic motivations explain the patterns we observe. In some cases, the occupational sorting was required for economic efficiency. Since strength was a scarce resource, the market paid a premium for it. In other cases occupational sorting was the result of a powerful group seeking to limit women's opportunities in order to improve its own economic position, at the expense of women, and at the expense of economic efficiency. The case of the Glasgow cotton spinners illustrates the second case. Women were excluded from the highly paid occupation of cotton spinning, not because they were incapable of doing the job, or because employers refused to hire them, or because social disapproval, combined with violence, kept them at home, but because the male cotton spinners' union was effective in excluding them, thus reducing the supply and increasing the equilibrium wage of cotton spinners.

In seeking to understand the causes of gender differences in wages and occupations, this book will focus on actuality rather than ideology. I am mainly interested in what work women actually did, rather than how people thought or spoke about this work. Both ideology and actuality are important topics of study, and one may influence the other, but we must not confuse the two. Many researchers are primarily interested in the ideology of the period. For example, Davidoff and Hall note, "The suitability of field work, indeed any outdoor work for women, was almost always discussed in moral terms."[6] This statement provides some insight into how people in the Industrial Revolution *discussed* women's work. By contrast, I am primarily interested in what people *did*. Which jobs did women do, and what were they paid?

We can ask two related but different questions about women's work: "What did people think women should do?" and "What work did women actually do?" What people *say* does not always match what they actually do, so evidence on the first question will not answer the second question. While social expectations influence behavior, they are not the whole story. People have an amazing ability to say one thing and do another, particularly when they can benefit from doing so. Nineteenth-century employers could hire married women at the same time they claimed to be opposed to the employment of married women. For example, in 1876 Frederick Carver, the owner of a lace warehouse, told a parliamentary committee: "we have as a rule an objection to employing married women, because we think that every man ought to maintain his wife without the necessity of her going to work." However, he seems to have been willing to break this rule without too much difficulty. Carver admitted that "As to married women, in one particular department of our establishment we have forty-nine married women and we wish that the present state of things as regards married women should not be disturbed."[7] Because preconceived notions of women's work and actual employment often conflicted, we must make a clear distinction between the two when trying to analyze women's employment opportunities.

Amanda Vickery has warned us against taking Victorian ideology at face value. She asks:

Did the sermonizers have any personal experience of marriage? Did men and women actually conform to prescribed models of authority? Did prescriptive literature contain more than one ideological message? Did women deploy the rhetoric of submission selectively, with irony, or quite critically? ... Just because a volume of domestic advice sat on a woman's desk, it does not follow that she took its strictures to heart or whatever her intentions managed to live her life according to its precepts.[8]

---

[6] Leonore Davidoff and Catherine Hall, *Family Fortunes: Men and Women of the English Middle Class, 1780–1850* (Chicago: University of Chicago Press, 1987), p. 274.
[7] BPP 1876, XIX, p. 258, quoted in Sonya Rose, *Limited Livelihoods: Gender and Class in Nineteenth-Century England* (Berkeley: University of California Press, 1992), p. 32.
[8] Amanda Vickery, "Golden Age to Separate Spheres? A Review of the Categories and Chronology of English Women's History," *Historical Journal* 36 (1993), pp. 385, 391.

This study will heed Vickery's warning, and will not assume that statements of gender ideology are evidence of how employers actually made economic decisions. The fact that some jobs were labeled "men's work" is not proof that women were excluded because the gender label attached to a job and the sex of the person who filled the job did not necessarily match. An 1833 parliamentary investigation finds that "In the Northern Counties, the Women engage in Men's work much more than in the Southern Districts."[9] While there was a clear category of jobs designated "men's work," it was not true that men always filled those jobs.

Of course, customary expectations often did accurately describe the gender division of labor. Michael Roberts has suggested that the debate between custom and market is not productive because the two are compatible.[10] It is true that market efficiency and custom usually prescribed the same outcomes, and I believe that this was no accident, but the result of the close relationship between the two. In theory the relationship between custom and market could run in either direction. Custom could determine the work that people did, or the work that people did could determine which customs would emerge, or both. Most historians believe that custom shaped economic outcomes. Some believe that economic outcomes shaped custom. Heidi Hartmann, for example, claims that women's low social status has its roots in the gender division of labor and can only be ended by ending occupational segregation.[11] I believe that economic outcomes matched custom so closely because custom was created to explain and justify the existing patterns of work and pay. In some cases the gender division of labor resulted from economic forces that promoted the most efficient outcome. However, since most people did not understand those economic forces, they relied on gender ideology to explain the patterns they observed. In other cases the gender division of labor was not efficient but benefited a particular group; in these cases the group benefiting from occupational segregation created and used gender ideology to promote their own economic interests.

By emphasizing the economic motivations for gender differences, I am providing a materialist explanation for the gender division of labor. This is meant to be an alternative to the prevailing ideological explanation, which gives priority to ideas about gender roles. I do believe that such

---

[9] BPP 1834 (44) XXX, Whitburn, Durham, p. 169.
[10] Michael Roberts, "Sickles and Scythes Revisited: Harvest Work, Wages and Symbolic Meanings," in P. Lane, N. Raven, and K. D. M. Snell, eds., *Women, Work and Wages in England, 1600–1850* (Woodbridge: Boydell Press, 2004), p. 89.
[11] Heidi Hartmann, "Capitalism, Patriarchy, and Job Segregation by Sex," *Signs* 1 (1976), pp. 137–69.

ideologies were present, but I don't think they were the driving cause of the differences we observe. Distributional coalitions could take advantage of such ideologies, and even expand them, in order to justify their inefficient policies. The Glasgow cotton spinners called the women spinners whores, not because they were driven by a concern for sexual purity, but because, by generating outrage, they could increase public support for their campaign to remove the women from their jobs. The question is not whether gender ideology existed, but whether it was the engine driving the train or just the caboose. Most research on the subject makes ideology the engine; I think it was the caboose.[12]

Even if patterns of work and pay were determined by economic forces, that does not mean that people understood them that way. Customary explanations are created partly because people do not understand economic forces. During the Industrial Revolution sudden changes in technology caused custom and the market to diverge, creating discomfort for the people involved when new realities did not match the customary explanations that had been created for a different reality. We can see an example of this discomfort in a passage by Friedrich Engels describing the husband of a factory worker:

[a] working-man, being on tramp, came to St. Helens, in Lancashire, and there looked up an old friend. He found him in a miserable, damp cellar, scarcely furnished; and when my poor friend went in, there sat Jack near the fire, and what did he, think you? why he sat and mended his wife's stockings with the bodkin; as soon as he saw his old friend at the door-post, he tried to hide them. But Joe, that is my friend's name, had seen it, and said: "Jack, what the devil art thou doing? Where is the missus? Why, is that thy work?" and poor Jack was ashamed and said: "No, I know that this is not my work, but my poor missus is i' th' factory; she has to leave at half-past five and works till eight at night, and then she is so knocked up that she cannot do aught when she gets home, so I have to do everything for her what I can, for I have no work, nor had any for more nor three years ... There is work enough for women folks and childer hereabouts, but none for men; thou mayest sooner find a hundred pound in the road than work for men ... when I got married I had work plenty ... and Mary need not go out to work. I could work for the two of us; but now the world is upside down. Mary has to work and I have to stop at home, mind the childer, sweep and wash, bake and mend." ... And then Jack began to cry again, and he wished he had never married.[13]

Both gender ideology and market forces were very real for Jack. Gender ideology told him that he should earn the income while his wife worked

---

[12] For an alternative view, see Rose, *Limited Livelihoods*, pp. 12–13.
[13] Frederick Engels, *Condition of the Working Class in England in 1844* (London: George Allen and Unwin, [1845] 1926), pp. 145–6.

in the home, and the fact that this ideology did not match his situation made him miserable. Market forces, however, determined the actual pattern of work; his wife worked at the factory while Jack worked in the home.

Many studies of women's work have chosen to focus on ideology, on how people thought and talked about women workers.[14] This focus may arise from an interest in ideology for its own sake, or from a belief that ideology drives action, that what people actually do is determined by the categories of how they think. My focus on actuality comes from a belief that the chain of causation more often runs the other way, that actuality drives ideology. Economic actors respond to economic incentives, and use ideology as a cover for their naked self-interest.

The relative strength of ideological and economic motivations is best seen when the two conflict. Humphries has suggested that occupational segregation was supported because concerns about sexuality required keeping the sexes apart.[15] In spite of this concern, however, men were admitted to the intimate setting of childbirth. Though midwifery had historically been a female activity, men began to enter the profession as man-midwives in the seventeenth century. By the nineteenth century male physicians were favored as birth attendants in spite of the Victorians' prudishness that considered it "indelicate" for a father to be present at the birth of his own child.[16] Men who otherwise would consider it dangerous to allow men and women to work together hired men to attend at the births of their children. The medical profession deflected any concerns about indelicacy by stressing male skill and supposed female incompetence. Where male jobs were at stake, impropriety did not seem to be a problem.

The existence of gender ideology sometimes makes it more difficult to discover the actuality of what work women did. Unfortunately, the ideologies that were present affected the accuracy of the historical records. Because a woman's social status was determined by her relationship to men, the census does not accurately describe the work women did. Many working women were not listed as having any occupation. The 1841 census instructed enumerators to ignore the occupations of a large fraction of women; its instructions state, "The professions &c. of wives, or of sons or daughters living with and assisting

---

[14] For example, see Deborah Simonton, *A History of European Women's Work* (London: Routledge, 1988) and Pamela Sharpe, "Commentary," in P. Sharpe, ed., *Women's Work: The English Experience 1650–1914* (London: Arnold, 1998), pp. 71–2.

[15] Jane Humphries, "'... The Most Free from Objection ...' The Sexual Division of Labor and Women's Work in Nineteenth-Century England," *Journal of Economic History* 47 (1987), pp. 929–50.

[16] Jean Donnison, *Midwives and Medical Men* (London: Historical Publications, 1988), p. 64.

their parents but not apprenticed or receiving wages, need not be inserted."[17] In practice, census enumerators seem to have ignored women's employment even when they were receiving wages; Miller and Verdon have both found examples of women who were paid wages for agricultural labor but had no occupation listed in the census.[18] Whether an occupation was categorized as "skilled" was also socially determined. Bridget Hill found that census officials were unwilling to categorize occupations employing women and children as skilled.

Albe Edwards, the man responsible for the reclassification, met with a problem when he found certain occupations which technically were classified as "skilled" had to be down-graded to "semi-skilled," "because the enumerators returned so many children, young persons, and women as pursuing these occupations." Edwards did not hesitate to lower the status of certain occupations when he found women and young people worked in them in large numbers.[19]

In this case the categorization of occupations as skilled or semi-skilled reflects ideology rather than characteristics of the job.

The ability of ideology to alter the historical record is not limited to the nineteenth century. Sanderson finds that in Edinburgh women were actively involved in many skilled occupations, and that historians have devalued their contributions by assuming that women's occupations were "merely extensions of domestic skills" or by failing to recognize that women's occupations were skilled occupations. The most telling example of such devaluation of women's work is from:

the entry in the printed Marriage Register for eighteenth-century Edinburgh where the advocate John Polson is recorded as married to "Ann Strachan, merchant (sic)". The fact is that Ann Strachan was a merchant, but the modern editor, because he assumed that an advocate was unlikely to have a working wife, recorded this as an error. In a Commissary Court process it was stated during evidence on behalf of the defender, that Polson had married Ann Strachan, the defender's sister-in-law, "who at that time had a great business and served the highest in the land."[20]

We must avoid making the same mistake as the editor of the marriage register, who took the gender ideology so seriously that he assumed Ann

[17] Quoted in Edward Higgs, *Making Sense of the Census* (London: HMSO, 1989), p. 81.

[18] C. Miller, "The Hidden Workforce: Female Fieldworkers in Gloucestershire, 1870–1901," *Southern History* 6 (1984), 139–61, and Nicola Verdon, *Rural Women Workers in Nineteenth-Century England: Gender, Work and Wages* (Woodbridge: Boydell Press, 2002), pp. 117–19.

[19] Bridget Hill, "Women, Work and the Census: A Problem for Historians of Women," *History Workshop Journal* 35 (1993), p. 90.

[20] Elizabeth Sanderson, *Women and Work in Eighteenth-Century Edinburgh* (New York: St. Martin's Press, 1996), p. 105.

Strachan's occupational title must be a mistake. If Ann Strachan the merchant disappears from history, we have lost any hope of discovering the true place of women in the economy. Because what people *said* about work is liable to be filtered through the lens of ideology, I will try wherever possible to use other types of evidence, such as statistical evidence, to determine what people actually did.

Part of this book will be devoted to documenting the gender differences in wages and occupations. However, the main question I wish to address is not whether differences occurred, but *why* they occurred. What caused the gender differences in wages and occupations that we observe? The question is not new, and many answers have been offered. The most common explanation for gender differences in the labor market is ideology: social institutions enforced socially determined gender roles, and women were confined to low-paid and low-status work. These social constraints could operate even if people were not aware of them.[21] Differences between the genders were socially constructed. Both the gender division of labor and women's lower wages were determined by gender ideology. For example, Deborah Simonton claims that "customary practices and ideas about gender and appropriate roles were instrumental in delineating tasks as male work and female work."[22] Sonya Rose focuses on the expectation that women were not supporting a family, and therefore did not need to be paid as much as a man; she claims that "Women were workers who could be paid low wages because of an ideology which portrayed them as supplementary wage earners dependent on men for subsistence."[23]

The ideological explanation of gender differences has some strengths. People did express ideas about femininity and masculinity that implied women should do certain jobs, and men others. We can observe these ideas being expressed. And we have seen abrupt changes in the gender division of labor that suggest artificial barriers existed in the past. If the percentage of law degrees earned by women increased from 5 percent in 1970 to 30 percent just ten years later, this suggests that women were eager to become lawyers, and some barrier besides interest or inclination kept the number of female lawyers low in 1970.[24] Surely gender ideology

---

[21] Sonya Rose notes that "Social actors often are unaware that these assumptions are guiding their activities." *Limited Livelihoods*, p. 13.

[22] Simonton, *European Women's Work*, p. 35

[23] Sonya Rose, "'Gender at Work': Sex, Class and Industrial Capitalism," *History Workshop Journal*, 21 (1986), p. 117.

[24] The percentage of law degrees earned by women continued to rise, reaching 42 percent in 1990 and 47 percent in 2001. US Census Bureau, *Statistical Abstract of the United States: 2003* (Washington, DC: Government Printing Office, 2003), p. 194.

played some part in the Church of England's prohibition on the ordination of women, which lasted until 1994. However, while I do think that gender ideology is part of the story, in this book it will be cast as a supporting character rather than as the protagonist.

At the other extreme, Kingsley Browne has embraced biological difference as an explanation for all differences in labor market outcomes between men and women.[25] Evolution, through sexual selection, created differences between men and women. Women, who can have only a few offspring, developed characteristics that led them to nurture these offspring, maximizing the chances of survival. Men, who can father a nearly unlimited number of children, developed strategies for winning competitions that would allow them to have access to more females. Scientific studies have shown that the sex hormones cause differences in aggressiveness, risk-taking, and nurturing behaviors. Kingsley Browne has argued that these differences between the sexes explain why men are more successful in the labor market than women. Men take more risks, are more aggressive, and choose to spend less time with their families. He argues that these are biological traits, against which it is futile to fight, and that they cause the observed differences in wages and occupations.

Even if Browne is right that evolution gives men a more competitive character, his explanation provides at best part of the story. His main focus is the "glass ceiling," the gap in success at the highest levels. He claims that men are more competitive and take more risks, and therefore are more likely to reach the top. However, this explanation doesn't tell us why there is so much occupational segregation farther down the occupational ladder. Also, Browne's explanation cannot account for sudden changes in the occupational structure. If there was something in the female character, created by evolutionary sexual selection, that made women reluctant to be lawyers, the number of women entering law would not have changed so radically in the space of a couple of decades.

Happily, we have recently seen a few authors who neither assume men and women must be biologically identical because they wish it to be so, nor suggest that biological differences make any attempts to change the status quo futile. Steven Pinker notes the emergence of a new left that acknowledges both human nature and the possibility of improving our social institutions.[26] In his chapter on gender differences, Pinker acknowledges biological differences that might lead men and women to choose

---

[25] Kingsley Browne, *Divided Labours: An Evolutionary View of Women at Work* (New Haven: Yale University Press, 1999).

[26] Steven Pinker, *The Blank Slate: The Modern Denial of Human Nature* (New York: Penguin Books, 2003), pp. 299–300.

different occupations, but also acknowledges the existence of gender discrimination.[27] Acknowledging differences does not imply that one sex is better than the other or must dominate over the other. Leonard Sax notes that

The bottom line is that the brain is just organized *differently* in females and males. The tired argument about which sex is more intelligent or which sex has the "better" brain is about as meaningful as arguing about which utensil is "better," a knife or a spoon. The only correct answer to such a question is: "Better for what?"[28]

Sax suggests that the outcomes are more likely to be equal if we admit gender differences than if we don't.

[Y]ou can teach the same math course in different ways. You can make math appealing to girls by teaching it one way, or you can make it appealing to boys by teaching it in another way. Girls and boys can both learn math equally well if you understand those gender differences.[29]

However, ignoring gender differences and teaching math only one way is likely to disadvantage one gender. Differences between the sexes are important and must be acknowledged if we are to understand our world and work to improve it.

There are also economic historians who allow biology to have a role in shaping economic activity, without admitting it the power to determine every observed difference. Some historians allow strength to have a role in determining the sexual division of labor. Judy Gielgud notes that "there are understandable reasons for a wage differential. For example, a man's strength might enable him to accomplish more of a given task than could a woman in the same time, where both were working at full stretch."[30] Merry Wiesner claims that the gender division of labor in agriculture in the early modern period was partly, though not completely, due to differences in physical strength, "with men generally doing tasks that required a great deal of upper-body strength, such as cutting grain with a scythe."[31] Mary Friefeld's story about the male domination of mule-spinning points to the male union as the factor excluding women after 1834, but acknowledges strength as the excluding

[27] *Ibid.*, pp. 354–7.
[28] Leonard Sax, *Why Gender Matters: What Parents and Teachers Need To Know about the Emerging Science of Sex Differences* (New York: Broadway Books, 2005), p. 32.
[29] *Ibid.*, p. 33
[30] Judy Gielgud, "Nineteenth Century Farm Women in Northumberland and Cumbria: The Neglected Workforce," unpublished PhD thesis, University of Sussex, 1992, p. 85.
[31] Merry Wiesner, *Women and Gender in Early Modern Europe*, 2nd edn (Cambridge: Cambridge University Press, 2000), p. 106.

factor in the early period. Pamela Sharpe admits a role for strength in the occupation of wool-combing.[32] Other historians have noted the effect of women's role in child-bearing on their work opportunities. Brenner and Ramas, for example, note that "[b]iological facts of reproduction – pregnancy, childbirth, lactation – are not readily compatible with capitalist production," so that as factories replaced home production women were marginalized.[33] These explanations all allow biology an important role, without making the current division of labor the only one biologically possible.

This book is also located between the extremes; it neither refuses to acknowledge biological differences, nor sees observed gender differences as completely determined by biology. I believe the importance of biological differences must be acknowledged if we are to have any hope of understanding the gender division of labor, but I do not attempt to ascribe all differences to biology. There is exclusion in this story, but it's not the whole story. We don't have to deny the importance of biological differences, or minimize their importance in the labor market, but neither do we have to accept all observed differences as the inevitable result of our evolutionary heritage.

Men and women are different in ways that affect their productivity, so we must not assume that differences in wages and occupations are necessarily due to discrimination. If we accept even the least controversial differences between men and women, much of the difference in wages is explained. The biological differences that I focus on are the least controversial. Kingsley Browne has argued that gender differences in personality, created by the evolutionary process of sexual selection, explain the differential success of men and women, but it may be difficult to say whether traits such as competitiveness are determined by biology or by culture. My argument does not rely on differences in cognition or personality, and requires only two differences between the sexes, neither of which is controversial. First, men are stronger than women, and second, women give birth and breast-feed their infants, while men do not. These two differences are sufficient to explain much of the occupational segregation and gender wage gap that we observe in Industrial Revolution Britain. While I do suggest that in many cases the gender gap in wages was the result of biological differences between men and women, that does not mean that I oppose attempts to reduce the

---

[32] Pamela Sharpe, *Adapting to Capitalism: Working Women in the English Economy, 1700–1850* (London: Macmillan, 1996), p. 24. She notes that both strength and guild restrictions kept this occupation male.

[33] Johanna Brenner and Maria Ramas, "Rethinking Women's Oppression," *New Left Review* 144 (1984), pp. 33–71.

gender gap. Referring to the assumption that biological explanations of the gender gap must support the status quo, Steven Pinker points out that, "This makes about as much sense as saying that a scientist who studies why women live longer than men 'wants old men to die'."[34]

While I take biology seriously, I don't think it can be the whole story. I differ from Kingsley Browne in not accepting that all differences in labor market outcomes are simply the result of biology, and therefore good. I am skeptical of claims that women will never choose career over family, especially when I see so many women doing so today. Kingsley Browne claims, rather broadly, that

Women care less about climbing hierarchies and about objective forms of recognition such as money, status, and power than men. They place more importance on a high level of involvement with their children. These conclusions are consistent with evolutionary theory, biological fact, and psychological data. It is simply the case that women tend to fit work to families, while men fit families to work.[35]

However, this statement clearly does not describe all women. I read the following in the *Guardian*: "I always expected to regret not having children ... So it comes as something of a surprise to discover that now, in my 40s, I do not regret that I never gave birth ... Instead, I feel more liberated than I could ever have imagined."[36] It could be that the columnist, Laura Marcus, is an unusual case, but it could also be that Browne has overestimated the role of evolutionary biology in determining women's choices.

The main conclusion of this book is that economic motivations caused the gender differences we observe in the labor market of Industrial Revolution Britain. In some cases these economic forces were beneficial, and in other cases they were harmful, but in either case both women and the economy in general would have benefited from more competitive markets. In the relatively competitive sectors of the labor market, strength was an important input in production, and men's higher wages represent the premium paid for strength. In order to economize on the scarce resource of strength, men were sorted into occupations requiring more strength, and women into occupations requiring less strength. Economic motivations led employers to hire men for jobs requiring strength, and hire women for jobs requiring less strength. When technology changed, the gender division of labor changed too, always allocating men to the more strength-intensive jobs. Employers were not

[34] Pinker, *The Blank Slate*, p. 353.   [35] Browne, *Divided Labours*, p. 53
[36] Laura Marcus, "The Joys of Childlessness," *The Guardian* August 22, 2002, p. 18.

constrained by gender roles, but switched between men and women workers when prices signaled that they should. While these forces did result in gender differences in wages and occupations, they were beneficial in the sense of improving the efficiency of the economy, and in the sense that they minimized the gender wage gap. Women's role in child-bearing reduced the time women had available for market work, and probably encouraged them to remain in the low-wage cottage industry sector, but overall child-bearing was probably not as important as strength in determining women's productivity.

Unfortunately, economic motivations were not always beneficial. The desire for gain sometimes leads groups with economic power to alter the market to favor themselves at the expense of others. Mancur Olson called such groups distributional coalitions.[37] While such groups take many forms, common forms are unions and professional organizations. These organizations often attempt to limit the supply of their services and thus raise their own wages. One way that occupational groups tried to limit labor supply was by excluding women from the occupation. While those in the occupation would benefit from high wages, society as a whole would suffer a loss of efficiency, and women would be harmed by having their occupational choices restricted. Heidi Hartmann has also argued that women were excluded from certain occupations because men wanted to protect their own economic interest.[38] Hartmann adds that men wanted not only to maintain their own high wages, but also to protect their own power within the family by ensuring that women remained dependent. I agree with Hartmann, and will argue that most of the real discriminatory constraints that women faced were restrictions put in place by men who were trying to protect their own economic position. Of course, not every group of men was able to enforce restrictions against women. Only those occupations with some source of market power, such as possession of a specialized skill, were successful in excluding women.

I offer different explanations for different parts of the labor market, but the explanations have a common strain: the importance of economic self-interest. I do not believe that self-interest is always good. In fact, one half of my story illustrates how self-interest could be harmful to both women and the economy. Self-interest is beneficial if disciplined by competition, but most economic actors would prefer to take the easier

---

[37] Mancur Olson, *The Rise and Decline of Nations: Economic Growth, Stagflation, and Social Rigidities* (New Haven: Yale University Press: 1982).
[38] Hartmann, "Capitalism, Patriarchy, and Job Segregation." See also Cynthia Cockburn, *Brothers: Male Dominance and Technological Change*, 2nd edn (London: Pluto Press, 1991), pp. 34–5.

route of monopoly and, if allowed, will use their power to benefit themselves at the expense of others. Competition was the most powerful force protecting women's opportunities, and barriers to women's employment appeared where competition was weakest. In competitive labor markets, market forces led to occupational sorting, but this sorting benefited women because it minimized the economic costs of their lesser strength. The main source of barriers to women's employment was groups of men, or "distributional coalitions" to use Mancur Olson's term, who wished to monopolize an occupation to raise their own wages. Where competition was strong these rules were ineffective; only where competition was limited would unions and professional organizations effectively bar women from employment. If there had been more competition, women would have been able to work in a wider variety of occupations, and would have had opportunities to earn higher wages.

In Industrial Revolution Britain men and women tended to work in different occupations, and received different wages. This book explores the reasons for those differences. I conclude that gender ideology played a supporting role, but was not the driving force behind most of the occupational segregation or wage gaps. Gender ideology had the most influence in institutions that did not have to compete to survive, such as the family and the government. Comparative advantage and productivity differences determined the division of labor and wages in the most competitive sectors of the labor market. In other sectors, where one group was able to amass enough economic power to stifle competition, men erected barriers to the employment of women in order to reduce the competition for their jobs. These men used gender ideology to increase public support for the entry barriers they erected, but their primary motivations were economic.

1   Women's occupations

Before we can discuss the causes of occupational segregation, we must first have an accurate understanding of what work women did. While this may seem to be a simple task, it presents some challenges to the historian. Measures of occupational distribution are less than perfect, and occupational patterns were changing rapidly during the Industrial Revolution. Census data on individuals begins only in 1841, and when it does exist it is not an accurate measure of women's employment. This leaves us without any aggregate measures of employment, so a glance at the statistical abstract will not suffice; instead, we must build a picture of women's employment from numerous incomplete sources. This chapter will examine the evidence and determine what work women did during the Industrial Revolution. Section I will discuss the limited statistical evidence available on the pattern of occupational sorting by gender, and Section II will examine the anecdotal evidence on women's occupations. Though the evidence is neither comprehensive nor perfectly reliable, it is clear that men and women tended to work in different occupations. However, it is also clear that the sorting was not perfect, and that women were frequently found in occupations not generally considered to be "women's work."

When examining women's employment, we must keep in mind that many of women's productive contributions remain invisible to the historian. Women at all levels of the labor market assisted their husbands but received no official recognition for their productive contributions. Frequently a marriage was also a business partnership, sometimes explicitly. An advertisement in the *Dorset County Chronicle* specified, "Wanted, A Man and his Wife, to manage a Dairy of Sixteen Cows."[1] In the parish workhouses, which separated all inmates by sex, the master took charge over the male inmates and the matron over the female inmates. The workhouse of Melton, Suffolk, paid a salary of £50 a year

---

[1] *Dorset County Chronicle*, December, 1860, quoted in Pamela Horn, "The Dorset Dairy System," *Agricultural History Review* 26 (1978), p. 100.

to the "governor and his wife."[2] In this case, a married couple shared these responsibilities and received a joint salary. We do not know how often the salary was simply given to the husband, with the understanding that the wife would contribute her services too. In many cases where a husband and wife worked as partners, the contribution of the wife was not officially acknowledged. One eighteenth-century observer noted a farmer who was assisted by his wife: "a large occupier of £17,000 a year, who was able to manage without a steward or bailiff, because he had the assistance of 'his lady, who keeps his accounts'."[3] A farmer's wife was frequently his business partner, taking over the management of the dairy and the poultry. Wool manufacture was also a family business; Joseph Coope, a Yorkshire clothier, noted that he had a servant and two apprentices, "which is the whole I employ, except my wife and myself."[4] We have enough evidence of this type to confirm that many wives worked with their husbands. In cottage industry the value of the output, such as a piece of cloth woven, was often counted as the man's earnings, even though much of the work was actually done by his wife or children. Unfortunately, we do not have the means to measure the extent of this work. In most cases the contribution of the wife to the family business went unnoticed and unrecorded.

I.   Measuring occupational segregation

The first problem I will address is how to measure occupational sorting. The statistical evidence is unfortunately inadequate; the only aggregate data on employment comes from the census, which does not list occupations of individuals before 1841. Even at this late date, the census systematically underrecords female employment. Left without a comprehensive measure of employment, I use other measures to establish occupational sorting by gender. First, I show that the percentage of women employed varied greatly by industry. Then I use commercial directories to measure occupational segregation for a specific segment of the labor market – business owners. Both of these measures confirm that men and women tended to work in different occupations.

---

[2] F. M. Eden, *State of the Poor* (London: Davis, 1797), vol. II, p. 687. In other cases, married couples working as governor and governess received separate salaries. It was fairly common, however, to give one salary to a husband and wife team. John Moss and his wife received £50 a year to be master and mistress of the Preston workhouse. BPP 1816 (397) III, p. 181.

[3] Ivy Pinchbeck, *Women Workers and the Industrial Revolution 1750–1850* (London: Routledge, 1930), p. 8. The observer was Marshall, *Rural Economy of Norfolk, 1782*.

[4] BPP 1806 (268) III, p. 31.

A.   The census

The census is usually the first place a historian looks for information on employment patterns because it provides the only complete measures of employment in the entire economy. Table 1.1 shows the occupational distribution from both the 1841 and 1851 censuses. These numbers suggest low rates of female labor force participation: in the 1841 census only 25 percent of females over age 10 had an occupation, and in the 1851 census only 35 percent. Women who did work were heavily concentrated in a few occupations. Three categories – domestic services, textiles, and clothing – accounted for 85 percent of the female workers in 1841 and 80 percent in 1851. The same categories held only 22 percent of male workers in 1841 and 20 percent in 1851. This stark contrast has been noted by many historians.[5]

Unfortunately, the census numbers are not an accurate measure of women's employment. While Hatton and Bailey conclude that the censuses of the early twentieth century accurately measured women's labor force participation, the same cannot be said of the 1841 and 1851 censuses.[6] Edward Higgs has studied the censuses extensively and concluded that the census numbers should not be considered raw data, but rather cultural objects generated by ideology.[7] The census data were collected by men who built some of their cultural ideology into the data. The assumption that the household, rather than the individual, was the working unit is reflected in the way the census data were collected. The 1811 to 1831 censuses collected information on the number of families, not individuals, in three broad occupational categories.[8] Individual enumeration began with the 1841 census, but knowledge of the occupation of the household head was considered sufficient. The 1841 census instructed the enumerators to ignore a large fraction of women workers; the instructions state, "The professions &c. of wives, or of sons or daughters living with and assisting their parents but not apprenticed

---

[5] For example, see Elizabeth Roberts, *Women's Work, 1840–1940* (Cambridge: Cambridge University Press, 1988), ch. 2, and Jane Rendall, *Women in an Industrializing Society: England 1750–1880* (Oxford: Basil Blackwell, 1990), pp. 55–6.

[6] Timothy Hatton and Roy Bailey, "Women's Work in Census and Survey, 1911–1931," *Economic History Review* 54 (Feb. 2001), pp. 87–107.

[7] "If the census reveals itself as part of the process by which gender divisions were defined, it cannot be used uncritically to study gender divisions in Victorian society. Such quantitative data is not necessarily 'raw material' for unbiased scientific analysis, it is also a human construct and therefore a worthy, and indeed necessary, subject for historical analysis." Edward Higgs, "Women, Occupations and Work in the Nineteenth Century Censuses," *History Workshop Journal* 23 (1987), pp. 76–7.

[8] The categories were "agriculture; trade, manufactures, and handicraft, and the number not occupied in the preceding classes." Higgs, *Making Sense of the Census*, pp. 22–3.

Table 1.1. *Occupations in the 1841 and 1851 censuses: Great Britain*

Occupational category	1841 census Males		1841 census Females			1851 census Males		1851 census Females		
	1000s	%	1000s	%	Percent female	1000s	%	1000s	%	Percent female
Public administration	40	0.8	3	0.2	7.0	64	1.0	3	0.1	4.5
Armed forces	51	1.0	0	0	0.0	63	1.0	0	0.0	0.0
Professions	113	2.2	49	2.7	30.2	162	2.5	103	3.6	38.9
Domestic services	255	5.0	989	54.5	79.5	193	2.9	1135	40.1	85.5
Commercial	94	1.8	1	0.1	1.1	91	1.4	0	0.0	0.0
Transport and communications	196	3.8	4	0.2	2.0	433	6.6	13	0.5	2.9
Agriculture	1434	28.2	81	4.5	5.3	1788	27.3	229	8.1	11.4
Fishing	24	0.5	0	0.0	0.0	36	0.6	1	0.0	2.7
Mining	218	4.3	7	0.4	3.1	383	5.9	11	0.4	2.8
Metal manufacture	396	7.8	14	0.8	3.4	536	8.2	36	1.3	6.3
Building and construction	376	7.4	1	0.1	0.3	496	7.6	1	0.0	0.2
Wood and furniture	107	2.1	5	0.3	4.5	152	2.3	8	0.3	5.0
Bricks, cement, pottery, glass	48	0.9	10	0.6	17.2	75	1.1	15	0.5	16.7
Chemicals	23	0.5	1	0.1	4.2	42	0.6	4	0.1	8.7
Leather and skins	47	0.9	3	0.2	6.0	55	0.8	5	0.2	8.3
Paper and printing	44	0.9	6	0.3	12.0	62	0.9	16	0.6	20.5
Textiles	525	10.3	358	19.7	40.5	661	10.1	635	22.4	49.0

Table 1.1. (cont.)

Occupational category	1841 census					1851 census				
	Males		Females			Males		Females		
	1000s	%	1000s	%	Percent female	1000s	%	1000s	%	Percent female
Clothing	358	7.0	200	11.0	35.8	418	6.4	491	17.3	54.0
Food, drink, lodging	268	5.3	42	2.3	13.5	348	5.3	53	1.9	13.2
Other	476	9.3	41	2.3	7.9	445	6.8	75	2.6	14.4
Total occupied	5093	100.0	1815	100.0	26.3	6545	100.0	2832	100.0	30.2
Total unoccupied	1604		5369			1060		5294		
Total individuals over age 10	6697		7184		51.8	7605		8126		51.7
Labor force participation rate	76.0		25.3			86.1		34.9		

Note: % = percentage of all occupied males or females in this occupational category.
Percent female = percentage of individuals in this occupational category who were female.
Source: B. R. Mitchell, *Abstract of British Historical Statistics* (Cambridge: Cambridge University Press, 1962), p. 60.

or receiving wages, need not be inserted."[9] Because of this aspect of the culture, the work of women was seriously undercounted, particularly in 1841. Table 1.1 suggests that female labor force participation rates were 25 percent in 1841, but 35 percent in 1851. On the surface this difference looks like a large increase in labor force participation, but it would be an error to conclude that this represents a real change, or that three-fourths of women did not work in 1841. The apparent increase just reflects how drastically women were undercounted in 1841. The 1851 census is an improvement in this respect, since it does ask that the occupations of wives be included. Even in 1851, however, the problem was not eliminated; women workers continued to be undercounted because women workers were more likely than men to be part-time, seasonal, and home workers, and because census enumerators expected women to be dependents.

Historians have debated the extent of errors in the census counts. Edward Higgs has suggested there are serious errors in the counting of domestic servants that would make the occupational distribution of females appear more skewed than it actually was, while Michael Anderson claims the problem is overstated by Higgs. In a survey of the returns of Rochdale, Lancashire, Higgs found that only 56 percent of people recorded as servants were "servants in relationship to the head of the household in which they lived."[10] Some of these people were probably servants working elsewhere but living at home. Many of these, however, would be better described as housewives; they were just female family members who did the housework. Higgs found that "For some enumerators 'housekeeper' and 'housewife' were synonymous."[11] While these women were clearly workers, they were not domestic servants in the sense in which we generally use the term. While the exact amount of overcounting is not known, the potential for error is very large. For example, if the number of servants was reduced by taking out family members designated as "servants," the number of servants in Rochdale in 1851 would be reduced by one-third.[12] Even among those who were actually hired servants, many were allocated to the wrong industry; many of the female servants recorded in the domestic service industry spent more time working in agriculture or trade rather than in domestic work.[13]

[9] Quoted in *ibid.*, p. 81.

[10] Edward Higgs, "Domestic Service and Household Production," in Angela John, ed., *Unequal Opportunities* (Oxford: Basil Blackwell, 1986), p. 130.

[11] *Ibid.*, p. 131.   [12] *Ibid.*, p. 132.

[13] Higgs, "Women, Occupations and Work." Among farm servants, men were most likely to be allocated to the agricultural sector, while women were likely to be classified as domestic servants.

Table 1.2. *The occupations of women workers: Higgs's revisions of census data (percentage of occupied women)*

| | 1841 | | 1851 | |
Sector	Census	Revised	Census	Revised
Agriculture	3.9	33.2	7.0	27.4
Mining	0.4	0.3	0.4	0.3
Building	0.1	0.1	0.0	0.0
Manufacture	32.0	28.0	42.7	39.4
Transport	0.2	0.1	0.5	0.4
Dealing	3.8	11.4	4.5	10.3
General laborers	0.8	0.7	0.3	0.3
Public service/professions	3.1	2.7	4.1	3.8
Domestic service	55.7	23.4	40.4	17.9

Note: The "census" figures are not directly from the census, but were revised to allow comparability across all nineteenth-century censuses. The revision adds corrections for the wives of tradesmen and the wives of agricultural workers, who are assumed to work one-sixth of the year, and moves some women from the "domestic service" category to the agricultural, retailing, and "dependent" sectors.
Source: Higgs, "Women, Occupations and Work," Tables 4 and 5.

While a male servant hired by a farmer would be counted as an agricultural worker, a female servant hired by a farmer might be counted as a domestic servant even if she did agricultural work. Thus Higgs suggests that the census data understate the participation of women and overstate the skewedness of the occupational distribution. Higgs revised the census figures to correct for seasonal work in agriculture, the under-counting of working wives, and the overcounting and mis-allocation of domestic servants. The results of this revision, shown in Table 1.2, tell a much different story. If Higgs is correct, the occupational distribution was not so heavily skewed toward domestic service, and had more women in agriculture, which was the most common occupation for men.

Michael Anderson, however, has questioned whether the problem is as bad as Higgs suggests. Rochdale does not seem to be representative of the entire country. Anderson finds that a national sample of census enumeration books suggests much lower numbers of women related to the household head who were recorded as "servant" or "housekeeper."[14] Servants who were related to the household head may have been visiting their families, since the 1851 census was taken on Mothering Sunday.[15]

---

[14] Michael Anderson, "Mis-Specification of Servant Occupations in the 1851 Census: A Problem Revisited," *Local Population Studies* 60 (1998), pp. 59–60.
[15] *Ibid.*, p. 61.

Anderson's evidence suggests that the overcounting of servants was much smaller than Higgs suggested, but not entirely absent. Anderson estimates that 11 percent of those listed as "domestic servant" and 58 percent of those listed as "housekeeper" were related to the head of household.[16] Higgs's corrections, then, are too extreme, and should not be taken as an accurate measure of the occupational distribution, but they do demonstrate that the errors present in the census data could potentially distort the occupational distribution.

Overcounting of domestic servants is not the only problem with the census data. There is reliable evidence that many women who were employed outside the home for wages were not listed as employed in the censuses. Andrew Walker notes that, while the owner of a Darfield stone quarry is listed in the 1881 census as employing nine women, no women in that enumeration district are listed as having the occupation of stone worker, suggesting that the census enumerator probably failed to record the occupations of some women.[17] Miller used evidence from Gloucestershire farm wage books to show that female employment in agriculture was underenumerated in the censuses of the late nineteenth century. Individual women who were clearly employed in agriculture, and received wages that were recorded in an account book, are not recognized by the census as employed. Miller matched the names of females in the farm wage books to the 1871 censuses and found that eleven of the seventeen women matched were returned by the census as having no occupation. For example, Anne Westbury worked 221½ days at a farm in Fairford, but the 1871 census does not list an occupation for her.[18] Nicola Verdon has done the same for a farm in the East Riding of Yorkshire; fourteen women were employed on this farm but not listed as agricultural laborers in the 1881 census. My own estimates suggest that the 1851 census records less than half of the female out-door laborers in agriculture.[19] Leigh Shaw-Taylor has defended the reliability of census on female employment, claiming that the employment of women who worked regularly was well recorded. He notes that irregular employment was underrecorded, but does not consider that a serious fault because

---

[16] *Ibid.*, p. 63.

[17] Andrew Walker, "'Pleasurable Homes'? Victorian Model Miners' Wives and the Family Wage in a South Yorkshire Colliery District," *Women's History Review* 6 (1997), pp. 317–36.

[18] Miller, "The Hidden Workforce," p. 146. See also Helen Speechley, "Female and Child Agricultural Day Labourers in Somerset, c. 1685–1870," unpublished PhD thesis, University of Exeter, 1999.

[19] Joyce Burnette, "The Wages and Employment of Female Day-Labourers in English agriculture, 1740–1850," *Economic History Review* 57 (2004), pp. 664–90.

the censuses were not meant to measure irregular work.[20] However, if we wish to obtain an accurate picture of women's employment we cannot afford to ignore irregular work. Much of the work women did was irregular, and confining ourselves to regular work will produce a skewed picture of female participation in the labor market.

The nature of women's work during the Industrial Revolution means that it could not be well recorded by the census. The censuses recorded each individual as either having an occupation or not, and generally only one occupation was listed per person.[21] This was not a good system for recording women's work during the Industrial Revolution period, which has been described as an "economy of makeshifts."[22] Many women did not pursue one type of employment exclusively, but survived by combining many different kinds of employment with other sources of income. Peter King estimated that, by gleaning, women and children could earn between 3 and 14 percent of a laborer's family income, and Steven King has argued that poor women combined poor law payments with work income in order to make ends meet.[23] Women who worked as agricultural day-laborers usually worked only a few days in a year. Of the seventy-one different women who appear in the wage book of the Estcourt farm in Gloucestershire between 1828 and 1849, fifty-nine women (83 percent) were casual workers in the sense that they worked fewer than sixty days in a year.[24] At the Oakes farm in Derbyshire, approximately half of all days worked by women were worked during the two-week hay harvest, so the vast majority of women hired at this farm

---

[20] "However, it is very clear that irregular work by women was under-recorded in 1851, but largely because the G.R.O. did not want to know about such work." Leigh Shaw-Taylor, "Diverse Experience: The Geography of Adult Female Employment in England and the 1851 Census," in Nigel Goose, ed., *Women's Work in Industrial England: Regional and Local Perspectives* (Hatfield: Local Population Studies, 2007), p. 40.

[21] This point was made by Andrew August, "How Separate a Sphere? Poor Women and Paid Work in Late-Victorian London," *Journal of Family History* 19 (1994), p. 288.

[22] See Steven King, " 'Meer pennies for my baskitt will be enough': Women, Work and Welfare, 1700–1830," in P. Lane, N. Raven, and K. D. M. Snell, eds., *Women, Work and Wages in England, 1600–1850* (Woodbridge: Boydell Press, 2004), p. 126, and Samantha Williams, "Caring for the Sick Poor: Poor Law Nurses in Bedfordshire, c. 1700–1834," in Lane *et al.*, eds., *Women, Work and Wages*, p. 156. The term was first used by Olwen Hufton in reference to the poor in France. Olwen Hufton, *The Poor of Eighteenth-Century France, 1750–1789* (Oxford: Clarendon Press, 1974).

[23] Peter King, "Customary Rights and Women's Earnings: The Importance of Gleaning to the Rural Labouring Poor, 1750–1850," *Economic History Review* 44 (1991), 461–76. King, "Meer pennies," pp. 119–40.

[24] Joyce Burnette, "Married with Children: The Family Status of Female Day-Labourers at Two South-Western Farms," *Agricultural History Review* 55 (2007), pp. 75–94.

worked no more than two weeks in the year.[25] These farm accounts do not tell us what these women were doing the rest of the year, but they may have worked at other farms, or in non-agricultural work. Describing the annual cycle of female labor, Mary Collier mentions both agricultural work and charring:

> The Harvest ended, Respite none we find;
> The hardest of our Toil is still behind:
> Hard Labour we most chearfully pursue,
> And out, abroad, a Charing often go.[26]

Given the many different forms of employment that one woman would engage in during the year, it is not surprising that the occupations listed in the census are an inadequate description of female employment.

B.   Employment ratios

Since the census data are unreliable, and are in any case not available before 1841, it is important to look for other data to corroborate the story of occupational sorting. Employment ratios in specific occupations provide an alternative to census data and, while not as complete as the census because they do not describe the occupational distribution across the entire economy, do establish that men and women worked in different jobs, and thus provide evidence of occupational sorting.

I have collected evidence on the percentage of employees who were female in a variety of occupations, from a variety of different sources, and this material is presented in Table 1.3. Some sources are very detailed and give the exact number of persons of each sex employed. Other sources are more impressionistic and give estimates or ratios. The evidence demonstrates that there was substantial occupational sorting by gender.

Many women were employed in textile factories and potteries, but women were scarce in the copper industry of South Wales, and non-existent in the dyehouses of Leeds. Handloom weaving employed both men and women, but mining was mostly a male occupation. Glovers and screw-makers were mostly female, while stocking weavers and calico printers were mostly male. If we look more closely at particular occupations, more segregation appears. In cotton factories 50 to 70 percent of the workers were female, but within the factory men and women

---

[25] Joyce Burnette, "'Labourers at the Oakes': Changes in the Demand for Female Day-Laborers at a Farm near Sheffield during the Agricultural Revolution," *Journal of Economic History* 59 (1999), p. 51.

[26] Mary Collier, "The Woman's Labour" (London: Roberts, 1739), reprinted by the Augustan Reprint Society, No. 230, 1985.

Table 1.3. *Employment ratios*

Year	Location	Occupation	Adults		Percent women	Percent children	Src
			Men	Women			
Factories							
Wool							
1813	Leeds	Wool factory	426	152	26.3	24.1	a
1830	Leeds	Wool factory	605	314	34.2	18.0	a
1833	Leeds	16 wool factories	1667	1034	38.3	46.1	b
1833	Gloucestershire	17 wool factories	667	466	41.1	43.2	b
Cotton							
1816	Scotland	Cotton factories	1776	3820	68.3	44.0	c
1816	Nottinghamshire	Cotton factories	327	572	63.6	49.4	c
1833	Lancashire	29 cotton factories	2010	2065	50.7	46.5	b
1833	Glasgow	46 cotton factories	2413	4016	62.5	46.8	b
1833	Lancashire & Cheshire	Cleaners & spreaders			71.7		d
	cotton factories	Carders			59.8		d
		Mule spinners & piecers			18.7		d
		Throstle spinners			78.0		d
		Reelers			94.6		d
		Weavers			56.9		d
		Engineers, mechanics			0.8		d
Other textiles							
1816	Nottinghamshire	2 worsted factories	32	74	69.8	31.6	c
1833	Leeds	4 flax factories	514	585	53.2	57.8	b
1833	Derbyshire	10 silk factories	439	873	66.5	49.5	b
1833	Norfolk, Suffolk	6 silk factories	16	418	96.3	74.1	b
Paper mills							
1833	Aberdeenshire	3 paper mills	45	38	45.8	14.4	b
1833	Valleyfield, Scotland	Paper mill	86	43	33.3	26.3	e
1843	West of Scotland	Paper mill	32	63	66.3		g
Potteries							
1833	Staffordshire	7 potteries	462	244	34.6	37.7	b
1843	Staffordshire	Earthenware pottery	4544	2648	36.8		g
Handloom weaving							
1838	Norwich		2211	1648	42.7		h
1838	Spitalfields	Silk velvets (skilled)	1871	526	21.9		h
1838	Spitalfields	Plain silk	2820	2790	49.7		h
1840	Spitalfields	Silk weaving	5098	3395	40.0	8.7	i
1840	Norwich	Weaving	1863	1383	42.6	4.5	i

Table 1.3. (*cont.*)

			Adults				
Year	Location	Occupation	Men	Women	Percent women	Percent children	Src
1840	Diss, Norfolk	Flax	40	3	7.0	31.8	i
1840	Gloucestershire	Wool	665	167	20.1		k
Mining							
1842	Cornwall	Metals	15,500	2700	14.8		l
1842	Yorkshire	Coal			2.2	39.8	l
1842	Lancashire	Coal			7.9	37.6	l
1842	Derbyshire	Coal			0.0	28.9	l
1842	West Scotland	Coal			0.0	24.4	l
1842	Pembrokeshire	Coal			29.7	33.0	l
Agriculture							
1751	England	Day laborers			13.6		m
1851	England	Day laborers			10.6		m
pre-1800	England	Servants			45.4		n
1851	England	Servants			32.0		n
Employers							
1824	Liverpool	Master shipwrights	26	1	3.7		o
1839	Montgomeryshire	Flannel weaving	82	3	3.5		k
Other							
1767–1834	Bedfordshire	Sick nurses	16	77	82.8		p
1786		Sun Fire Insurance agents	113	5	4.2		q
1795	Northampton	Servants	203	280	58.0		r
1795	Overingham, Notts.	Stocking weavers	37	3	7.5		r
1807	Woodstock	Gloves	65	1450	95.7		s
1818	Coventry	Ribbon weavers	5056	4365	46.3		t
1833	Devonshire	Lace factories	299	234	43.9	34.8	b
1833	Leeds	Dyehouses	125	0	0.0		b
1843	Birmingham	Screw manufacture	90	402	81.7		g
1843	North England	Calico printers	8620	184	2.1	55.1	f
1842	South Wales	Copper works	1605	57	3.4		l
1844		Gloves	2803	4401	61.1	21.9	u
1845		Framework knitting	722	64	8.1	15.8	v

Sources:
a. H. Heaton, "Benjamin Gott and the Industrial Revolution in Yorkshire," *Economic History Review*, 3 (1931), pp. 45–66. Adult = 21 and over.

did different jobs. Throstle-spinners were mostly women, and mule-spinners were men (most of the females in the "mule-spinners and piecers" category were assistants). While women handloom weavers were common, most of the workers weaving flax were men. Men dominated the professional jobs of engineers and mechanics, while almost all reelers were female.

The data on employment ratios not only confirm that there was substantial occupational segregation, but suggest that grouping workers by broad categories, as in Table 1.1, understates the amount of segregation. Within the textile industry, silk mills employed more women than cotton mills, which generally employed more women than woollen mills. Within a particular mill men and women did different jobs. Clearly workers were not randomly assigned to jobs; gender mattered.

C.   Commercial directories

An additional source of data on occupational sorting, though only for a portion of the workforce, is the commercial directory. Commercial directories listed the names and addresses of all the tradesmen and tradeswomen of a town and served as a type of Yellow Pages for customers. The commercial directories, then, measure ownership and authority, but not necessarily everyday work. Only the head of the

Sources to Table 1.3 (cont.)
b. "Report of Dr. James Mitchell," BPP 1834 (167) XIX. Adult = 18 and over.
c. BPP 1816 (397) III.
d. Frances Collier, The Family Economy of the Working Classes in the Cotton Industry (Manchester: Manchester University Press, 1964).
e. BPP 1833 (450) XX.
f. BPP 1843 (431) XIV p. 3. Adult = 18 and over.
g. BPP 1843 (430) XIII.
h. Pinchbeck, Women Workers.
i. Mitchell report, BPP 1840 (43) XXIII.
k. From report by W. A. Miles, Esq, BPP 1840 (217) XXIV.
l. BPP 1842 (380) XV.
m. Burnette, "Wage and employment."
n. Kussmaul, Servants in Husbandry.
o. BPP 1824 (51) V.
p. Williams, "Caring for the Sick Poor."
q. Phillips, Women in Business, p. 124.
r. Eden, State of the Poor, vol II, pp. 534 and 579.
s. Young, General View of Oxfordshire, p. 329.
t. BPP 1818 (134) IX.
u. Neff, Victorian Working Women, p. 263.
v. Rose, "Gender Segregation, p. 166."

business was listed, so this source will not tell us anything about women working for their husbands or fathers, or even about wage-earning women. Many women worked in partnership with their husbands but do not appear in the directories. Subsidiary workers, both men and women, do not appear in these directories. Thus this source only measures economic activity relatively high on the ladder. While the directory listings are limited to a small portion of the labor force, they do provide a comprehensive listing of individuals in that category, and they have not been fully exploited by historians.

The evidence provided by commercial directories is difficult to interpret because ownership of a business did not necessarily imply active participation, whether the owner was male or female. Some women who are listed as owners of businesses were owners only and not active managers; many widows remained the nominal head of the business even if their sons did the work. William Lambert, an overlooker employed by Mrs. Vanderplank of Gloucestershire in 1806, notes that "She has got two sons who carry on the business."[27] The sons seem to have been the active proprietors. However, we must not be too quick to assume that female business owners were inactive. Robert Cookson makes contradictory statements about his mother's business. He first claims to be "carrying on the business in my mother's name; after my father's death I had the management of the business,"[28] implying that his mother contributed only her name. Later, however, he stated that after his father's death "my mother and I fell to cloth making," implying that his mother did participate in the business. Perhaps such statements about the participation of women are not accurate statements of economic activity, but social judgments, reflecting the fact that women's real contributions were often undervalued or ignored by men. There is evidence that women were actively involved in their businesses. The mother of George Holyoake carried on a button-making business separate from her husband, and George recalled that

She received the orders; made the purchases of materials; superintended the making of the goods; made out the accounts; and received the money besides taking care of her growing family. There were no "Rights of Women" thought of in her day, but she was an entirely self-acting managing mistress.[29]

---

[27] BPP 1806 (268) III, p. 330.   [28] *Ibid.*, p. 67.

[29] G. J. Holyoake, *Sixty Years of an Agitator's Life* (London, 1900), p. 10, quoted in Leonore Davidoff and Catherine Hall, "'The Hidden Investment': Women and the Enterprise," in P. Sharpe, ed., *Women's Work: The English Experience, 1650–1914* (London: Arnold, 1998), p. 274.

There were also cases of businesses that seem to be owned by men but were actively managed by women, as is the case with the following example:

The case came up in Essex quarter sessions in 1795 of woolcards being stolen from Messrs Suter and Sansom of Colchester, woolcard makers. The "Messrs" were, in fact, Hannah Sansom and her partner Mary Suter ... Hannah Sansom was a spinster, a daughter or granddaughter of Philip Sansom, a card-maker who was mentioned in petty sessions in 1765 in a case regarding a servant let to him. Mary Suter was the wife of one John Suter who would have legally owned the business. Yet the menfolk nowhere directly appear in the court case; clearly their names were a front for a mainly women's operation.[30]

Davidoff and Hall note the underrecording of female merchants in Birmingham:

A sample from the directories for Birmingham, for example, does not list a single female merchant after 1800, yet as late as the 1830s evidence from only a sample of wills produces a bone, timber and marble merchant who left instructions for their wives to take over the business.[31]

So the listings in the commercial directories may be inaccurate measures of the gender of the active business manager, but they are as likely to underestimate female participation as they are to overestimate it.

Commercial directories provide underestimates of women's real participation because they are less likely to record individuals of lower social status. This effect is particularly strong in the field of medicine. Most women who provided medical care were not listed in directories because they did not have professional status of male physicians.[32] Midwives might also be considered too low in status to list in a directory. In the 1824–5 directory of Manchester, no midwives are listed in the directory of tradesmen, but the description of the lying-in hospital lists twenty-four midwives working alongside seven men-midwives, one physician, and one apothecary.[33] This omission leads the directory to understate the involvement of women in the professional activities.

Business owners included married as well as single women. D'Cruze found that Colchester milliners "took apprentices and made out bills in their own names even when married."[34] For example, "When Michael Boyle, school master, married Mary Walford, milliner in 1775, not only

[30] Sharpe, *Adapting to Capitalism*, p. 12.
[31] Davidoff and Hall, "The Hidden Investment," p. 277.   [32] *Ibid.*
[33] *Pigot and Dean's Directory for Manchester, Salford, &c. for 1824–5* (Manchester: J. Pigot and W. Dean, 1825), p. 277.
[34] Shani D'Cruze, " 'To Acquaint the Ladies': Women Traders in Colchester c. 1750–c. 1800," *The Local Historian* 17 (1986), p. 159.

Table 1.4. *Comparison of commercial directories and population*

	Male	Female	Percent female	Total
Birmingham				
Persons 20 and over	61,276	65,545	51.7	126,821
Persons 20 and over listed with occupations in the 1851 census	59,949	25,725	30.0	85,674
Persons listed in the 1850 commercial directory	16,534	2,219	11.8	18,753
– as percent of population	27.0	3.4		19.8
– as percent of employed	27.6	8.6		21.9
Manchester and Salford				
Persons 20 and over	104,906	120,821	53.5	225,727
Persons 20 and over listed with occupations in the 1851 census	103,055	55,964	35.2	159,019
Persons listed in the 1846 commercial directory	14,043	1,437	9.3	15,480
– as percent of population	13.4	1.2		6.9
– as percent of employed	13.6	2.6		9.7

Sources: BPP 1852–3 (1691) LXXXVIII, pp. 504–9, 648–53; *Slater's National Commercial Directory of Ireland* (Manchester: Isaac Slater, 1846); *Slater's Royal, National and Commercial Directory, 1850.* Population figures for 1841 and 1851 were averaged to estimate the population in 1846.

did Mary continue in millinery but a few years later Michael opened a silk ribbon manufactory, the produce of which was sold in the milliner's shop along with stocks purchased by Mary on frequent trips to London."[35] Mary Boyle is just one example of married women actively engaged in the business world. For eighteenth-century Edinburgh, Elizabeth Sanderson documents 106 cases where wives had different occupations from their husbands.[36]

We can see what segment of the population appears in commercial directories by comparing the number of persons in a directory to the town's population. Table 1.4 compares the number of persons in commercial directories for Birmingham and Manchester to population figures from the 1851 census. Since commercial directories record only business owners, they record a smaller number of people where firms are larger. The Birmingham directory of 1850 lists 20 percent of the population over age 20, but the Manchester directory for 1846 lists only 7 percent. Manchester's industries were factories, so a larger portion of

[35] *Ibid.*, p. 160.   [36] Sanderson, *Women and Work*, pp. 126–7.

Table 1.5. *Number of independent tradeswomen, from commercial directories*

Date	Place	Men	Women	Unknown	Percent women	Percent unknown	Percent of pop. listed
More complete directories							
1774	Sheffield	545	28	74	4.9	11.4	2.3
1788	Manchester	2033	199	321	8.9	12.6	3.6
1791	Coventry	395	39	104	9.0	19.3	3.5
1824–5	Manchester	4185	297	1671	6.6	27.1	3.1
1835	Coventry	1090	110	118	9.2	9.0	3.9
1846	Manchester	11,942	1222	2316	9.3	15.0	5.3
1850	Birmingham	15,054	2020	1677	11.8	8.9	10.8
1850	Derby	2415	332	194	12.1	6.6	6.7
"Principal tradesmen" only							
1787	Staffordshire	146	2	49	1.4	24.9	0.1
1787	Cheshire	94	3	13	3.1	13.4	0.1
1787	Lancashire	525	1	153	0.2	29.1	0.1

Sources: Sketchley's Sheffield Directory (Bristol, 1774); *Topographical Survey of Stafford, Chester, and Lancaster; Lewis's Manchester Directory for 1788*; *The Universal British Directory of Trade, Commerce and Manufacture* (London: Chapman and Withrow, 1791); *Pigot and Dean's Directory for Manchester, 1824–5; Pigot & Co.'s National Commercial Directory, 1835; Slater's National Commercial Directory of Ireland, 1846; Slater's Royal National and Commercial Directory, 1850.* Population data from E. A. Wrigley, *People, Cities, and Wealth* (Oxford: Blackwell, 1987), p. 159; and BPP 1852–3 (1691) LXXXVIII.

the population were wage-earners. Birmingham's toy trades had more small businesses, and thus a larger portion of the population was self-employed and appeared in the directory.

Women were less likely to own businesses than men. In Birmingham 27 percent of the male population were listed in the directory, while only 3 percent of women were listed. Table 1.5 gives the percentage of persons listed in commercial directories who are female.[37] In Manchester in 1788 only 8.9 percent of the listed "tradesmen" were female, and in 1846 only 9.3 percent. In Birmingham in 1850, 11.8 percent of those listed were female. There is also some evidence of a glass ceiling making it difficult for women to reach the highest status among business owners. Generally the more selective listings included fewer women. A 1787 select listing of merchants and manufacturers in Staffordshire, Chester, and Lancaster, which listed only one tenth of 1 percent of the population

---

[37] The sex of each person was determined by the first name, with the help of Patrick Hanks and Flavia Hodges, *A Dictionary of First Names* (Oxford: Oxford University Press, 1990) for the difficult names. If there was any doubt, the individual was counted as "unknown."

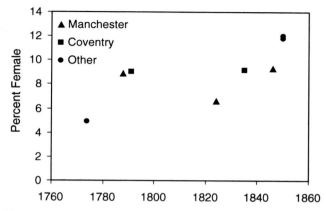

Figure 1.1 The prevalence of women in commercial directories
Source: Table 1.5.

of those counties, included very few women; less than 1 percent of the "principal tradesmen" listed were female.[38] This suggests that women were less likely than men to make their way into the highest class of business owners.

Table 1.5 suggests that around one in ten business owners was female, which means that women were less likely to be business owners than employees. Table 1.3 suggests that in textile factories and handloom weaving close to half of the adult workers were women. While the percentage of day laborers who were female was similar to the percentage in commercial directories, women were much more prevalent among farm servants. These patterns suggest that there was occupational segregation by gender; men and women did not do the same jobs.

For the trades listed in commercial directories, there is no evidence of declining female employment. Figure 1.1 graphs the percentage female in each of the more complete commercial directories against time. This graph suggests that, if anything, the trend was toward greater relative female participation. The relative number of women appearing in the Coventry directory stayed stable between 1791 and 1835, at 9 percent and 9.2 percent. Relative female participation in Manchester appears to have fallen between 1788 and 1824, and then risen between 1824 and 1846. However, the decline in 1824–5 may be the result of decisions

[38] *A Topographical Survey of the Counties of Stafford, Chester, and Lancaster* (Nantwich: E. Snelson, 1787), reprinted by Neil Richardson (Manchester, 1982).

about who to include in the directory; the 1824–5 directory includes no specific category for shopkeepers and includes relatively fewer persons in retailing than the other two Manchester directories. The Sheffield directory for 1774 included fewer women than the Birmingham or Derby directories for 1850. However, it is not clear if this difference results from increased opportunities for women, or from other factors such as difference between the towns, or the fact that the 1774 Sheffield directory is somewhat more selective than the other directories. Regression analysis confirms that there is no evidence of a decline in the presence of women in this segment of the workforce. While the percentage of the population listed in the directory does have a significantly positive effect on the percentage of listed "tradesmen" who were female, there is no statistically significant trend.[39]

Commercial directories also reveal the extent to which women who did run businesses were segregated into certain occupations. Females do seem to have been concentrated into a smaller number of trades than men. Table 1.6 shows the ten most popular occupational categories for men and women in each of the six directories. Some occupations were important for both sexes – publican and shopkeeper appear on both lists. Some occupations were clearly female specialties; milliner, dressmaker, and straw bonnet maker are found only on the female lists. A few occupations were exclusively male, but a handful of women appear in most occupational categories; only fifteen of the sixty listed top male occupations had no women at all. Women were also likely to share their occupations with men. Only seven of the sixty listed top female occupations were 100 percent female. Women do appear to be more concentrated in a few occupations than men, as evidenced by the fact that the percentage of women in the directory accounted for by the top ten occupations is much greater than the equivalent number for men. Women in the top ten occupations account for 88 percent of all the

---

[39] The data from Table 1.5 give the following regression results (the dependent variable is the percent female; standard errors are given in parentheses).

	Including 1787 directories	Excluding 1787 directories
Intercept	− 22.414 (64.714)	− 33.139 (47.979)
Year	0.014 (0.036)	0.022 (0.027)
Percent of population	1.000* (0.339)	0.526 (0.303)
R^2	0.78	0.693
N	11	8

Table 1.6. *The top ten most common occupations for men and women in commercial directories*

	Male	Female	Unknown	Percent female
A. Manchester 1788				
Top 10 male occupations				
Manufacturer cloth	257	4	118	1.5
Public house/inn/tavern	126	13	2	9.4
Shopkeeper	107	16	4	13.0
Grocer and tea dealer	91	16	12	15.0
Boot and shoe maker	87	0	1	0.0
Warehouse	64	0	14	0.0
Tailor	59	0	1	0.0
Merchant	58	1	18	1.7
Fustian cutter/shearer	54	2	0	3.6
Draper, mercer, dealer of cloth	46	15	19	24.6
Top 10 female occupations				
Milliner	0	24	0	100.0
Grocer and tea dealer	91	16	12	15.0
Shopkeeper	107	16	4	13.0
Draper, mercer, dealer of cloth	46	15	19	24.6
Public house/inn/tavern	126	13	2	9.4
Black worker	1	11	0	91.7
Mantua-maker	0	10	2	100.0
Schoolmaster/mistress	18	10	0	35.7
Corn and flour dealer	45	4	5	8.2
Manufacturer cloth	257	4	118	1.5
B. Manchester 1824–5				
Top 10 male occupations				
Manufacturer cloth	475	1	309	0.0
Tavern and public house	296	53	48	15.2
Baker and shopkeeper	178	19	8	9.6
Cotton spinner	137	0	122	0.0
Merchant	134	0	138	0.0
Calico printer	132	0	112	0.0
Grocer	105	10	16	8.7
Joiner	104	1	11	1.0
Attorney	96	0	38	0.0
Agent and commission dealer	85	0	33	0.0
Top 10 female occupations				
Tavern and public house	296	53	48	15.2
Milliner	0	20	14	100.0
Baker and shopkeeper	178	19	8	9.6
Pawnbroker	67	19	6	22.1
Academies	18	17	7	48.6
Straw-hat maker	9	14	4	60.9
Confectioner	18	10	4	35.7

Table 1.6. (*cont.*)

	Male	Female	Unknown	Percent female
Grocer	105	10	16	8.7
Furniture broker	32	9	0	22.0
Tea dealer	26	8	16	23.5
C. Coventry 1835				
Top 10 male occupations				
Tavern and public house	105	11	1	9.5
Retailer of beer	74	3	0	3.9
Ribbon manufacturer	72	2	27	2.7
Butcher	70	1	0	1.4
Shopkeeper	61	11	0	15.3
Maltster	34	2	0	5.6
Boot and shoe maker	31	3	0	8.8
Tailor	28	0	1	0.0
Baker and flour dealer	28	2	2	6.7
Grocer and tea dealer	26	0	1	0.0
Top 10 female occupations				
Milliner	0	19	0	100.0
Academies and schools	15	19	4	55.9
Shopkeeper	61	11	0	15.3
Tavern and public house	105	11	1	9.5
Straw-hat maker	4	10	0	71.4
Boot and shoe maker	31	3	0	8.8
Staymaker	3	3	0	50.0
Retailer of beer	74	3	0	3.9
Wine and spirit merchant	12	2	2	14.3
Linen and woollen draper	13	2	5	13.3
D. Manchester 1846				
Top 10 male occupations				
Shopkeeper	776	128	4	14.2
Manufacturer cloth	740	8	363	1.1
Tavern and public house	496	91	42	15.5
Butcher	464	43	2	8.5
Boot and shoe maker	321	7	7	2.1
Merchant	265	1	184	0.4
Cotton spinner	262	0	118	0.0
Tailor	239	1	18	0.4
Grocer and tea dealer	208	8	12	3.7
Agent and commission dealer	192	1	64	0.5
Top 10 female occupations				
Milliner and dressmaker	12	245	18	95.3
Schoolmaster/mistres	156	167	12	51.7
Shopkeeper	776	128	4	14.2
Tavern and public house	496	91	42	15.5

Table 1.6. (*cont.*)

	Male	Female	Unknown	Percent female
Smallware dealer	83	47	6	36.2
Butcher	464	43	2	8.5
Straw-bonnet maker	12	30	6	71.4
Confectioner	59	28	7	32.2
Pawnbroker	142	23	16	13.9
Linen draper and silk mercer	127	19	10	13.0
E. Birmingham 1850				
Top 10 male occupations				
Shopkeeper and dealer in groceries	880	168	9	16.0
Boot and shoe maker	709	16	4	2.2
Retailer of beer	629	53	1	7.8
Tavern and public house	505	75	4	12.9
Tailor	382	7	7	1.8
Butcher	365	14	3	3.7
Coal merchant and dealer	323	20	18	5.8
Button manufacturer	254	4	38	1.6
Jeweler – manufacturing	231	8	33	3.3
Baker and flour dealer	212	16	7	7.0
Top 10 female occupations				
Milliner and dressmaker	11	492	13	97.8
Schoolteacher	142	365	5	72.0
Straw-bonnet maker	10	193	6	95.1
Shopkeeper and dealer in groceries	880	168	9	16.0
Tavern and public house	505	75	4	12.9
Staymaker	6	60	5	90.9
Retailer of beer	629	53	1	7.8
Haberdasher and dealer in smallwares	86	40	4	31.7
Hosier and glover	74	33	5	30.8
Coal merchant and dealer	323	20	18	5.8
F. Derby 1850				
Top 10 male occupations				
Shopkeeper and dealer in groceries	187	49	1	20.8
Boot and shoe maker	172	0	1	0.0
Tavern and public house	154	20	2	11.5
Tailor	116	1	0	0.9
Butcher	112	2	2	1.8
Carrier	67	2	3	2.9
Baker and flour dealer	65	6	1	8.5
Agent	58	0	6	0.0
Retailer of beer	55	4	1	6.8
Jeweler – working	53	0	5	0.0
Top 10 female occupations				
Milliner and dressmaker	0	97	4	100.0
Schoolteacher	43	58	8	57.4

Table 1.6. (*cont.*)

	Male	Female	Unknown	Percent female
Shopkeeper and dealer in groceries	187	49	1	20.8
Straw-bonnet maker	0	26	0	100.0
Tavern and publichouse	154	20	2	11.5
Staymaker	4	12	0	75.0
Baker and flour dealer	65	6	1	8.5
Berlin wool repository	0	6	2	100.0
Fruiterer and greengrocer	43	5	0	10.4
Tea dealer	2	4	0	66.7

Sources: Lewis's Manchester Directory for 1788; Pigot and Dean's Directory for Manchester, 1824–5; Pigot & Co.'s National Commercial Directory, 1835; Slater's National Commercial Directory of Ireland, 1846; Slater's Royal National and Commercial Directory, 1850.

women in the Derby directory and 74 percent of all the women in the Birmingham directory, while men in the top ten occupations account for only 45 percent of all men in the Derby directory and 30 percent of men in the Birmingham directory.

Commercial directories reveal that women were less likely than men to have their own businesses in retail trade and manufacturing. Among the women who were listed as business owners, a large portion were concentrated in typically female occupations such as dressmaking and millinery. Women were overrepresented in school teaching; about half of school teachers listed were women. While women were concentrated in these occupations, many women did work in occupations not typically considered women's work. Most towns had women butchers, chemists, coopers, and ironmongers. Women were certainly not confined to a handful of occupations.

Commercial directories, the employment ratios in Table 1.3, and Higgs's corrected census data in Table 1.2 all support the same general conclusion. Men and women clearly did not have the same occupational distributions. Men were more likely to be found in some occupations, women in others. We can be confident that the labor market of the Industrial Revolution was characterized by extensive occupational sorting by sex. The cause of this sorting, however, remains undetermined.

II.   Survey of women's work

While the statistical evidence is limited, anecdotal evidence on women's work is abundant. This section will provide a description of the various types of work that women did during the period 1750 to 1850. Textiles, cottage industries, agriculture, and domestic service receive the most attention because they employed the largest numbers of women, but I also note that women were employed in a wide variety of occupations.

A.   Textiles

At the onset of the Industrial Revolution, textile production was the largest employer of women. Wool cloth was England's most important export, and women had an important part in the industry. The most important single shock to women's employment opportunities during the Industrial Revolution was the disappearance of hand spinning. Before mechanization, spinning employed vast numbers of women. It took so many spinners to supply enough yarn for one weaver that spinning could provide employment for nearly all the women in textile districts. A 1741 pamphlet on the wool industry estimates that out of 1187 workers needed to perform all processes for 1200 pounds of wool, 900 (75.8 percent) were spinners.[40] Parliamentary investigator H.S. Chapman, reporting on handloom weavers in 1840, claimed, "In 1715, with the old single-spindle it took 10 spinners to keep one stuff-loom at work."[41] In 1770 Arthur Young calculated that there were twenty spinners for every weaver in the sacking manufacture of Warrington.[42] Lavenham, Suffolk, had 150 wool-combers, each of whom furnished enough wool for thirty spinners.[43] This implies 4500 spinners in the neighborhood of this one town. The most common description of the extent of employment in spinning was that spinning employed "all" the women in an area. In the "Rural Queries" of 1833, a Norfolk farmer reported, "formerly, all the Women and Children had spinning to do, and they brought in as much as the Man did."[44] A Suffolk farmer stated in 1843, "Formerly, all the women and children in the neighboring villages, from 10 to 15 miles round, used to be employed in spinning yarn, and the wife and children, on an average, could earn nearly as much as the husband."[45] Of course spinning did not literally

---

[40] Alice Clark, *Working Life of Women in the Seventeenth Century* (London: Routledge, 1919), p. 98.

[41] BPP 1840 (43) XXIII, p. 586.

[42] Arthur Young, *A Six Months' Tour through the North of England* (Dublin: P. Wilson, 1770), vol. II, p. 255.

[43] *Reports of Special Assistant Poor Law Commissioners on the Employment of Women and Children in Agriculture*, BPP 1843 (510) XII, reprinted by W. Clowes (London: W. Clowes, For Her Majesty's Stationery Office, 1843), p. 228.

[44] BPP 1834 (44) XXX, Costessey, Norfolk, p. 318. The "Rural Queries" was an extensive survey sent out by the Poor Law Commissioners. Over a thousand parishes responded, and the complete responses are printed in an appendix to the Commissioners' report.

[45] *Women and Children in Agriculture*, p. 228.

employ *all* women, but it may have come close, and these descriptions do provide a clear indication that spinning was the most important employer of women.

The Industrial Revolution, however, made this employment obsolete. The invention of the water frame (1769), the jenny (1770), and the mule (1779) changed spinning technology so drastically that hand spinners could not possibly compete and hand spinning disappeared. Before industrialization, wool was the most prominent fiber, and the spinning of wool occupied countless women across the country. Cotton spinning was the first to be mechanized, but this change in technology still had a substantial impact on the traditional wool spinning. Since the different types of cloth competed as substitutes, cotton's success as cheap cloth reduced the demand for wool and flax cloth. The shift to cotton cloth and the adaptation of the cotton machinery to wool and flax made hand spinning, long the largest employer of English women, unprofitable. The impact of this change was extensive; indeed, the collapse of an industry that employed "all" the women and children in some districts could not help but be significant.

As spinning became mechanized on an increasingly large scale, spinning employment was reduced, and male workers eventually replaced female workers. The spinning wheel was replaced by the spinning jenny, the water frame, and later the spinning mule. The early machines were worked by women and children. The spinning jenny was a small machine and was used in the home. The water frame, since it used water power, moved spinning into the factory, but was still operated by women. The switch from female to male spinners came only with the third machine, the mule. The mule, so named because it was a combination of the jenny and the water frame, became the dominant technology and grew in size. In 1788 one pamphlet writer estimated that Britain contained 143 water mills for spinning, 550 mules of 90 spindles each, and 20,070 jennies of 80 spindles each.[46] Women were employed on all these machines. Women were not, however, employed on the larger mules that appeared in the early nineteenth century. A woman could operate a mule of 90 spindles, but one of 500 spindles was beyond her strength. Spinning mules required so much strength that even older men did not have the strength for peak performance. Male productivity peaked in the early thirties, and declined thereafter. From a parliamentary study we learn of one mule spinner whose weekly earnings

---

[46] *An Important Crisis in the Callico and Muslin Manufactory in Great Britain, Explained*, 1788, quoted in Eden, *State of the Poor*, vol. II, p. 478.

(on piece-rate work) declined 14 percent between his late twenties and mid-thirties:

Alexander Pitcairn, aged thirty-four, solemnly sworn, depones, that he is a mule-spinner at this work, and at present makes about 25s. a week; that his wheels contain five hundred and twenty-eight spindles; that seven or eight years ago he, at this work, made from 28s. to 30s. per week, but at wheels containing seven hundred and twelve spindles.[47]

Normally we expect earnings to increase with age as workers acquire more skill. In this case it is clear why Alexander's earnings decreased – he used to work on a larger machine. By age 34 Alexander was no longer able to work as large a machine as he could in his late twenties. This suggests that mule spinning required a great deal of strength.

A combination of high strength requirements and specific actions by male spinners led mule spinning to become an exclusively male occupation. The strength required for the larger mules made women less productive as mule spinners. A woman could operate a smaller mule, but smaller mules produced less yarn, so a female spinner's productivity was less than a male spinner's productivity.[48] The ability to operate the larger mules gave male spinners an advantage over female spinners. The actions of male unions also contributed to the elimination of women from mule spinning. Male spinners also used violence, if necessary, to prevent female workers from being employed. The introduction describes an example of such violence in Glasgow. The strength requirement was eliminated in 1833 with the invention of the self-actor, which completely mechanized mule spinning.[49] By this time it was too late, though. Women, who had been eliminated from the trade, did not have the skills required, and male spinners refused to teach them. Mule spinning remained an exclusively male trade after the mule was fully mechanized because the male mule-spinning union maintained a monopoly on the skills and did not admit women spinners.[50]

Technological change in spinning altered the regional pattern of women's employment. Employment decreased in hand spinning and

---

[47] BPP 1833 (450) XX, A1, p. 112.

[48] If a 500-spindle mule produced twice as much yarn per hour as a 250-spindle mule, then a male spinner who could operate the former was twice as productive as a female spinner who could only operate the latter.

[49] The change to the self-actor in factories did not happen immediately; George Henry Wood, *The History of Wages in the Cotton Trade during the Past Hundred Years* (London: Sherratt and Hughes, 1910), p. 27, suggests "The change from hand-mule spinning to self-actor minding has taken place gradually, and commenced about 1836."

[50] Mary Freifeld, "Technological Change and the 'Self-Acting' Mule: A Study of Skill and the Sexual Division of Labour," *Social History* 2 (1986), 319–43. For further discussion, see Chapter 5.

increased in factories, but the increase in employment was smaller than the decrease and was concentrated in a few northern counties. In towns where the new factories opened, the demand for women workers increased. Women in these areas could earn good wages. An inhabitant of Settle, Yorkshire, claimed "The lowness of the Poor's Rates is here ascribed to the introduction of the cotton manufacture; which has raised the demand for labor, and afforded full employment to the wives and children of the industrious Poor."[51] Other areas, however, experienced a decline in employment. To some extent the unemployed spinners moved into handloom weaving, the demand for which increased with the reduced price of yarn. However, many women were still left unemployed. Women in areas of industrialization did well, while many other women were left without work in regions of distress, such as the south-east, where spinning disappeared but no factories appeared.

While women were spinners in the pre-industrial period, men were weavers. Employment in weaving, too, changed during the Industrial Revolution. With the mechanization of spinning, women who had lost their spinning work became handloom weavers in large numbers. Since most handloom weaving was relatively unskilled, women found it easy to enter this occupation when they could no longer find employment spinning. Parliamentary investigator J. Symons concluded that one of the reasons for low wages in handloom weaving was "the extreme and peculiar facility with which weaving is learnt."[52] The result was that the number of women handloom weavers soon matched the number of men. However, handloom weaving, too, disappeared in the face of new technology. The powerloom was invented in 1785, but did not work well enough to be useful until about 1815.[53] Even then, the adoption of the powerloom was slow because of its imperfections.[54] Handloom weavers persisted, but by mid-century they were clearly a dying breed, barely earning enough to survive.[55]

By the mid-nineteenth century, textile production had changed from a domestic industry to a factory industry, so that the women who were

[51] Eden, *State of the Poor*, vol. III, p. 867.   [52] BPP 1839 (159) XLII, p. 53.
[53] Joel Mokyr, *The Lever of Riches: Technological Creativity and Economic Progress* (Oxford: Oxford University Press, 1990), p. 100.
[54] Duncan Bythell, *The Handloom Weavers* (Cambridge: Cambridge University Press, 1969), pp. 76–8.
[55] In 1835 the factory inspectors found 103,564 powerlooms in England: 96,679 in cotton, 5105 in wool, 1714 in silk, 41 in flax, and 25 in mixed goods. BPP 1840 (220) XXIV, p. 591. See also Bythell, *The Handloom Weavers*, and John Lyon, "Family Response to Economic Decline: Handloom Weavers in Early Nineteenth-Century Lancashire," in R. Ransom, ed., *Research in Economic History*, vol. XII (London: JAI Press, 1989).

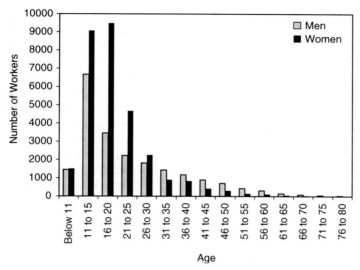

Figure 1.2 The age distribution of textile factory workers
Note: Includes cotton, wool, flax, and silk factories.
Source: BPP 1834 (167) XIX.

employed in this industry were doing very different work than women
had done in 1760. Spinning entered the factories early, and weaving
somewhat later. By mid-century, then, the textile industry was a factory
industry. Figure 1.2 shows the pattern of employment, by sex and age, in
textile factories sampled by parliamentary investigator James Mitchell.[56]
This figure shows that women, mainly young women, were extensively
employed in textile factories.

By 1850, then, women's employment in textiles was still important, but
was less extensive and of a different kind than it had been in 1760. Women's employment in textiles changed greatly between 1750 and 1850. In
1750 a large portion of the female population worked in hand spinning.
This work was done at home by women of all ages. By 1850 this work had
disappeared. In some regions women in their teens and twenties could find
work in textile factories, but in others textile work simply disappeared.

New technologies changed not only the gender patterns of employment, but the geographical patterns as well. While the very visible cotton
factories increased opportunities for women workers in the areas where
they appeared, in other areas the demand for women workers decreased
substantially. Labor markets were local, and migration failed to completely

[56] BPP 1834 (167) XIX.

equate real wages in different areas. Williamson and Hunt both find large and persistent regional differences in real wages, even correcting for price differences, compensating differentials, and poor law payments.[57] Women's work opportunities, then, depended on the state of the local industry. In England, most of the factories were located in Lancashire and the West Riding, but there were factories elsewhere. In James Mitchell's 1833 survey of factories, which is neither a complete nor a random sample, 56 percent of English employment was located in Lancashire and the West Riding, 24 percent was located in the southwest, 14 percent in the west midlands, and only 6 percent in the southeast.[58] English cotton factories were concentrated in Lancashire, flax factories in Leeds, wool factories in the south-west, silk factories in Derbyshire, lace factories in Devonshire and Derbyshire, and potteries in Staffordshire. Scotland also had substantial factory employment, especially in Glasgow.[59] Locations that did have factories had relatively high demand for female labor. In 1833 the overseer of Stroud claimed, "The Women and Children are employed in the woollen manufacture, and, generally speaking, their labor is more in demand than that of the Men."[60] At the same time, areas where no factories were built experienced a decline in the demand for women workers, as hand spinning disappeared. While not all factories were located in Lancashire and the West Riding, factory employment was still more concentrated than hand spinning had been, and many locations found themselves with suddenly reduced employment opportunities. Many areas reported that there was little or no work for women; one Norfolk parish reported, "Since spinning and knitting have been nearly superseded by the use of machinery, our Women and Children have little to do except in harvesttime."[61] Thus new technologies had important effects on work opportunities for women, opportunities that varied from one town to another.

B. Cottage industries

Cottage industry, in which employers gave out raw materials for their workers to work up at home, was an important employer of women

---

[57] Jeffrey Williamson, "Did English Factor Markets Fail during the Industrial Revolution?" *Oxford Economic Papers* 3 (1987), 641–78, and E. H. Hunt, *Regional Wage Variations in Britain, 1850–1914* (Oxford: Clarendon Press, 1973).

[58] "Report from Dr. James Mitchell to the Central Board of Commissioners," BPP 1834 (167) XIX.

[59] In Mitchell's survey, total Scottish factory employment was 75 percent of total English factory employment.

[60] Thomas Shill; BPP 1834 (44) XXX, Stroud, Gloucestershire, p. 208.

[61] John Ayton, JP; BPP 1834 (44) XXX, Scole, Norfolk, p. 329

in the eighteenth century.[62] It rose to prominence in the eighteenth century and was replaced by the factory system during the Industrial Revolution. Important cottage industries were spinning, weaving, lace-making, framework knitting, and straw-plaiting. Because the demise of the cottage industry is so much better documented than its rise, we tend to think of it as sector with very poor pay. Parliamentary reports of the nineteenth century examine in excruciating detail the starvation wages in industries such as handloom weaving and framework knitting. By the mid-nineteenth century, relatively few women still worked in cottage industries, and those who did earned very low wages. In their day, though, cottage industries employed large numbers of women at relatively high wages.

Lace

In the late eighteenth century pillow-lace making was a thriving cottage industry, and the women employed in it made good wages.[63] By the mid-nineteenth century, however, the pillow-lace trade had dwindled and lace-makers earned extremely low wages. This decline was due both to the increasing factory production of lace and to competition with France.

In the eighteenth century lace making employed substantial numbers of women in the midlands. Defoe, in his 1724 tour, noted that lace-making was widespread in Bedfordshire.[64] In 1770 Arthur Young noted, "The town of Bedford is noted for nothing but its lace manufactory, which employs above 500 women and children."[65] The lace industry prospered during the Napoleonic Wars because imports were cut off. Women could find ample employment making lace and thus were not found in agriculture. In 1813 women in Buckinghamshire worked at lace making and straw plaiting and could "earn by such work from 7s. to 30s. per week."[66]

After the war, the industry started to decline because of competition from the Continent and, more importantly, from increasing mechanization. Mechanization did not immediately replace the domestic industry; machine lace-making and pillow-lace making existed side by side for a long time. At first the machines could only do limited tasks,

---

[62] See Maxine Berg, *The Age of Manufacture* (Oxford: Oxford University Press, 1986).

[63] The making of lace by hand was termed "pillow-lace" because the lace was formed on pins that were stuck in a pillow.

[64] Daniel Defoe, *A Tour through the Whole Island of Great Britain*, abridged and edited by Pat Rogers (Harmondsworth: Penguin, 1986), p. 427. Lace-making was centered in the midlands, and was most prominent in Bedfordshire.

[65] Young, *Northern Tour*, vol. I, p. 26.

[66] St. John Priest, *General View of the Agriculture of Buckinghamshire* (London: Sherwood, Neely, and Jones, for the Board of Agriculture, 1813), p. 346. Pinchbeck also quotes wages as high as £1 to 25s. during the Napoleonic Wars. Pinchbeck, *Women Workers*, p. 207.

and many types of lace could still only be made by hand. As the machines improved, more types of lace could be made by machine, and the pillow-lace trade gradually disappeared.

The first lace machine, the bobbinet machine invented by John Heathcoat, appeared in 1809. This machine had the obvious effect of lowering the prices of lace, so that the wages of lace makers were reduced, and workers were thrown out of employment. Spenceley claims that the number of lace makers in one town declined from 2000 to only 300.[67] However, since the bobbinet machine could only make lace net, only workers making plain lace net were so affected. Hand work was still necessary to make more complicated types of lace and to embroider designs on the lace net.[68] This employment, called tambouring, continued to employ many women.

Though employment declined, pillow-lace making continued to be a large domestic industry in the early nineteenth century. It was one of the most important non-agricultural occupations cited for women in the 1833 "Rural Queries" of the Poor Law Commission, even though the industry was in decline at this time. Lace work was most common in Bedfordshire, where thirteen of sixteen responding parishes reported that their women did lace work, and in Buckinghamshire, Northampton, and Derbyshire. The respondents all agreed, however, that the trade was in decline. The pillow-lace trade was said to be "excessively bad,"[69] "not a thriving trade,"[70] and "reduced by one-half."[71] Wages were very low in 1833, and many women continued to work for wages as low as 1s. to 4s. a week.

A brief respite was granted when exports of lace boomed from 1840 to 1844, adding to the industry's prosperity. After this boom, however, the pillow-lace trade went into a permanent decline, lasting until the 1880s. Power was increasingly used for the lace machines, especially after 1820.[72] The first lace factory was built in Tiverton, Devonshire. Machines were gradually improved and adapted to making all types of lace. In the 1840s the Jacquard system was adapted to the lace machinery, increasing the ability of these machines to make patterned lace. It was not until the 1860s, however, that machines could successfully make

[67] The town was Honiton. G. F. R. Spenceley, "The English Pillow Lace Industry 1840–80: A Rural Industry in Competition with Machinery," *Business History* 19 (1997), p. 70.
[68] Some types of lace were made in two stages – the net was woven, and then the design was embroidered onto that net. The bobbinet machine could do only the first operation, but it did so much more efficiently and hand-workers making the net were replaced.
[69] BPP 1834 (44) XXX, Medmenham, Buckinghamshire, p. 45
[70] BPP 1834 (44) XXX, Easton Mawdit, Northamptonshire, p. 341.
[71] BPP 1834 (44) XXX, Watlington, Oxfordshire, p. 390.
[72] William Felkin, *A History of the Machine-Wrought Hosiery and Lace Manufactures* (London: Longmans, Green, and Co., 1867), p. 331.

Table 1.7. *Wages in lace making*

Year	Place	Earnings		Ratio	Src
		Women in lace	Men in agriculture		
1770	Bedford	8d.–10d./dy	6s./wk*	0.75	a
1770	Maidenhead, Berkshire	10d.–1s./dy	7s./wk	0.79	a
1795	Leighton Buzzard, Bedfordshire	8d.–10d.	6s.–7s./wk*	0.69	b
1795	Buckingham	8d.–9d./dy	1s.–1s.6d./dy	0.57	b
1795	Roade, Northamptonshire	8d.–10d./dy	1s./dy	0.75	b
1833	Cardington, Bedfordshire	2s.6d./wk	12s./wk	0.21	c
1833	Kempston, Bedfordshire	2s.6d./wk	10s./wk	0.25	c
1833	Thornton, Buckinghamshire	1s.–3s./wk	8s.–12s./wk	0.20	c
1833	Woodbury, Devon	6d./dy	9s.–10s./wk	0.32	c
1833	Sheepy Magna, Leicestershire	6d./dy	2s./dy	0.25	c
1833	Kettering, Northamptonshire	1s.6d.–3s.6d./wk	9s.–12s./wk	0.24	c
1843	Nottingham	3s.6d./wk			d

* *Wages in a neighboring town.*
Sources:
a. Young, *Northern Tour.*
b. Eden, *The State of the Poor*, vol. II, pp. 8, 24 and 544.
c. BPP 1834 (44) XXX, pp. 7, 8 and 49.
d. BPP 1843 (431) XIV.

Maltese lace.[73] With the move to factories, men began to work as lace makers, though women were also employed in the mechanized lace factories. Eventually, factory production completely replaced the making of lace by hand, and the pillow-lace industry disappeared.

The fortunes of the lace industry are reflected in the path of wages. Table 1.7 shows wages in domestic lace manufacture and, for comparison, wages of male agricultural laborers. A substantial fall in wages of lacemakers is evident. In 1770 women made good wages. Arthur Young noted that in Bedford "women that are very good hands earn 1s. a day, but in common only 8d. 9d. and 10d."[74] These wages were the same as what male agricultural laborers in the neighborhood could earn in the winter.[75] The industry boomed at the end of the eighteenth century. Spenceley claims that in 1795 workers in Honiton made £1 a week.[76]

[73] Spenceley, "The English Pillow Lace Industry," p. 79.
[74] Young, *Northern Tour*, vol. I, p. 26.
[75] Wanden 8d. to 1s.; Broughton 10d.; Biddenham 9d.; labourers, of course, earned more in the summer. These wages are also from Young, *Northern Tour.*
[76] Spenceley, "The English Pillow Lace Industry," p. 70.

This would have been quite a high wage, particularly for women, and was likely the result of restrictions on imports imposed by war. By 1833, after a period of decline, wages were much lower, generally around 3s. a week, a low wage and less than women generally earned in agriculture.

Straw plaiting

Straw plaiting, like lace making, provided extensive employment for women in the late eighteenth century, but dwindled to insignificance by the mid-nineteenth century. The straw industry had provided women with work since at least 1724, when Defoe mentioned its existence in Bedfordshire.[77] The industry grew and, by the turn of the nineteenth century, employed a substantial number of women. In 1784 the invention of a tool for splitting straw increased the wages in straw-plaiting.[78] Straw-plaiting was encouraged as a replacement for lost spinning work, leading to further growth in employment. In 1795 Eden found that in Dunstable, Bedfordshire, straw work "has given employment, for the last 20 years, to every woman, who wished to work," and he claimed that an adult woman could earn from 6s. to 12s. per week.[79] These wages, though, were probably higher than at other times. As in the lace trade, the Napoleonic Wars cut off competition from the Continent and led to a boom in the English industry. With peace came foreign competition, and the industry declined.

By 1833, the state of the straw-plaiting industry was quite different. Competition from Italian straw hats put the industry into decline. In the "Rural Queries," a respondent from Sible Hedingham, Essex, replies, "There is a little straw plaiting, which now goes on very badly."[80] At this time straw plaiters in Essex were making only 3s. per week.[81] Some women were still employed in straw plaiting in 1851, but their numbers were relatively few. The census reports a total of 14,425 straw plaiters in England and Wales, which is only 0.14 percent of the population age 20 and over.[82]

Gloves

Women also lost employment in glove making as fashion changed and glove making became a branch of the factory lace industry rather than a

---

[77] Defoe, *Tour*, pp. 427–8.
[78] Duncan Bythell, *The Sweated Trades* (New York: St. Martin's Press, 1978), p. 119.
[79] Eden, *State of the Poor*, vol. II, p. 2.   [80] BPP 1834 (44) XXX.
[81] *Ibid.* Ten years later straw plaiters in Suffolk were earning approximately the same wages, 6d. to 8d. per day. *Women and Children in Agriculture*, p. 229.
[82] BPP 1852–3 LXXXVIII.

cottage industry. Making of leather gloves was centered in Woodstock, Yeovil, and Worcester. Generally men cut the gloves, and the women sewed them.[83] In 1807 Arthur Young found the male leather cutters earning 21s. to 30s. a week and the women earning 8s. to 12s. a week sewing the gloves.[84]

This industry declined when restrictions on trade with France were eliminated. Restrictions on the importation of French gloves were lifted in 1826, and by the early 1830s the decline was evident. In Worcester the trade was in 1832 only one-third what it had been in 1825.[85] The "Rural Queries" of 1833 find the glove-making areas complaining of decline. We learn that in Wootton, Oxfordshire, the glove trade was "much fallen off," and in Ledbury, Herefordshire, "owing to the free trade system, this source of employment is greatly diminished." The overseer of Claines, Worcester, complains, "We had [employment for women], in the Glove trade, until the *free trade* system ruined it." In Ledbury, in 1833, women earned 3s. to 4s. a week sewing gloves. This was a typical wage for women at the time, but it was much lower than previous wages in the industry – a quarter to a half the wage quoted by Arthur Young twenty-six years earlier. The overseer of Yeovil also estimated that "Females do not earn so much by half as formerly."[86] All this suggests a rapid decline in this industry.

The change in fashion from leather gloves to cloth gloves also contributed to the disappearance of the glove trade in the south-west. By 1840 the leather glove trade had disappeared. In 1840 in Hereford we find that, "John Hatton, glover ... has given up the trade within the last 12 months; it has been gradually declining ever since the importation of French gloves."[87] In the report of W. A. Miles, we find that in Ludlow "The glove trade in this town once occupied 100 persons, but owing to change of fashion, namely, the introduction of cotton, woollen, silk, and thread as a material, the leather glove trade decreased, and about 2 years ago became extinct."[88] After this the glove trade became a branch of the lace trade, the gloves being made of fabric knitted on a frame. An industry that had been an important employer of women ceased to exist.

---

[83] BPP 1834 (44) XXX, Yeovil, Somerset.
[84] Arthur Young, *General View of the Agriculture of Oxfordshire* (Newton Abbot: David and Charles, [1813] 1969), p. 329.
[85] Berg, *The Age of Manufactures*, p. 124.
[86] BPP 1834 (44) XXX, Yeovil, p. 417.   [87] BPP 1840 (220) XXIV, p. 544.
[88] BPP 1840 (220) XXIV, p. 542.

Buttons

The manufacture of buttons was concentrated in Dorset.[89] The industry employed 4000 women and children near the town of Shaftesbury in 1793. In 1812 a woman could earn between 6s. and 12s. a week making buttons.[90] The Dorset button industry declined when competition from pearl buttons reduced the demand for wire buttons. A draper from Blandford, Dorset, attributed the decline to the competition with pearl buttons

The introduction of the pearl-button has made a serious difference to the button makers; it has very considerably diminished the demand for wire-buttons, which were the most profitable to make, whilst it has increased, perhaps, the demand for the coarser articles, upon which the earnings are small. The demand for wire-buttons has diminished perhaps twenty-five per cent.[91]

The draper estimated that women could earn only 3s. per week making buttons.[92] Still, the trade was strong enough that a farmer from Whitchurch, Dorset, found it difficult to hire women at 4s. per week.[93] The Dorest button industry did not last past mid-century, when the industry was superseded by machinery.[94]

C.   Agriculture

Though its role was declining, agriculture was also an important employer of women in pre-industrial Britain. It employed about half of the labor force in 1760. By the 1801 census this had fallen to about a third, and by 1850 only a quarter of the labor force worked in agriculture.[95] While agriculture did not employ the majority of the population, it still employed a significant fraction. Women agricultural workers were occasionally farmers, but usually either unpaid family workers or hired workers, which were either annual servants or day-laborers.[96]

---

[89] In the 1833 "Rural Queries," seven out of sixteen parishes in Dorset mention button-making employment, while only one parish outside of Dorset (Biddulph, Staffordshire) mentions the trade. BPP 1834 (44) XXX.

[90] Pinchbeck, *Women Workers*, p. 231.

[91] Mr. Fisher, of Blandford, Dorset, Draper, *Women and Children in Agriculture*, p. 87.

[92] *Women and Children in Agriculture*, p. 87.

[93] "The women are much engaged in the buttoning in this village; it is with difficulty they can be got to work for 4s. a-week in harvest." Mr. Joseph Fowler, Farmer, Whitchurch, Dorset, *Women and Children in Agriculture*, p. 56.

[94] Pinchbeck, *Women Workers*, p. 232.

[95] Gregory Clark, "Agriculture and the Industrial Revolution, 1700–1850," in Joel Mokyr, ed., *The British Industrial Revolution: An Economic Perspective* (Boulder: Westview Press, 1993), p. 233.

[96] Young people were generally servants until marriage, becoming day-laborers thereafter.

Some women were tenant farmers managing their own farms. Eden reported a census of a Surrey town which included eight farmers, one of whom was a woman (a widow); she hired four servants, three male and one female.[97] In an 1829 directory of Derbyshire, 5 percent of the farmers listed in the county were female, so while women farmers were not common there were certainly more than one or two isolated examples.[98] In the 1841 census 7 percent of farmers and graziers in Britain were female.[99] Most of these women were probably widows who became farmers when their husbands died. An example is Mary Stimpson of Alderford, Norfolk. In the 1820s her husband Benjamin rented a farm of 94 acres for £141 per year.[100] After Benjamin died in 1831, Mary managed the farm until 1838.[101] While most of these women farmers were widows, some were not. Davidoff gives the example of "Louisa Fairhead of Wickham's Bishop in Essex [who] inherited the family farm and ran it 'with equal skill to that of male members of the family' throughout her long life."[102]

There is no reason to expect that these women farmers were not active managers. We do have evidence of women actively managing their farms. One woman, in a letter in the *Annals of Agriculture*, wrote of the management of her farm:

I bought a small estate, and took possession of it in the month of July, 1803. I mowed the crop immediately, and had only nine ton of hay off fifteen acres ... I had the rocks blown up, broken small, and laid in the drains: all the trees grubbed up. I had 576 perches of under-drains made, and as much open ditching ... In July following, I mowed the fifteen acres, and had thirty ton of hay.[103]

Arthur Young spoke with one farmer's wife who told him her opinion on feeding cabbages to cows: "Lady Darlington assured me, that she had attended particularly to the effect of the cabbages on the butter, expecting to find it taste, but was agreeably surprised at the fine flavour

---

[97] Eden, *State of the Poor*, vol. III, pp. 705–9.

[98] Stephen Glover, *The Directory of the County of Derby* (Derby: Henry Mozley and Son, 1829). Of the 3423 farmers listed in the directory, 3191 could be identified as male and 162 as female, so I estimate the number of female farmers at 4.8 percent of the total.

[99] BPP 1844 (587) XXVII. Davidoff reports that "In a 1851 sample from Essex and Suffolk, 9.3 per cent of farm households were headed by women, almost all widows." Leonore Davidoff, "The Role of Gender in the 'First Industrial Nation': Agriculture in England 1780–1850," in Rosemary Crompton and Michael Mann, eds., *Gender and Stratification* (Cambridge: Polity Press, 1986), p. 207.

[100] Norfolk Record Office MC 561/44 and MC 561/54.

[101] Receipts signed by Mary Stimpson show that she was actively managing the farm. Norfolk Record Office MC 561/55.

[102] Davidoff, "The Role of Gender," p. 207.

[103] *Annals of Agriculture*, vol. XLIV, p. 477, quoted in Pinchbeck, *Women Workers*, p. 30.

of it, so much superior to that commonly made in the winter."[104] In July 1773 a farmer named Sarah Simpson wrote to her landlord that she was too busy with farm work to visit him: "I am at present strongly engaged with the Hay harvest and probably shall be so for Two or Three weeks longer, but as soon as I can be spared from the present Hurry intend to do my self the pleasure of weitng upon you at Netherhall."[105] Eden wrote of two unmarried sisters who farmed:

Mrs. Sarah Spencer was the daughter of a gentleman in Sussex ... on the demise of her father, she found her whole fortune did not amount to quite £300. Her sister Mary ... was left in a similar predicament ... they could [not] marry advantageously ... at a loss what else to do, they took a farm; and, without ceasing to be gentlewomen, commenced farmers. This farm they carried on for many years, much to their credit and advantage ... and, not seldom, in one and the same day, have they divided their hours in helping to fill the dung-cart, and receiving company of the highest rank.[106]

Clearly these women were not just owners, but were active farmers.

Wives of tenant farmers were also actively engaged in the work of managing the farms. The wife of a farmer was typically responsible for feeding the family and servants, brewing beer, spinning wool, keeping the house and clothing clean, managing the dairy and pigs, poultry, and bees, and minding the children.[107] The mistress of a small farm might do many of these tasks herself, but the mistress of a large farm would spend a greater portion of her time supervising hired labor. In addition to directing the servants to their tasks, the farmer's wife also hired and fired servants. Mary Hardy, the wife of a Norfolk farmer, wrote in her diary for January 5, 1779, "Turned both the maids away for raking with Fellows & other misdemeanors." On January 7 she wrote, "Hired Jane Rece yesterday at 5/6 per month."[108] There is some disagreement in the literature about the extent to which dairywomen were replaced by men. Deborah Valenze suggests that commercial dairymen pushed women out of the business, but Sally McMurray finds more continuity.[109] By

---

[104] Young, *Northern Tour*, vol. II, p. 129.
[105] Gielgud, "Nineteenth Century Farm Women," p. 164.
[106] Eden, *State of the Poor*, vol. I, pp. 626–7.
[107] Nicola Verdon, "'... subjects deserving of the highest praise': Farmers' Wives and the Farm Economy in England, c. 1700–1850," *Agricultural History Review* 51 (2003), 23–39.
[108] Mary Hardy, *Mary Hardy's Diary* (London: Norfolk Record Society, vol. 37, 1968), p. 31.
[109] Deborah Valenze, "The Art of Women and the Business of Men: Women's Work and the Dairy Industry, c 1740–1840," *Past and Present* 139 (1991), 142–69; Sally McMurray, "Women's Work in Agriculture: Divergent Trends in England and America, 1800 to 1930," *Comparative Studies in Society and History* 34 (1992), pp. 248–70.

the middle of the nineteenth century, men had entered the dairy industry, but it was still common for the farmer's wife to run the dairy. In 1843 Alfred Austin reported that in the smaller dairy farms of the south-east

the most laborious part of the work is not performed by servants, but by the mistress herself. The prosperity of such a farm depends entirely on the quality of the cheese, or, in other words, upon the skill and attention bestowed on its making and subsequent management. The entire management of the dairy rests with the farmer's wife, and cannot be left to servants.[110]

A farmer's wife might also take over the management of the farm in her husband's absence. For example, Ann Lukin took over the management of a 142 acre farm when her husband, Captain Lukin, was called to sea.[111]

Ivy Pinchbeck suggests that the wives of better-off farmers withdrew from active participation in farm work. The evidence she provides is anecdotal. The author of *An Honest Farmer* complained that wives and daughters of farmers enjoyed leisure rather than working on the farm:

Our wives have their Toilettes, and their Entertainments; Trifles, Jellies, Syllabubs, and Sweetmeats, are become Things of course ... Our daughters, instead of being taught their Duty, and the Business of a Dairy at home, receive their Education at a Boarding School, are taught to dance, to speak French, and to play upon a Harpsicord.[112]

A satiric poem by John Robey suggests change over time in the activities of women, as well as men:

> 1743
> Man, to the Plough
> Wife, to the Cow,
> Girl, to the Yarn,
> Boy, to the Barn,
> And your Rent will be netted.

> 1843
> Man, Tally Ho
> Miss, Piano,
> Wife, Silk and Satin,
> Boy, Greek and Latin,
> And you'll all be Gazetted.[113]

---

[110] *Women and Children in Agriculture*, p. 5. A farmer from Othery, Somerset, claimed that nearly all the dairy work in that region was done by farmers' wives. *Women and Children in Agriculture*, p. 120.

[111] Norfolk Record Office WKC 5/233.

[112] Quoted in Pinchbeck, *Women Workers*, p. 36.   [113] *Ibid.*

Nicola Verdon, however, suggests that the withdrawal of farmers' wives was not universal, and was probably more common in East Anglia, where farms were growing larger, than in other regions.[114] Smaller farms, where wives' participation was still needed, remained numerous. Where women did cease to be engaged in farm work, this withdrawal was probably related to the increased wealth of the farmers as their farms grew larger. The Industrial Revolution was a time of concentration of land ownership, a phenomenon Allen calls the landlord's agricultural revolution.[115] Changes in mortgage law enabled landowners to run out copyholds and increase their property rights. Enclosures pushed small farmers off the land. These changes probably resulted in larger farms, where the farmer's wife could afford more leisure.

Wives of laborers also worked as self-employed agricultural producers. In 1785 a pamphleteer claims, "I have known instances of the wife's management of the live stock, together with the earnings of herself and her children in hay time, and harvest, &c., produce nearly as much money in the course of the year, as her husband by all his labor during the same time."[116] When a common was available, a laborer's wife could use it to raise animals such as geese or pigs, or a cow. The produce from a cow could mean a weekly income of 5s. to 6s. per week for the family, which was higher than a woman's usual weekly wage as a hired laborer. [117] The commons also provided raw material for making brooms, and women could also reduce household expenditures by collecting fuel, berries, and nuts there. Thus, the laborer's wife could earn substantial sums even if she rarely worked for wages. Unfortunately, the opportunities for such work diminished as a result of parliamentary enclosures, which reached a peak in the first few decades of the nineteenth century.[118] Enclosures prevented landless laborers from keeping livestock; the number of cows in Tutvy[Turvey], Bedfordshire, decreased from 110 to 40 after enclosure.[119]

---

[114] Verdon, "... subjects deserving."
[115] Robert C. Allen, *Enclosures and the Yeoman: The Agricultural Development of the South Midlands 1450–1850* (Oxford: Clarendon Press, 1992).
[116] *A Political Enquiry into the Consequences of Enclosing Waste Lands* (London: L. Davis, 1785), p. 46. Eden, *State of the Poor*, vol. I, p. 608 claims: "I have often observed, that when the circumstances of a laboring family have enabled them to purchase a cow, the good management of the wife has preserved them from the parish as long as the cow lasted."
[117] Jane Humphries, "Enclosures, Common Rights, and Women: The Proletarianization of Families in the Late Eighteenth and Early Nineteenth Centuries," *Journal of Economic History* 50 (1990), 17–42.
[118] Mark Overton, *Agricultural Revolution in England: The Transformation of the Agrarian Economy 1500–1850* (Cambridge: Cambridge University Press, 1996), pp. 150–1.
[119] Board of Agriculture, *General Report on Enclosures* (London: B. McMillan, 1808), p. 150.

The loss of the commons was partially replaced by the provision of allotments, small plots of land that laborers could rent. Allotments were first provided about 1795, but did not become common until the 1830s. By the mid-nineteenth century, nearly one quarter of English parishes had allotments, and these were more common in the south than in the north.[120] Burchardt estimated that an allotment of a quarter acre would increase family income by £4 to £5, which was about half of the profit that could have been derived from keeping a cow on the common.[121] Women provided much of the labor for allotments. Burchardt suggests that men did the heavy labor of digging during the winter when they were unemployed, while the lighter summer work of weeding and picking was done by women and children.[122] Many of the laborers' wives interviewed by Alfred Austin in 1843 mention farming small amounts of land, which they used to grow potatoes and sometimes wheat, and to keep a pig. Mrs. Sumble, the wife of a farm laborer from Calne, Wiltshire, reported in 1843: "We have an allotment of one acre all but ten rods. Last year we laid out half an acre in wheat, and had two sacks and a bushel; the rest in potatoes. We generally fat a pig to sell to pay the shoemaker's bill. This year the pig died, which is a bad job."[123] Jane Long, the wife of a laborer from Studley, Calne, had half an acre and raised potatoes and a pig; she notes "I work on the land myself."[124] Land was not always available, though, and some laborers expressed the desire for more land. The wife of a Wiltshire laborer reported:

We have also two small pieces of ground, together 65 perches, for which we pay 2l. 7s. a-year, and upon which we grow potatoes. We would like to have an acre more, for then we could raise a little corn, and have more bread than now at a cheaper rate. The land we have does not furnish potatoes enough; we have to buy some in the spring.[125]

In addition to allotments, farmers sometimes gave their laborers small "potato grounds" as a supplement to their cash wage.[126] A Somerset farmer noted that, instead of cider, he gave his laborers half an acre of

---

[120] Jeremy Burchardt, *The Allotment Movement in England, 1793–1873* (Woodbridge: Boydell and Brewer, 2002), p. 68.
[121] *Ibid.*, p. 232. [122] *Ibid.*, p. 146. [123] *Women and Children in Agriculture*, p. 68.
[124] *Ibid.*, p. 71. See also pp. 70, 270, and 271.
[125] Mrs. Wilshire of Cherill, Wiltshire. The Wilshire family also raised a pig. *Ibid.*, p. 69.
[126] "Many farmers give their regular laborers a potato-ground rent-free, where they have no allotments." Alfred Austin, in *Women and Children in Agriculture*, p. 14. Mrs. Bustler of Whitchurch, Dorset reports "My husband is carter to Mr. Fowler. He has 7s. a-week wages. We have also our cottage with a garden, and ten lugs of potato-ground, rent-free." *Ibid.*, p. 90.

potato ground, which was worked by their wives and children[127] After enclosure women retained the right to glean, and often the value of the gleanings was greater than what the woman could have earned in harvest work.[128] Thus, in spite of enclosures, poor women still had opportunities to be agricultural producers.

In the paid labor market, women were widely employed as agricultural servants, and did a variety of farm tasks. Kussmaul estimates that in pre-industrial Britain about 60 percent of the population between 15 and 24 years of age were servants.[129] This was a stage of life between childhood and marriage, through which men and women both passed. There were more male farm servants than female, but not by a wide margin; the ratio was 121 males to every 100 females.[130] Women also worked as agricultural day-laborers, but here they were greatly outnumbered by male workers. In 1851 there were about 840 male day-laborers (including boys) for every 100 female day-laborers.[131] The employment of female day-laborers varied a great deal from one region to another. Few women worked as agricultural laborers near London, or where there were thriving cottage industries, while more women worked as agricultural laborers in the north or the south-west.[132] Women were widely employed for hay making, and were also frequently employed for land-cleaning tasks such as weeding and stone-picking. Harvest employment for women was reduced when the scythe replaced the sickle.

The portion of agricultural day-labor worked by women decreased between 1750 and 1850. Women contributed about 13.6 percent of all days worked in 1751, and only about 10.6 percent of days worked in 1851.[133] Enclosures may have decreased the demand for female agricultural laborers; at one farm near Sheffield, the percentage of workdays worked by women fell from 18 percent in the 1770s (before enclosure) to 6 percent in the 1830s (after enclosure).[134] The portion of farm servants who were female may have declined, but the inaccuracies of the 1851 census make this uncertain. Kussmaul estimates that in the seventeenth and eighteenth centuries 45 percent of farm servants were female, compared to only 32 percent in the 1851 census.[135] However,

---

[127] Mr. Somers of Othery, Somersetshire, *ibid.*, 1843, p. 121.
[128] King, "Customary Rights."
[129] Ann Kussmaul, *Servants in Husbandry in Early Modern England* (Cambridge: Cambridge University Press, 1981), p. 3.
[130] *Ibid.*, p. 4. The difference may be partly due to the fact that women tended to marry younger.
[131] Burnette, "Wages and Employment," p. 683.
[132] *Ibid.*, p. 681. See also Verdon, *Rural Women Workers*, pp. 102–3, 142.
[133] Burnette, "Wages and Employment," p. 683.
[134] Burnette, "Labourers at the Oakes."   [135] Kussmaul, *Servants in Husbandry*, p. 4.

Higgs has shown that the 1851 census misallocated many farm servants as domestic servants. The errors in the 1851 census are large enough to leave open the possibility that the portion of farm servants who were female did not decline; Higgs's revisions of the 1851 census increase the number of women in agriculture by over four times.[136] However, the compositional effects of the decline in service surely did decrease female employment in agriculture. Since servants were much more likely than laborers to be female, the decline in the employment of farm servants would have reduced the number of female agricultural employees.[137]

Throughout the Industrial Revolution, women's opportunities for farming work varied with region. The south-east specialized increasingly in grain, and women workers were less in demand there because most of the tasks in arable agriculture were strength-intensive. In the west, dairy farming was more popular, and the demand for women workers was maintained in these areas. In the far north, labor in general was scarce, and women were more often employed in agriculture. This region developed its own institution to deal with the scarcity of labor. Male laborers who contracted to work for a farmer for a year were required to provide a "bondager," a woman who was available for work whenever the farmer wanted her, at a set wage. A man who had no wife or daughter to serve as a bondager often had to hire one – in effect, this was a decrease in the man's wage and an increase in the woman's. Without this system, farmers may have been forced to pay higher wages to get the workers they needed.

D.   Domestic service

Many women were employed in domestic service, though the number is probably overstated in the censuses. As we have seen, Edward Higgs claims that the 1841 and 1851 censuses exaggerate the extent to which women's paid work was concentrated in domestic service, partly because female farm servants, who were often called "maids," were frequently mis-categorized as domestic rather than agricultural workers. Edward Higgs's revisions, presented in Table 1.2, suggest that in 1851 only 18 percent of the female labor force was employed in domestic service. However, Higgs's revisions are too extreme, because they are based on detailed studies from Lancashire, which was not representative of the entire country.[138] The percentage of the female labor force employed in

---

[136] Higgs, "Women, Occupations and Work," pp. 59–80.
[137] Kussmaul, *Servants in Husbandry*, p. 15.
[138] Anderson, "Mis-Specification of Servant Occupations."

domestic service was probably somewhere between the 40 percent reported in the 1851 census and the 18 percent reported by Higgs.

A common form of employment in domestic service was as a live-in domestic servant. Servants received room and board in addition to an annual money wage. In the 1830s general servants typically earned about £10 per year for their money wage, and adding the value of in-kind payments would at least double this wage.[139] For these wages servants had to put up with long hours, limited freedom, and sometimes sexual harassment.[140] While the Duke of Bedford employed forty servants in 1753, such large retinues were rare.[141] In fact, less than half of all servants worked with another servant in the same household. Edward Higgs finds that in Rochdale, Lancashire, in 1851, 61 percent of servants were "the only resident domestic in the households in which they were enumerated."[142]

Live-in domestic servants were generally young and single. In Rochdale in 1871, 71 percent of servants were less than 30 years old, and 89 percent of female general servants were single. In London in 1851 only 2 percent of female servants were married.[143] Servants were often recruited from rural areas, and were more likely to have migrated away from their place of birth than typical town residents.[144] More females than males were hired as domestic servants; at the end of the seventeenth century 57 percent of servants in English towns were female.[145] The employment of female, as opposed to male, domestic servants was encouraged by a tax on male domestic servants which was in effect from 1777 to 1791.[146] If we accept the count of domestic servants given in the 1841 census, 79 percent of domestic servants were female. If we accept Higgs's claim that the number of female domestic servants is overstated

---

[139] Higgs, "Domestic Service," p. 138.
[140] Bridget Hill, *Women, Work, and Sexual Politics in Eighteenth-Century England* (Oxford: Basil Blackwell, 1989), p. 137.
[141] *Ibid.*, p. 129.   [142] Higgs, "Domestic Service," p. 136.
[143] Simonton, *European Women's Work*, p. 99.
[144] In 1851, 70 percent of women age 10 to 30 living in Rochdale, Lancashire, had been born there, while only 38 percent of female servants had been born in Rochdale. Higgs, "Domestic Service," p. 139.
[145] This estimate is based on returns from five large and five small English towns. David Souden, "Migrants and the Population Structure of Later Seventeenth-Century Provincial Cities and Market Towns," in Peter Clark, ed., *The Transformation of English Provincial Towns, 1600–1800* (London: Hutchinson, 1984), p. 150.
[146] Servants employed in "any trade or calling by which the master or masters of such servants earn a livelihood or profit" were exempt from the tax. In 1785 a tax on female servants was introduced, but the tax on female servants was always lower than the tax on male servants. John Chartres, "English Landed Society and the Servants Tax of 1777," in Negley Harte and Roland Quinault, eds., *Land and Society in Britain, 1700–1914* (Manchester: Manchester University Press, 1996), pp. 34–56.

by the census and should be reduced by about half, then we conclude that two-thirds of domestic servants were female.[147] Thus we can conclude that there were more female servants than male servants, and somewhere between 66 and 79 percent of servants were female in 1841. There was a gendered division of labor among domestic servants. Men were hired as footmen, butlers, grooms, coachmen, and gardeners, but not as kitchen maids or housemaids.[148]

Live-in servants, though, were not the only women engaged in domestic service occupations. Women were also employed "charring," which refers to housework, usually cleaning, done in the home of the employer and paid on a daily basis. When Mary Collier described her experience charring, she mentioned laundry, cleaning pewter, washing pots and pans, and brewing as work that she did. For these tasks she earned 6d. or 8d. per day.[149] Other women took in laundry, doing the washing in their own homes. The circumstances of such work are well described by Henry Mayhew, who entered the home of a London dock worker:

The room was about 7 feet square, and, with the man and his wife, there were eight human creatures living in it. In the middle of the apartment, upon a chair, stood a washing-tub foaming with fresh suds, and from the white crinkled hands of the wife it was plain that I had interrupted her in her washing. On one chair, close by, was a heap of dirty linen, and on another was flung the newly-washed ... On my observing to the woman that I supposed she dried the clothes in that room, she told me that they were obliged to do so, and it gave them all colds and bad eyes.[150]

This particular woman earned money both by taking in washing and by going out to do washing or charring at 3s. per week.[151] A laundress could earn more if she owned a mangle; a watercress seller told Henry Mayhew that his wife "takes in a little washing, and keeps a mangle ... The mangle we give 50s. for, and it brings us in now 1s. 3d. a day with the washing."[152] Ironing required more skill than washing and paid better; women could earn 15s. per week ironing.[153] While domestic servants were generally young and single, charwomen and laundresses were more likely to be middle-aged and married.[154]

---

[147] BPP 1844 (587) XXVII, and Higgs, "Women, Occupations and Work."
[148] Hill, *Women, Work, and Sexual Politics*, p. 127.
[149] Collier, "The Woman's Labour."
[150] Henry Mayhew, *London Labour and the London Poor* (London: Griffin, Bohn, and Co., 1861), vol. III, p. 306.
[151] *Ibid.*, vol. III, p. 307. [152] *Ibid.*, vol. I, p. 150.
[153] Sally Alexander, *Becoming a Woman and Other Essays in 19th and 20th Century Feminist History* (New York: New York University Press, 1995), p. 43; Patricia Malcolmson, *English Laundresses: A Social History, 1850–1930* (Urbana: University of Illinois Press, 1986), pp. 33–4.
[154] Alexander, *Becoming a Woman*, p. 42. Malcolmson, *English Laundresses*, p. 18.

Nursing, or tending the sick, could also be seen as a form of domestic service. Before the mid-seventeenth century the term "nursing" meant caring for children. After that time, however, the term also meant caring for the sick. Nurses would take care of and sit through the night with sick individuals, and would also help with household tasks such as cleaning or laundry.[155] Most nurses were women, but men were also employed as nurses. In a sample of nurses hired by poor law overseers in Campton, Bedfordshire, between 1767 and 1834, 17 percent of nurses were male.[156] Wages for nursing varied considerably. Sitting up with a sick person paid 6d. per night, and full-time nursing was paid from 4s. to 8s. per week.[157] In 1826 an Essex laborer wrote that "my wife expects to be confined and I cant Get a nus [nurse] for les then 4 shilen a weak."[158] Occasionally earnings were higher; one nurse earned 42s. for about three weeks work with smallpox patients in 1832.[159]

Using the statements of witnesses in court records from 1695 to 1725, Earle finds that 11 percent of women in London were engaged in charring or laundry, and another 9 percent in nursing. The numbers of women engaged in these more temporary forms of domestic service were only slightly smaller than the numbers employed as live-in domestic servants. While 25 percent of women were domestic servants, charring, laundry, and nursing together employed 20 percent of women. While most live-in domestic servants were single, most of the charwomen (63 percent) were married.[160]

E.   Variety

One oversimplified view of Industrial Revolution labor markets is that men and women never did the same work; men were only found doing "men's work," and women were only found doing "women's work." This view is false. The allocation of work between the sexes was less strict than most people imagine. The tendency to exaggerate the division

---

[155] Williams, "Caring for the Sick Poor," p. 149.
[156] Ibid., p. 150. Williams reports that 16 percent of nurses in her sample were male, and 8 percent were of unknown gender. I exclude those of unknown gender, and conclude that 17 percent of nurses of known gender were male.
[157] Ibid., pp. 147, 157.
[158] Quoted in Pamela Sharpe, " 'The bowels of compation': A Labouring Family and the Law, c. 1790–1834," in Tim Hitchcock and Peter King, eds., Chronicling Poverty: The Voices and Strategies of the English Poor, 1640–1840 (New York: St. Martin's Press, 1997), p. 98.
[159] Williams, "Caring for the Sick Poor," pp. 147, 156–7.
[160] Peter Earle, "The Female Labour Market in London in the Late Seventeenth and Early Nineteenth Centuries," Economic History Review 42 (1980), pp. 328–53.

of labor between the sexes and make general tendencies into strict rules probably arises from the failure to distinguish between ideology and reality. While occupations did tend to be dominated by one sex or the other, and contemporaries did label certain occupations "men's work," that doesn't mean men always did these jobs. Focusing on the ideological labels of jobs leads us to overlook the fact that such designations did not always reflect true employment patterns. We frequently find men doing "women's work" and women doing "men's work." For example, a Durham rector noted that "In the Northern Counties, the Women engage in Men's work much more than in the Southern Districts; serving the masons with mortar, bricks, &c. is not uncommonly done by Women in the Towns."[161] The actual distribution of labor, then, was much more flexible than the gender labels assigned to the work.

The impression one sometimes gets from reading histories of women workers is that they worked in only a handful of occupations, and never in positions of authority. Honeyman and Goodman suggest that "The central problem in the history of women's work is to explain ... the persistence of women in the lowest paid, least stable, and most unrewarding occupations."[162] Rose claims, "Women were often supervised by men, but men were never supervised by women."[163] While it is true that women workers were concentrated in a few low-skill occupations, a significant minority of women were employed in a wide variety of occupations – in industries not thought of as "women's work," and in positions of authority. We must not exaggerate the extent of the occupational sorting.

Women were not confined to a small number of occupations. In the 1841 census, which significantly underrecords women's participation, three-fourths of all the occupations listed contained both men and women. Of the 935 occupations, 219 (23 percent) were exclusively male and 5 (0.5 percent) were exclusively female.[164] Women were accoutrement-makers, actors, agents, agricultural implement makers, alkali manufacturers, alum manufacturers, anchor-smiths, animal and bird dealers, animal and bird preservers, anvil makers, archery-goods dealers, army clothiers, artists, auctioneers, aurists, and authors – and that's just the A's.

In agriculture the designations "women's work" and "men's work" do not accurately predict the sex of the worker. Certain tasks were regularly done by women and were considered "women's work." Dairying was

---

[161] BPP 1834 (44) XXX, Whitburn, Durham, p. 169.
[162] Katrina Honeyman and Jordan Goodman, "Women's Work, Gender Conflict, and Labour Markets in Europe, 1500–1900," *Economic History Review* 44 (1991), p. 608.
[163] Rose, *Limited Livelihoods*, p. 16.   [164] BPP 1844 (587) XXVII.

women's work, and women were said to do weeding, hoeing, and stone-gathering better than men.[165] Such labels, however, were descriptions rather than rigid rules. We often find men doing these tasks.[166] Men usually tended the animals, but in 1810 a Gloucestershire farm hired Elizabeth Selby to help with tending the sheep.[167] Dairy work was generally gendered as female, but men were frequently found doing all the tasks of the dairy. Men often milked cows.[168] Marshall notes that in Gloucestershire, "An indoor servant, by the name of a 'milking man,' is generally kept, in the larger dairies, for the purpose of milking, churning, and otherwise assisting in the business of the dairy."[169] Men were also employed in churning butter.[170] Women usually managed dairies, but in the nineteenth century dairymen began to take over the management of some dairies.[171] In the south west it was common for cows to be rented out to a dairyman and his wife.[172]

While cottage industry tended to be female, some of these industries employed mostly men. Even the male cottage industries, though, were accessible to women workers. Handloom weaving was primarily a male occupation in the eighteenth century, but when hand spinning was replaced by machine spinning, women moved easily into handloom weaving. Another typically male cottage industry was framework knitting. Women most often worked seaming the stockings, and the great majority of frames were worked by men, but in 1845 7 percent of frames were worked by females.[173]

Women workers were found in coal, lead, copper, and tin mines. In certain locations women and children were employed underground in collieries, mainly in transporting the coal. It was extremely rare for women to work hewing coal. Women were certainly not employed as frequently as men in coal mines, but they were not unknown; in Lancashire the ratio of

---

[165] Pinchbeck, *Women Workers*, p. 100.
[166] Examples of men hoeing: Norfolk Record Office MC 561/47, Devon Record Office 346M/E8, Hertfordshire Record Office D/EP EA50/2. Examples of men weeding: Devon Record Office 346M/E8.
[167] Gloucestershire Record Office D1571 A21.
[168] The autobiography of Joseph Mayett, a farm servant, tells us that he milked cows. See Kussmaul, *Servants in Husbandry*, p. 86. McMurry, "Women's Work in Agriculture," p. 254, claims: "Milking, of course, was done by men and women together; numerous published materials referred to farmers who hired men and women to milk."
[169] William Marshall, *The Rural Economy of Gloucestershire*, 2nd ed. (London: G. Nicol, 1796), vol. I, pp. 272–3.
[170] Deborah Valenze, *The First Industrial Woman* (Oxford: Oxford University Press, 1995), p. 60; Pinchbeck, *Women Workers*, p. 14.
[171] Pinchbeck, *Women Workers*, p. 41.   [172] Horn, "The Dorset Dairy System."
[173] Sonya Rose, "Gender Segregation in the Transition to the Factory: The English Hosiery Industry, 1850–1910," *Feminist Studies* 13 (1987), p. 166.

women to men employed underground was one woman for every twelve men.[174] The employment of women in coal mines varied greatly with region. According to the 1842 parliamentary report, coal mines in Leicestershire, Derbyshire, Durham, Northumberland, Monmouthshire, and the west of Scotland did not hire any female workers. Coal mines in Lancashire, Yorkshire, and Glamorganshire hired a few women, and mines in Pembrokeshire and the east of Scotland hired many.[175] The Mines Act of 1842 forbade the employment of females underground, but women continued to work at the pit brow. At lead mines, women washed the ore; they seem to have engaged in this occupation through the eighteenth century, and into the nineteenth. In the 1720s, Defoe talked to a woman in Derbyshire who earned 3d. a day washing ore.[176] In 1769, Arthur Young found that in the lead mines of North Yorkshire "the men earn at an average about 1s.3d.; the women 1s."[177] In 1833, women and children washing lead ore in North Yorkshire earned 4d. to 10d. a day.[178] In Cornwall and Devon women worked at the copper and tin mines. In 1827 there were an estimated 2276 women working in the copper and tin mines of Cornwall.[179] Their work was always above ground, and they generally broke up the ore to make it ready for the crushing machines. In 1833, women working at the copper and tin mines at St Agnes, Cornwall, earned 6d. a day.

Women were often employed in the manufacture of small metal goods. A parliamentary investigator stated in 1843:

I saw in some manufactures women employed in most labourious work, such as stamping buttons and brass nails, and notching the heads of screws: these are certainly unfit occupations for women. In screw manufactories the females constitute from 80 to 90 per cent of the whole number employed.[180]

This investigator's opinion that these were "unfit occupations for women" is striking, but despite such Victorian rhetoric, women were widely employed in these "unfeminine" tasks.[181] In Wolverhampton

---

[174] BPP 1842 (380) XV, p. 39.   [175] *Ibid.*, p. 38.   [176] Defoe, *Tour*, p. 464.

[177] Young, *Northern Tour*, vol. I, p. 357.

[178] BPP 1834 (44) XXX, Reeth, North Yorkshire, p. 613.

[179] Gill Burke, "The Decline of the Independent Bal Maiden: The Impact of Change in the Cornish Mining Industry," in Angela John, ed., *Unequal Opportunities* (Oxford: Basil Blackwell, 1986), p. 182.

[180] BPP 1843 (430) XIII, p. 16.

[181] Carol Morgan points out that observers seem to have been more concerned with the morality of female workers in the small metal industries than with their working conditions. Carol Morgan, "Work for Girls? The Small Metal Industries in England, 1840–1915," in Mary Jo Maynes, Birgitte Soland, and Christina Benninghaus, eds., *Secret Gardens, Satanic Mills: Placing Girls in European History, 1750–1960* (Bloomington: Indiana University Press, 2005), pp. 83–98.

women were widely employed in screw-making, japanning, and nail-making. Indeed, there is evidence that the employment of women in these trades was increasing. A workman stated in 1843, "Since the machines have been introduced in the weaving and spinning mills, ten times as many girls come to work at nails and chains ... The girls can make the nails well; some of them as well as a man."[182] In 1833 women were said to be employed making nails in Staffordshire, Warwickshire, Worcestershire, and West Yorkshire. Women made needles in Warwickshire and Worcestershire. In Tardebigg, Worcestershire, their earnings averaged 8s. a week.[183] In Brightside Bierlow, West Yorkshire, "Women and children are employed in most of the branches of the Sheffield trade, particularly the silver plated, white metal, nail-cutting." In Sedgeley, Staffordshire, women earned "From 3s. to 6s. per week in making nails and wood screws."[184] This was dirty work, as one observer explains: "In Staffordshire they make nails; and unless my readers have seen them, I cannot represent to the imagination the extraordinary figures they present – black with soot, muscular, brawny – undelightful to the last degree."[185] Though this type of work did not fit the cultural notion of women's work, women did it anyway.

The pin-making industry contained a high proportion of women workers throughout the Industrial Revolution. Arthur Young, in 1767, found a great number of women in pin-making in Gloucester and Bristol.[186] The 1841 census records 838 females and 492 males (of all ages) in pin manufacture, a ratio of 170 females for every 100 males. In 1843 a parliamentary committee found that this trade was still "carried on principally by female labor."[187] These females were mostly young, and averaged about 6s. a week.[188]

The work of women in textile factories is well known, but their work in other kinds of factories is less so. In 1833 women and children worked "in brick and tile manufactory" in Northallerton, North Yorkshire.[189] In

---

[182] BPP 1843 (430) XIII, p. 16.

[183] BPP 1834 (44) XXX, Alcester, Warwickshire and Tardebigg, Worcestershire, pp. 545, 602.

[184] Ibid., pp. 453, 621

[185] Bessie Rayner Parkes, *Essays on Women's Work*, 1865, quoted in Ellen Jordan, "The Exclusion of Women from Industry in Nineteenth-Century Britain," *Comparative Studies in Society and History* 31 (1989), p. 288.

[186] Arthur Young, *A Six Weeks' Tour through the Southern Counties of England and Wales* (London: W. Nicoll, 1768), pp. 109, 150.

[187] BPP 1843 (430) XIII, p. 17.

[188] Wanda Fraiken Neff, *Victorian Working Women: An Historical and Literary Study of Women in British Industries and Professions, 1832–1850* (London: George Allen and Unwin, 1929), p. 96.

[189] BPP 1834 (44) XXX, Northallerton, North Yorkshire, p. 612.

earthenware manufacture in Staffordshire, the number of adult women (over 21) was 58 percent the number of adult men. Many of these women were skilled workers. Skilled women were employed painting pottery and earned high wages; one woman earned 3s.6d. a day, which is approximately what women in cottage industry would earn in a week.[190] Women also worked in paper mills; in the 1833 "Rural Queries" six parishes in five different counties reported work opportunities for women in paper mills.[191] Older women were frequently employed as overlookers in the rag-room, whose workers were youths of both sexes.[192]

While the majority of the recorded tradeswomen did work in the typically "female" trades, many did not. A few skilled trades, particularly dressmaking, mantua-making, and millinery, were "women's work" and employed females almost exclusively. However, women were also widely involved in retail trade, keeping shops of all descriptions. They frequently ran taverns and inns. Sometimes these women were quite successful; in 1765, one London woman had saved £6000 from her boarding-house business.[193] While these trades account for most of the documented tradeswomen, women were certainly not limited to these few trades. Even among tradeswomen recorded as working on their own account, a significant minority worked in trades that were never considered "women's work." In Manchester in 1788 we find Elizabeth Turpin, wool-comber, Widow Brownson, butcher, Ann Chadwick, timber dealer, and Mrs. Horsefall, carter.[194] All of these women worked in occupations normally considered men's work.

There are also many examples of women in skilled work or in positions of authority. As noted above, some women were farmers who actively managed their farms. Sometimes women farmers took on duties of local government.[195] When her husband died, Mary Stimpson finished out Benjamin's half-year term as overseer of the poor, signing the rate book in March of 1832.[196] (However, she did not continue in

[190] This woman earned more than her husband. "Since the differentials applied to particular skills, particularly skillful women could substantially out-earn their less skillful husbands. Mrs. Wilcox, a skilled flower painter in Wedgwood's London workrooms, earned 3s.6d. a day ... her husband also a painter but less skilled, and employed on simpler, more repetitive tasks, earned 2s.6d. a day." Neil McKendrick, "Home Demand and Economic Growth: A New View of the Role of Women and Children in the Industrial Revolution," in Neil McKendrick, ed., *Historical Perspectives: Studies in English Thought and Society* (London: Europa, 1974), pp. 185–6.

[191] BPP 1834 (44) XXX.   [192] BPP 1843 (431) XIV, pp. a1–a30.

[193] Dorothy George, *London Life in the Eighteenth Century* (London: Kegan Paul, Trench, Trubner & Co., 1925), p. 89.

[194] *Lewis's Manchester Directory for 1788*, reprinted by Neil Richardson (Manchester: Neil Richardson, 1984).

[195] Davidoff, "The Role of Gender," p. 201.   [196] Norfolk Record Office MC 561/46.

Table 1.8. *The British proprietress*

Name	Business	Comments	Year of src
Miss Rachel Leach	Cotton mill, Keighley, West Yorks.	Built a cotton mill in the 1780s and operated it for a few decades	*
Mrs. Betty Hudson	Cotton mill, Keighley, West Yorks.	Built and operated a mill	*
Mrs. Vanderplank	Woollen clothier, Gloucestershire	Her 2 sons are managers	1806
Mrs. Elizabeth Lazenby	Owns Harvey's Fish Sauce, sells it wholesale from her warehouse in London	Inherited the trademark from her brother	1819
Mrs. Doig	Powerloom weaving factory, Scotland	60 employees, 50 female	1833
Mary Powell	Flannel handloom weaving, Wales	16 looms, 8 men employed	1840
Mrs. Ann Harris	Handloom weaving "factory," Wales	14 employees, 6 men	1840
Mrs. Ann Whiled	Handloom weaving "factory," Wales	9 employees	1840

Sources: * Crouzet, *The First Industrialists*, pp. 52. **1806**: BPP 1806 (268) III, pp. 328–31. **1819**: *The London Times*, Jan. 14, 1819. **1833**: BPP 1833 (450) XX, A1, p. 120. **1840**: BPP. 1840 (220) XXIV, pp. 562–73.

this position, but was replaced by William Copeman.) Female business proprietors were not common, but they were not unknown. Table 1.8 lists some examples of women business owners. Grove Mill in the booming town of Keighley, West Yorkshire, was owned and rented out by Mrs. Ann Illingworth.[197] In the neighborhood of Keighley, near Leeds, Miss Rachael Leach and Mrs. Betty Hudson built and operated cotton mills.[198] In the flannel trade in Llanidloes, Montgomeryshire, Mrs. Lucas and Ann Lewis each employed forty handloom weavers, most of whom were men.[199] In Manchester in 1788, we find the firm of Phebe Fletcher & Co., iron forger and founder, and the brickmaker Mrs. Wagstaff.[200] Women worked as iron casters in Staffordshire; in

[197] "Notes on Grove Mill," Keighley Reference Library.
[198] François Crouzet, ed., *The First Industrialists* (Cambridge: Cambridge University Press, 1985), p. 52.
[199] BPP 1840 (220) XXIV, p. 565.
[200] *Lewis's Manchester Directory for 1788*. J. Aiken, *A Description of the Country from Thirty to Forty Miles round Manchester* (London: John Stockdale, 1795), p. 177, also notes that "Mrs. Phebe Fletcher" was the head of one of Manchester's five iron foundries.

1866 it was noted that "Instances of women working as casters are still remembered in the trade."[201] Noting the women employed as insurance agents for the Sun Fire Office, Nicola Phillips states that these women "appear to have been accepted in their own rights as publicly recognised financial brokers."[202] Businesswomen were common in the pillow-lace trade; the "middle-men" in this trade were actually women. Lace-making was a cottage industry; women obtained the materials from their employers, manufactured the lace at home, and were paid a piece-rate. The employers who farmed out the work were women. In the 1840s in Nottingham, there were frequently three or even four layers of women giving out lace embroidery work. These lace mistresses were no better to their female employees than were male employers in other industries. They paid low wages, paid these wages in truck ("bread and candles"), and made their employees work on Sundays.[203]

Elizabeth Sanderson documents the prevalence of women in the Edinburgh business world. Women kept shops and were members of the Merchant Company. Many women were "roupers" or auctioneers who settled the estates of the deceased or of shopkeepers giving up business. Women provided lodgings for rent, and worked as sick-nurses and gravesclothes makers. Sanderson concludes that "far from being cocooned in a domestic world, women from all kinds of backgrounds, single, married, and widowed, were actively operating in the same world as their male counterparts."[204]

Women were also found as managers in factories, typically where the work was done by women or children. In 1833 a flax mill owned by Mr. Hammonds had a woman as an overlooker; a former overlooker told a parliamentary investigator, "I think he has got a young woman there now for overlooker."[205] George Courtland's daughters worked as overseers in his Essex silk mill.[206] Women overlookers were common in rag-cutting rooms of paper factories; an 1843 parliamentary study finds a number of them in Kent: Elizabeth Tirker, aged 40, at Springfield Mill; Sarah Bridgeland at Messrs. Smith and Allnutt; Harriett Lovelock at Hayle Mill; Mary Wright at Beech Mill.[207]

---

[201] W. Kendrick, "Cast Iron Hollow-ware, Tinned and Enamelled, and Cast Ironmongery," in Samuel Timmins, ed., *The Resources, Products, and Industrial History of Birmingham and the Midland Hardware District* (London: Robert Hardwicke, 1866), p. 109. He is quick to note that the use of women as casters "has, happily, been discontinued."

[202] Nicola Phillips, *Women in Business, 1700–1850* (Woodbridge: Boydell Press, 2006), p. 130.

[203] BPP 1843 (431) XIV, pp. 610–11.   [204] Sanderson, *Women and Work*, p. 2.

[205] BPP 1833 (450) XX, C1, p. 74, evidence of Mark Best.

[206] Davidoff and Hall, *Family Fortunes*, p. 251.

[207] BPP 1843 (431) XIV, pp. a2, a5, a6, a30.

If all of the work done by women was recorded, the distribution of women workers would be more evenly spread across the trades. Unfortunately, many of the women who worked in trades remain invisible because they worked with their husbands and were never counted as working on their own account. In his autobiography, James Hopkinson said of his wife, "I found I had got a good and suitable companion one with whom I could take sweet council and whose love and affections was only equall'd by her ability as a business woman."[208] Many of these women worked in trades where recorded women workers are infrequently found. Women rarely worked independently in printing, but some women did assist their husbands in this trade. The memoirs of one printer briefly mention this type of assistance: "How she labored at the press and assisted me in the work of my printing office, with a child in her arms, I have no space to tell."[209] In heavier trades wives probably participated less in the actual production process. Jordan claims, "In most such trades [millwrights, blacksmiths], a master craftsman's wife might handle much of the business side of the enterprise, but male apprentices, rather than wives and daughters, were used as assistants."[210] But in trades where strength was less important, wives seem to have acted as assistants to their husbands. Since women were so closely involved in their husbands' trades, they were often able to continue these businesses as widows. Most guilds acknowledged the right of a widow to become a freewoman in her husband's trade, based on the assumption that she had learned the trade while assisting her husband.[211]

In the professions, women were most commonly found as teachers. Women taught as governesses, as schoolmistresses in schools run by others, and in schools they ran themselves. Anyone could open a school, and many women who had no other opportunities did just that. For example, when Mrs. Weeton, wife of a sea captain, was widowed in 1782 she supported her two children by opening a school in Up Holland, Lancashire.[212] In 1840 the wife of James Hitching, a Gloucester weaver, earned 2s. a week by running a school. She had twelve students and charged 2d. each.[213] Schoolmistresses could be found

---

[208] James Hopkinson, *Victorian Cabinet Maker: The Memoirs of James Hopkinson, 1819–1894*, ed. Jocelyne Baty Goodman (London: Routledge & Kegan Paul, 1968), p. 96.

[209] Memoirs of J. B. Leno, quoted in Sonya Rose, "Gender Antagonism and Class Conflict: Exclusionary Strategies of Male Trade Unionists in Nineteenth-Century Britain," *Social History* 13 (1988), p. 203.

[210] Jordan, "The Exclusion of Women," p. 295.   [211] See Chapter 5.

[212] Catherine Hall, *White, Male and Middle-Class: Explorations in Feminism and History* (New York: Routledge, 1992), p. 172.

[213] BPP 1840 (220) XXIV, p. 426.

throughout the whole range of the social scale, from cheaper schools for the working class, to Mrs. Harvest's "ladies boarding school" in Manchester.[214] Neither sex dominated in this occupation; in Manchester in 1788, 37 percent of the school teachers were women, and in Derby in 1850, 57 percent were women.[215] Teachers and schoolmasters were 56 percent female in the 1841 census and 63 percent female in the 1851 census.[216]

In other professions, women were less common, but still participated. Though their number was diminishing, women still practiced various forms of medicine in the late eighteenth century. Female midwives were being replaced by male practitioners, but still existed. These women were less well paid for their services than male physicians. Eden includes in the budget of a poor family 5s. as the price of a midwife.[217] By contrast, in 1819 the "Medical Gentlemen of Blackburn" recommended fees of 15s. to 21s. for midwifery services.[218] The lower status of female midwives may have caused them to be underrecorded. The 1824–5 directory of Manchester lists no female midwives, but the directory's description of the Lying-In Hospital includes twenty-four female midwives and only nine male midwives. Importantly, the men listed are given much greater importance in the listing; the men are listed near the top, and the women are listed after the "Ladies Auxiliary."[219] Though the more prestigious occupation of physician was closed to them, women could become apothecaries or surgeons by apprenticeship.[220] Wyman documents the case of a girl apprenticed to a surgeon in 1729, and gives examples of payments made to women for cures throughout the eighteenth century.[221] Women's employment in these areas was declining, though, and the 1841 census lists only 1384 female midwives and no female physicians, surgeons or apothecaries, compared with 1476 male physicians and 18,658 male surgeons, apothecaries, and

---

[214] *Lewis's Manchester Directory for 1788.*

[215] *Ibid.*, and *Slater's Royal, National and Commercial Directory and Topography of the Counties of Derbyshire, Herefordshire, Leicestershire, Lincolnshire, Monmouthshire, Northamptonshire, Nottinghamshire, Rutlandshire, Shropshire, Staffordshire, Warwickshire, and Worcestershire* (Manchester: Isaac Slater, 1850).

[216] BPP 1844 (587) XXVII and 1852–3 (1691) LXXXVIII.

[217] The family is from Cumwhitton, Cumberland. Eden, *State of the Poor*, vol. II, p. 74.

[218] *Rules and Regulations Agreed and Entered into by the Medical Gentlemen of Blackburn*, 1819, quoted in Anne Digby, *Making a Medical Living: Doctors and Patients in the English Market for Medicine, 1720–1911* (Cambridge: Cambridge University Press, 1994), p. 255.

[219] *Pigot and Dean's Directory for Manchester*, p. 277.

[220] Digby, *Making a Medical Living*, p. 16.

[221] A. L. Wyman, "The Surgeoness: The Female Practitioner of Surgery 1400–1800," *Medical History* 28 (1984), pp. 22–41.

medical students.[222] The 1851 census does not list opticians as a separate category, but we know there was at least one female optician; Mary Ann Godfrey worked as an optician in Birmingham in 1850.[223] Women sometimes worked as veterinarians. In the farm accounts of a Shropshire farm in 1746 we find a woman veterinarian; the farmer paid 2s. 6½d. "To the Widdow Walker for curing the Sick Cattle."[224] In 1824–5, Ann Cooper was one of four veterinary surgeons in Manchester.[225]

Women authored both fiction and non-fiction books. Some of the most famous novelists of the period were women. Charlotte and Emily Brontë, George Eliot, and Jane Austen are well known, but there were other women novelists who are not as well known today, including Fanny Burney, Sarah Fielding, Elizabeth Gaskell, Eliza Haywood, and Frances Trollope. Hannah More's writing included works on religion and morals, and she was an influential intellectual figure.[226] Catherine Macaulay wrote *History of England from the Accession of James I to the Elevation of the House of Hanover*, volume I of which appeared in 1763. The book was immediately recognized as an authoritative history and was widely used in dissenting academies.[227] Mrs. Jane Marcet wrote books on chemistry and economics.[228] Her chemistry book was so popular that it went through at least eight editions in England and nine in America.[229] These women authors were generally from the higher classes, as education was necessary for this work. A woman could make good money as an author; Jane Taylor earned £150 in 1810 for her book *Hymns for Infant Minds*.[230] Women also published books; 10 percent of publishing houses were run by women.[231] The first daily English newspaper, *The Daily Courant*, was started by Elizabeth Mallett in 1702.[232]

If we look closely, we find women working in occupations not considered "women's work," some of them in skilled occupations and in positions of authority. While men and women generally worked in

---

[222] BPP 1844 (587) XXVII.   [223] *Slater's Royal, National Commercial Directory.*
[224] Rural History Centre, Reading, SAL 5/1/1. April 16, 1746.
[225] *Pigot and Dean's Directory for Manchester.*
[226] Davidoff and Hall, *Family Fortunes*, pp. 167–72.
[227] Because the *History* was written from a republican point of view, it was widely read in dissenting academies. See Bridget and Christopher Hill, "Catherine Macaulay and the Seventeenth Century," *Welsh History Review* 3 (1967), pp. 381–402.
[228] Her books include *Conversations on Political Economy* (London: Longman, Hurst, Rees, Ormen and Brown, 1819); *John Hopkin's Notions on Political Economy* (Boston: Allen and Ticknor, 1833); *Mary's Grammar* (London: Longman, Hurst, Rees, Ormen and Brown, 1835); and *Conversations on Nature and Art* (London: J. Murray, 1837–8).
[229] Jane Marcet, *Conversations on Chemistry*, 9th American edn from the 8th London edn (Hartford: Oliver Cooke, 1824).
[230] Davidoff and Hall, *Family Fortunes*, p. 67.
[231] Simonton, *European Women's Work*, p. 61.   [232] Phillips, *Women in Business*, p. 207.

different occupations, we must not forget that this generalization describes only central tendencies, and not every working woman. The wide spread of women's work suggests that the barriers to women's employment were not absolute or ubiquitous.

Conclusion

While the occupational distributions of male and female workers differed widely in the Industrial Revolution labor market, the participation of women was widespread and not strictly confined to a small set of occupations. Work patterns changed during the Industrial Revolution, as textile factories emerged and replaced older cottage industries. The flexibility of the employment patterns suggests that work patterns were able to respond to changes in economic incentives, but gender seems to have played an important role in determining an individual's occupation. Chapter 3 will present two closely related models explaining why there was such a pronounced division of labor by gender, but before moving to explanations of occupational sorting we will first consider women's wages. The next chapter will examine how women's wages compared with men's wages, establishing the size of the wage gap, and offering some explanations for it.

2 Women's wages

> It is not easy to account for so striking an inequality; and still less easy
> to justify it.   F. M. Eden, 1797[1]

> The strength required for the work performed by men effectively prevents
> women from being employed in it; and the lower rate of wages for which
> they work has not had any tendency, therefore, to make them more
> generally employed.   Alfred Austin, parliamentary investigator, 1843[2]

In the last chapter we saw that women and men tended to work in
different occupations, though the sorting was not perfect and we find
women working in a great range of occupations. This chapter will
investigate gender differences in wages. I will first establish the size of the
wage gap, and then move on to the question of why it existed. Measuring
the size of the wage gap may seem straightforward, but it is in fact
complicated because, as we shall see, measurement error in many cases
leads to an incorrect assessment of the gap. Understanding the causes of
the wage gap is even more difficult because both custom and market
forces pushed women's wages below men's wages, making it difficult to
determine which was the fundamental cause of wage differences.

Women's wages were clearly lower than men's. Historians generally
accept that women's wages were between one-third and one-half as
much as men's wages. Here are some examples of historians' conclusions about the gender wage gap:

If we compare male and female average day rates in nineteenth-century agriculture,
women usually earned between one-third and a half of the male day rate.[3]

It is generally assumed that women by custom received one-third to one-half of
the wage of men.[4]

Women's wages average out at a third of a comparable male wage across the time
period 1780–1840.[5]

---

[1] Eden, *State of the Poor*, vol. II, p. 47.   [2] BPP 1843 (510) XII, p. 27.
[3] Verdon, *Rural Women Workers*, p. 126.
[4] Maxine Berg, "What Difference Did Women's Work Make to the Industrial Revolution?"
History Workshop Journal 35 (1993), p. 31.
[5] Sharpe, *Adapting to Capitalism*, p. 146.

Much of the evidence of women's wages in the early period of industrialization is partial and piecemeal, yet that which does exist suggests levels of at most 50 per cent to the male wage.[6]

Table 2.1 gives male and female wages in a variety of occupations and generally supports the conclusions given above. There are numerous cases where the wage ratio is above, and sometimes well above, 50 percent, but women never earned the same wages as men. The wages are compiled from contemporary sources, most of them from parliamentary committees or observers such as Arthur Young. As much as possible, I have tried to compare male and female wages for the same work, but the work done may not match exactly. For example, the agricultural wages may have been given to men for ploughing and to women for weeding. All the evidence confirms that women's wages were less than men's wages, and the wage ratio usually ranged somewhere between one-third and two-thirds.

Table 2.1 is divided into separate sections for time-rate wages and piece-rate wages (plus a third section for cases where the type of payment is not known) because each type of wage must be interpreted differently. Time-rate wages were paid for a unit of labor measured by the day or week. Differences in male and female time-rate wages could occur because the definition of the day or week differed, or because men and women were paid different wages for the same unit of time input. If the latter was the case, the wage differences may have resulted from differences in productivity or from wage discrimination, or from a combination of both.

Many workers during this period, though, were paid per unit of output rather than per unit of time. For example, weavers were paid per yard of cloth, rather than per day. In domestic industry employers could not accurately measure the amount of time the workers put in, and paid the workers for their output. The "piece-rate" wages in Table 2.1 are reported as daily or weekly earnings because contemporary observers were concerned about the workers' living standards and generally reported the typical earnings of piece-rate workers rather than the price per unit of output. A parliamentary committee investigating the economic distress of weavers was more interested in what a typical weaver earned in a week than the specific prices paid for each type, width, and length of cloth. Gender differences in these weekly earnings could be due either to differences in the piece-rate paid to men and women, or to differences in the amount of output they produced in a typical week.

---

[6] Katrina Honeyman, *Women, Gender and Industrialization in England, 1700-1870* (New York: St. Martin's Press, 2000), p. 54.

Table 2.1. *Women's wages compared to men's*

Year	Place	Task	Women	Men	Ratio	Src
A: Time-rate wages						
Agriculture						
1650	Somerset	Hay	8d./dy	12d./dy	0.67	a
		Corn harvest	1s./dy	1s.2d./dy	0.86	a
1684	West Yorkshire	Reaping	11d./dy	13d./dy	0.85	b
1686	Staffordshire	Reaping	6d./dy	12d./dy	0.50	c
1696	West Yorkshire	Harvest	8d./dy	12d./dy	0.67	b
		Hay	6d./dy	12d./dy	0.50	b
1706	West Yorkshire	Reaping	8d./dy	12d./dy	0.67	b
1730s	Westmorland	Winter	4d./dy	6d./dy	0.67	d
		Summer	6d./dy	8d./dy	0.75	d
1752	Leyburn, North Yorkshire	Reaping	6d./dy	10d./dy	0.60	e
1770	Howden, North Yorkshire	Hay	6d./dy	1s.2d./dy	0.43	f
1770	Schorton, North Yorkshire	Winter	5d./dy	1s./dy	0.42	f
1770	Gilling, North Yorkshire	Harvest	1s.3d./dy	2s.6d./dy	0.50	f
		Winter	5d./dy	10d./dy	0.50	f
1789	Hertfordshire		6d./dy	8s./wk	0.38	g
1790s	Perthshire	Harvest	5.8s./wk	8s./wk	0.73	h
1795	Hothfield, Kent	Winter	8d./dy	1s.6d./dy	0.44	g
		Summer	10d./dy	2s./dy	0.42	g
1795	Orton, Westmorland	Harvest	10d./dy	1s./dy	0.83	g
1796	Northumberland		8d./dy	10s./wk	0.40	g
1796	Nuneham, Oxfordshire		3s./wk	8s./wk	0.38	g
1796	Walton Upon Thames, Surrey		1s./dy	10s.–12s./wk	0.55	g
1796	Southam, Warwickshire	Summer	6d./dy	7s./wk	0.43	g
1796	Sneed, Wiltshire	Hay harvest	8d./dy	1s.6d./dy	0.44	g
1700s	Near London	Market gardens	5s.–7s./wk	10s.–12s./wk	0.55	i
1807	Clifton, Oxfordshire		8d./dy	9s./wk	0.44	k
1807	Tetsworth, Oxfordshire	Spring	8d./dy	10s./wk	0.40	k
1807	Bignal, Oxfordshire	Harvest	1s.6d./dy	20s./wk	0.45	k
1807	Heyford, Oxfordshire	Hay	8d./dy	12s./wk	0.33	k
1807	Wormsley, Oxfordshire	Winter	8d./dy	10s./wk	0.40	k
		Spring	8d./dy	11s./wk	0.36	k
1807	Average of Oxfordshire	Spring & hay	9d./dy	11s.6d./wk	0.39	k
		Harvest	1s.2d./dy	19s./wk	0.37	k

Table 2.1. (*cont.*)

Year	Place	Task	Women	Men	Ratio	Src
1833	Cumrew, Cumberland	Summer	6s./wk	12s./wk	0.50	l
1833	Ingatestone, Essex	Summer	5s./wk	11s./wk	0.45	l
1833	Starstone, Norfolk		7d./dy	10s./wk	0.35	l
1833	Llandillo, Brecon	Summer	8d./dy	9s./wk	0.44	l
1838	Bath, Somerset	Summer	1s./dy	2s.2d./dy	0.46	m
		Winter	10d./dy	1s.9d./dy	0.48	m
1838	Frome, Somerset		8d./dy	1s.4d./dy	0.50	m
1838	Bromsgrove, Worcestershire		8d./dy	1s.8d./dy	0.40	m
1838	Martley, Worcestershire		6d./dy	1s.4d./dy	0.38	m
1838	Pershore, Worcestershire		6d./dy	1s.4d./dy	0.38	m
1838	Worcester, Worcestershire		9d./dy	1s.6d./dy	0.50	m
1838	Gloucestershire average		8.5d./dy	17.25d./dy	0.49	m
1843	Wiltshire		3s.–4s./wk	9s./wk	0.39	n
1843	Scotland average		4.3s./wk	9.1s./wk	0.47	h

Domestic labor

Year	Place	Task	Women	Men	Ratio	Src
1766	Kent	Servants	£3/yr	£12/yr		o
1776	Kent	Servants	£4/yr	£8.8s./yr		o
1796	Kent	Servants	£5.12s./yr	£8.8s./yr		o
1800	Middlezoy, Somerset		8d./dy			p
1833	Kirk Langley, Derbyshire	Washing	1s./dy			l
1833	Springfield, Essex	Washing	3s.–4s./wk			l
1833	Clifton, Gloucestershire	Charring, washing	1s.–1s.6d./dy			l
1833	Mortlake, Surrey	Charring	2s./dy			l
1833	Mortlake, Surrey	Washing, ironing	3s./dy			l
1833	Fenny Compton, Warwickshire	Charring	6d.–9d./dy			l
1833	Potter Newton, W. Yorks.	Washing	1s./dy			l
1839	Crosdale, Co. Durham	Washing	1s.6d./dy			q

Schoolmaster / schoolmistress

Year	Place	Women	Men	Ratio	Src
1816	Parochial Charity School, Spitalfields	£38/yr	£85/yr	0.45	r
1816	Protestant Dissenters School, Spitalfields	£40/yr	£60/yr	0.67	r
1819	Charity School, New Town, nr Spitalfields	£35/yr	£60/yr	0.58	r
1820	Bethnal Green National School	£40/yr	£70/yr	0.57	r
1840	Witham National School, Essex	£35/yr	£55/yr	0.64	s

Table 2.1. (*cont.*)

Year	Place	Task	Women	Men	Ratio	Src
Workhouse master / matron						
1783	Isle of Wight		£30/yr	£40/yr	0.75	g
1787	Manchester		£36/yr	£45/yr	0.80	g
1788	Birmingham		£20/yr	£52.10s./yr	0.38	g
1791	Bristol		£30/yr	£50/yr	0.60	g
1792	Wolverhampton, Staffordshire		£10/yr	£30/yr	0.33	g
1793	Isle of Wight		£30/yr	£50/yr	0.60	g
1795	St. Martin in the Fields, Middlesex		£20/yr	£50/yr	0.40	g
1795	Gressinghall, Norfolk		£25/yr	£65/yr	0.38	g
Other salaried						
1787	Birmingham	Vestry clerk		£52.10s./yr		g
1790	Sheffield	Vestry clerk		£20/yr		g
1790	Sheffield	Collector of rates		£60/yr		g
1790	Sheffield	Surgeon of workhouse		£50/yr		g
1794	Kendal, Westmorland	Apothecary		£50/yr		g
B: Earnings on piece-rate work						
Spinning						
1737	South of England		6d./dy			g
1767	Witney Woolle		10d.–1s./dy			t
1770	Leeds, West Yorks.	Wool	2s.6d.–3s./wk			f
1770	Kiplin	Flax	4d./dy			f
1770	Kendal, Westmorland	Wool	4s.6d.–5s./wk			f
1770	Manchester	Cotton	2s.–5s./wk			f
1787	South of England		7d./dy			g
1795	Cumberland	Wool	4d.–6d./dy			g
	Derby	Cotton	3s.–5s./wk			g
	Lancashire	Wool	3s.–4s./wk			g
	Leicester	Worsted	6d.–10d./dy			g
	Worcester		4d.–9d./dy			g
	Yorkshire		3d.–5d./dy			g
1795	Oldham, Lancashire	Jenny spinning	16s.–17s./wk			u
Factory						
1830	Manchester	Mule spinning	12s.–14s./wk	25s.–30s./wk	0.47	v
1833	Perthshire	Mule spinning	9s.–11s./wk	13s.–16s./wk	0.69	w
1833	Perthshire	Mule spinning	10s.–14s./wk			w
		Throstle spinning	6s.–7s./wk			w

Table 2.1. (*cont.*)

Year	Place	Task	Women	Men	Ratio	Src
Handloom weaving						
1795	Norwich		5s.–6s./wk	7s.–8s./wk	0.73	g
1795	Kendal, Westmorland		4s./wk	8s.–12s./wk	0.40	g
1824	Knaresborough	Linen	5s.6d./wk	11s.–12s./wk	0.48	x
1840	Braintree, Essex	Silk	5s.1d./wk	7s.2d./wk	0.71	y
1840	Gloucestershire	Wool	7s./wk	11s.10d./wk	0.59	y
Lace						
1795	Buckinghamshire		8d.–9d./dy			g
	Bedford		8d.–10d./dy			g
1833	Bedfordshire		2s./wk			l
Straw-plaiting						
1795	Bedfordshire		6s.–12s./wk			g
1833	Bedfordshire		5s.–10s./wk			l
1833	Essex		3s./wk			l
1843	Blything, Suffolk		6d.–8d./dy			z
Gloves						
1770	Worcester		4s.–5s./wk	7s.–9s./wk	0.56	f
1807	Woodstock, Oxfordshire	Leather cutters		21s.–30s./wk		k
		Sewing	8s.–12s./wk			k
1840	Torrington, Devon	Sewing	3s.6d./wk			y
Metals						
1790s	Birmingham	Toy trades	7s.–10s./wk	20s.–30s./wk	0.34	g
Mining						
1724	Derbyshire	Lead mining	3d./dy	5d./dy	0.60	aa
1769	North Yorkshire	Lead mining	1s./dy	1s.3d./dy	0.80	f
1795	Derbyshire	Washing lead ore	6d./dy			u
1833	Cornwall	Copper and tin mines	6d./dy			l
Sewing						
1800	Colchester	Milliners, journey women	6s./wk			s
1813	London	Soldiers' coats	5d./dy			i
1843	Blything, Suffolk		6d.–1s./dy			z
1800	London	Tailors		27s./wk		y
1816	London	Tailors		36s./wk		y
C: Wage type unclear						
Factories						
1770	Knutsford, Cheshire	Silk mill	4s.–5s./wk			f
		Thread factory		6s.–8s./wk		f

Table 2.1. (*cont.*)

Year	Place	Task	Women	Men	Ratio	Src
1824	Glasgow	Mule spinning	15s.–18s./wk	23s.–24s./wk	0.70	x
1840	Norwich	Silk mill	5s.5d./wk	14s.10d./wk	0.37	y
Misc.						
1770	Burslem	Pottery workers	5s.–8s./wk	7s.–12s./wk	0.68	f
		Pottery gilders	7s.6d./wk	12s./wk	0.63	f
1770	Newcastle	Hatters	3s.–6s./wk	7s.–10s./wk	0.53	f
1770	Sheffield	Plating and cutlery	4s./wk	13s.6d./wk	0.30	f
1813	London	Compositors		33s./wk		y
1843	London	Bookbinders	12s./wk			bb

Sources:
a. Assessed wages. Kelsall, "Wage Regulations," p. 160.
b. West Yorkshire Archives Service, Leeds, TN/EA/12/11.
c. Roberts, "Sickles and Scythes."
d. Gielgud, "Nineteenth Century Farm Women," p. 150A.
e. Gilboy, "Labor at Thornborough."
f. Young, *Northern Tour*.
g. Eden, *State of the Poor*.
h. Ian Levitt and Christopher Smout, "Farm Workers' Incomes in 1843," in T. M. Devine, *Farm Servants and Labour in Lowland Scotland, 1770–1914* (Edinburgh: John Donald, 1984).
i. George, *London Life in the Eighteenth Century*.
k. Young, *General View of Oxfordshire*.
l. BPP 1834 (44) XXX.
m. BPP 1837–8 (526) XVIII, Part III, Minutes of Evidence for June 25, 1838.
n. BPP 1843 (431) XIV.
o. Cash book of Lee Warly of Blean, Rural History Centre, KEN 14/2/1.
p. Devon Record Office, 880M/E3. Oct 29, 1800.
q. Durham Record Office, D/Sa/E181.
r. Phillip McCann, "Popular Education, Socialization, and Social Control: Spitalfields 1812–1824," in Phillip McCann, ed., *Popular Education and Socialization in the Nineteenth Century* (London: Methuen, 1977).
s. Davidoff and Hall, *Family Fortunes*.
t. Young, *Southern Tour*.
u. Aiken, *A Description of the Country round Manchester*.
v. Kirby and Musson, *The Voice of the People*, p. 109.
w. BPP 1833 (450) XX.
x. BPP 1824 (51) V.
y. BPP 1840 (43) XXIII.
z. *Women and Children in Agriculture*.
aa. Defoe, *Tour*.
bb. BPP 1843 (430) XIII.

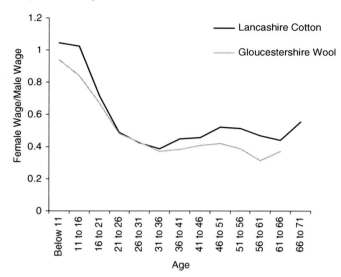

Figure 2.1 The female–male wage ratio by age in textile factories
Source: BPP 1834 (167) XIX.

The wage gap between females and males was not constant through the working life, but appeared in the teenage years and declined in old age. Figure 2.1 shows how the wage gap varied with age for a sample of factory workers in 1833, and Figure 2.2 shows the same relationship for agricultural workers. Girls earned the same wages as boys, and occasionally more, since girls mature earlier than boys. However, after age 16 boys quickly surpassed girls, and continued to earn more than women throughout their lives. In older ages, however, the size of the wage gap declined as male wages fell.

The existence of the wage gap between men and women is well known and not disputed. What *is* disputed is the interpretation of this fact. On one side there are those, generally economists, who assume that markets function fairly well, and that wage differences must reflect differences in productivity. On the other side are those who are more skeptical of the degree to which wages were determined by markets, who emphasize the customary nature of wages and interpret the wage differences as the result of an ideology devaluing women.

Economic theory suggests that, in competitive markets, wages must equal the marginal product of labor. Employers are assumed to maximize profits, and if the marginal product of labor was higher or lower than the wage, employers would not be maximizing profits because they could increase their profits by increasing or decreasing employment. In a

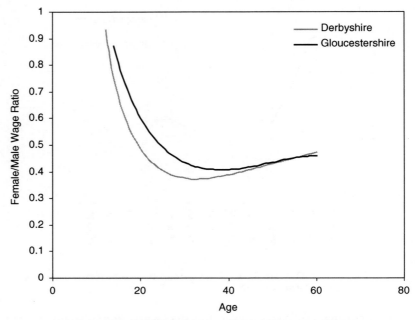

Figure 2.2 The female–male wage ratio by age in agriculture
Source: Joyce Burnette, "How Skilled Were English Agricultural Laborers in the Early Nineteenth Century?" *Economic History Review* 59 (2006), p. 714.

competitive market employees are price-takers, but will adjust their hiring so that the marginal product of labor equals the wage. The actions of employers determine the demand for labor, and the wage is determined by the interaction of this demand for labor and the supply of labor. An alternative to the competitive model is the monopsony model. A monopsony occurs when there is only one employer who can hire the worker, and in this situation the employer can use his market power to pay wages lower than the marginal product of labor. However, economists generally do not believe the monopsony model has a wide application.[7] If there is evidence that workers have a choice of possible employers, economists generally assume that markets are competitive and wages are equal to the marginal product of labor.

Economists who believe that markets are competitive use the gender wage gap as evidence of productivity differences between men and

---

[7] For an attempt to apply the monopsony model more broadly, see David Card and Alan Krueger, *Myth and Measurement: The New Economics of the Minimum Wage* (Princeton: Princeton University Press, 1995).

women. While it is possible to measure productivity using production functions, it is much easier to use observed wage differences to measure productivity differences. Goldin and Sokoloff, for example, assume that the relatively low female wage in the US North indicates that female workers had a relatively low marginal product, and they use this observation to explain the rise of textile manufacturing in the North.[8] When aggregating the amount of labor used by manufacturing firms, Sokoloff counts an adult woman as the equivalent of half an adult man because women's wages were about half of men's wages.

Females and boys have been treated as equal, in terms of their labor input, to one-half of an adult male employee, with these weights having been drawn from evidence on the relative wages of the groups prevailing near the end of the period.[9]

In a comment on this article, Jeffrey Williamson questions whether assuming a constant productivity ratio over time is valid, but does not question the assumption that the wage ratio is an accurate measure of the productivity ratio.[10] Similarly, Atack, Bateman, and Margo assume, based on the wage ratio, that an adult female worker is equal to 60 percent of an adult male worker.[11] Doraszelski also assumes that relative wages measure relative productivity when he uses wage rates to calculate the contributions of female and child workers to aggregate labor in his study of French industry.[12]

Not everyone agrees that the wage gap is evidence of productivity differences. On the other side of the debate are those who believe that women's lower wages were not justified by productivity differences, but were set by custom. For example, Pamela Sharpe claims that the wages of female servants were "a matter of custom bearing little relationship to economic determinants."[13] Sonya Rose claims that "Women could be

---

[8] Claudia Goldin and Kenneth Sokoloff, "The Relative Productivity Hypothesis of Industrialization: The American Case, 1820 to 1850," *Quarterly Journal of Economics* 99 (1984), pp. 461–87.

[9] Kenneth Sokoloff, "Productivity Growth in Manufacturing during Early Industrialization: Evidence from the American Northeast, 1820-1860," in Stanley Engerman and Robert Gallman, eds., *Long-Term Factors in American Economic Growth* (Chicago: University of Chicago Press, 1986), pp. 702–3.

[10] Jeffrey Williamson, "Comment," in Stanley Engerman and Robert Gallman, eds., *Long-Term Factors in American Economic Growth* (Chicago: University of Chicago Press, 1986), pp.729–33.

[11] Jeremy Atack, Fred Bateman, and Robert Margo, "Productivity in Manufacturing and the Length of the Working Day: Evidence from the 1880 Census of Manufactures," *Explorations in Economic History* 40 (2003), pp. 170–94.

[12] Ulrich Doraszelski, "Measuring Returns to Scale in Nineteenth-Century French Industry," *Explorations in Economic History* 41 (2004), pp. 256–81.

[13] Sharpe, *Adapting to Capitalism*, p. 114.

paid low wages because they were women. They earned a customary wage, not one which was generated out of open competition in a sexually neutral labor market."[14] Similarly, Deborah Simonton claims that, for nineteenth-century women, "Wages, like the gendered character of many jobs, rested on custom rather than real labor value."[15] While Woodward finds early modern male wages responding to supply and demand, he thinks female wages were different:

> The low rates of pay given to most women were rooted in convictions about their physical, economic and social, intellectual, and political inferiority which characterized English society into the present century, and which were underscored by biblical authority. Their rates of pay were not simply reflections of the supply of and demand for female labor.[16]

This group of historians explains women's wages not in terms of their productivity, but in terms of social expectations of women's inferiority.

There are three main ideological assumptions about women that are usually blamed for keeping women in low-paid work: women were assumed to be weak, unskilled, and dependent on men. Some historians suggest that assumptions about women's physical weakness justified low wages and kept them confined in certain occupations. Michael Roberts suggests two reasons why seventeenth-century farmers saw women as "the weaker vessel" and thus allocated them the lightest tasks. One was the physical weakness caused by pregnancy, and the other was the moral weakness evident in the biblical story of the fall, where Eve gave in first to temptation.[17] An important point is that the assumption of female weakness is not tied to physical reality; Deborah Simonton claims that "The association of women with weakness was not necessarily a biological notion, since the association of woman as the 'weaker vessel' was as much an ideological construction as it was physical."[18]

Women might also be assigned to low-paying jobs because they were assumed to be unskilled workers. Sonya Rose suggests that women factory workers were paid less than men and were not given jobs with the potential for advancement because it was assumed that they could not acquire the necessary technical skills.

Employers considered mechanical aptitude to be a purely masculine trait. They talked about men's "natural" technical ability and women's mechanical

---

[14] Rose, "Gender Antagonism," p. 208.   [15] Simonton, *European Women's Work*, p. 170.
[16] Donald Woodward, "The Determinants of Wage Rates in the Early Modern North of England," *Economic History Review* 47 (1994), p. 37.
[17] Michael Roberts, "Sickles and Scythes: Women's Work and Men's Work at Harvest Time," *History Workshop* 7 (1979), p. 11.
[18] Simonton, *European Women's Work*, p. 34.

ineptitude as though this was a gender difference everyone recognized; it was common sense. The belief that women naturally lacked facility with machinery was in fact widely held, and employers used it to justify paying women less than men for the same jobs.[19]

The assumption that women were unskilled was strong enough to lead to the relabeling of work done by women. Bridget Hill found that census officials were unwilling to categorize occupations hiring women and children as skilled.

Albe Edwards, the man responsible for the reclassification, met with a problem when he found certain occupations which technically were classified as "skilled" had to be down-graded to "semi-skilled," "because the enumerators returned so many children, young persons, and women as pursuing these occupations." Edwards did not hesitate to lower the status of certain occupations when he found women and young people worked in them in large numbers.[20]

In this case the categorization of occupations as skilled or semi-skilled reflects ideology rather than characteristics of the job.

Women's low wages are often said to result from the fact that, being dependent on men, they "needed" less income. Sonya Rose, for example, emphasizes the expectation that women were secondary earners, who did not need to support a family, and whose wages were only supplementary to the wages of the men on whom they were dependent: "Women were workers who could be paid low wages because of an ideology which portrayed them as supplementary wage earners dependent on men for subsistence."[21] Deborah Valenze also claims that "the level of a woman's earnings was determined by an assumption that her wage was a supplement to some other (most likely a breadwinner's) wage."[22]

However, while it is true that contemporaries did hold these beliefs about women's inferiority and dependence, it does not necessarily follow that these beliefs were the *cause* of women's low wages. While I do not question the claim that contemporaries believed women to be weak, unskilled, and dependent on men, I do question whether these ideologies were the real motivations behind the actions of employers, or whether they were simply the justifications given by employers to disguise their true motivations. Unfortunately it is difficult to determine whether women's wages were set by markets or by custom because both theories suggest that women would earn lower wages than men. The

---

[19] Rose, *Limited Livelihoods*, p. 27.   [20] Hill, "Women, Work and the Census," p. 90.
[21] Rose, "Gender at Work," p. 117.
[22] Valenze, *The First Industrial Woman*, p. 108; see also p. 89.

remainder of this chapter examines the wage data carefully and argues that in competitive portions of the labor market women's lower wages were the result of their lower productivity, and were set by the market rather than custom.

I.   Interpreting piece-rate wages

For piece-rate wages, wage discrimination exists only if women and men are paid different piece-rates. If women earned less than men but were paid the same piece-rates, then the difference in earnings is clearly due to differences in output. While there are a few examples of piece-rates that differ by gender, such examples of wage discrimination are the exception rather than the rule. In most cases men and women were paid equal piece-rates when they worked at the same tasks.

Even for workers who were paid by the piece, many historical sources report daily or weekly earnings rather than the actual piece-rates. Section B of Table 2.1 gives examples of such reported earnings. One reason this is true is that piece-rates could be very complex. In mule-spinning there was a different piece-rate for every count, or fineness, of yarn. In handloom weaving there was a different piece-rate for each type of cloth. Reporting all these numbers might confuse the reader.[23] Also, contemporary readers were usually concerned about the living standards of the workers, and thus were interested in the earnings of the workers rather than the piece-rates per se. Daily or weekly earnings, though, do not tell us whether there was gender discrimination. The gap between women's and men's earnings on piece-rates seen in section B of Table 2.1 may have a variety of causes, including mismeasurement, differences in hours worked, differences in output per hour, and differences in piece-rates paid. I will discuss these four possibilities in turn.

One possible reason for the wage gap observed in piece-rate earnings is measurement error. Wages given for work done in the home often conflate the earnings of different members of the family. Even if the whole family contributed labor, the entire amount gained may be counted as the man's wage. In his parliamentary report on handloom weavers, H. S. Chapman states,

On one occasion I saw a piece of shalloons woven under the following circumstances: 1. The man was in the loom weaving. 2. A boy of 10 years of age was winding bobbins. 3. The wife was at her husband's elbow picking the work.

---

[23] For an example of a parliamentary committee being confused by wage evidence presented by a witness, see the minutes of evidence from the 1808 *Report on the Cotton Weavers' Petition*. BPP 1808 (177) II, p. 10.

4. His daughter was at the back of the loom taking up the broken threads of the warp, for it was not a good warp. When the piece was taken home, the wages would be paid as the earnings of *one man*, yet the piece was really the work of a family.[24]

This type of mismeasurement would systematically raise estimates of men's earnings and lower those of women's earnings. In the reports of parliamentary committees we find specific examples of this mismeasurement occurring. Witness the following exchange between a parliamentary committee and a hatter from London:

How much do you earn a week now? – Perhaps £2.8s.

Out of that what payment have you to make? – If I had not a wife I should have to pay 6s. out of that for picking, if ovals; if flat 9s.4d.

What do you mean by picking? – The women are employed in picking the coarse hairs out that are in the stuff, that my wife does.[25]

Note that the hatter claimed to earn 48s. per week, though by his own admission at least 6s. of this (one-eighth) represents value of work done by his wife.

The following example further illustrates this point. In 1824 Joseph Sherwin, a handloom weaver from Stockport, told a parliamentary committee that he usually earned 6s.6d. a week, and his wife 3s. by winding bobbins for two other looms.[26] However, he failed to subtract from his wage, and add to hers, the value of her winding services for his loom. Mrs. Sherwin received for winding 3d. out of every shilling earned by each of two weavers who hired her services; each of these weavers, then, earned only 9d. for every 1s. worth of cloth.[27] Since she could wind for three looms (her husband's plus two others), Mrs. Sherwin could earn the same amount as these two weavers, (9d. = 3 × 3d.). Joseph Sherwin admitted, "I must pay three pence out of every shilling, if I had no wife."[28] His true wage, then, was only 4s.10½ d. (=0.75 × 6s.6d.), and his wife's true wage was 4s.7½ d. (= 3s. + [0.25 × 6s.6d.].). (The difference arises only because Joseph weaves cloth worth 6s.6d. a week, while each of the other two weavers complete only 6s. worth of cloth in a week.) What by his statement appeared to be a wage ratio of 0.46 (3s./6s.6d.) turns out to be, in truth, approximately equal wages.

---

[24] BPP 1840 (43) XXIII, p. 561. He also says, "when a manufacturer says 'such a weaver can earn so much,' it may happen that the sum is really, as already explained, the wages of two persons" (p. 559).
[25] BPP 1824 (51) V, p. 97.   [26] *Ibid.*, pp. 419–20.
[27] Since a shilling was worth 12 pence, 3d. out of every shilling was 25 percent.
[28] BPP 1824 (51) V, p. 419.

If women were credited with the work that they did, the wage ratios would appear slightly higher, but women would still earn less than men. A second possible reason for the wage gap in piece-rate earnings is the difference in hours worked per day or per week. Most women had domestic duties that reduced the amount of time available for market work, so on average women generally worked fewer hours than men. In 1840 parliamentary investigator James Mitchell found that women hand-loom weavers working in weaving shops earned an average of 5s.5d. a week, while those working at home averaged only 4s. He attributed this difference to a difference in hours worked: "The lower average of the wages of the women working at home is, in a considerable degree, attributable to the circumstance that many of them are married women, and their time is partly occupied by their domestic duties."[29] When investigators presented weekly wages, they probably did not assume that women worked as many hours as men. Davies makes his calculations for hand spinning explicit: "When she sits closely to her wheel the whole day, she can spin 2 lbs. of coarse flax for ordinary sheeting and toweling, 2½ d. per lb."[30] Davies then assumes four days of work in a week, for earnings of 1s.8d. a week. Usually we are simply given the estimated earnings, with no mention of time input. If we were told only that the earnings were 1s.8d. a week, we might erroneously assume this was for a full week's work and seriously underestimate the daily wage.[31] Unfortunately we do not know how many hours women in domestic industry spent at their paid work. Even their employers did not know how many hours they worked. These workers would often keep secret or even misrepresent the number of hours they spent working, for fear that employers would demand faster work, or to make their wages appear lower.[32]

[29] BPP 1840 (43) XXIII, p. 317. The same was true in the hosiery industry; see Rose, "Gender Segregation," p. 167.

[30] David Davies, *The Case of Labourers in Husbandry Stated and Considered* (London: Robinson, 1795), p. 85.

[31] Pinchbeck, *Women Workers*, p. 138, noted the need to correct for hours of work: "Labor at the hand wheel was often a by-employment, and the time given to it varied according to the housewife's preoccupation with other duties. The small amounts earned by laborers' wives and others who span to supplement the family income cannot, therefore, fairly be described as spinner's wages, and must not be confused with the earnings – for the most part adequate – of those who regarded it as a full time occupation."

[32] In response to a parliamentary survey, the overseer of Gestingthorpe, Essex, states, "It is very difficult to get at the amount of earnings of that part of the family which is not employed by the farmer, as they conceal them for fear of having their allowances diminished." BPP 1834 (44) XXX, p. 175a. The motivation for concealing or exaggerating hours worked might be to get poor relief from the parish, or to convince the parliament to mandate a minimum wage, as it did for the Spitalfields silk weavers. For handloom weavers, investigator J. Mitchell spoke of "many of the weavers and their ill-judging friends endeavouring to make it appear, that from dire necessity the weaver

The problem of differences in hours worked was most acute in domestic industry, but even in some kinds of factory work we occasionally find women working fewer hours than men. In 1816 Henry Houldsworth, a cotton manufacturer from Glasgow, noted that the women who picked the cotton for him could come and go as they pleased, and "as they are a very irregular set of hands, time is not noticed."[33] Since he paid them only for their output, and no machinery was used in this process, he had no reason to insist on regular hours. The result was lower average working hours for these women. Houldsworth estimated that these women averaged seven hours a day: "Some of them, in summer time, will work as much as eleven or twelve hours; but taking them altogether, I do not conceive they average seven hours, summer and winter."[34] Seven hours was a little more than half the twelve hours fifty minutes that Houldsworth's regular mill-hands worked. Such a large difference in hours, even for only a portion of the workers, could easily bias female–male ratio of factory wages.

A third possible reason for women's lower earnings in piece-rate work was that women may have produced fewer units per hour. Unfortunately, we do not have evidence on output per hour of piece-rate workers because the time worked was not recorded. However, we do know that in US manufacturing women produced fewer units per hour than men. Claudia Goldin reports that women in manufacturing earned less than men in spite of working the same hours and being paid the same piece-rate, which implies lower output per hour.[35]

While it is difficult to measure output per hour, we can observe the actual piece-rates more readily. If the piece-rates paid to men and women were the same, then men and women were paid the same wage for the same output, even if they earned different amounts per week. Wage discrimination existed only if men and women were paid different piece-rates. The majority of the evidence suggests that, when men and women did the same work, they were paid the same piece-rate. For example, Table 2.2 shows the amounts paid for reaping at Gooseacre Farm in Radley, Berkshire. This group of reapers clearly contained both men and women, and all workers, regardless of their sex, received the

works a far greater number of hours than it would be supposed that human nature could endure." BPP 1840 (43) XXIII, p. 238. From the report of W. A. Miles on handloom weavers we learn, "The weavers did not like the masters to know in what time a chain could be woven, because they considered if the master knew that they could earn a given sum in a short time, the price of the next chain would be lowered." BPP 1840 (220) XXIV, p. 383.
[33] BPP 1816 (397) III, p. 233.   [34] *Ibid.*
[35] Claudia Goldin, *Understanding the Gender Gap: An Economic History of American Women* (Oxford: Oxford University Press, 1990), p. 104.

Table 2.2. *Payments for reaping at Gooseacre Farm, Radley, Berkshire*

Name of worker	Area Reaped A-r-p	Payment £ s d	Payment per acre (s.)
John Fisher	2-3-0	1-4-9	9
G. Comely	3-0-37	1-9-1	9
Ann Waters	1-3-28	0-17-4	9
J. Minns	3-0-39	1-9-2½	9
Wm Stinson	3-2-15	1-12-4	9
Wm House	3-1-0	1-9-3	9
Mary Minns	1-0-36	0-11-1	9
T. Gunter	2-1-27	1-1-8½	9
Mary Grimes	1-0-16	0-9-11¼	9

Source: Rural History Centre, University of Reading, BER 13/5/2.

same price per acre. The women earned notably less than the men (the three workers who were clearly women earned on average only 12s.9d., which is less than half the 28s.9d. earned on average by the three workers who were clearly men), but this is because they reaped fewer acres. There is no way to tell from this source why the women reaped fewer acres – because they worked fewer hours, because they accomplished less per hour, or because they had fewer unnamed assistants than the male workers. But the reason for the difference in earnings in clear: the women earned less because they reaped fewer acres, not because they were paid at a different rate per acre than the men.[36]

Gooseacre Farm was not unusual; other evidence also points to equal piece-rates in agriculture. On the few occasions where we observe both men and women doing the same agricultural tasks on piece-rates, they are paid the same wages. In 1773 both Thomas Cook and Mary Dawson were paid 1s. per load for picking stones.[37] In 1778, William Thompson of Staffordshire paid Betty Sillito, John Dunn, William Rowley, Dolly Matthews, Betty Baker, and Nanny Greenbrough the same rate for reaping wheat ($4\frac{1}{2}$d. per thrave).[38] Helen Speechley found that women and men were paid the same rates for piece-work on Somerset farms.[39]

Equal piece-rates were observed in manufacturing as well. The 1845 report on framework knitters explicitly stated that women were employed "at the same rate of wages" as men.[40] In 1840 a Welsh weaver

---

[36] Rural History Centre, Reading, BER 13/5/2. The bill is undated, but is from sometime in the 1820s or 1830s.
[37] Records Hitchin farm of the Ratcliffe estate. Hertfordshire Record Office D/DE E110.
[38] Rural History Centre, Reading, microfilm P262.
[39] Speechley, "Female and Child Agricultural Day Labourers," ch. 6.
[40] BPP 1845 (609) XV, p. 101.

told a parliamentary committee that women and girls could weave as well as men, and received the same rate of wages.[41] Even when rates were set by law, the piece-rates applied equally to men and women. Female silk weavers received the same piece-rates specified for "journeymen" in the Spitalfields Acts. In 1811 one employer threw the trade into confusion by refusing to pay a journeywoman the rates specified in the Spitalfields Acts, claiming that the law applied only to male workers. To clear up the confusion, an amendment was added to the Act specifically stating that women were to receive the same piece-rates as men.[42]

If the work was done in the worker's home rather than the factory, the employer often did not even know who the worker was, and paid the head of the family for the work of the whole family. The finished product was generally brought in for payment by the head of the household, and the employer would not know if the piece was woven by the man of the house, by his wife or one of his children, or by any other worker. When asked whether the handloom weavers he employed were men, women, or children, Adam Bogle of Glasgow replied, "we do not know whether they are children, or men or women; the work is generally brought to the works by a man; they are generally men, and their families, and apprentices I believe."[43] If he did not know the sex of the worker, he could not pay a price that differed by gender.

Some historians claim that female mule-spinners in Manchester were paid lower piece-rates than male spinners. Though I have not seen any actual piece-rates quoted (wages are always quoted as weekly earnings), this does appear to be true because in 1829 the male spinners urged the female spinners to form a separate union, and promised to support their effort to obtain the same rates as the men.[44] Piece-rates that differed by gender would certainly seem like compelling evidence of discrimination, but in this case we do have more detailed information on the industry that suggests that the women may not have been underpaid. The male and female mule spinners were not really doing the same job. Men hired

---

[41] BPP 1840 (220) XXIV, p. 557.   [42] Pinchbeck, *Women Workers*, pp. 177–8.
[43] BPP 1816 (397) III, p. 167.
[44] R. G. Kirby and A. E. Musson, *The Voice of the People: John Doherty, 1798-1854, Trade Unionist, Radical and Factory Reformer* (Manchester: Manchester University Press, 1975), p. 94. Many historians have called attention to the lower wages of female mule-spinners. See Freifeld, "Technological Change and the 'Self-Acting' Mule," p. 334, and Paul Johnson, "Age, Gender and the Wage in Britain, 1830-1930," in Peter Scholliers and Leonard Schwarz, eds., *Experiencing Wages: Social and Cultural Aspects of Wage Forms in Europe since 1500* (New York: Berghahn Books, 2003), p. 230. Weekly earnings for women were about half as much as men's earnings, but it is unclear how much of this was due to lower output, and how much to lower piece-rates.

and disciplined their own assistants (piecers), while the women did not. Huberman notes that when the cotton spinning firm M'Connel and Kennedy hired women mule-spinners, responsibility for disciplining piecers shifted to overlookers, and the firm incurred additional costs in recruiting piecers. Problems with supervision of piecers led to increases in the amount of cotton wasted. M'Connel and Kennedy began hiring women spinners in 1810, and between 1809 and 1817 its wastage rates increased 63 percent. This trend was reversed in the 1820s when the firm returned to hiring male spinners.[45] If women mule-spinners in fact were equally productive and were paid less, then the firm's profits should have increased. In fact, the firm found its profits falling, in spite of the fact that it paid the female spinners lower piece-rates. So it turns out that in this case the difference in piece-rates was justified by differences in productivity.[46]

Instances of women being paid lower piece-rates than men did exist, but were not the norm. A survey of wages by Sidney Webb, while not from the Industrial Revolution period, is instructive. Webb examined a wide variety of industries in Britain and France at the end of the nineteenth century, and he found twelve industries where men and women earned equal piece-rates and only two where women earned lower piece-rates than men.[47] For the 1750–1850 period I have found only one example of women being paid a lower piece-rate than men for doing the same work. In the 1840 report on handloom weavers in the west we find an employer, Mr. Peter Payne, who claims:

A woman receives 3s. a piece less on the white work than a man, and 4s. less on coloured. This has always been the case, and the example was set by the master weavers. Women are not so regular in their time as men, nor so able to perform the work in the same time. Thirty men will do as much work as forty women, and the outlay for looms, buildings, &c. is greater for a number of females than for the male weavers, but that this outlay for looms, buildings, &c. is not considered to be equal to the difference in pay to the same extent.[48]

He suggests that part of the difference is justified by the cost to the manufacturer of slower work, but that part of it is not justified.

Of course a cloth finished in three weeks *is* a different good from a cloth finished in four weeks, and these goods may reasonably have

[45] Michael Huberman, *Escape from the Market: Negotiating Work in Lancashire* (Cambridge: Cambridge University Press, 1996), p. 39.

[46] *Ibid.*, pp. 25–9.

[47] Sidney Webb, "The Alleged Differences in the Wages Paid to Men and to Women for Similar Work," *Economic Journal* 1 (1891), 635–62. In one of the later industries, compositing, women were disadvantaged by legal restrictions on the hours they could work.

[48] BPP 1840 (220) XXIV, p. 401.

different prices. Mr. Payne was right to be concerned about the number
of weeks a worker keeps the cloth, because if the worker ties up the
material for an extra week, the employer loses one week's worth of
interest on the value of the raw material. The interest rate faced by these
employers would have been fairly high, given the imperfections in the
capital market, and the high cost of the yarn.[49] The input costs of one
piece of cloth is given in the 1840 report:

Value of the wool	£17.10s.4d.
Labor	£5.12s.
Materials	£2.16s.10d.
Rent, wear and tear	£0.18s.[50]

The cost of the raw wool alone accounts for two-thirds of the total cost
of the cloth. The yarn given to the weaver would also include the value of
some of the labor, materials, and rent. The value of the yarn, then, was
many times greater than the weaver's wage. Mr. Payne's description
suggests that in this case the employer was providing buildings and
looms as well, so lower wages for women might represent implicit rent
for the capital equipment. The cost of delayed weaving was high, and
thus we should expect the employer to pay a lower price for cloth kept
out longer. A woman generally took longer than a man to weave a given
cloth, both because of her lower productivity and because she was likely
to devote less time to the work. Some idea of this time difference is given
in another report on handloom weaving, which claims that a man would
take three weeks to weave a piece of 46 yards, while his wife would take a
month. On cloth that took a man a fortnight to weave, his wife would
take two days longer.[51]

Completion time, however, is clearly observable and there is no reason
for the manufacturer to use sex as a signal for this quality. If the
employer was really concerned with completion time rather than the
gender of the worker, it is not clear why he would pay according to sex
and not specifically according to weaving time. In fact, employers elsewhere specified in their wage contracts that they would reduce the price
of a piece that was out longer than a specified time period. A "ticket"
specifying the wage contract, given out by a Carlisle manufacturer in 1838
states, "6d. per day deducted off work kept out longer than 28 days."[52]

---

[49] See Joel Mokyr, "Editor's Introduction: The New Economic History and the Industrial
Revolution," in J. Mokyr, ed., *The British Industrial Revolution: An Economic Perspective*
(Boulder: Westview Press, 1993), p. 109.
[50] BPP 1840 (220) XXIV, p. 374.   [51] BPP 1840 (43) XXIII, pp. 435–6.
[52] BPP 1840 (220) XXIV, p. 597. Another example of such a ticket from Londonderry
specifies a 3d. per day deduction for work kept over twenty-one days.

Employers in the west of England had no valid reason to use sex as a signal of completion time, because time was perfectly observable; they seem to have chosen a noisy signal (gender) over the actual variable of interest (time). The story of paying women less because they take longer does not hold up. We can only conclude that this practice was an example of wage discrimination against women.

If wage discrimination exists, economic theory tells us that two forces will be at work to eliminate it: the substitution of women for men, and the failure of firms who continue to employ men at higher rates. If women do the same work cheaper than men, the economic incentive to employ them in preference to men is great. Only an employer with a "taste for discrimination" will not do so. Discriminating employers, however, will be vulnerable to bankruptcy if the market is competitive. Discrimination may exist in disequilibrium, but it will not be a dominant characteristic of the labor market. In this case competitive forces do seem to have been eroding the wage difference by removing men from the occupation of handloom weaving. Anthony Austin, reporting on handloom weaving in Somerset, Wiltshire, Devon, and Dorset, says of serge weaving:

> women are employed, who will readily undertake it, at a lower price than men receive ... indeed, it appears to be a custom in every trade to pay women at a lower rate than men for the same article. I have found it in the broad-cloth trade, in the blanket trade, and in the silk-velvet trade. By this process (unless the men consent to take the lower rate of wages) the whole of the weaving is gradually put into the hands of women ... and the men are compelled to seek other work.[53]

As economic theory tells us, and as Austin suggests, such a difference in piece-rate wages is not an equilibrium. If women are paid less than men for the same output, women workers will be substituted for men. Thus, wage discrimination will lead to no men being employed in that occupation.

Male workers were aware of these economic forces, and they sometimes demanded equal wages for this reason. A ban on women workers was preferable, but if women were to work, they must earn the same wage as men, since this was the only way to maintain male employment. In 1833 David Sloan, manager of the Bridgetown Mills in Calton, Glasgow, reported:

> that the women originally agreed to spin for wages at a rate one thirteenth lower than the males, but the association having heard of their being engaged to work had emissaries on the way on the very first day ... that a deputation of the association waited upon him the same day, to tell him that if they could help it, they would not allow the women to be employed at all as spinners, but that in all

---

[53] BPP 1840 (43) XXIII, p. 442.

events they would fall on means to prevent their being employed for lower rates than those which they had fixed.[54]

The male workers of Bridgetown Mills rioted, and the female spinners had to be escorted to and from work. The riots ceased when the firm announced that male and female spinners would be paid at the same rate, and the female spinners continued to work in peace. A male spinner commented that "the chief reason was to prevent the lowering of wages, in which the association in the end succeeded."[55] The male workers were well aware that their jobs could not be maintained if women were allowed to work at lower wages. The position of the Bridgetown union was not unique; Sonya Rose has found a number of similar examples in the second half of the nineteenth century. In hosiery factories, the men voted for an equal piece-rate because when the rate was not equal, men were replaced by women.[56] During a strike over women carpet workers in Kidderminster, the union said "If the looms are supposedly within the compass of a women, let her do it and be paid like a man."[57] Since unequal piece-rates reduced male employment, men actively opposed such differences.

While I have found piece-rate wage discrimination in handloom weaving in the south-west, the most common practice was to pay men and women the same piece-rate. In all the instances where men and women were paid the same piece-rate, we can confidently say that there was no wage discrimination. Any differences in weekly earnings arose because of differences in time devoted to work, or from differences in productivity. Unfortunately, it is more difficult to identify wage discrimination in time-rate wages, but even there differences in productivity seem to have been the main cause of the wage gap.

II.   Interpreting time-rate wages

While time-rate wages must be examined separately from piece-rate wages, I conclude that the reasons for the wage gap in time-rate wages were essentially the same as for the earnings gap observed where piece-rate wages were paid. The time-rate wages in Table 2.1 suggest a wage ratio of between one-third and three-fourths. However, a portion of this wage gap is the result of measurement error. Women often worked fewer hours per day than men, so the ratio of daily wages understates the ratio

---

[54] BPP 1833 (450) XX, A1, p. 84. The self-actor had just been invented, but it was probably not in use yet.
[55] Ibid., p. 85.   [56] Rose, "Gender Segregation."
[57] Rose, "Gender Antagonism," p. 200.

of hourly wages. In other cases, the failure to include in-kind payments led to an underestimate of the wage ratio. The bondager system used in Northumberland also led to quoted wages which understated the real compensation to women workers. If these biases are taken into account, the wage ratio looks closer to two-thirds than to one-third. Even if these measurement errors are accounted for, a substantial wage gap remains. Some historians interpret this wage gap as evidence of discrimination, but the evidence suggests that women's relative productivity was at least approximately equal to their relative wage. This section will explore the reasons for the wage gap in time-rate wages and argue that wage discrimination was not an important cause of the wage gap.

In agriculture, female day-laborers frequently worked shorter days than male wage-laborers, a fact that accounts for some (though not all) of the wage difference.[58] In 1843 a farmer from Dorset reported why he did not hire more women: "I consider their labor dear; they want 8d. a day, and they don't come till nine, and are away again at five."[59] Men generally worked 6 a.m. to 6 p.m.[60] so if women worked eight hours a day, they worked only two-thirds as many hours as men. In this case, a daily-wage ratio of 0.5 would imply an hourly-wage ratio of 0.75. If such a difference in hours was widespread, correcting for hours reduces the wage gap considerably. In fact, it does appear that women commonly worked fewer hours than men. The 1843 parliamentary report *Women and Children in Agriculture* shows that it was a common practice for women to start an hour later than men, so they could get breakfast for their families, and to return home sooner in the evening.[61] The same is found in the "Rural Queries," a questionnaire sent out by the Poor Law Committee in 1833. In one Cornwall parish we find that women in agriculture worked from 8 a.m. to 6 p.m., and Leicester women are said to work only eight or nine hours a day.[62] Gilboy finds the same thing in the eighteenth century – the women began work at 8 a.m. rather than 6 a.m.[63] Differences in hours worked were common, so earnings ratios will understate the wage ratios. The 1843 report on *Women and Children in Agriculture*

---

[58] Gielgud, "Nineteenth Century Farm Women," p. 102, suggested that difference in hours worked might explain the wage gap, though she does not attempt to measure the difference in hours worked.

[59] BPP 1843 (510) XII, p. 88.

[60] See, for example, Eden, *State of the Poor*, vol. III, p. 876; BPP 1824 (392) VI, p. 22; BPP 1843 (510) XII, pp. 120, 169–71.

[61] BPP 1843 (510) XII.

[62] BPP 1834 (44) XXX, St. Anthony of the East, Cornwall, and Sheepy Magna, Leicestershire.

[63] Elizabeth Waterman Gilboy, "Labour at Thornborough: An Eighteenth Century Estate," *Economic History Review* 3 (1932), pp. 388–98.

provides 109 observations on daily hours of work for women. Women's hours ranged from eight to twelve hours per day, and averaged 9.66 hours.[64] If men worked twelve-hour days, then equal hourly wages would imply a daily-wage ratio of 0.805, and if a woman's daily wage was 40 percent of a man's daily wage, then her implicit hourly wage was 50 percent of a man's. Thus daily wages reported in Table 2.1 overstate the size of the wage gap.

In the case of washerwomen, on the other hand, failing to control for the number of hours worked in a day makes the female wage appear much too large. Wages for women going out washing by the day were as high as 2s.6d. a day in London,[65] but were lower in areas farther from London. The "Rural Queries" record of 1834 gives wages ranging from 6d. to 3s. per day, but 1s. seems to have been more typical. Some of these wages appear to be very high relative to the wages of women in other occupations, but most of the apparent difference is a result of the fact that these women worked long hours, perhaps even double the hours of other workers. A day's work of washing might begin at 1:00 a.m. and continue to the next evening.[66] These long days of washing were recognized as "a day and a half's work."[67] In London in 1839 women could earn 2s.6d. for nearly twenty hours' work, which would put the wage at about 1½ pence an hour.[68] This hourly wage is still higher than agricultural labor, which often paid about 1d. an hour, but the difference is not nearly as great as it first appears, and we would expect wages to be higher in London than in the country.

In-kind payments to servants also lead to an overstatement of the wage gap for some workers. Many workers, particularly in domestic service and agriculture, were employed as live-in servants. These workers were given room and board in addition to a cash wage, and the value of these in-kind payments was frequently greater than the cash wage. Ignoring the in-kind portion of the wage will bias the wage ratio down. Table 2.3 shows wages paid to agricultural servants. Two wage ratios are presented – the first is the ratio of money wages, and the second is the ratio of full wages, with the value of board included.[69] The value of board was a large portion of the wage, and including it has a large impact on the wage ratio. Since women require fewer calories than

---

[64] *Women and Children in Agriculture*. Women's hours of work are inclusive of breaks for meals, as is the twelve-hour day for men.
[65] Hill, *Women, Work, and Sexual Politics*, p. 159.   [66] *Ibid.*, p. 158.
[67] George, *London Life in the Eighteenth Century*, p. 20.   [68] *Ibid.*, p. 208.
[69] Arthur Young's estimate includes the value of room, but the others do not. This omission is less serious than the omission of board because the value of the room was small compared to the value of board.

Table 2.3. *Servants' wages (£ per year)*

Employer	Servant	Male wages		Female wages		Ratio1	Ratio2	Src
		Money	Board	Money	Board			
Robert Loder, Harwell, Berkshire								
1613	Robert Earnold, carter	3	10.25					a
	Dick, shepherd	2	10.25					a
	Johan C., maid			2.38	10.25	0.79	0.95	a
	Alice K., maid			1.5	10.25	0.75	0.96	a
1614	Robert Andrewes, carter	3.33	7					a
	Johan Colle, maid			2.35	7	0.71	0.91	a
	Mary, maid			2	7	0.60	0.87	a
1615	Ned, carter	3	11.83					a
	Dick, shepherd	2.4	11.83					a
	Mary			2	11.83	0.67	0.93	a
	Margaret			2.25	11.83	0.94	0.99	a
1620	London Baker's journeyman & maid	6.5	10.4	2.17	10.4	0.33	0.74	b
1761	Bury, Lancashire, agric. servant	6.5		3		0.46		c
1770								
Danby	More skilled	15.0	9.1	5.5	5.5	0.37	0.46	d
Kabers	More skilled	9.0	9.1	3.0	6.1	0.33	0.50	d
	Less skilled	5.0	9.1	2.25	6.1	0.45	0.59	d
Ormskirk, Lancs.	More skilled	7.0	9.0	3.0	6.0	0.43	0.56	d
Shenstone	More skilled	11.0	9.0	4.0	6.0	0.36	0.50	d
	Less skilled	6.5	9.0	2.5	6.0	0.38	0.55	d
Hagley	More skilled	10.0	10.0	3.5	6.7	0.35	0.51	d
	Less skilled	6.75	10.0	2.75	6.7	0.41	0.56	d
Bends-worth	More skilled	10.0	12.0	4.0	8.0	0.40	0.55	d
	Less skilled	8.0	12.0	2.75	8.0	0.34	0.54	d
1791	Bury, Lancashire, agric. servant	9.45		4.5		0.48		c
1795	Cumberland, common servant	9		3.25		0.36		c
1795	Northamptonshire, age 20	7.5		3		0.40		c
1821	William Stickney, Yorkshire	16.5	27	7	18	0.42	0.57	e

Ratio1 = ratio of money wages.
Ratio2 = ratio of full wage, including in kind payments.
Sources:
a. Fussel, Robert Loder's Farm Accounts. Where there are multiple wages for each sex, I compare the highest-wage females to the highest-wage males.
b. Bakers of London, quoted in S. Paul Garner, *Evolution of Cost Accounting* (University of Alabama Press, 1954), p. 32.
c. Eden, *State of the Poor*, vol. II, p. 294.
d. Young, *Northern Tour*. Danby gives an estimate for a maid's board; the others are two-thirds of the male value, which Young suggests is the correct ratio, in vol. III, p. 288. "More skilled" servants are the headman and a dairy maid.
e. BPP 1821 (668) IX.

men (about 73 percent of what a man requires), the cost of board for a woman was less than for a man.[70] However, since the ratio of cash wages was well below half and thus lower than the ratio of food intake, including board in the calculation of wages will still raise the wage ratio.

The cases presented in Table 2.3 demonstrate the error introduced by using only cash wages. In the seventeenth century, Robert Loder of Berkshire calculated a value for board by dividing total expenditures on food by the number of people at his table. Including this value in the wages of his servants raises the female–male wage ratio. This calculation somewhat overstates the ratio, however, since the men would have eaten more than the women. In fact, if women ate only 73 percent as much as men, then adding board would not significantly alter the wage ratio. In the eighteenth century, however, the ratio of cash wages was much lower, and including the value of board increases the wage ratio even if women received less than men. Arthur Young, on his northern tour, asked a few farmers what value they gave to a man's board, lodging, and washing. The costs of lodging and washing were relatively small, so most of this value was the cost of board. Young assumed that a woman received two-thirds as much as a man in in-kind payments, and this ratio is used to value these payments in Table 2.3. Even if the in-kind payments received by women were only two-thirds as much as those received by men, including these payments increases the wage ratios from a little more than a third to over a half.[71] The same pattern is observed for Yorkshire in 1821; here the wage ratio rises from 0.42 to 0.57 when the value of board is included. The wage gap remains substantial, but the difference is not as extreme as it first appears. If we wish to discuss the causes of the wage gap, we must first find its correct size, which requires including the value of in-kind payments.

A different kind of mis-measurement occurred in northern counties that used the bondager system. Male and female laborers were hired together, and the compensation package overstated the portion earned by the male, and understated the portion earned by the female. In this system the male laborer, called the "hind," was required to provide a woman worker, the "bondager," to work whenever the employer desired at a specified rate. Usually this woman was a family member, but if the

[70] Geert Bekaert, "Caloric Consumption in Industrializing Belgium," *Journal of Economic History*, 51 (1991), p. 638. Ogilvie finds that in Germany female agricultural laborers' meals were valued at 67 to 79 percent as much as male laborers' meals. Sheilagh Ogilvie, *A Bitter Living: Women, Markets, and Social Capital in Early Modern Germany* (Oxford: Oxford University Press, 2003), p. 287.

[71] I use the ratio of two-thirds because this is the ratio that Young used to calculate the value of a woman's board. Young, *Northern Tour*, vol. III, p. 288.

hind could not provide a bondager from his own family, he had to hire one. The bondager was paid a lower daily rate than other women workers.[72] For example, a Northumberland farmer paid Jane Thompson, a bondager, 10d. per day, but paid Isabella Thompson, who was not a bondager, 1s. per day.[73] The farmer was able to pay the bondager 2d. less than the market wage because John Thompson's contract specified that, as a condition of employment, he must provide a bondager. Hinds complained about the bondager system because if they had no suitable relative to provide as a bondager, hiring a bondager cost them money. When hiring a bondager, the hind had to pay the bondager an annual wage and provide her food for the year as well. The hind received from the farmer the daily wage for the bondager's work, but this was less than he spent to hire and feed the bondager. The cash wage paid to the bondager was nearly as much as she earned from the farmer, and the hind had to provide her food for the year as well.[74] When the bondager was a family member the hind did not pay the bondager a wage, but it was still true that part of the hind's wage was compensation for work of the bondager. This system disguised part of the female bondager's earnings as compensation of the male hind.

Women's wages were lower than men's. However, the available wage quotes often overstate the gap. Correcting for measurement error biases can increase our estimate of the wage ratio substantially. Initially women's wages appear to be between one-third and one-half of men's wages, but correcting for measurement error suggests that women's wages were closer to one-half to two-thirds of male wages. The wage gap does not disappear, and there still remains the question of why this gap occurred. As discussed above, the wage gap has been interpreted either as evidence of women's lesser productivity, or as evidence that women's wages were set by custom rather than the market. Evidence on the size of the wage gap is abundant, but this evidence cannot distinguish between the two theories because both theories suggest that women's wages would be lower than men's. To test the assumption that the wage gap matches women's lower productivity we need independent evidence on male and female productivity. Unfortunately evidence on productivity is much scarcer than evidence on wages. However, since we do not want to rely on prejudice to answer this question, we must look at what limited evidence is available. The existing evidence suggests that, at least for

---

[72] Gielgud, "Nineteenth Century Farm Women," p. 145.

[73] The farmer is Mr. Hindmarsh, "an extensive farmer in the neighbourbood of Wooler." *Women and Children in Agriculture*, p. 297.

[74] Gielgud, "Nineteenth Century Farm Women," p. 330.

manual workers, women were not as productive as men, and that the
wage gap may indeed have been justified by productivity differences.

Quotes from contemporaries have been used to evaluate relative
female productivity, but if we look at a variety of such quotes we can see
that they conflict with each other. A farm bailiff from Kent estimated
that women and boys were less productive than men in reaping: "The
boys begin to do this at about 12 years of age; a boy in this time of life
will reap about a quarter of an acre in two days, while a man would be
reaping three-quarters of an acre in the same time, and a woman half an
acre, if she worked as many hours as the man."[75] This implies that a boy
of age 12 was one-third as productive as a man, and a woman was two-
thirds as productive as a man. Another nineteenth-century author gives a
contradictory assessment. Henry Stephens claimed that a woman could
reap as much as a man: "The reapers may all be men, or all women, the
women being able to cut down as much as the men."[76] Frederick Eden
claimed that in Bromfield

The wages of men-servants employed in husbandry, who are hired from half-
year to half-year, are from 9 to 12 guineas a year; whilst women, who here do a
large portion of the work of the farm, with difficulty get half as much. It is not
easy to account for so striking an inequality; and still less easy to justify it.[77]

While Eden was unable to explain the wage differences he observed,
individuals interviewed by Alfred Austin and Mr. Vaughn for the 1843
report on *Women and Children in Agriculture* were less mystified by the
wage differences. One Dorset farmer referred to women's shorter hours
of work (see p. 94), but others suggested that women accomplished less
work than men when working at the same tasks. When asked if women
and men worked together in the fields, a Wiltshire farm manager replied,
"The women generally work together; they don't get on so fast as the men
in their work, particularly in reaping and hoeing turnips."[78] A Surrey
landlord claimed that, in poling hops, "The value of the woman's labor
is rather more than a third of the man's."[79] Joseph Henley noted that
women workers in Northumberland did various tasks, including "in some
instances forking (pitching) and loading hay or corn, though when such is
the case two women are put to the work of one man."[80] Robert Loder

---

[75] *Women and Children in Agriculture*, p. 185.
[76] Henry Stephens, *The Book of the Farm*, 2nd edn (Edinburgh and London: William
Blackwood and Sons, 1845), vol. II, p. 331.
[77] Eden, *State of the Poor*, vol. II, p. 47.   [78] *Women and Children in Agriculture*, p. 62.
[79] *Ibid.*, p. 198.
[80] Report of Joseph Henley, 1867, quoted by Gielgud, "Nineteenth Century Farm Women,"
p. 11.

found women less productive than men in the early seventeenth century; he had hired women to harvest cherries, but noted that "I think it were a better course to hire men, for they would doe twice so much I think."[81] Given these conflicting statements by contemporary observers, whom should we trust? The best way to resolve the question of who was right is to look for evidence that is not the expression of someone's opinion, but is direct evidence from output.

One of the simplest pieces of evidence for differences in productivity is earnings differences among workers paid piece-rate wages. When workers were paid piece-rates, their earnings depended directly on their output, and any differences in productivity would translate directly into differences in earnings. Claudia Goldin has noted that, in nineteenth-century manufacturing in the US, when men and women worked together "males earned 25% more than females, even when the work was identical, the piece-rate was the same, and both worked for the same firm."[82] If these workers were paid the same rate per unit of output, the differences in their earnings must have come from differences in output; Goldin's findings suggest that women were 80 percent as productive as men.

Direct measures of cotton picked by individual slaves in the US South suggest that a woman picked less cotton than a man in a day. Olmstead and Rhode collected over 600,000 observations of the weight of cotton picked in a day by individual workers from 113 plantations in the period 1801–62. A girl could pick as much as a boy until about age 15, at which point a gender gap began to emerge. For prime-age adults, a man picked about 18 percent more cotton per day than a woman.[83] This may seem like a relatively small difference, but cotton picking was not a particularly strength-intensive task where we would expect to find large gender differences in productivity. Goldin and Sokoloff suggest that manufacturing emerged in the US North because women were relatively less productive in northern agriculture than in southern agriculture, and therefore had a lower opportunity cost. The South grew cotton and tobacco, which could make better use of female workers. They note that a woman's disadvantage relative to a man was comparatively small in cotton picking: "Even though males (over age 16) had an absolute advantage over females in cotton picking, females had a comparative advantage and therefore picked a greater percentage of the man-days

[81] G. E. Fussell, ed., *Robert Loder's Farm Accounts, 1610–1620*, Camden Society, Third Series, vol. 53 (London: Royal Historical Society, 1936), p. 148.

[82] Goldin, *Understanding the Gender Gap*, p. 104.

[83] Alan Olmstead and Paul Rhode, "'Wait a Cotton Pickin' Minute!' A New View of Slave Productivity," presented at the Economic History Association Annual Meeting in Pittsburgh, Sept. 17, 2006.

allocated to that task."[84] If we could directly measure output in other agricultural tasks, we would expect to find a larger gender gap.

Slave prices are consistent with Olmstead and Rhode's measures of productivity. Slaves were sold in a competitive market, and the price paid for a slave should represent the current value of the slave's future output. If slave prices included any value put on the sexual services or children produced by female slaves, this would increase the value of women relative to men. In spite of their potential reproductive benefits, we find that slave women had lower prices than slave men. Girls had higher prices than boys, but after age 16 the prices of male slaves rose above those of female slaves. At age 32 a man cost 18 percent more than a woman.[85] Slave owners were willing to pay more for male slaves because males were more productive.

Another way to measure women's relative productivity is to estimate production functions using historical data. This method consistently finds that women were less productive than men in agriculture. Using US census data, Craig and Field-Hendrey find that women were about 60 percent as productive as men in agriculture.[86] Toman estimates the marginal product of slaves and finds that the marginal product of female slaves was 40 percent of male productivity in the task system, and 60 percent of male productivity in the gang system.[87] The same seems to be true in other areas of the world as well. Benjamin and Brandt use a 1936 household survey in China to estimate the contribution of men and women to family income in general and crop income specifically; they find that women contributed 62 percent as much as men to farm production.[88] Women are also less productive than men in agriculture in developing countries today; Jacoby found that women were 46 percent as productive as men in Peruvian agriculture in the 1980s.[89]

---

[84] Goldin and Sokoloff, "The Relative Productivity Hypothesis," p. 473.
[85] Laurence Kotlikoff, "Quantitative Description of the New Orleans Slave Market, 1804 to 1862," in R. W. Fogel and S. L. Engerman, eds., *Without Consent or Contract: The Rise and Fall of American Slavery, Markets and Production: Technical Papers*, vol. I (New York: Norton, 1989), pp. 42–5.
[86] Lee A. Craig and Elizabeth Field-Hendrey, "Industrialization and the Earnings Gap: Regional and Sectoral Tests of the Goldin–Sokoloff Hypothesis," *Explorations in Economic History* 30 (1993), pp. 60–80.
[87] J. T. Toman, "The Gang System and Comparative Advantage," *Explorations in Economic History* 42 (2005), p. 320.
[88] Dwayne Benjamin and Loren Brandt, "Markets, Discrimination, and the Economic Contribution of Women in China: Historical Evidence," *Economic Development and Cultural Change* 44 (1995), pp. 63–104.
[89] Hanan Jacoby, "Productivity of Men and Women and the Sexual Division of Labour in Peasant Agriculture of the Peruvian Sierra," *Journal of Development Economics* 37 (1992), pp. 265–87.

Studies that estimate production functions for manufacturing also consistently find that women are less productive than men. Craig and Field-Hendrey estimate that women were 40 to 50 percent as productive as men in US manufacturing in 1860.[90] Cox and Nye use data on nineteenth-century French manufacturing firms to estimate the marginal product of male and female workers and find productivity ratios ranging from 0.37 to 0.63. When they test for wage discrimination, they find no evidence of it.[91] Studies of late twentieth-century manufacturing find a smaller gap, but still conclude that women were less productive than men. Haegeland and Klette find that women were 83 percent as productive as men in Norwegian manufacturing, while Hellerstein, Neumark, and Troske find that women were 84 percent as productive as men in the US.[92]

Evidence from production functions suggests that, in agriculture and manufacturing, differences in productivity were large enough to explain the portion of the wage gap that is not explained by measurement error. Section III examines possible reasons for these productivity differences. Before moving on, though, it is important to note that not all wage differences could be explained by productivity differences. In less competitive areas of the economy wage discrimination could persist. Of all the wages in Table 2.1, the most likely candidates for wage discrimination are the salaried professions. While the lower salaries of schoolmistresses may have resulted from their lower skills, those of workhouse matrons do not seem to be justified by productivity differences.

Teachers may have experienced employer discrimination, but it is also possible that the wage differences reflected productivity. When hired by schools, female teachers earned lower salaries than male teachers. The examples in Table 2.1 suggest that schoolmistresses earned one-half to two-thirds the salaries of schoolmasters. However, some of this wage gap reflects the fact that women teachers had fewer skills and thus taught fewer subjects. Schoolmistresses were generally not expected to teach

---

[90] Craig and Field-Hendrey, "Industrialization and the Earnings Gap."
[91] Donald Cox and John Vincent Nye, "Male–Female Wage Discrimination in Nineteenth-Century France," *Journal of Economic History* 49 (1989), pp. 903–20.
[92] Torbjorn Haegeland and Tor Jakob Klette, "Do Higher Wages Reflect Higher Productivity? Education, Gender and Experience Premiums in a Matched Plant-Worker Data Set," in J. Haltwanger, J. R. Lane, J. Spletzer, J. Theeuwes, and K. Troske, eds., *The Creation and Analysis of Employer–Employee Matched Data* (Amsterdam: Elsevier, 1999), pp. 231–59. Judith Hellerstein, David Neumark, and Kenneth Troske, "Wages, Productivity, and Worker Characteristics: Evidence from Plant-Level Production Functions and Wage Equations," *Journal of Labor Economics* 17 (1999), pp. 409–46. Hellerstein, Neumark, and Troske find evidence that women were underpaid, but Haegeland and Klette do not.

writing or arithmetic. One set of rules for a charity school required the master to be "One who can write a good hand, and who understands the grounds of arithmetic," but did not require the same of a schoolmistress.[93] At one Lancashire school the girls were taught by a schoolmistress, except in writing and arithmetic, which the schoolmaster taught.[94] Women were less likely than men to be able to write or do arithmetic and therefore they generally did not teach these subjects. Without measures of output it is difficult to say whether the difference in skills justified the difference in salaries, but it is at least possible.

The differences in the salaries of workhouse administrators are more difficult to explain. The position did not require extensive education. If anything, women were better trained in the skills required to run a household. The master and matron of the workhouse had similar responsibilities. At Bristol, both the master and the matron had money on hand at the end of the fiscal year, suggesting that both had financial responsibilities.[95] Women seem to have been paid less for doing the same job. Wage discrimination could exist for workhouse administrators because the market was not competitive. A workhouse did not go bankrupt if it lost money. The gender difference in salaries did not even result in an all-female workforce because each workhouse hired exactly one master and one matron, the former to watch over the men, and the latter to watch over the women. Because the workhouse inmates were strictly segregated by sex, the parish could not substitute a matron for a master. Segregation of inmates, and the fact that there was no competition between workhouses, allowed the persistence of wage discrimination.

III.   Productivity differences

The evidence presented above suggests that in the past women were less productive than men, but the question of *why* they were less productive still remains. The argument that women's wages were commensurate with their productivity is convincing only if there are plausible reasons for women's lower productivity. Two important reasons for such productivity differences were strength and human capital. Strength was an important component of productivity during the Industrial Revolution, and since women have on average less strength than men, they

---

[93] Asher Tropp, *The School Teachers: The Growth of the Teaching Profession in England and Wales from 1800 to the Present Day* (London: William Heinemann, 1957), p. 6.

[94] John Roach, *A History of Secondary Education in England, 1800–1870* (London: Longman, 1986), p. 15.

[95] Eden, *State of the Poor*, vol. II, p. 198. However, the master had more money in his possession than the matron.

were less productive. Women also had less human capital. Since human capital is chosen rather than biologically determined, identifying discrimination becomes more complicated in this case because human capital differences may be both a result of and a cause of wage differences. While strength differences are largely exogenous, skill differences are largely endogenous.

A.   Strength

The impact of strength on sex differences in employment has been noted by many historians. Merry Wiesner claims that the gender division of labor in agriculture in the early modern period was partly due to differences in physical strength, "with men generally doing tasks that required a great deal of upper-body strength, such as cutting grain with a scythe."[96] Judy Gielgud notes that "Individual women could and did use a scythe, but it was too heavy an implement for them to use all day keeping level with the other mowers, as was essential at harvest" and that, more generally, "a man's strength might enable him to accomplish more of a given task than could a woman in the same time, where both were working at full stretch."[97] Edward Shorter notes that "spading and ploughing the fields was too much for women to manage as a rule – great strength being necessary to maneuver a Norfolk plow behind a team of percherons."[98] Joan Lane suggests that strength requirements influenced occupational sorting: "Older boys were a minority in textile factories because they could work in trades requiring physical strength."[99] More generally, Brian Harrison suggests that the gender division of labor:

is older by far than the "capitalism" to which it is sometimes ascribed. It occurs wherever manual labor is at a premium, and reflects the fact that on average men surpass women in sheer muscle-power. Whenever heavy labor was involved, the sexes had rarely worked together in the past.[100]

Sometimes strength is included as one factor among many. Mary Freifeld's story about the male domination of mule-spinning faults the male spinners' union for excluding women following the adoption of the

[96] Wiesner, *Women and Gender in Early Modern Europe*, p. 106.
[97] Gielgud, "Nineteenth Century Farm Women," pp. 67–8, 85.
[98] Edward Shorter, "Women's Work: What Difference Did Capitalism Make?" *Theory and Society* 3 (1976), p. 517.
[99] Joan Lane, *Apprenticeship in England, 1600–1914* (Boulder: Westview Press, 1996), p. 15.
[100] Brian Harrison, "Class and Gender in Modern British Labor History," *Past and Present* 124 (1989), p. 125.

self-actor in the 1840s, but blames the strength requirements of the machines for pushing out women in the 1830s.[101] Pamela Sharpe blames both strength and guild restrictions for keeping women out of wool-combing.[102] Sheilagh Ogilvie notes that in Germany gender differences in strength were "one factor influencing women's choice of work," but that this influence was marginal because of "countervailing institutional influences, such as guild rules excluding females from sedentary industrial pursuits, thereby pushing them into farmwork and laboring."[103]

However, while strength is sometimes offered as a possible explanation of the division of labor, often it is either ignored, or discussed but ultimately rejected. Elizabeth Roberts notes that strength was sometimes used as justification for men's higher wages, but she rejects this explanation, arguing that women sometimes did heavy labor, and that "In some cases these assumptions appear to have been based on gender stereotyping rather than on reality."[104] Deborah Simonton discusses the role of strength in determining the gender division of agricultural work, but argues that strength is not sufficient to explain the results observed, since "the persistence of woman as 'the weaker vessel' was as much an ideological construction as it was physical." Simonton concludes that custom and gender roles were "instrumental" in determining who did what, not biological strength.[105] While Sandy Bardsley suggests that older men may have earned lower wages because they were "less capable of hard physical labour," she rejects strength as an explanation of gender differences and suggests that "social conventions" rather than physical strength prevented women from mowing with the scythe. Bardsley even warns the reader against the "dangers in assuming that physical strength, rather than gender, determined division of labor in the late medieval economy."[106] Gay Gullickson also doubts that differences in strength between the genders were large or important.

Whether women were significantly weaker than men in the early nineteenth century is debatable, however. Studies of women's farm labor demonstrate that rural women were as accustomed to strenuous farm work as men were, and the size and strength differences between the sexes were probably not large. In fact, it seems more likely that the paeans to male strength (and intelligence) which began to appear in the nineteenth century are more a reflection of male

---

[101] Freifeld, "Technological Change and the 'Self-Acting' Mule."
[102] Sharpe, *Adapting to Capitalism*, p. 24.   [103] Ogilvie, *A Bitter Living*, pp. 286, 326.
[104] Roberts, *Women's Work*, p. 14.   [105] Simonton, *European Women's Work*, pp. 31–4.
[106] Sandy Bardsley, "Women"s Work Reconsidered: Gender and Wage Differentiation in Late Medieval England," *Past and Present* 165 (1999), p. 21 and footnote 20 on p. 11.

psychological distress over the entry of women into weaving and knitting then they are evidence of women's inferiority.[107]

By referring to claims that have been made in the past about women's lesser intelligence, Gullickson hopes to convince us that differences in strength were equally fictional. However, strength and intelligence are very different things, and there is a great deal of evidence that gender differences in strength are very real and very large.

Because the miracles of modern technology have made our own lives so easy, we can underestimate the importance of strength in determining wages in the past. For most of history, manual occupations dominated, and in manual occupations biological differences in strength matter. Strength was a scarce factor of production, and was rewarded in the market. Women could do, and did do, physically demanding jobs, but as long as men could produce more output per day, men would earn more. The ubiquity of the wage gap across time and place makes sense if it is not an arbitrary difference created by society, but a reflection of women's lower productivity in manual labor. This section will present evidence establishing that the difference in strength between the sexes is large, and will argue that this difference in strength led to differences in productivity.

Numerous physiological studies have measured various kinds of strength, including arm, leg, and hand grip strength. Adult women clearly have less strength than adult men. Figure 2.3 shows relative female strength from two studies of adults. Strength is originally measured as torque or force exerted, but the results are presented here as ratios of female to male strength. The study by Lindle et al. examines the leg strength of 654 individuals, and the study by Lynch et al. examines both leg and arm strength of 703 individuals.[108] Women have 46 percent as much arm strength as men at age 20, and their relative position increases with age as male arm strength deteriorates. Women's relative leg strength is fairly constant between ages 20 and 75, at about 60 percent of male leg strength. This strength gap between the sexes appears during adolescence. Figure 2.4 shows relative strength in a number of activities for teenage girls and boys. At ages 8–12 girls are only slightly behind

---

[107] Gay Gullickson, "Love and Power in the Proto-Industrial Family," in Maxine Berg, ed., *Markets and Manufacture in Early Industrial Europe* (London: Routledge, 1991), pp. 218–19.

[108] R. S. Lindle et al., "Age and Gender Comparisons of Muscle Strength in 654 Women and Men aged 20–93," *Journal of Applied Physiology* 83 (1997), pp. 1581–7; N. A. Lynch et al., "Muscle Quality. I. Age-associated Differences between Arm and Leg Muscle Groups," *Journal of Applied Physiology* 86 (1999), pp. 188–94.

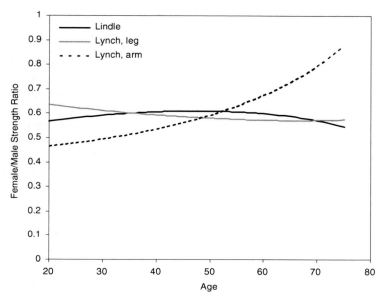

Figure 2.3 Female–male strength ratios: adults
Sources: Lindle, "Age and gender comparisons," Lynch, "Muscle quality."

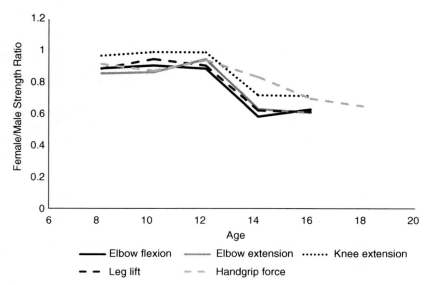

Figure 2.4 Female–male strength ratios: teens
Source: Roy Shephard, *Physical Activity and Growth* (Chicago: Year Book Medical Publishers, 1982), Table 5–11.

boys; female strength by various measures ranges from 86 to 99 percent of male strength. After age 12, though, boys rapidly pull ahead and the ratio drops rapidly to about 60 percent.

Part of the male advantage is due to the fact that male bodies are larger. Men are taller than women and weigh more. Throughout the world, men are about 7 percent taller than women.[109] Longer bones give men better leverage, so that the same muscle movement will do more work.[110] Not only are men larger, but a greater proportion of their weight is devoted to muscles. Muscles are about 42 percent of body weight for men, but only 36 percent for women.[111] Men also have larger hearts and lungs and can use oxygen more efficiently.[112] Women's bodies have other advantages, such as greater resistance to disease, but they are inferior when it comes to brute strength.

Differences in muscle strength result in differences in the work that individuals can do. Gender differences in the performance of exercise tasks are as well documented as gender differences in muscle strength. Table 2.4 shows sex differences in the performance of certain tasks among US Army soldiers.[113] Because they have smaller bodies, women are less disadvantaged in tasks requiring individuals to move their own bodies, such as running or sit-ups. The gender difference in sit-ups is not statistically significant. In running time the gender difference is statistically significant, but the female mean is less than two standard deviations above the male mean. In lifting, however, the difference in ability between the sexes is large. Men can lift twice as much as women, and the gap is more than three times the standard deviation. Thus the largest gap between the sexes in physical ability occurs in the ability to move external objects, which is exactly what is required for heavy manual labor.

These differences do not seem to be the result of differences in fitness, since the gaps appear among soldiers, who are required to be fit. Table 2.5 compares the gender gap in running time and sit-ups among army

[109] John Nicholson, *Men and Women: How Different are They?* (Oxford: Oxford University Press, 1984), p. 28.

[110] John Cooper, Marlene Adrian, and Ruth Glassow, *Kinesiology* (St. Louis: C. V. Mosby, 1982), p. 142.

[111] Franz Frohse, Max Brodel, and Leon Schlossberg, *Atlas of Anatomy* (New York: Barnes and Noble, 1961), p. 39.

[112] George Brooks and Thomas Fahey, *Exercise Physiology* (New York: John Wiley, 1984), p. 642.

[113] James Vogel and Karl Friedl, "Army Data: Body Composition and Physical Capacity," in Bernadette Marriot and Judith Grumstrup-Scott, eds., *Body Composition and Physical Performance* (Washington, DC: National Academy Press, 1992).

Table 2.4. *Differences in physical performance by sex*

| | Male | | Female | | Gap/ | Gap/ | |
	Mean	(SD)	Mean	(SD)	SD*m*	SD*f*	$P(F \geq \mu m)$
All ages							
Two-mile run (minutes)*	15.1	(2.0)	17.9	(2.4)	1.4	1.2	0.12
Sit-ups	52	(14)	51	(13)	0.1	0.1	0.47
Maximum lift capacity (kg)*	59.2	(11.8)	29.7	(6.2)	3.5	4.8	<0.001
By age group							
Two-mile run (minutes)							
17–20*	14.0	(1.6)	17.2	(2.4)	2.0	1.3	0.09
21–27*	14.4	(1.8)	18.0	(2.0)	2.0	1.8	0.04
28–39*	15.8	(2.0)	18.4	(3.0)	1.3	0.9	0.19
Maximum lift capacity (kg)							
17–20*	61.3	(11.7)	30.4	(8.1)	2.6	3.8	<0.001
21–27*	61.0	(12.0)	29.3	(4.8)	2.6	6.6	<0.001
28–39*	56.6	(11.0)	30.3	(7.2)	2.4	3.7	<0.001
40 +	53.0	(8.3)					

* *= difference between males and females is significantly different from zero at the 5% level. The difference in means divided by the standard deviation is a measure of effect size known as "Cohen's d," and values above 0.8 are considered large. See* Jacob Cohen, *Statistical Power Analysis for the Behavioral Sciences*, 2nd edn (Hillsdale, NJ: Lawrence Erlbaum Associates, 1988), ch. 2.

Source: Vogel and Friedl, "Army Data," p. 93. The sample consists of 1126 male and 265 female soldiers.

recruits to the gender gap among soldiers in their twenties.[114] Soldiers are fitter than the recruits; running time decreases and sit-up performance increases as we move from trainees to soldiers. There is some support for the hypothesis that among the civilian population women are relatively less fit, since women's relative sit-up performance increases from 77 to 91 percent of male performance. In running time, however, the gender gap does not narrow as fitness improves. The performance measures in Table 2.4 control for issues of physical fitness because they

[114] Data on army trainees are from Bruce Jones, Matthew Bovee, and Joseph Knapik, "Associations among Body Composition, Physical Fitness, and Injury in Men and Women Army Trainees," in B. Marriott and J. Gumstrup-Scott, eds., *Body Composition and Physical Performance* (Washington, DC: National Academy Press, 1992). This study uses 2245 trainees at Fort Jackson, South Carolina, in 1988. Data on soldiers are from Vogel and Friedl, "Army Data." This study uses a sample including both soldiers from Fort Hood, Texas, and students from the Army War College at Carlisle Barracks, Pennsylvania.

Table 2.5. *Gender gaps in performance for recruits and soldiers*

	Males	Females	Ratio
Army trainees			
Two-mile run (minutes)	16.4	20.3	1.24
Sit-ups	44.3	33.9	0.77
Soldiers, age 21–27			
Two-mile run (minutes)	14.4	18.0	1.25
Sit-ups	57.0	52.0	0.91

Source: Army trainees from Jones, Bovee, and Knapik, "Body Composition, Physical Fitness, and Injury," pp. 141–73. Soldiers from Vogel and Friedl, "Army Data," pp. 89–103.

are results from a sample of soldiers, who are more uniformly physically fit than the general population. Even for this highly fit population, though, differences in lift capacity are large.

Unfortunately we do not have similar direct measures of performance for tasks done by eighteenth- and nineteenth-century workers. We do, however, know that much of the work available during this time required lifting objects or exerting force. Strength was an important component of productivity in a large percentage of the work available in the first half of the nineteenth century. Lane notes that "muscle power was essential in most trades ... a wide range of artisans were obliged to lift, carry and move very heavy weights as a normal part of their work."[115] Francis Place notes that his father, a baker, was strong enough to carry two sacks of flour at the same time.[116] While industrialization did reduce the need for strength, it did not necessarily do so immediately. Humphries doubts that strength requirements can explain the occupational sorting of women workers found in the 1851 census because industrialization decreased the requirements for strength; she claims, "Technical change in the eighteenth and nineteenth centuries tended to reduce the need for human muscle power and hence would logically widen female opportunities."[117] Similarly, Hudson and Lee claim that:

In theory one might expect that technological change would increase the opportunities for women to work on a greater parity with men. By removing or lightening tasks requiring great physical strength, more efficient tools and

[115] Lane, *Apprenticeship in England*, p. 51.
[116] Mary Thale, ed., *The Autobiography of Francis Place* (Cambridge: Cambridge University Press, 1972), p. 20.
[117] Humphries, "Most Free from Objection," p. 934.

mechanization might have changed that aspect of the sexual division of labor grounded in or at least justified by the notion of female physical inferiority.[118]

However, while industrialization eventually eliminated the need for strength in most industries, it is not true that strength was irrelevant by 1851. Strength continued to be important. In coal-mining, for instance, machines were introduced for ventilation and draining, but throughout the nineteenth century the most physically demanding work, hewing the coal, still relied on shovels, picks, and human muscle.[119] Samuel noted that the new machines of the Industrial Revolution required a great deal of strength and called it "a cruel caricature to represent machinery as dispensing with toil."[120]

The change in strength requirements was not even monotonic; in at least a few cases the strength requirement *increased* substantially before it decreased. The industrial innovations with the greatest impact on women's work were those in spinning. Spinning had been the largest employer of women, but mechanization reduced total employment, and eventually women spinners were replaced with men. The mule, a combination of the earlier jenny and water frame, started as a relatively small machine that could be worked by women, but it rapidly increased in size. Soon the mule was so large that it required too much strength for women to work it. A mule carriage with 336 spindles for spinning coarse yarn weighed 1400 pounds, and this had to be moved by the spinner three and a half times per minute.[121] Thus, until the mule was fully mechanized in 1830, mechanization increased the strength requirements of spinning. A similar increase in the size of a machine occurred in framework knitting. In 1833 a parliamentary investigator reported:

The labour of working the hand-machines must be very severe; and as fresh experiments seem to be constantly making on the degree of toil which the human frame is capable of sustaining, some of the recently constructed machines are such as none but the most athletic can manage. In 1829 the widest machine known was a twelve-quarter; that is capable of making a piece of net three yards

---

[118] Pat Hudson and W. R. Lee, "Women's Work and the Family Economy in Historical Perspective," in Hudson and Lee, eds., *Women's Work and the Family Economy in Historical Perspective* (Manchester: Manchester University Press, 1990), p. 9.

[119] Raphael Samuel, "Mechanization and Hand Labour in Industrializing Britain," in Lenard R. Berlanstein, ed., *The Industrial Revolution and Work in Nineteenth-Century Europe* (London: Routledge, 1992), p. 30.

[120] Raphael Samuel, "Workshop of the World: Steam Power and Hand Technology in mid-Victorian Britain," *History Workshop* 3 (1977), p. 8.

[121] William Lazonick, "Industrial Relations and Technical Change: The Case of the Self-Acting Mule," *Cambridge Journal of Economics* 3 (1979), p. 235.

wide. Since that time they have progressively enlarged, and I saw one man at work on a stupendous hand-machine twenty quarters or five yards wide.[122]

An increase in strength requirements can also be seen in agriculture. During the early nineteenth century, the need for strength in harvesting increased because of the gradual replacement of the sickle with the scythe.[123] The scythe was much heavier than the sickle, and the mower who used it benefited from both height and strength. Harvesting required large amounts of strength until it was mechanized in the late nineteenth century.[124] In the early part of the nineteenth century, mechanization had by no means freed women from their natural disadvantages.

The fact that women can occasionally be observed doing a task proves that their productivity was greater than zero, but it does not prove that it equaled male productivity in the same job. Women rarely plowed, but on occasion have been observed to do this task. Most cases of women plowing seem to have occurred in the north, where labor was relatively scarce. In 1794 Andrew Pringle noted that, in Westmorland, female servants "drive the harrows, or the plow, when they are drawn by three or four horses."[125] Judy Gielgud interviewed women from the north who had plow with horses in the early twentieth century.[126] This proves that women *could* plow, but it does not prove that they did the job as well as men. If men were scarce, or if small farm size limited the possibilities for division of labor according to comparative advantage, women may have been set to work plowing even though they did the job more slowly than men.

We must also keep in mind that what matters is not the effort put in by the worker, but the work output. The market rewards workers for what they produce, not for how hard they try. Elizabeth Roberts dismisses the claim that men's greater strength justified their higher wages because "Women expended prodigious amounts of strength and energy in, for example, the mining industry, in agriculture and in domestic work."[127]

---

[122] BPP 1833 (450) XX, C1, p. 35.

[123] See E. J. T. Collins, "Harvest Technology and Labour Supply in Britain, 1790-1870," *Economic History Review* 22 (1969), pp. 453–73, and Roberts, "Sickles and Scythes."

[124] The mechanical reaper, which was widely adopted in the US in the 1850s, was not well adapted to the small fields and rough, wet terrain of Britain. Paul David estimates that "in 1874 probably more than 53 percent of the British corn-harvest was still being cut by the sickle and scythe." Paul David, *Technical Choice, Innovation and Economic Growth* (Cambridge: Cambridge University Press, 1975), p. 236.

[125] Andrew Pringle, *General View of the Agriculture of the County of Westmoreland* (Edinburgh: Chapman and Co., for the Board of Agriculture, 1794), p. 41.

[126] Gielgud, "Nineteenth Century Farm Women," pp. 108–9.

[127] Roberts, *Women's Work*, p. 14.

She seems to be suggesting that women should be paid as much as men because they put a great deal of effort into their jobs. However, even the woman who strains herself to the limit will not be able to produce as much output as a man. If paid a market wage, the man will earn more because he produces more.

Contemporary observers were aware of the importance of strength for productivity. Alfred Austin, who investigated agriculture for a parliamentary committee in 1843, concluded: "The strength required for the work performed by men effectively prevents women from being employed in it; and the lower rate of wages for which they work has not had any tendency, therefore, to make them more generally employed."[128] Interpreting such statements is difficult. Do these statements reflect what work was really like, or are they simply reflections of ideology that connects male work with strength? It may be useful to note that such statements about physical strength limiting productivity came not only from those who accepted women's lesser social status, but also from those trying to improve women's status. William Thompson, a supporter of socialism and equal political rights for women, connected this physical disadvantage to lesser productivity in work. He noted that, "Two circumstances – permanent inferiority of strength, and occasional loss of time in gestation and rearing infants – must eternally render the average exertions of women in the race of the competition for wealth less successful than those of men."[129] The early feminist Mary Wollstonecraft admitted that: "In the government of the physical world it is observable that the female in point of strength is, in general, inferior to the male ... A degree of physical superiority cannot, therefore, be denied."[130] Even those who thought that women were equal to men in intellect, and should be equal to men politically, agreed that women were disadvantaged in the world of work by their lesser strength.

Could differences in strength really have created differences in productivity large enough to account for the wage differences observed? In certain cases the answer is clearly yes. Even among men, strength differences caused substantial differences in wages. From a framework knitter we learn that, "The strong man can earn 18s. or 20s. a week on

---

[128] BPP 1843 (510) XII, p. 27.
[129] William Thompson, *Appeal of One Half of the Human Race, Women, against the Pretensions of the Other Half, Men, to Retain them in Political and thence in Civil and Domestic Slavery* (New York: Source Book Press, [1825] 1970), p. x. He goes on to say that since women are disadvantaged in this way, they must have the protection of political rights.
[130] Mary Wollstonecraft, *A Vindication of the Rights of Woman* (New York: Norton, [1792] 1967), p. 32.

the wide work, while another poor man sits for 6s."[131] In this case, strength could increase a man's wage by a factor of three. In light of such differences in productivity, the gender wage differences of the Industrial Revolution no longer seem surprising. Indeed, if in some cases differences in strength might alter earnings by a factor of three, then an efficient allocation of jobs was necessary to keep the gender wage gap from being even larger than it actually was.

Wage premiums for occupations requiring strength have been interpreted as efficiency wages. Allen noted that wages in occupations requiring strength remained high while those in occupations not requiring strength were eroded. He interpreted this as an efficiency wage; the excess wages in the "privileged sectors" were necessary to "secure a work-force that was sufficiently nourished."[132] This point reinforces my claim that individuals who had more strength were more productive and thus could earn higher wages, but it adds a circularity to the argument, since according to this argument differences in strength were partially the result of higher wages. This raises the question of whether the differences in strength themselves were the result of discriminatory practices that gave men privileged access to food. While I admit the possibility that high wages in strength-intensive jobs may have an efficiency wage component, I do not believe that differences in access to food is sufficient to explain the differences between men and women. The evidence presented above documents large gender differences in strength among well-fed modern populations. Evidence from army soldiers and recruits presented in Table 2.5 suggests that differences in performance between fit and unfit individuals are smaller than differences between men and women. While efficiency wages may have been part of the story, productivity differences between men and women were not simply the result of men's privileged access to food.

This section has provided clear evidence that men are stronger than women, and that these strength differences lead to large differences in certain types of performance such as the maximum amount of weight an individual can lift. Since Industrial Revolution technology required a great deal of strength, and wages differed among members of the same gender according to their strength, it seems reasonable that strength was an important reason for the differences in productivity documented in Section II.

---

[131] BPP 1833 (450) XX, C1, p. 25. Evidence of George Goode. Wages also differed among women according to strength. The parliamentary investigator Alfred Austin found that "a woman who is strong and active, a good work-woman, is paid higher than one of inferior strength." *Women and Children in Agriculture*, p. 6.

[132] Allen, *Enclosure and the Yeoman*, p. 300.

B.   Training

While strength was important, it was not the only reason for differences in productivity. Differences in skill also affected productivity. Women certainly did not lack skills, but on average they had less training than men, and they tended to acquire different skills than men. This section will discuss both formal training, through schooling and apprenticeship, and informal on-the-job training through work experience. Women received less schooling than men, and were less likely to be apprenticed, so they had less formal training. Women were probably as likely as men to acquire skills through experience, but they acquired different skills than men, and the value of women's skills fell during the Industrial Revolution.

During the Industrial Revolution women received less formal education than men. While many girls were taught to read, few learned more than this. Girls were often kept home from school to help with the housework, and rarely progressed beyond primary subjects. In 1792 Mary Wollstonecraft argued that the intellectual inferiority of women was the result of inadequate education rather than natural ability.[133] Few women, whatever their ability, had any opportunity to become well educated. Beyond the elementary level, boys and girls were educated very differently. Grammar schools, which provided a classical education, were only open to boys.[134] Exceptions were rare. A few girls were admitted to a Blackburn grammar school in 1830, but in 1833 the school's governors ruled that no girls were to be admitted without a special vote.[135] Roach concludes that, "It is probable ... that it became more and more uncommon as time went on for girls to receive classical training."[136] Girls were taught basic literacy in elementary schools, but additional education was limited to household arts such as sewing and "accomplishments" meant to attract a husband. The wealthiest girls had governesses, but they were likely to learn subjects such as music and French, subjects designed to help them in society rather than the workplace because these girls were not expected to enter the workforce. The boarding schools for girls were generally finishing schools that did not teach academic subjects. Music and embroidery were more common at girls' schools than Latin or science.[137]

Women's opportunities for higher education were severely limited. Oxford and Cambridge were closed to women until the twentieth century.

---

[133] Wollstonecraft, *A Vindication of the Rights of Woman*.
[134] Davidoff and Hall, *Family Fortunes*, p. 290.
[135] Roach, *A History of Secondary Education*, p. 82.   [136] *Ibid.*
[137] Rosemary O'Day, *Education and Society, 1500–1800* (New York: Longman, 1982), p. 189.

Women were not fully admitted to Oxford until 1920.[138] Cambridge admitted women to exams in 1882, but did not allow them full privileges until 1948.[139] A degree from Oxford or Cambridge was a requirement for entry into the professional elite. The Royal College of Physicians, for example, admitted only graduates from these two universities.[140]

Differences in schooling led to marked differences in literacy levels. Measuring literacy by the ability to sign the marriage register, Schofield found large differences in the illiteracy rate by gender. In the 1750s, 60 percent of women and 40 percent of men could not sign the marriage register. In 1840 the rates were lower, but women were still less literate than men; 50 percent of women and 33 percent of men could not sign their names.[141] Because reading was taught before writing, and many women stopped attending school before they learned to write, differences in the ability to read were smaller than differences in the ability to write. While factory workers are not a random sample of British workers, an 1816 survey conducted by a parliamentary committee studying children's employment shows that, at least among factory workers, females were less literate. Among these workers females were almost as likely as males to be able to read; 84 percent of women over age 18 could read, compared to 89 percent of men. For writing, however, the gap is much larger; only 32 percent of the women could write, while 70 percent of the men could.[142]

While literacy was not required for most jobs, it was required for many of the best jobs. Literacy improved the chances of upward mobility for both men and women, and women who wished to escape manual labor and enter the most skilled occupations would find literacy valuable. Mitch divided occupations into four categories: those requiring literacy, those where literacy was likely to be useful, those where literacy may have been useful, and those where it was unlikely to be useful. He found

---

[138] L. Grier, "Women's Education at Oxford," in *Handbook of the University of Oxford* (Oxford: Oxford University Press, 1969), p. 286. The first women came to Oxford to study in 1878, but the road was long. By 1895 examinations were open to women. In 1896 an attempt to allow women to take the BA degree failed.

[139] Christopher Brooke, *A History of the University of Cambridge* (Cambridge: Cambridge University Press, 1993), vol. IV.

[140] W. J. Reader, *Professional Men: The Rise of the Professional Classes in Nineteenth-Century England* (London: Weidenfeld and Nicolson, 1966), p. 16.

[141] R. S. Schofield, "Dimensions of Illiteracy, 1750–1850," *Explorations in Economic History* 10 (1973), p. 443. Schofield claims that the signature is a good measure of moderate literacy skill, because "school curricula had been so phased that reading was taught before writing, and the intermittent nature of school attendance thus ensured that large numbers of children left school having acquired some reading ability, but little or no ability to write" (p. 440).

[142] BPP 1816 (397) III.

that women were less likely to be found in the top two categories. In 1841, only 7.4 percent of women workers were in occupations where literacy was required or likely to be useful, while 27.4 percent of working men were.[143] In a sample of marriage registers, literate brides were more likely than illiterate brides to be dressmakers, proprietors, or professionals, and they were less likely to be textile workers or unskilled laborers.

To some extent, women's lack of schooling was a rational investment choice. Since they would spend less time in the labor force, girls would receive lower returns from education than boys. To some extent, however, women's low education levels reflect discrimination in families and in schools themselves. Families may have made their investment decisions based on gender roles rather than the expected returns of the investment. Also, many schools discriminated against women by not admitting them. Even those women who wanted to could not attend grammar schools or universities.

Apprenticeship was another important method of obtaining job skills, though it became less important during the Industrial Revolution period. Girls could be apprenticed and often were, but they were much less likely than boys to receive this training. Parish apprentices were about 30 percent female.[144] Parish apprentices, though, often received little training because they were apprenticed mainly to save the parish the expense of maintaining them. A more accurate measure of human capital acquisition is the number of girls apprenticed by their parents, and these percentages are much lower. In the sixteenth and seventeenth centuries only 3 to 4 percent of private apprentices were female.[145] For the eighteenth century, estimates range from 3 to 8 percent, but average 5 percent.[146] Clearly girls were not gaining the same human capital as boys through apprenticeship.

---

[143] David Mitch, *The Rise of Popular Literacy in Victorian England: The Influence of Private Choice and Public Policy* (Philadelphia: University of Philadelphia Press, 1992), p. 15.

[144] K. D. M. Snell, *Annals of the Laboring Poor: Social Change and Agrarian England, 1660–1900* (Cambridge: Cambridge University Press, 1985), Table 6.1. Steve Hindle finds the same sex ratio among pauper apprentices in the 1630s. Steve Hindle, " 'Waste' Children? Pauper Apprenticeship under the Elizabethan Poor Laws, c. 1598–1697," in P. Lane, N. Raven, and K. D. M. Snell, eds., *Women, Work and Wages in England, 1600–1850* (Woodbridge: Boydell Press, 2004), p. 35.

[145] Michael Roberts finds that 4 percent of apprentices in Bristol 1532–65 were female, while Sue Wright finds 3 percent for Bristol 1542–53, and 3.6 percent for Salisbury 1603–14. Michael Roberts, " 'Words They Are Women, and Deeds They Are Men': Images of Work and Gender in Early Modern England," and Sue Wright, "'Churmaids, Huswyfes and Hucksters': The Employment of Women in Tudor and Stuart Salisbury," in Lindsay Charles and Lorna Duffin, eds., *Women and Work in Pre-Industrial England* (London: Croom Helm, 1985).

[146] Roberts finds the percentage of female apprentices to be 8 percent in Wiltshire 1710–60, 3 percent in Sussex 1710–60, 4 percent in Warwickshire 1710–60, 5 percent in

Some of women's lower productivity, then, seems to be the result of deliberate choices to provide less formal training for girls, both through education and through apprenticeship. To some extent these choices were influenced by gender roles that assigned girls more domestic tasks. Girls were more likely than boys to be absent from school. In one public school, between 1832 and 1834, boys had a 21 percent chance of being absent, and girls a 27 percent chance.[147] This difference was in large part due to the expectation that girls would help with the housework. A parliamentary investigator in Ireland found that "the services of females are more frequently required at home than those of boys, and the consequence is, their attendance at school is more irregular."[148] Gender roles that assigned domestic work to girls rather than boys thus led them to receive less education.

Even if parents were in principle willing to provide training for their daughters, calculation of costs and benefits would have discouraged it. Apprenticeship was often a substantial investment; Table 2.6 shows some examples of apprenticeship premiums paid. Parents were more willing to invest in sons because doing so brought a larger reward. A girl would be expected to spend less time in the labor market over her lifetime, lowering the potential value of human capital.[149] Also, a woman's place in the economy was more often determined by the man she married. Wives of tradesmen often helped their husbands rather than engaging in independent work. In the guild system, wives had the special position of being allowed to work in the trade without having been apprenticed to it. A woman was likely to give up the trade in which she had been trained when she got married. An example is the wife of James Hopkinson; she had learned dressmaking and was managing a business when she became engaged, but gave it up when she got married in order to help James with his cabinet-making shop.[150] If a girl was likely to abandon her training to work in her husband's shop, this would reduce the potential payoff to her human capital and thus discourage investment.

Women's lower level of human capital was to some extent due to circular reasoning. Women needed less education because they were less

Bedfordshire 1711–20, and 5 percent in Surrey 1711–31. Roberts, "Words They Are Women." See also Snell, *Annals of the Labouring Poor*, Table 6.4.

[147] Beryl Madoc-Jones, "Patterns of Attendance and Their Social Significance: Mitcham National School, 1830–39," in Phillip McCann, ed., *Popular Education and Socialization in the Nineteenth Century* (London: Methuen, 1977), p. 58.

[148] BPP 1840 (43) XXIII, p. 673.

[149] Women's lower labor force participation may have been partially due to their lower skill levels and lower wages, but it was also at least partially due to women's role in child-bearing.

[150] Hopkinson, *Victorian Cabinet Maker*, pp. 85, 88, 96.

Table 2.6. *Examples of apprenticeship premiums*

Date	Location	Occupation	Premium	Sex	Src
1710	London	Carpenter	£4	F	a
1713	London	Grocer	£180	M	b
1715	London	Apothecary	£50	M	c
1720	Birmingham	Baker	£15	M	c
1733	London	Mercer	£126	M	c
1737	Yarmouth	Cordwainer	£6	M	d
1741	Chippenham	Saddler	£20	M	c
1741	Dorchester	Joiner	£18	M	c
1743	Hertford	Butcher	£20	M	d
1750	Salisbury	Milliner	£40	F	c
1759	Westminster	Mantua-maker	£10	F	e
1767	Colchester	Milliner	£25	F	f
1773	Coventry	Surgeon	£130	M	c
1778	London	Bookbinder	£4	M	g
1785	London	Surgeon	£420	M	b
1792	London	Bookbinder	£15.15s	M	g
1796	Hertford	Grocer	£50	M	d
1800	London	"Wholesale manufacturing"	£100	M	h
1800	Essex	Wholesale draper	£500	M	i
1819	London	Stationer	£156	M	k
1824	Dublin	Cabinet maker	£100	M	l
1833	Leeds	Dressmaker	10s.6d. per year	F	m
1834	Nottingham	Cabinet maker	£20	M	n
1840		Wool sorter	£70	M	o
1843	Nottingham	Dressmaker	£50–60	F	p

Sources:

a. E. B. Jupp and W. W. Pocock, *Company of Carpenters* (London: Pickering and Chatto, 1887).

b. Harold Perkin, *The Origins of Modern English Society* (London: Routledge and Kegan Paul, 1969).

c. Lane, *Apprenticeship in England*, pp. 117, 122, 124, 138, 143.

d. O. Jocelyn Dunlap, *English Apprenticeship and Child Labour* (New York: Macmillan, 1912).

e. George, *London Life in the Eighteenth Century*.

f. D'Cruze, "To Acquaint the Ladies," p. 161.

g. Ellic Howe, *A List of London Bookbinders* (London: The Bibliographical Society, 1950).

h. *The Times*, February 16, 1819.

i. Davidoff and Hall, *Family Fortunes*.

k. *The Times*, January 14, 1819.

l. BPP 1824 (51) V, p. 456.

m. BPP 1833 (450) XX, C1, p. 73.

n. Hopkinson, *Victorian Cabinet Maker*.

o. BPP 1841 (296) X, p. 41.

p. BPP 1843 (430) XIV.

likely to work outside the home, but women were less likely to work outside the home because their wages were lower, and these lower wages were partially due to lower levels of education and training. If this trap was purely due to socially determined gender roles, then we would call it discriminatory. However, there were biological as well as ideological forces keeping women in this trap. Women give birth and breast feed infants, while men don't. This is one factor, in addition to lower wages, that makes women more likely than men to fulfill the domestic role. As discussed above, in many occupations women's lower wages were the result of their lesser strength. Thus women's lower levels of formal training were only partially, and not wholly, due to discrimination.

Formal training, though, was not nearly as important during the Industrial Revolution period as it is today. While a few of the most prestigious occupations required formal education, most occupations did not. Mitch calculates that, in 1841, 5 percent of males worked in occupations where literacy was required and a further 23 percent worked in occupations where literacy was likely to be useful. The bulk of the male labor force, approximately three-fourths of male workers, worked in occupations where literacy was not useful or only possibly useful.[151] Women do seem to be underrepresented in occupations requiring literacy, but differences in literacy can explain occupational segregation for only a minority of workers.

Differences in apprenticeship rates are likely to be a relatively minor reason for occupational segregation because apprenticeship was becoming increasingly irrelevant during the Industrial Revolution period. Even before the Industrial Revolution, apprenticeship was not the only way to acquire skills. In her study of female apprentices in Bristol, Ben-Amos notes that "training and skills were also acquired by young women in the town without a formal, recorded apprenticeship."[152] Many individuals acquired their job skills through practical experience. Apprenticeship was a legal requirement for entry into a trade under the Elizabethan Statute of Artificers until this law was repealed in 1814.[153] Even before 1814, though, the law was widely evaded. The Hammonds conclude that, in the woollen industry, "The practice of enforcing a seven years' apprenticeship for weavers and cloth workers had fallen into disuse by 1802."[154] In 1803 only 13 percent of the weavers hired by a Gloucester manufacturer,

---

[151] Mitch, *The Rise of Popular Literacy*, p. 15.
[152] Ilana Krausman Ben-Amos, "Women Apprentices in the Trades and Crafts of Early Modern Brisol," *Continuity and Change* 6 (1991), p. 228.
[153] Peter Kirby, *Child Labor in Britain, 1750–1870* (Basingstoke: Palgrave, 2003), p. 95.
[154] J. L. Hammond and B. Hammond, *The Skilled Laborers, 1760–1832* (London: Longmans, Green and Co., 1920), p. 170.

and none of the cloth workers, had served an apprenticeship.[155] In the nineteenth century apprenticeship continued largely through parish apprenticeship, which was an institution for providing for the poor rather than for human capital acquisition.

Both men and women acquired valuable skills through work experience, but, because they did different work, they tended to acquire different skills. One occupation where women acquired significant skills, and were paid good wages for their skills, was in dairy management. Skilled dairywomen could earn more than male agricultural laborers. In 1821 a Gloucestershire bailiff paid £3.14s.3½d. to "Jos. Wilcox for his wife attending the Dairy 7 weeks."[156] Even assuming that she worked seven days per week, Mrs. Wilcox earned more than 18d. per day for this work. At the same date the modal wage for male laborers was 16d. per day, so Mrs. Wilcox earned a wage that was higher than the majority of the male laborers.

Women were more likely than men to work at tasks requiring manual dexterity rather than strength, and they acquired superior skills in spinning and sewing. Though people sometimes interpreted these skills as "natural" female skills, they were learned rather than innate. (To check this, simply try asking a twenty-first-century woman to spin or sew.) Women learned these skills through practice. Men learned skills too, but they tended to learn different skills. Skills in hand spinning, for example, were acquired by women but not men. Sometimes young boys would spin, but they do not seem to have done this work often enough to acquire the same skills as women. Men, it seems, could not spin as well as women. In the early seventeenth century the town officials of Bocking noted that spinning was the only work available for employing the poor, and that "spinning work will not yield maintenance to those that want work, they being for the most part men that have not been exercised in the art of spinning."[157]

When women's skills were highly valued, women did well. An example is the boom in the straw-plaiting industry during the Napoleonic Wars;

[155] *Ibid.*

[156] Estcourt accounts, Gloucestershire Record Office, D1571 vol. A36, Feb. 17, 1821. In 1821 Mrs. Wilcox was paid £13.16s. for a half year, which is the same weekly wage. The 1821 payment for seven weeks of work was made when the Estcourts closed their dairy. There are other examples of high wages given to dairywomen. A large farmer from Worcestershire claimed that he paid the woman in charge of his dairy "55l. per year for herself and servant, including maintenance." In this case, unfortunately, the wages of the dairywoman and her assistant were combined, but this case confirms that dairywomen could earn relatively high salaries. *Women and Children in Agriculture*, p.125.

[157] Quoted in Sharpe, *Adapting to Capitalism*, p. 31.

women's wages reportedly rose to 21s. per week, about twice the weekly wage of a male agricultural laborer.[158] Women lace-makers in late seventeenth-century Devon also earned twice as much as male agricultural laborers.[159] In most cases where women's wages rose above male laborers' wages, the high wages were short-lived.[160] Maxine Berg claims that high wages in lace-making were more enduring.

Wages in the seventeenth and early eighteenth century were high, higher than those for wool spinners and much higher than those for local male agricultural labor. Yet despite the evident prosperity of this occupation for a time, men were not employed in it, neither did they seek to enter it.[161]

If the high wages earned by women in lace-making were indeed sustained over a long period of time, this does suggest some skill barrier preventing men from pursuing this occupation.

Unfortunately, the Industrial Revolution was not good to women. The machinery of the Industrial Revolution replaced many hand skills with machines. Sometimes this happened to men such as the cloth dressers and woolcombers (who resisted strongly). But none of these occupations could match hand spinning in terms of numbers employed. Recall that, before the arrival of machinery, spinning was said to employ all the women in certain areas. What had been a valued skill for most women suddenly became worthless as the jenny, water frame, and mule replaced hand spinning. To some extent, then, women's low wages reflected their bad luck in having their most important skills replaced by machines. Unfortunately for women, the Industrial Revolution led to a collapse in the value of women's skills. The fact that women's wages fell relative to men's wages during the Industrial Revolution was probably due to bad luck; the Industrial Revolution eroded the value of certain skills, and women happened to be more heavily invested in the hardest-hit skills than men.

To some extent women's lower productivity can be explained by women's lower levels of human capital. Women received less schooling than men, and had lower apprenticeship rates. If these women were paid wages equal to their productivity, then there was no discrimination in

---

[158] Sharpe, *Adapting to Capitalism*, p. 57.

[159] Pamela Sharpe, "Literally Spinsters: A New Interpretation of Local Economy and Demography in Colyton in the Seventeenth and Eighteenth Centuries," *Economic History Review*, 44 (1991), p. 52.

[160] Maxine Berg, "What Difference Did Women's Work Make," p. 37.

[161] *Ibid.*, pp. 32–3. Here Berg refers specifically to Sharpe's article on lace-makers at Colyton. While Sharpe gives only one wage citation, she does show that lace-making affected sex ratios and marriage patterns over a long period of time.

the labor market, but the wage gap may still reflect discrimination if the differences in education were the result of pre-market discrimination that limited women's schooling and apprenticeship. Women also suffered from bad luck; they acquired significant skills through work experience, but certain skills such as hand spinning lost their market value during the Industrial Revolution.

IV.   Did women earn customary wages?

As noted above, economic historians do not agree about how to explain the gender wage gap. Some assume that the wage gap is evidence of differences in productivity, while others suggest that women were paid customary wages, which were lower because women were assumed to be inferior to men. There are now quite a few articles discussing the question of whether women's wages were market wages or customary wages, and many of these conclude that women's wages were customary. Pamela Sharpe argues that "there is evidence for the importance of cultural factors outweighing rational economic decision-making."[162] Penelope Lane claims that the level of women's wages must have been set by custom because the wage gap cannot be entirely explained by differences in productivity.[163] Sonya Rose emphasizes the expectation that women were secondary earners, who did not need to support a family, and whose wages were only supplementary to the wages of the men on whom they were dependent.[164]

Unfortunately the claim that women were paid customary wages is difficult to evaluate because the claim is not clearly defined. Different historians seem to mean different things when they use the term. For some historians, inflexibility is an important characteristic of customary wages. Sharpe suggests that: "On the whole these women's wages were highly inelastic and could remain unchanged across generations regardless of other factors taking place in the economy. This suggests that women's wages had a large customary element."[165] Penelope Lane, however, suggests that wages may be customary even if they are flexible: "Historians are aware of the effect produced on female wage levels by male labor shortages, or the availability of alternative employment, but a

---

[162] Pamela Sharpe, "The Female Labor Market in English Agriculture during the Industrial Revolution: Expansion or Contraction?" *Agricultural History Review* 47 (1999), pp. 161–81.

[163] Penelope Lane, "A Customary or Market Wage? Women and Work in the East Midlands, c. 1700–1840," in P. Lane, N. Raven, and K. D. M. Snell, eds., *Women, Work and Wages in England, 1600–1850* (Woodbridge: Boydell Press, 2004).

[164] Rose, "Gender at Work."   [165] Sharpe, *Adapting to Capitalism*, pp. 145–6.

flexibility that breaks with custom is not evidence of a market wage."[166] It is not clear whether inflexibility is a necessary characteristic of customary wages.

If we want to determine whether women's wages were customary wages, we must first define what that term means. In this section I present five possible definitions for "customary wages" and examine whether each definition fits the facts. Wages might be customary in the sense that they were set by the government, or in the sense that they did not respond to changes in supply and demand. Wages might be customary in the sense that they were lower than fair market wages would have been. Wages might be customary in the sense that, when custom and market forces conflicted, custom took precedence. Finally, wages might be customary in the sense that society developed ideologies and customs designed to justify the wage differences that were created by the market, and most people thought about wages in these terms. I find that the evidence does not support the first four definitions of customary wages, and only the fifth definition matches the evidence.

Definition 1: Wages were set by government regulation
Wages might be fairly described as customary if they were set by law rather than the free market and legal wages were determined by customary ideas about the relative worth of males and females. England did have a legal apparatus for setting wages until 1813. The Elizabethan Statute of Artificers empowered local justices to set maximum wages for various kinds of work; it was passed in 1563 and not repealed until 1813.[167] In principle this would mean that wages were set by local authorities rather than the market, but the evidence suggests that the laws were not effective. Woodward suggests that wage regulations were effective in the first half of the sixteenth century, but largely ineffective in both the second half of the fifteenth century and the second half of the sixteenth century. He concludes that after 1563 "official attempts to control wage rates were largely unsuccessful."[168] Certainly the system was little used in the eighteenth century. Examining the evidence that compares actual wages to assessed wages, Kelsall concludes that "there is clearly a tendency for assessed and actual rates to diverge in the

---

[166] Lane, "A Customary or Market Wage?" p. 118.
[167] The Statute of Artificers was not the first English law to provide for maximum wages. Wage regulation began with the Statute of Laborers of 1349. R. H. Tawney, "The Assessment of Wages in England by the Justices of the Peace," reprinted in W. E. Minchinton, ed., *Wage Regulation in Pre-Industrial England* (Newton Abbot: David and Charles, 1972), p. 38.
[168] Woodward, "The Determination of Wage Rates," pp. 26, 28.

eighteenth century."[169] By 1813 the law was so irrelevant that members of parliament did not even know of its existence. The Hammonds report that, when the Lancashire cotton weavers appealed to parliament to have wages set according to the law:

In moving the second reading of the repealing Bill in the House of Lords, Lord Sidmouth remarked that at the time that recent petitions for regulating wages had been discussed in the House of Commons it was not known that there were Acts in existence for regulating the rate of wages "but in the course of the last year, it had been discovered that there were Acts both in England and Scotland rendering it imperative on magistrates to fix the rate of wages." Sidmouth assumed – and rightly assumed – that it was only necessary to mention the existence of this legislation to secure its repeal.[170]

While the law permitting justices to set wages was not repealed until 1813, the law had fallen out of use in the eighteenth century, so wages were not set by government regulation during the Industrial Revolution period.

Definition 2: Wages did not respond to the forces of supply and demand
Some historians have specifically stated that women's wages were not set by supply and demand. For example, Hudson and Lee claim that "The labor-market was segmented so that excess demand for female labor did not translate itself into higher female wages."[171] Pamela Sharpe focuses on the inflexibility of women's wages: "Whenever the women worked and whatever they did, the most likely sum they would be paid was 6d. This ... must beg the question of the extent to which the payment is an arbitrary, or customary figure rather than representing a market value."[172] Scholliers and Schwarz claim that "For most of the eighteenth and earlier nineteenth centuries the pay of women in agriculture was set at 6d. a day over most of England, irrespective of price movements, but also irrespective of a surplus or shortage of female labor."[173] While he shows that male wages did respond to supply and demand, Woodward claims that women's wages "were not simply reflections of

[169] R. Keith Kelsall, "Wage Regulations under the Statute of Artificers," reprinted in W. E. Minchinton, ed., *Wage Regulation in Pre-Industrial England* (Newton Abbot: David and Charles, [1938] 1972), p. 118.
[170] Hammond and Hammond, *The Skilled Labourer*, p. 87.
[171] Hudson and Lee, "Women's Work and the Family Economy," p. 18.
[172] Sharpe, *Adapting to Capitalism*, p. 80.
[173] P. Scholliers and L. Schwarz, "The Wage in Europe since the Sixteenth Century," in Scholliers and Schwarz, eds., *Experiencing Wages: Social and Cultural Aspects of Wage Forms in Europe since 1500* (New York: Berghahn, 2003), p. 9.

the supply of and demand for female labor."[174] Paul Johnson identifies customary wages as stable wages, in contrast to market wages, which are flexible:

> Has the labor market in Britain since early industrialization been characterized by customary and stable wage differentials, or by flexible wages that have reflected the marginal productivity of the worker and which have readily adjusted to changing supply and demand conditions?[175]

Sometimes the claim that wages did not respond to market forces is a claim about general tendency rather than an absolute rejection of any responses to market conditions. In her 1996 study of women in Essex, Pamela Sharpe also claims that wages were not responsive to economic conditions. She notes that the wages of unskilled domestic servants "were a matter of custom bearing little relationship to economic determinants."[176] In a 1999 article, though, she acknowledged that the market could occasionally affect wages: while women's wages were "sticky" at 6d. per day, in a few cases higher wages were paid, "which shows that the market certainly had some effect."[177] Thus wages might on occasion respond to market forces, but this was the exceptional case, and on the whole they were inflexible and unresponsive to the market.

Were women's wages inflexible, with only a few rare exceptions? If we look at a large sample of women's wages over time it is clear that women's wages were not fixed for generations. Figures 2.5 and 2.6 show the wages paid to women in winter and summer at a sample of ninety-five farms. There is a great deal of geographical variation in wages at any one point in time, and there is also movement in wages over time. Figures 2.5 and 2.6 combine wages from many different farms, but even if we confine ourselves to wages paid at a particular farm we find that women's wages were flexible over time. Buckland Abbey in Devon paid all its female workers the same wage. In 1798 and 1799 they earned 6d. per day year-round; by 1803 this wage had risen to 7d. in the winter and 8d. in the summer.[178] A farm in Lilistock, Somerset, owned by the Marquis of Buckingham, also paid uniform wages to its female laborers; this was 10d. in 1815 and 8d. in 1816 and 1817.[179] At a farm in Mangursbury, Gloucestershire, the female summer wage was 9d. per day in 1823 and

---

[174] Donald Woodward, "The Determination of Wage Rates in the Early Modern North of England," *Economic History Review* 47 (1994), p. 37.
[175] Johnson, "Age, Gender and the Wage," p. 229.
[176] Sharpe, *Adapting to Capitalism*, p. 114.
[177] Sharpe, "The Female Labor Market," p. 174.
[178] Devonshire Record Office, Drake 346M/E8–E11.
[179] Rural History Centre, BUC 11/1/11.

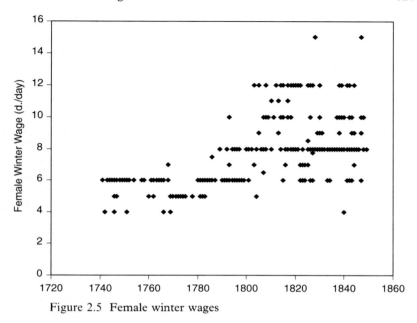

Figure 2.5 Female winter wages

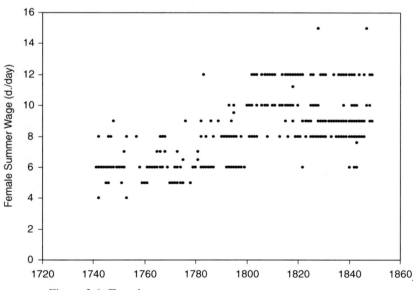

Figure 2.6 Female summer wages

1824, and rose to 10d. in 1825. The winter wage rose at the same time from 6d. to 7d., but fell back to 6d. in 1826.[180] At the Oakes farm in Derbyshire, the female non-harvest wage remained at 8d. between 1837 and 1846, but in 1847 rose to 10d.[181] These are just a few of the individual farms at which the female daily wage changes over time.

To further examine wage persistence I made use of the fact that about half of the farms in my sample have wage observations from more than one year. Table 2.7 shows the number of wage pairs in my data set categorized by the number of years between the observations. There were 131 cases where female summer wages were available for two consecutive years at the same farm. In 102 of these cases the two wages were the same, and in twenty-nine cases the two wages were different. I conclude that the probability of the female wage changing over the course of one year is 22 percent, and that the probability of wage persistence is 78 percent. Figure 2.7 graphs the probability of wage persistence from Table 2.7 against the number of years between wage observations. Wage persistence declines as the number of years increases. After one year most farms, 78 percent, are still paying the same wage. After fifteen years half of the farms are paying the same wage, and half of the farms have changed the wage. After three decades the probability a farm was still paying the same wage is only 10 percent. Thus there were some farms where the female wage remained fixed for decades, but these farms were not in the majority.

Women's agricultural wages not only changed, but did so in a way that responded to supply and demand conditions. Regions that had high demand for female labor in alternative occupations should have higher wages in agriculture, since the presence of other work decreased the supply of women available to agriculture. In my sample of farm accounts I find that counties with more cottage industry had higher female wages. Moving from an average county to Bedfordshire, where cottage industry was most prevalent, increased female wages in agriculture by 20 percent. The appearance of textile factories in the north-west also increased female agricultural wages. The north-west region, including (for my purposes) Lancashire, Cheshire, and the West Riding of Yorkshire, had lower female wages than the south-east in the second half of the eighteenth century, but in the first half of the nineteenth century wages were about 50 percent higher than in the south-east.[182] Clearly a high demand for female labor in competing industries increased the wages earned by females in agriculture.

---

[180] Rural History Centre, GLO 1/2/1.   [181] Sheffield Archives, OD1518, OD1531.
[182] Burnette, "Wage and Employment," p. 677.

Table 2.7. *Wage persistence, female summer wages*

Number of years between observations	Number of pairs	Number of pairs with equal wages	Persisting percent
1	131	102	78
2	98	71	72
3	88	65	74
4	66	51	77
5	62	47	76
6	50	39	78
7	48	34	71
8	44	29	66
9	37	26	70
10	39	27	69
11	30	20	67
12	25	14	56
13	23	14	61
14	23	14	61
15	22	11	50
16	19	9	47
17	19	9	47
18	18	9	50
19	18	8	44
20	16	8	50
21	17	7	41
22	13	2	15
23	13	4	31
24	13	3	23
25	13	3	23
26	13	3	23
27	11	2	18
28	13	2	15
29	11	1	9
30	10	1	10

If the claim that women's wages were unresponsive to the market was an absolute one, then it could be disproven with one example. If the claim is not absolute, and admits some exceptions, it is harder to disprove. I have shown that women's wages were not fixed over the period 1740 to 1850, and that they responded to regional opportunities for women's employment. I have also measured the extent of wage persistence, and have shown that, while most farms paid women the same wage after one decade, most farms had changed the female wage by the

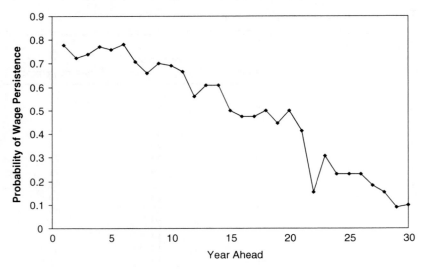

Figure 2.7 Wage persistence

end of three decades. I hope this is enough to convince the reader that instances of wages responding to market forces were not rare.

Definition 3: Wages were customary in the sense that they were lower than fair market wages
Wages, even if flexible, might be said to be customary wages if they were lower than market wages would have been. Sometimes the claim that wages were customary boils down to a claim that women were paid too low a wage. Penelope Lane, for example, acknowledges that female wages responded to market conditions, but notes that "flexibility that breaks with custom is not evidence of a market wage."[183] Lane believes that women's wages were discriminatory because, even after correcting for hours worked, "the gap that remains cannot be accounted for by differences in productivity."[184] Lane specifically points to the case of weeding, where she argues that "it could be argued that women were actually more efficient at this task, since weeding was so closely associated with them in any century, and therefore they should have received higher wages than men."[185]

---

[183] Lane, "A Customary or Market Wage?" p. 118.   [184] *Ibid.*, p. 112.
[185] *Ibid.*, pp. 111–12. Note, however, that the association of women with weeding implies that women had the comparative advantage in this task, but does *not* imply that women were absolutely more productive than men in this task.

Here the claim is not that women's wages were inflexible, but that they were too low relative to women's productivity.

Supporters of customary wages simply do not believe that women were half as productive as men. If it is true that women's wages were lower than their marginal product, then wage discrimination in the sense defined by Gary Becker existed.[186] Evaluation of this claim requires an evaluation of the relative productivity of male and female workers. Evidence presented in Section II suggests that women were less productive than men, and that the gaps were large enough to explain the wage gaps. Women were 85 percent as productive as men in picking cotton, but in agricultural more generally only about 60 percent as productive. In manufacturing, women were about half as productive as men in the nineteenth century. Today women are still not as productive as men in manufacturing, though their relative productivity is higher, at 83 to 84 percent of male productivity. Econometric estimates of productivity suggest that the productivity differences were large enough to explain the wage gap.

Definition 4: Wages were customary in the sense that they were determined by custom even when custom conflicted with market forces
Perhaps wages only seem to follow the dictates of the market because custom and market did not often conflict. Michael Roberts speaks of the "lack of incompatibility" between custom and market.[187] Certainly it is true that custom and market usually prescribed the same thing. Custom led people to expect that women should be paid less, and, as we have seen, productivity differences also suggested that women's wages should be lower than men's. If custom and market pushed in the same directions, perhaps evidence of flexible wages does not disprove the importance of custom in setting wages. But if there is any meaning to the debate about whether wages were market or customary, then there must have been some occasions when market and custom suggested different outcomes, so that it is still meaningful to ask which was the main determinant of wages. Which was the locomotive, and which the caboose? Pamela Sharpe argues that custom was the determining force for wages: "there is evidence for the importance of cultural factors outweighing rational economic decision-making."[188] The evidence I find, though, supports the opposite conclusion.

---

[186] Gary Becker, *The Economics of Discrimination* (Chicago: University of Chicago Press, 1957).
[187] Roberts, "Sickles and Scythes Revisited," p. 89.
[188] Sharpe, "The Female Labor Market," p. 178.

To find evidence of whether custom or market was pulling the train, we need to find evidence of cases where custom and market conflicted, and see which prevailed. One such area of conflict is cases where the market pushed women's wages above men's wages. It is generally agreed that society expected women's wages to be lower than men's, so if the market suggested women's wages should be higher than men's, there was a conflict between the prescriptions of custom and the market. When market forces increased the demand for occupations where women had skills, we occasionally do see women earning wages higher than men earned. An example is in the lace and straw industries during the Napoleonic Wars. War with France cut off imports, increasing the demand for domestically supplied lace and straw. In response to this demand, women's wages rose. In some cases women in these industries earned more than male agricultural laborers (who couldn't switch to making lace because they didn't have the skills). In the straw-plaiting industry, women's wages reportedly rose to 21s. per week, about twice the weekly wage of a male agricultural laborer.[189] High demand for females in cottage industry meant that female agricultural servants could earn as much as some men in Buckinghamshire in 1813.[190] Unfortunately these high wages were short-lived, and the end of the wars brought lower wages. Similarly, the invention of the spinning jenny for a brief time allowed a woman using this machine to make more than a man weaving cloth.[191] This situation was short-lived, though, because the spinning mule soon made the jenny obsolete.

Deborah Valenze explains the relatively low wages earned by female spinners in the eighteenth century as the result of the assumption that the spinners were supported by men:

Stigmatized by its association with women's work, spinning never earned wages commensurate with the demand for thread ... Purchasers of spun thread, whether middleman or manufacturer, assumed that spinners came from households where male wages provided the primary means of support; thus they deliberately set wages for spinning low, often in complete disregard of other factors involved in the trade.[192]

However, she also presents evidence that high demand for female labor could overcome such concerns and push women's wages above men's. When the invention of the flying shuttle caused a shortage of thread, increasing its price, Valenze notes that, "Decrying the fact that at times

---

[189] Verdon, *Rural Women Workers*, p. 143. See also Sharpe, *Adapting to Capitalism*, p. 57.
[190] Female annual wages were £10.10s., and male annual wages were £10.10s. to £12.12s. Verdon, *Rural Women Workers*, p. 50.
[191] Valenze, *The First Industrial Woman*, p. 79.   [192] *Ibid.*, p. 72.

women obtained more for their work than weavers, contemporaries called attention to the seeming injustice of it all."[193] If it is true that spinning wages were set by the expectation that women were supported by male wages, then how can we explain the fact that for a time women's wages for spinning were *higher* than male wages? The high prices paid to spinners conflicted with custom, leading to complaints from contemporaries, but the high prices were paid anyway.

Similar conflicts arose in seventeenth-century Devon, where women lace-makers could earn 7s. per week, while male agricultural laborers earned only 6d. to 8d. per day.[194] In this case the high female wages had important social consequences. The sex ratio of burials fell to around 75 males per 100 females as male workers migrated out of the region and female workers migrated in. Age at marriage was high for women, higher even than for men, and few widows remarried, leaving large numbers of women living independently.[195] High female wages did not fit with cultural expectations, and caused social changes that were probably unsettling to some, but the market prevailed. In this case, where market valuations conflicted with cultural expectations, market wages were paid. Thus, while women's wages were justified by appeals to religion and women's roles in the family, these justifications do not seem to have prevented women from earning high wages when the demand for their services was high.

Definition 5: Wages are set by market forces but justified by custom
It is possible that wages were governed by market forces, but explained and justified by appeals to custom and gender ideology. I do believe that women's wages were customary in this sense. Most people do not understand how economic forces set prices, and tell other stories about how prices are determined. When gasoline prices rise, conspiracy theories emerge.[196] Increases in gasoline prices prompt Congressional investigations. In a 2004 poll, 77 percent of Californians thought that high gasoline prices were due to the greed of the oil companies, and only 14 percent thought that the high prices were due to "legitimate changes

---

[193] *Ibid.*, p. 79.   [194] Sharpe, "Literally Spinsters," p. 52.   [195] *Ibid.*, pp. 49, 55.
[196] In 2000, Congress asked the Federal Trade Commission to investigate whether high gasoline prices were caused by illegal price-fixing. See the "Interim Report of the Federal Trade Commission, Midwest Gasoline Price Investigation," July 28, 2000, www.ftc.gov/os/2000/gasprice.htm. In May 2007, MoveOn.org asked for support of a bill against price-gouging, noting that "As consumers suffer, the oil industry continues to reap the windfall – breaking profit records on an almost quarterly basis. It's outrageous! ... Hearings start today on H.R. 1252, a House bill that would make gas price-gouging a federal crime, punishable by 10 years in prison."

in market conditions."[197] Similarly, individuals who did not understand market forces sought alternative explanations of women's lower wages. Sonya Rose suggests that wages must have been set by custom because, when asked, employers could only justify women's wages by appealing to what women usually earn.

Industrialists evidently paid women a customary wage rate based on their gender. A study of women's work and wages in Birmingham in 1906 reported that "employers can usually give no other reasons for the actual wage than the fact that such and such a figure is what women usually get in Birmingham."[198]

However, wages may be set by the market even if employers do not understand how the market works. In fact, the competitive models suggest that employers should be price takers, paying the going rate for labor. One of the strengths of the market system is that it works even if the individual decision-makers have very little information. I may not understand *why* the price of milk is $2.94 per gallon, but that does not prevent it from being a market price. Buyers of milk do not need to know why the current price is $2.94 – that's one of the greatest strengths of the capitalist system. The fact that these employers could not explain how wages were determined does not contradict the claim that they were market wages.

If people do not understand how market forces work, they can be expected to appeal to other factors to explain the levels of wages. In nineteenth-century Britain women's wages were explained in terms of custom, or in terms of their domestic role. For example, James Mitchell, reporting on the wages of factory workers in 1834, noted the fact that women's wages were lower than men's wages, and commented:

Some persons feel much regret at seeing the wages of females so low, in some cases full grown women averaging under 6s., and comparatively few more than 8s., but perhaps such persons are wrong; and nature effects her own purposes more wisely and more effectually than could be done by the wisest of men. The low price of female labor makes it the most profitable as well as the most agreeable occupation for a female to superintend her own domestic establishment, and her low wages do not tempt her to abandon the care of her own children. Nature thereby provides that her designs shall not be disappointed.[199]

Mitchell clearly was seeking some explanation of what struck him as gross inequality. He did not have access to economic explanations of the wage gap, and he justified women's lower wages as a means to encourage them to pursue domestic duties. However, that does not mean he was

---

[197] Field Poll #2117, http://field.com/fieldpollonline/subscribers/.
[198] Rose, "Gender Antagonism," p. 197.   [199] BPP 1834 (167) XIX, p. 39.

correct in his assessment. Even if custom or ideology was invoked to justify the wage gap, that does not mean that custom or ideology was necessarily the *cause* of the wage gap. While I would agree that women's wages were customary in the sense that they were justified by appeals to ideology and understood by contemporaries in these terms, I do not believe that ideology really determined the level of women's wages.

I do not believe that women's wages were inflexible, unresponsive to supply and demand, or set lower than women's productivity. I do believe that contemporaries understood women's lower wages through the lens of gender ideology rather than through the lens of economic models. However, individuals do not always understand the true causes of phenomena they observe. If the Greeks, observing lightning, explained it as a thunderbolt thrown by Zeus, that was part of their culture, but it doesn't mean that the lightning really did come from Zeus. Similarly, nineteenth-century Britain could interpret women's lower wages as the result of their inferiority or dependency on men, without those being the real causes of the low wages. I conclude that both the level of wages and changes in wages over time were the result of market forces, thus that women's wages should be called market wages, even if contemporaries did not understand them that way. Customary explanations for women's wage were part of the culture, but they did not cause the gender wage gap.

3 Explaining occupational sorting

> Two circumstances – permanent inferiority of strength, and occasional loss of time in gestation and rearing of infants – must eternally render the average exertions of women in the race of the competition for wealth less successful than those of men.   William Thompson, *An Appeal*, 1825[1]

The previous two chapters have documented large gender differences in wages and occupations. These differences are well known and easy to document, but explaining why these differences occurred is a more difficult task. Most historians attribute occupational sorting by gender to some form of discrimination. However, this conclusion is too hasty if we have not first explored whether a non-discriminatory labor market would produce the observed results. This chapter will present some models of market-based occupational sorting, and will argue that in the most competitive parts of the labor market the division of labor between the sexes matched would have been produced by the market.

In the last chapter we saw that sex differences in wages could be explained by differences in productivity. Of course, discrimination could still be the cause of women's low wages if gender discrimination confined women to a limited number of occupations, where their productivity was low. One way to explain the observed occupational sorting and wage differences is the crowding hypothesis formulated by Barbara Bergmann.[2] This theory states that because women are prevented from entering many occupations, the few occupations which they are permitted to enter become overcrowded, lowering the marginal productivity of workers in these occupations and thus also their wages. This model implies that the occupational sorting is based on gender discrimination, on barriers that prevented women from entering the male occupations.

---

[1] Thompson, *Appeal of One Half of the Human Race*, p. x.
[2] Barbara Bergmann, "The Effect on White Incomes of Discrimination on Employment," *Journal of Political Economy* 79 (1971), pp. 294–313, and "Occupational Segregation, Wages and Profits when Employers Discriminate by Race or Sex," *Eastern Economic Journal* 1 (1974), pp. 103–10.

Bergmann's crowding model assumes that workers are paid wages equal to their marginal product, and thus is consistent with the results of the last chapter.

This chapter will present alternative models of occupational segregation based on comparative advantage. In the first section I assume that, owing to their lesser strength, women were less productive than men in some occupations, and then ask what division of labor a competitive market would produce. These models, like Bergmann's crowding model, predict occupational segregation by gender. Unlike Bergmann's model, however, the occupational segregation results in a smaller wage gap than would have been the case without such segregation. In Bergmann's model, occupational segregation is harmful to women, reducing their wages below what they would have been without segregation. In the models presented here, occupational sorting is beneficial to women, saving them from feeling the full force of their lower productivity. Women's role in child-bearing may also lead them to choose different occupations than men. The second section of this chapter will examine the implications of women's role in child-rearing and suggest that women were more likely to choose occupations in cottage industry because these occupations were more easily combined with their child-care responsibilities.

The explanations for occupational segregation provided in this chapter are not meant to apply to all occupations, only to occupations without barriers to entry that blocked competition. Later chapters (5 and 6) will address less competitive occupations with barriers to entry and will explain why circumstances were different in those occupations. Although such a split at first seems unproductive and even misleading in a study discussing occupational segregation, I believe that in this case such a distinction allows a better description of the complex Industrial Revolution labor market. In more competitive parts of the labor market, where jobs were relatively easily entered, the gender division of labor was one that promoted efficiency. In other areas, where it was possible to monopolize occupations, men found it to their advantage to create artificial barriers to women's employment, and both women and the efficiency of the economy were reduced. One explanation for occupational segregation does not suffice for the whole labor market – in certain areas women were excluded from male occupations, but in other areas they competed with men. The claim that unifies these two strains is that women benefited from competition. Where the labor market was competitive, occupational sorting reduced the wage gap. Women only suffered from gender discrimination in those parts of the labor market that were not sufficiently competitive.

The gender division of labor among workers in openly competitive industries seems to have been a response to two basic gender differences: differences in strength, and differences in child-rearing roles. Both of these differences had profound implications for labor, and both have at least some biological basis. Social institutions were important for determining child-rearing roles, but at least two parts of child-rearing, pregnancy and breast-feeding, are biologically female. Differences in strength and child-bearing are the only two biological differences between the sexes that I assume; nowhere in this analysis do I assume that women are any different from men in either intellectual ability or personality. The remainder of this chapter discusses how the market's response to these two biological differences created the gender division of labor that we observe in much of the labor market.

I.   Occupational sorting based on strength

In the last chapter we saw that sex differences in strength caused substantial differences in productivity. Having recognized these differences in productivity, we can move on to discuss whether the observed division of labor between the sexes can be explained by gender differences in strength. This section will show that the simple fact that men are generally stronger than women is sufficient to explain much of the observed division of labor between the sexes. It will also show that this division of labor was beneficial to women in the sense that it allowed them to earn higher wages than they would have earned without sorting. I will first present models of sorting, and then argue that these models are good descriptions of the competitive portions of the labor market.

A.   Models of sorting

In his classic paper, Roy claimed that workers are sorted into occupations according to comparative advantage. Workers differ by ability, and those with more ability are sorted into those occupations where productivity is most responsive to ability. He offered this model as an argument against the view that "the distribution of incomes is an arbitrary one that has developed by the process of historical accident."[3] Applying this model to the division of labor between the sexes suggests that women should be sorted into occupations requiring less strength and men into occupations requiring more. This allocation of labor is

---

[3] A. D. Roy, "Some Thoughts on the Distribution of Earnings," *Oxford Economic Papers* 3 (1951), pp. 135–46.

efficient, rather than arbitrary. I will first present models of sorting for piece-rate and time-rate work, and then examine whether the evidence is consistent with these models.

A model is, by definition, a simplification of reality. The models presented here make a number of simplifying assumptions. They abstract from reality by assuming that individuals differ only by strength. Gender is relevant only because it is strongly correlated with strength. In reality workers differ in many other ways, including cognitive ability and skill. However, since I do not believe cognitive ability is correlated with sex, it cannot explain gender differences. Skill is correlated with gender, but it is endogenous. I assume that individuals of either sex could acquire equal amounts of skill if they had the incentive to do so. In these models I assume that skill does not determine the division of labor among the sexes because individuals of either sex could obtain the skills necessary for any occupation. If there are barriers that prevent women from acquiring skill in a certain occupation, then the market is not competitive. Chapters 5 and 6 discuss what happens when such barriers exist. In the models presented below, strength imposes the only exogenous constraint on individuals. Strength is to some extent endogenous, but as we saw in Chapter 2 changes in fitness levels do not erase the male strength advantage, so I will assume that the male strength advantage is exogenous, a biological given.

Model A: Job choice with piece-rate wages[4]

In some cases the employer could observe output and thus could pay each worker a wage equal to his or her true marginal product. This description applies to work done on piece-rate wages, where the worker was paid for his or her output rather than for time input. In these cases employers were generally indifferent to who their workers were. In handloom weaving, for example, the employers paid for output and had relatively little contact with their workers. The finished product was generally brought in for payment by the head of the household, and the employer would not know if the piece was woven by the man of the house, by his wife or one of his children, or even by a journeyman renting a loom. When asked whether the handloom weavers he employed were men, women, or children, Adam Bogle of Glasgow replied, "we do not know whether they are children, or men or women; the work is generally brought to the works by a man; they are generally

---

[4] For similar models see Roy, "The Distribution of Earnings," and Michael Sattinger, "Assignment Models of the Distribution of Earnings," *Journal of Economic Literature* 31 (1993), pp. 831–80.

men, and their families, and apprentices I believe."[5] In a case like this, where the employer did not even know who produced the cloth, workers could choose the occupation best suited to their strength endowment. This section models the individual's choice of occupation in a market where each worker is paid a set price times the number of units he or she produces, and can freely choose his or her occupation. Given gender differences in strength, and variations in the return to strength across industries, the model predicts gender differences in wages and occupations that match observed outcomes. The model can also be used to predict gender patterns of wages and occupations, and to examine how changes in the occupational distribution and the wage gap result from changes in demand or technology.

Models are simplifications of reality that allow us to understand reality better, so I begin my discussion of this model by describing the assumptions on which it is based. First I assume that workers have a range of different levels of strength. We can imagine giving each worker a percentile score "S" indicating where he or she falls relative to others in terms of strength (i.e., the person with a score of 20 is stronger than 20 percent of the workforce and weaker than 80 percent of the workforce). If we compared strength scores across the sexes, women would have lower scores than men. For the purposes of this model I will assume that the male and female strength distributions do not overlap, and that all individuals below the median are female, and all individuals above the median are male. In reality there would be some overlap, though measures of strength suggest the amount of overlap would be quite small. Table 3.1 shows, for men and women age 30 to 34, three measures of strength at the 90th, 50th, and 10th percentiles. In every case the 90th percentile for females is well below the 10th percentile for males. Thus, assuming that all females have strength scores lower than all males is not too far from the truth. Those concerned about this assumption can turn to the appendix to this chapter (pp. 336–7) for a more general model which allows the male and female distributions to overlap.

I also assume that an individual may choose any occupation, and will earn in that occupation an income equal to the number of units he or she produces (q_i) times the piece-rate in that occupation. An individual's output in a particular job is a function of the worker's strength score. Since jobs differ in their use of strength, the relationship between output (q_i) and strength (S) will be different for different occupations. In some jobs strength is no advantage; in others it is very important. We can

[5] BPP 1816 (397) III, p. 167.

Table 3.1. *Male and female strength distributions*

	Grip strength (kg)	Arm strength (kg)	Strength index
Male			
90th percentile	124	114	234
50th percentile	102	94	198
10th percentile	82	74	161
Female			
90th percentile	65	60	123
50th percentile	49	49	102
10th percentile	36	36	77

Strength scores for individuals aged 30–34.
Source: Henry Montoye and Donald Lamphiear, "Grip and Arm Strength in Males and Females, Age 10 to 69", *Research Quarterly* 48 (1977), pp. 109–20.

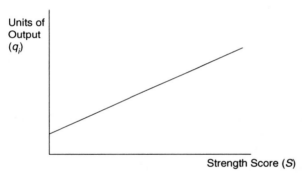

Figure 3.1 A general example of a strength–productivity relationship

imagine graphing the relationship between strength and output in a particular job; Figure 3.1 shows an example of such a relationship. The relationship between strength and productivity is increasing in this example, but it need not be. If strength does not affect output, then the strength–productivity relationship will be a flat line. It is theoretically possible that greater strength might actually reduce output, though if this did occur it would be rare. In general the relationship need not be linear, but in this section I will use linear functions for simplicity.

The worker takes the piece-rate as given and chooses the occupation that gives him or her the highest income. To take a specific numerical example, we can imagine two occupations, A and B, whose products are good A and good B. Strength is not valuable in occupation A, and any

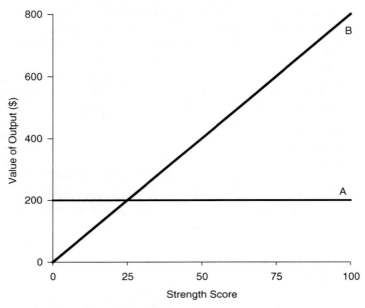

Figure 3.2 A specific example: productivity as a function of strength in occupations A and B

individual can produce twenty units of good A in a week. In occupation B, however, strength is advantageous, and those with more strength can produce more output; in this case the number of units an individual can produce is equal to twice that individual's strength score ($q_i = 2S_i$). We can graph both functions on the same graph if we value the output in money. If the piece-rate paid in occupation A is $10 per unit of good A, then any individual can earn $200 per week in occupation A. If the piece-rate paid in occupation B is $4 per unit of good B, then the income an individual can earn is a function of S, and is equal to eight times the strength score ($8S_i$). The relationships between strength and income in each occupation are graphed in Figure 3.2.

If individuals are free to choose their occupations, then the competitive market will produce the outcome that is optimal both in terms of maximizing each individual's income, and in terms of maximizing society's total output. If each individual chooses the occupation that gives him or her the highest income, then in the case depicted in Figure 3.2 anyone below the 25th percentile in strength would choose occupation A, and anyone above the 25th percentile would choose occupation B. This outcome is optimal for individuals; any individual who changes

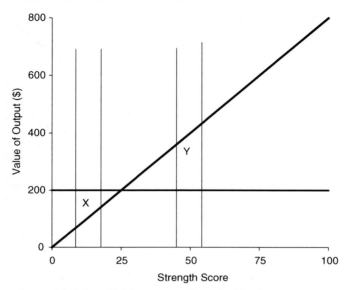

Figure 3.3 The efficiency costs of moving workers

occupations would earn less. The outcome is also optimal in the sense that the total value of the output is maximized; if any individual changes jobs it will reduce the total value of the goods produced in the economy. Suppose that we tried to make the gender division of labor more equal and moved women with strength scores between 10 and 20 from occupation A to occupation B, while at the same time moving men with strength scores between 45 and 55 from occupation B to occupation A. The women, who had been producing goods worth $200 each, would now produce goods worth between $80 and $160 each. The men, who had been producing between $360 and $440 worth of output each, would now produce only $200 worth of output each. Both the men and the women would be worse off, and the total value of society's output would also be lower, so the outcome would be inefficient. In Figure 3.3, area X is the amount of value lost by moving the women to occupation B, and area Y is the amount of value lost by moving the men to occupation A. There are no compensating gains. Both men and women earn less, and the total value of output produced has declined by the sum of these two areas.

A change in demand for the goods would alter the piece-rate prices, and change the incentives to workers, thus changing the output mix. If consumers decide they don't want as many units of good B, then there

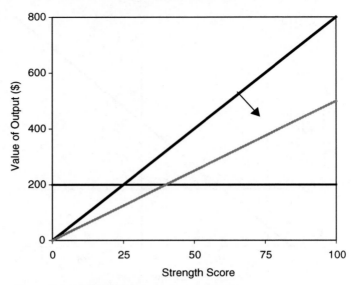

Figure 3.4 A decline in the price of good B

will be an excess supply of good B in the market, and the price of good B will fall. Suppose, for example, the price of good B falls to \$2.50 (see Figure 3.4). Individuals who work in occupation B will now earn their strength score times five ($5S_i$), and individuals between the 25th and 40th percentile will find it to their advantage to switch from occupation B to occupation A. As a result, society produces more of good A and less of good B.

This model allows us to examine the implications of strength for gender differences in occupations and wages, and to examine how those differences would respond to changes in demand or technology. If we assume that individuals below the 50th percentile are female, and individuals above the 50th percentile are male, then, in the case in Figure 3.2, workers in occupation A are all female, and workers in occupation B are one-third female. The women in occupation A all earn \$200 per week. The women in occupation B earn different incomes, but average \$300.[6] The men in occupation B earn on average \$600 per week.[7] Within occupation B the female–male wage ratio is 0.5. Averaging women in both occupations, the female wage is \$250 per week, so

---

[6] The average income is calculated by taking the midpoint on the line segment between $S = 25$, where income would be 200, and $S = 50$, where income would be 400.

[7] 600 is the midpoint between 400 and 800.

the female–male wage ratio for the workforce as a whole is 0.42 (250/600). Note that, in spite of the fact that all individuals in occupation B earn more than all individuals in occupation A, the wage gap is not caused by barriers preventing women from entering occupation B.

If occupational segregation is the result of sorting by comparative advantage, it reduces the size of the wage gap rather than increasing it. If, in Figure 3.2, we moved all the women below the 25th percentile from occupation A into occupation B, their earnings would fall from $200 to an average of $100, and the female–male wage ratio would fall to 0.33 (200/600). Moving to the male-dominated occupation would make the women worse off, not better off. Division of labor according to comparative advantage improves women's relative productivity because it allows them to work where the penalty to their lesser strength is smallest. Specialization improves the productivity of women relative to men. Toman has found evidence of this phenomenon among slaves in the US South. Plantations large enough to use the gang system could increase output per worker because they could divide the labor according to comparative advantage, giving the most strenuous tasks to the strongest workers, and using the weaker workers for less strenuous tasks. Under the tasks system, which did not allow for such sorting, female slaves were only 40 percent as productive as male slaves. Under the gang system, which allowed for sorting according to comparative advantage, the marginal productivity of a female slave was 60 percent as much as a male slave.[8] The model presented here implies that occupational sorting raised women's productivity, and thus their earnings, by sorting them into occupations that were to their comparative advantage. This is the opposite of the conclusion implied by Bergmann's crowding model, where reductions in occupational segregation would decrease the wage gap.

This model can also explain how the gender division of labor or the size of the wage gap can change in response to changes in the demand for goods, or the introduction of new technology. Changes in the gender division of labor are sometimes interpreted as evidence that custom determined this allocation. For example, Laurel Thatcher Ulrich, observing the movement of women into weaving in New England, concludes that: "The shift in the division of labor described here … demonstrates an essential feminist argument – that gender is socially rather than biologically determined."[9] However, this occupational shift

[8] Toman, "The Gang System."
[9] Laurel Thatcher Ulrich, "Wheels, Looms, and the Gender Division of Labor in Eighteenth-Century New England," *William and Mary Quarterly* 55 (1998), p. 34.

need not be the result of shifts in social expectations. The movement of women into handloom weaving can be explained by the combination of biological difference and technological change. In the model just described we would expect changes in technology or demand to alter both the division of labor between the sexes and the wage ratio. Suppose that, as in Figure 3.4, the demand for good B falls. Women between the 25th and 40th percentile would move into occupation B. Occupational segregation increases as the representation of women in occupation B falls to one-sixth, but the wage gap also falls. In the new case, women in occupation B earn only $225 on average, but the average earnings of the men falls even more, to $375. Women in occupation B now earn 60 percent as much as men. The improvement in their relative wage is the result of the movement of the weakest women into occupation A, and of the decrease in the demand for the strength-intensive product which reduced the market return to strength.

Taking a case more closely related to the Industrial Revolution, suppose that a new strength-intensive technology is introduced for producing good A. The new occupation, occupation C, produces the same good as occupation A, but has a steeper strength–productivity line. An individual working in occupation C can produce $(2S_i-60)$ units of output per week. The ease with which high-strength individuals can produce good A will increase the supply of this good and decrease its price. Suppose the price of good A falls so that the piece-rate for producing a unit of good A is only $5. If the price of good B is $2.50 as in Figure 3.4, individuals in that occupation earn $5S_i$, and women with strength scores between the 20th and 50th percentiles will choose occupation B. Occupation C produces the same output as occupation A, so the price of good C is also $5. Individuals in that occupation will earn $5(2S_i - 60) = 10S_i - 300$. Individuals with a strength score above the 60th percentile will choose occupation C (see Figure 3.5). In this case, occupation A contains only women, occupation B contains both women and men, and occupation C contains only men. The overall wage gap increases, and women on average earn only 32 percent as much as men.[10]

While this is a hypothetical example, it does bear some resemblance to what happened in textile manufacturing during the Industrial Revolution. Hand spinning, like occupation A, did not require strength.

---

[10] Two-fifths of women earn $100 in occupation A, and the three-fifths of women in occupation B earn on average $175. Overall women earn on average $145. The one-fifth of men in occupation B earn on average $275, while the rest earn on average $500 in occupation C. Overall, men earn on average $455.

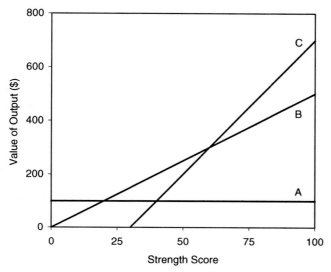

Figure 3.5 Entry of a new occupation

During the Industrial Revolution, however, this old technology was replaced by a new technology that did require strength. The earliest spinning machines, the jenny and the throstle, did not require much strength and were worked by women. However, the spinning mule, which did require a great deal of strength, could produce a better quality of yarn and became the dominant machine. Women were initially used for mule-spinning, but as the mules grew larger men came to dominate that occupation.[11] Men became mule spinners, and women moved out of hand spinning as the wage in that occupation dropped. Young women and boys were used as assistants to mule spinners, but overall the demand for female workers in spinning fell substantially, partly because the total number of workers required to spin yarn fell. Many of the women who were no longer employed in hand spinning moved into handloom weaving, whose strength requirements were greater than in hand spinning but less than in mule spinning. The introduction of a new strength-intensive technology, which replaced an old technology requiring no strength, made women worse off and increased the overall wage gap in the economy.

---

[11] Men continued to dominate mule spinning even after the self-actor reduced the need for strength because the mule spinners' union was able to exclude women. See Chapter 6, and Freifeld, "Technological Change and the 'Self-Acting' Mule."

Model B: Time-rate wages with sex as a signal of strength

In many cases the employer could not readily observe individual output and thus could not pay piece-rate wages. For the second model I make an extreme informational assumption – that employers observe only the worker's sex and know nothing else that would help them measure the worker's productivity. Where output of an individual worker is not observed, the employer must pay a time-rate wage. The employer can observe sex, which is a signal of strength, and in a competitive market must pay each worker his or her expected productivity given sex. With insufficient information on individual productivity, each woman is assumed to have the average female strength endowment, and each man the average male strength endowment. The result is statistical discrimination; workers of each sex will be treated as a homogenous quantity, and all persons of the same sex will receive the same wage, regardless of their individual productivity.

Firms produce a product, and the amount that an individual can produce in a day is a function of strength, though not necessarily proportional to strength. If strength increases productivity, then the employer will expect that men on average will produce one level of output, and women another. The ratio of average female output to average male output will be different at different firms, and I will call it r_i, where the subscript i indicates that each firm has its own female–male productivity ratio. We can imagine arranging firms by r_i, starting with the firm with the lowest r and progressing to those firms with higher levels of r. We can then construct an "r-profile," which is a step function, as in Figure 3.6. The length of the x-axis (the origin to point L) is the total amount of labor employed in the economy, and the length of each step on the r-profile is proportional to the number of workers hired by each firm. The market wage ratio will be the wage ratio that clears the market, that is, where firms' demand for female workers equals the supply of females, and firms' demand for males equals the supply of males. Point X divides the workforce into males and females. The distance between the origin and point X is the number of males in the workforce, and the distance between point X and point L is the number of females in the workforce.

Each firm will compare its productivity ratio to the market wage ratio. If $r_i < w_f/w_m$ the firm will hire males, since females are too expensive relative to their productivity. If $r_i > w_f/w_m$ the firm will hire females, since their relative productivity is greater than their relative wage. A firm is willing to hire both males and females only if $r_i = w_f/w_m$, so that the firm is indifferent between male and female workers. Figure 3.6 shows how the market wage ratio is determined. The vertical line through point X intersects the r-profile at the seventh firm, which has an r of 0.55. This

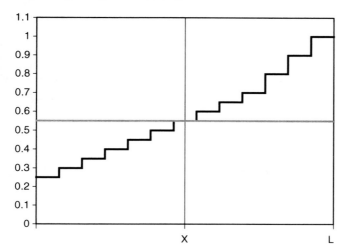

Figure 3.6 Determination of the wage ratio in Model B

means that the market wage ratio must be 0.55 to clear the market. The six firms with r's lower than 0.55 will hire only males, and the six firms with r's higher than 0.55 will hire only females. The seventh firm is indifferent to hiring males and females, and will hire both. Note that this model predicts nearly complete occupational segregation. Only firms whose r_i is exactly equal to the market wage ratio will hire both men and women. Thus even high levels of occupational segregation are consistent with efficient sorting in a competitive market. While only 9 percent of occupations in the 1904 report of the US Commission of Labor were integrated by gender, this fact is not proof of discriminatory constraints on occupational choice.[12]

The entry and exit of firms, or expansion and contraction of employment at existing firms, will cause the r-profile to shift and may change the market wage ratio. Suppose that a low-r firm replaces a high-r firm, as when mule-spinning replaces hand spinning. If we remove the firm whose r is 1.0, and replace it with another firm whose r is 0.3, then the new r-profile shifts down and to the right, as depicted in Figure 3.7. At the old wage ratio of 0.55, there would be women unemployed and an excess demand for men. To clear the market the wage ratio will fall. The vertical line originating at point X intersects the new r-profile at a firm whose r is 0.5, so the new market wage ratio is 0.5. Thus we find that, as in Model A, the replacement of a low-strength technology with a

---

[12] This statistic comes from Goldin, *Understanding the Gender Gap*, p. 77.

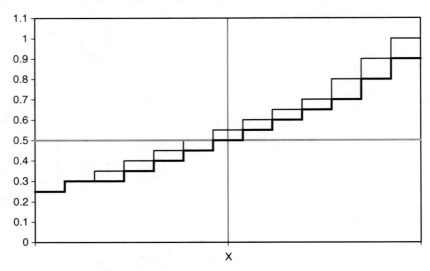

Figure 3.7 A change in technology

higher-strength technology (as happened in spinning) would cause the relative wages of women to fall.

The two models presented here depict two extremes. In the first model, the output of each worker is perfectly observable, while in the second model the employer cannot observe individual output at all, and knows only the gender of the worker. Even when time-rate wages were paid, we might think that the employer received some information about the individual productivity of the workers. Output, though not perfectly observable, may be observable with some error. If the employer initially knows only the gender of the worker, but over time learns more about the individual productivity of that worker, then the employer will be able to tailor the wage more closely to the individual's ability. A third model presented in the appendix (Model C) describes this case in greater detail. An important prediction of this third model is that casual workers are more likely to have uniform wages than regular workers. This matches the pattern of wages we observe in agriculture. Female day-laborers were usually casual workers hired for only a few weeks, so employers did not have much information about individual productivity, and their wages were uniform. Often all women received the same wage. Male laborers were more likely to work regularly, and we do observe more individual variation in wages for male workers. Table 3.2 shows the wages paid to all workers on July 15, 1836 at the Apley Park farm in Shropshire. All the women were paid the same wages, but only eight of

Table 3.2. *Wages paid to laborers at the Apley Park farm,*
July 15, 1836

Name	Daily wage (d.)
MALES	
Sam Partridge	36
Sam Pace	24
Richard Piver	22
John Hadley	20
Samuel Crump	20
John Rhods	20
William Pace	20
John Blackshaw	20
Henry Barret	20
Thomas Littleport	20
Jim Brown	20
Moses Davis	18
William Childs	12
Edward Hollans	8
FEMALES	
Sarah Hadley	10
Eliz. Crump	10
Sarah Brown	10
Mary Barret	10
Jane Pace	10
Sarah Harris	10
Jane Parton	10

Source: Shropshire Record Office 5586/5/17/28.

the fourteen men earned the modal wage. The uniformity of female
wages has sometimes been interpreted as evidence of the importance of
custom in setting wages, but it may be that farmers paid all women the
same wage because they were casual workers and thus the employer had
little information about individual productivity.

Before looking for evidence that these models describe the labor
market during the Industrial Revolution, I will point out a few things
that are *not* implied by the models of occupational sorting presented
here. First, it is *not* necessary for the strength requirements of jobs to be
so great that women cannot do these jobs at all. Women were capable of
plowing, but that doesn't mean that a woman would do the job as well or
as quickly as a man. In both of the models presented above, I assume
that women can do all of the jobs, but sometimes have lower productivity than men (an exception is occupation C in Figure 3.5, where
women below the 30th percentile have zero productivity). Nor is it
necessary that the differences in productivity be large. Gullickson argues

that since the difference in the strength needed for weaving different types of cloth was small, the occupational sorting by type of fabric could not have been based on this difference. She claims, "The difference in strength requirements, as well as the actual strength of men and women, was slight, however, and the assertion of male superiority was far more important in this new sexual division of labor than was physical strength."[13] However, the size of the productivity difference need not be large. A small difference in productivity can lead to complete occupational segregation as easily as a large difference. Even if the differences in productivity were relatively small, maximum efficiency could only be achieved if each person was assigned to the task where he or she would be most productive. Differences in strength can lead to complete occupational segregation even if the differences in productivity are relatively small, and women simply work more slowly than men.

Nor does the fact that women can be observed doing heavy work disprove the strength hypothesis. The fact that women sometimes did strength-intensive tasks does not prove that they were as productive as men in those tasks. Women were capable of plowing, but rarely did so. Gielgud concludes that, "Most women were too sensible to take on a job they knew to be beyond their strength unless particular circumstances required them to do it ... and it seems that men recognized it as work which was too physically difficult for most women and did not expect it of them."[14] When women did plow, it was usually on small family farms that did not hire laborers.[15] Deborah Simonton claims that, "The continued involvement of women across a broad spectrum of field tasks, including the most arduous, undermines the notion that purely biological characteristics or maternal functions determined female agricultural roles."[16] However, if the demand for strength is high in the economy, or if institutional restrictions prevent women from entering more suitable occupations, women will be assigned to strenuous tasks even if they are less productive than men in those tasks.[17]

---

[13] Gay Gullickson, *Spinners and Weavers of Auffay: Rural Industry and the Sexual Division of Labor in a French Village, 1750–1850* (Cambridge: Cambridge University Press, 1986), p. 109.

[14] Gielgud, "Nineteenth Century Farm Women," p. 110.

[15] Pinchbeck, *Women Workers*, p. 9. If her husband was busy with other work a woman might end up plowing because hiring a laborer rather than employing a family member created principal-agent problems.

[16] Simonton, *European Women's Work*, p. 130. See also Hudson and Lee, "Women's Work and the Family Economy," p. 9.

[17] In Germany, where institutional restrictions were tighter and markets were less competitive, women seem to have done more plowing than in Britain. Ogilvie, *A Bitter Living*, pp. 119, 151, 200.

These models also do *not* imply that the gender division of labor will remain fixed over time. Laurel Thatcher Ulrich, noting that weaving shifted from being men's work to women's work in eighteenth-century New England, claims that this shift proves "that gender is socially rather than biologically determined."[18] However, the models presented here demonstrate that changes over time in the gender division of labor or wage ratio are compatible with a biologically-based explanation of the division of labor. Even if differences in strength are biologically based, and the wage gap is the direct result of those differences in strength, this does not imply that the wage gap must remain fixed over time. Strength was a scarce good, which received a premium in the market, but the value of strength, and the size of that premium, varied over time. In fact, we should expect the wage ratio to change with changes in demand and technology. While I do assume that gender differences in strength are biologically based, I do not expect these strength differences to produce the same division of labor, or the same wage ratio, in all times and places. The secret to this puzzle is to realize that the same underlying strength ratio is converted into different productivity ratios in different occupations. Some technologies are very strength-sensitive, so that the underlying strength differences cause large differences in productivity. Other technologies are less sensitive to strength, and in those cases differences in productivity by gender are small or non-existent.

The models also make it clear that we should not expect men and women to earn the same wage even when they do the same task. Commenting on farm accounts from seventeenth-century Devon, Pamela Sharpe notes that "women agricultural workers were paid less than the rates of pay for men, even when they appear to have done directly comparable work. For example, in May 1683, Jone Clements and her husband were both paid for a day's threshing. She was paid 4d. and he was paid 5d."[19] Even if both of the Clements worked the same hours, we should not expect men and women to earn the same wage because we cannot expect them to have threshed the same amount of grain. Threshing was a strenuous job, and unless Jone was very unusual she had less strength than her husband, and would have threshed less grain over the course of the day.[20] Both of the models above predict that, when men and women work in an occupation where strength increases

---

[18] Ulrich, "Wheels, Looms and the Gender Division of Labor," pp. 34–5.
[19] Pamela Sharpe, "Time and Wages of West Country Workfolks in the Seventeenth and Eighteenth Centuries," *Local Population Studies* 55 (1995), pp. 67–8.
[20] For evidence that threshing was a job requiring strength, see Stephen Duck's poem, "The Thresher's Labor," in *Poems on Several Occasions* (London, 1736).

productivity, the women will produce less because they have less strength, and will earn less than men doing the same job.

B.   Anecdotal evidence of market-based sorting by strength

A closer look at the historical facts shows that the models of occupational sorting presented in the previous section are helpful for understanding the occupational distribution during the Industrial Revolution, at least for the competitive sectors of the economy. The models predict that we should observe men in strength-intensive occupations, and women in occupations requiring less strength. Much of the occupational pattern of the early nineteenth century is consistent with this sorting prediction. To show that the models presented above are good descriptions of how the gender division of labor was determined, I will examine whether the strength-intensity of the job determined whether men or women were employed. I look first at the overall distribution of labor between the sexes, showing that men did the most strenuous tasks. Then I show that some unusually strong women can be found doing male jobs. Next I examine regional differences in the pattern of sorting, and show that in regions where the demand for strength was lower women earned higher relative wages. I also show that the division of labor between the sexes changed in response to technological changes that altered the strength requirements of certain jobs.

1.   Patterns of occupational sorting

In general women tended to congregate in occupations requiring little strength. In Chapter 1 we saw that hand spinning was one of the largest employers of females during the pre-industrial period. Women also monopolized such industries as lace making and straw plaiting which required dexterity but not strength. Heavy industries, on the other hand, employed men. To support her claim that "androcentric blindness" prevented employers from hiring women, Jordan points to the absence of women in certain new industries, specifically iron and steel manufacture, engineering, railways, and mining.[21] However, we would not expect these industries to employ women in a competitive market. They are called "heavy industries" for a reason – the materials are heavy and the work requires strength. Many occupations requiring heavy work were male preserves. In the 1841 census, dock workers and firemen (those who tended furnaces) were exclusively male. Quarriers were 99.5 percent male, wood cutters 95.5 percent, sawyers 99.93 percent,

---

[21] Jordan, "The Exclusion of Women," pp. 294–5.

and ship builders 99.95 percent.[22] The lack of women workers in these occupations is not surprising given the strength required for the work.

Both men and women worked in agriculture, but they typically did different tasks, and the men's tasks generally required more strength than women's tasks. In the eighteenth-century records of an estate in the North Riding of Yorkshire, Gilboy found that the jobs done exclusively by men were threshing, hedging, and plowing – the most strenuous of the agricultural jobs.[23] Plowing is strongly associated with male workers, to the point that the use of the plow is an important factor in determining whether agricultural work is done by men or women. Ester Boserup notes that "the advent of the plow usually entails a radical shift in sex roles in agriculture; men take over plowing even in regions where the hoeing had formerly been women's work."[24] Farm women interviewed by Judy Gielgud did some plowing, but only with difficulty:

From the women I have interviewed who have plowed with horses ... it is plain that the weight of the plow, particularly when turning it at the headlands at the end of the furrow, is what needed particular strength; the share and coulter must be lifted clear of the furrow and the handles born down upon to swing the plow round. Most said they simply did not weigh enough to do this with comfort.[25]

Women were more likely to do jobs such as spreading manure and weeding. Henry Best, a Yorkshire farmer, summarized the harvest labor needs of his farm in 1641. Breaking the tasks into three categories according to the sex of workers:

Women only	Both sexes	Men only
Gathering after the mower	Reaping	Mowing
Raking	Pulling peas	Binding
		Stooking (stacking)

All of these tasks required at least moderate amounts of strength. Mowing (harvesting with a scythe) required a great deal of strength.

[22] BPP 1844 (587) XXVII. On the strength required for these jobs, see Samuel, "Workshop of the World."
[23] Gilboy, "Labor at Thornborough."
[24] Ester Boserup, *Women's Role in Economic Development* (New York: St. Martin's Press, 1970), p. 33. In Africa, where the hoe is the main tool for cultivation, agricultural work is primarily done by women.
[25] Gielgud, "Nineteenth Century Farm Women," pp. 108–9. Note that the fact that women occasionally did plow does not contradict the claim that it was not generally the most efficient use of scarce resources. Cases of women plowing usually come from labor-scarce regions, such as the north.

Reaping (harvesting with a sickle) required strength, but less than mowing. The men-only tasks other than mowing required lifting the hay, and the women-only tasks did not require lifting. Even within each task, Best instructs his readers to take account of individual strength in assigning workers; thus, "the strongest and ablest of your shearers [reapers] you shoulde allways putte to the ridge, because there the corne is rankest and strongest."[26]

The sickle was used by both men and women, but the scythe was used only by men. Michael Roberts examined 125 illustrations from Europe in the period from the second century to the sixteenth century and found no examples of women using scythes, though he found many examples of women using sickles. Though Roberts was skeptical of employers' assumptions about women's strength, he noted that, "The strength or stature required of the mower appears to provide the most plausible explanation why women were so rarely employed in this way."[27] Men mowing with a scythe remained standing and swung the scythe. They benefited from greater strength, because the scythe was heavier than the sickle, and from greater stature, because this provided more leverage. By contrast, shorter stature was beneficial to the reaper, who stooped to cut with the sickle. While reaping required less strength than mowing, it required more strength than other tasks done by women. Mary Haynes, a laborer from Wiltshire, noted that "I think reaping the hardest of all the work I have ever done."[28] She mentions having worked at stone-picking, weeding, haymaking, and turnip-hoeing, as well as reaping, so reaping was more demanding than all these other tasks. This suggests that reaping required more strength than other types of farm work done by women. Reaping required enough strength that not every woman could do it. A farm laborer from Devon noted that his wife worked regularly in the fields, but "she can't reap, she is not strong enough."[29]

Model A predicts that, when women are observed doing relatively strength-intensive jobs, we should also observe them earning more than other women. This prediction holds true for reaping. Reaping was relatively well paid work for women, and for much of English history the female–male wage ratio was higher at harvest than at other times of year. Among the agricultural wage ratios in Table 2.1, the wage ratio for harvest work tends to be higher than the wage ratio for work in other

---

[26] Henry Best, *Rural Economy in Yorkshire in 1641*, Surtees Society, vol. 33 (Durham: George Andrews, 1857), p. 44.

[27] Roberts, "Sickles and Scythes," p. 12.

[28] Evidence of Mary Haynes, widow, of Calne, Wiltshire, *Women and Children in Agriculture*, p. 69.

[29] George Moxey of Shillingford, near Exeter, *Women and Children in Agriculture*, p. 112.

seasons, at least in the seventeenth and eighteenth centuries. For the seventeenth century, the harvest wage ratios average 0.72, while the wage ratios for hay time average 0.59. In the eighteenth century all the wage ratios are lower, but the wage ratio is still higher at harvest (0.67) than at other times of the year (0.48). By the nineteenth century, this effect has disappeared, and the harvest wage ratios are no higher than wage ratios at other times of year. This reduction in the harvest wage ratio was probably due to the disappearance of opportunities for work reaping. In the eighteenth century (and before) most grains were cut with the sickle. Women could do this task fairly well, and were paid accordingly. In the nineteenth century, however, the scythe replaced the sickle for cutting grains, and women worked only in less well paid subsidiary activities.[30]

While some agricultural tasks, such as hedging and threshing, were always assigned to men, many tasks were done by both men and women. While we sometimes observe both men and women doing the same task at the same farm at the same time, more often we observe a task moving back and forth between male and female workers depending on the circumstances. Hoeing was an example of a task that was done sometimes by women and sometimes by men. Marshall explains how the task of weeding could vary in intensity depending on various conditions:

[T]he requisite labor varies with the state of the crop, and the nature of the soil. A full clean crop, on a free soil, wants little labor. Nor, on such a soil, though foul with seed weeds, is the labor difficult, provided that crop has not been suffered to run up, and hide the surface. On the contrary, a thin tall crop, foul with couchgrass, on a stubborn soil, in a dry season, requires more labor than is paid for. I have seen a man hoing wheat, under the last mentioned circumstances, at 3s. an acre. But he barely earned day wages ... If the soil be tolerably free, the season kind, and the crop taken in a proper state, as to growth, notwithstanding it may be foul with seed weeds, there are women who will hoe half an acre, a day. Such a crop is not unfrequently done, at 2s. an acre.[31]

Note that Marshall suggests men are used for the more laborious hoeing tasks, and women for the less laborious hoeing tasks. Whether men or women were used for hoeing might also depend on the local labor demand conditions. In the discussion of Model B we saw that an increase in demand for labor in a less strength-intensive job may change the marginal occupation. Regions with better alternative employments for women should be less likely to employ women for hoeing.

The agricultural task most closely associated with women was dairying, but even in the dairy the gender division of labor responded to

[30] On the increased use of the scythe, see Chapter 7, and Collins, "Harvest Technology."
[31] Marshall, *The Rural Economy of Gloucestershire*, vol. I, pp. 123–4.

comparative advantage. Male assistants were frequently hired to do the most strength-intensive tasks, such as turning and washing the large cheeses, and churning the butter.[32] Milking, which required less strength than some agricultural jobs, was commonly a female task, but when women workers could find work in non-agricultural occupations requiring even less strength, men did the milking. John Broad notes that "In areas such as Buckinghamshire where women were more fully and profitably employed in lace and straw plait manufacture than the men in agriculture, men took over the subsidiary task of milking cows, leaving women in charge of the indoor work."[33]

Turning to textile manufacture, we also find the division of labor among tasks to be consistent with the models presented. The employment of women in the Leeds cloth industry in 1769, as described by Arthur Young, matches the predictions of Model A. Young mentions women employed in three different occupations: weaving broad cloths, weaving "stuffs," and spinning.[34] The weaving of broad cloths required the most strength. The reason for this is succinctly described in the 1841 parliamentary report on handloom weavers: "In proportion to the width of a fabric must be the size of the loom, and therefore the strength of the workman."[35] Weaving stuffs required little strength, and hand spinning required no strength. A graph of this situation would look something like Figure 3.5, with spinning as occupation A, weaving stuffs as occupation B, and weaving broad cloths as occupation C. As the model predicted, Young observed that women in Leeds were more likely to work in spinning and in weaving the lighter cloths. However, Young did find a few women working even in the strength-intensive broad cloths, and these women earned as much as the men. Men weaving broad cloths could earn 10s.6d. if fully employed, but usually earned 8s. a week. The wages of women who did this work were similar. Young noted that "some women earn by weaving as much as the men."[36] Other women, working in other occupations, earned much less. Women weaving stuffs earned 3s.6d. or 4s. a week, and those spinning earned 2s.6d. or 3s. This difference in wages is predicted by the model, and is the result of the women's individual abilities. According to Model A, the women who worked as spinners could not have earned 8s. a week weaving broad cloths because they did not have the same characteristics as the women

[32] Pinchbeck, *Women Workers*, pp. 13–14; Valenze, *The First Industrial Woman*, p. 60.
[33] John Broad, "Regional Perspectives and Variations in English Dairying, 1650–1850," in R. Hoyle, ed., *People, Landscape and Alternative Agriculture* (Exeter: British Agricultural History Society, 2004), pp. 106–7.
[34] Young, *Northern Tour*, vol. I, p. 89.   [35] BPP 1841 (296) X, p. 3.
[36] Young, *Northern Tour*, vol. I, p. 89.

who did, and the spinners did not choose to move to broad cloth weaving because it would not have improved their wages. Occupational assignment, and wages, seem to have been based on individual ability rather than strictly on gender.

In Norwich, where the cloths woven required little strength, the men who wove them earned low wages. Young noted that "Men on average do not exceed 5s. a week; but then many women earn as much: and boys of 15 to 16 likewise the same."[37] This suggests that women may have earned slightly less than men, but that the earnings of men and women were similar. The men who worked in this industry must have been unable to earn high wages elsewhere, and must have had relatively low endowments of strength, as the women weaving broad cloths in Leeds must have had high strength endowments, allowing them to earn high wages.

There are numerous other examples where the allocation of women workers within weaving reflects their comparative advantage in cloth not requiring strength. Women were concentrated in the lighter and nar-rower cloths, leaving men predominant in the heavier and wider cloths that required more strength. Fewer women were engaged in flax weaving than in other types of weaving because it required more strength. In the 1840 *Reports from Assistant Hand-Loom Weavers' Commissioners*, James Mitchell reports, "The work is too heavy for women in general, and hence the very small number of women in the trade. For the same cause there are very few boys or girls."[38] Similarly, the manager of a bed-quilt weaving shop in Bolton noted that he only employed men: "they must be stout, able-bodied men to do the work; and ours is the best paid work on the hand-loom weaving line."[39] Parliamentary investigator Symons noted that:

Where wide, as in broad cloths and damask table cloths, a degree of strength is required which no very young, very old, or weak persons can apply. Women are debarred from entering into competition with men in these factories, not by the material used, but the physical force required.[40]

Men, rather than women, worked looms for patterned ribbons, where shuttles could weigh as much as 130 pounds.[41] In Spitalfields, women were concentrated in plain silks, which required less strength than vel-vets.[42] The ratio of women to men weavers was 0.23 in velvets, but 0.99

---

[37] Arthur Young, *The Farmer's Tour through the East of England* (London: W. Straham, 1771), vol. II, p. 75.
[38] BPP 1840 (43) XXIII, p. 351.   [39] BPP 1840 (220) XXIV, p. 585.   [40] *Ibid.*, p. 615.
[41] Simonton, *European Women's Work*, p. 144.
[42] The comparison of strength requirements is given by parliamentary investigator J. Symons. BPP 1840 (220) XXIV, pp. 616–17.

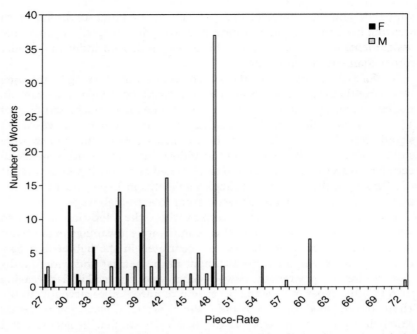

Figure 3.8 The distribution of male and female workers across cloths
of various piece-rates
Source: University of Leeds Archives, Clough 19.

in plain silks. While women were able to weave velvets, few did so
because of the greater strength requirement.

We can see the distribution of male and female workers over different
types of cloth by looking at the accounts of Robert Clough of Grove
Mill, Keighley.[43] Clough owned Grove Mill, a spinning mill which used
water power until 1836. He also employed out-workers, male wool-
combers, and both male and female weavers. The weavers produced
many different types of cloth, and each type had its own piece-rate. If
cloths with higher piece-rates required more strength, and workers
sorted themselves according to their individual abilities, then we should
observe that women tend to work on cheaper cloth, but that a few
women were able to work on the higher-priced cloths dominated by
men. That is exactly what we observe. Figure 3.8 shows the distribution
of male and female workers across the different piece-rates in October
of 1824. Men and women can be observed over most of the range of

[43] University of Leeds Archives, Clough 19.

cloths. Both male and female weavers produced the cloth with the lowest piece-rate (27s). No woman worked at a cloth with a piece-rate higher than 48s., but only 10 percent of men did so. While different types of cloth do not seem to have been assigned solely on the basis of gender, there is a definite gender pattern. Women tended to work on cloths with lower piece-rates. The median piece-rate was 36s. for women and 42s. for men.

The same pattern of a small number of women engaged in a pre-dominately "male" occupation is found in the hosiery industry. In general, men operated the knitting frames and women seamed the stockings. This division of labor matched the comparative advantages of the sexes because the knitting frame required strength. Osterud has pointed out the "heaviness of the physical labor involved in the oper-ation of wide frames," noting that the strength necessary prevented youths and older men from being employed on wide frames.[44] While in general work was allocated along gender lines, the barrier was not strict. Although few in number compared to the men, women did work at the knitting frames. Rose notes that women were occasionally knitters, especially in Nottinghamshire and Leicestershire. In 1845, 7 percent of frames were worked by females.[45] When women did work as knitters, this was most commonly on narrow frames, which required less strength. This distribution of employment is consistent with the model's predic-tion that a few women with high strength endowments should be found working with the men. No discriminatory constraints prevented women from becoming framework knitters. Both boys and girls were apprenticed to the trade.[46] Women were hired at the same piece-rates as men, and no combination of male workers opposed their employment. In 1819 a union of framework knitters was formed in Nottinghamshire, and women were included.[47] Women could easily move into knitting if they found it advantageous. William Felkin describes such a movement in 1833. When the wages in embroidering fell because of foreign competition, many women quit that trade and took up the stocking frame.

I believe the average wages of embroiderers in the bobbin-net trade have fallen one half since September 1831 ... I think runners are now earning from 9d. to

---

[44] Nancy Grey Osterud, "Gender Divisions and the Organization of Work in the Leicester Hosiery Industry," in Angela John, ed., *Unequal Opportunities* (Oxford: Basil Blackwell, 1986), p. 50.

[45] Rose, "Gender Segregation," p. 166.

[46] Felkin described the trade as suffering from a "constant influx of too many apprenticed boys and girls." Felkin, *A History of the Machine-Wrought Hosiery*, p. 115.

[47] *Ibid.*, pp. 441–3. In the first three months of 1821, 2172 knitters received benefits for unemployment; 1559 were men, and 613 were women and boys.

3s.6d. a week. I know that several young women are now putting into the stocking-frame because they can earn more in it than at lace-running.[48]

These women had not been segregated into the embroidery trade; they chose that occupation because it was the most profitable for them, and they moved to another occupation when it ceased to be profitable. The only disadvantage a woman had was her lack of strength. The 1845 parliamentary report on framework knitters emphasized this equality of opportunity: "Vast numbers of women and children are working side by side with men, often employed in the same description of frames, making the same fabrics, at the same rate of wages, the only advantage over them which the man possesses being his superior strength."[49] This statement clearly describes a competitive market.

The one exception to the rule that men always did the jobs requiring strength is laundry. Laundry work required heavy lifting and wringing. An Exeter woman who had worked in both agriculture and washing thought that "washing is harder than working in the fields."[50] One laundress remarked, "You had to be as strong as a man to lift the great wooden wash tubs."[51] Since the work was so heavy, men sometimes helped their wives with the heaviest parts of it. A London street-seller told Henry Mayhew that he helped his laundress wife turn the mangle: "She earns about 1s. 3d. a day. She takes in a little washing, and keeps a mangle. When I'm at home I turn the mangle for her."[52] The husband of another laundress, an often-unemployed dock worker, reported to Mayhew that "the party my wife works for has a mangle, and I go sometimes to help; for if she has got 6d. worth of washing to do at home, than I go to turn the mangle for an hour instead of her – she's not strong enough."[53] A Manchester schoolmaster was "liable to interruption in his academic labors, as his wife keeps a mangle, and he is obliged to turn it for her."[54] The fact that men often helped their wives with laundry work suggests that laundry was a strength-intensive job that might have been better suited to men.

In spite of the strength required for laundry work, men rarely did it.[55] The 1841 census lists only 583 males in laundry work, as compared to

[48] BPP 1833 (450) XX, C1, pp. 50–1. Report of Mr. Drinkwater, evidence of William Felkin.
[49] BPP 1845 (609) XV, p. 101.
[50] Mary Puddicombe of Exeter, *Women and Children in Agriculture*, p. 109.
[51] Malcolmson, *English Laundresses*, p. 26.   [52] Mayhew, *London Labor*, vol. I, p. 150.
[53] *Ibid.*, vol. III, p. 307.
[54] *Manchester Statistical Society*, 1837, quoted in Phil Gardner, *The Lost Elementary Schools of Victorian England* (London: Croom Helm, 1984), p. 122.
[55] Ruth Schwartz Cowan, *More Work for Mother: The Ironies of Household Technology from the Open Hearth to the Microwave* (New York: Basic Books, 1983), p. 20, noted the fact that women were assigned this strength-intensive task in the early US.

50,706 females, so that only about 1 percent of laundry workers were male. Laundry work may have appealed to women because it was often done at home, so that it was easy to combine with domestic duties such as child care (see Section II). In the later nineteenth century when factory-like steam laundries replaced laundry work done in the home there was some increased use of men in laundries, but women still did much of the work, and did some of the heavy work. The employment of men increased from 1 to 5 percent of the workforce, and many men were employed in loading and unloading the washing machines, which was a heavy task.[56] Women were employed for ironing, which was a light task, but were also employed calendering, which was a heavy task.[57] While there was some movement toward the employment of men, women still dominated the workforce. The prominence of women in laundry work, a task requiring strength, suggests that this may be one case where gender roles were strong enough to overrule comparative advantage. Gender roles associating women with housework were so strong that women did the laundry even when the work was better suited to men's strength. Comparative advantage encouraged husbands to help their wives with the most arduous tasks, but laundry as a whole remained a female industry. It should be noted, though, that when women worked as laundresses, they received relatively high wages. Even accounting for the long hours, wages in laundry work were about 50 percent higher than in agricultural work.[58] When women did strength-intensive work, they received a wage premium.

Except for laundry work, which should have employed more men, all the patterns of occupational sorting that we have examined here comply with the predictions of the sorting models. Workers in strength-intensive occupations were primarily men, and workers in occupations requiring little strength were primarily women. The gender division of labor was one of general tendencies, not absolute barriers. A few women were found in strength-intensive tasks such as framework knitting, suggesting that women could do such work if they found it advantageous.

2.   *Unusual women*

When discussing Model A above, I assumed that all women had less strength than all men. While this is usually true, there will be cases when it does not hold. There will be a few exceptional women who are stronger than some men. An interesting test of the labor market, then, is what happens to these women. If the competitive market is functioning well, then exceptional women ought to be able to do the same work as

---

[56] Malcolmson, *English Laundresses*, pp. 140–1.   [57] *Ibid.*, pp. 143, 145.   [58] See Chapter 2.

men and earn as much as men. We do occasionally observe unusually strong women doing work typically done by men, and being well paid for it. In seventeenth-century Oxfordshire, Alice George claims that "she was able to have reaped as much in a day as any man, and had as much wages."[59] In the 1840s Mary Haynes, a farm laborer from Wiltshire, claimed: "I am a good reaper, as good as many men; and in harvest, when I have worked by the job, I have earned 2s., sometimes 2s.6d. a-day." We don't know how her harvest wages compared to the wages of male reapers, but we do know that Mary earned more at reaping than her husband's normal summer wage of 10s. per week, or 1s.8d. per day.[60]

In coal-mining, the work was by piece-rate, and employers took little interest in who their workers were. One employer told the parliamentary investigators, "I exercise no control over them. I merely pay the men for the coal which they bring to the bank."[61] Miners were paid by weight for the coal they brought up, and paid their assistants themselves. This gave the miners freedom to allocate the different mining tasks among themselves. This suggests that Model A should describe the allocation of labor in mining. The allocation of tasks in mining fits the prediction that men should do the more strength-intensive jobs. Hewing the coal (wielding the pick) required more strength than pushing or drawing containers of coal through the tunnels, so in general men hewed, and women and children "hurried" (transported the coal).[62] This division of labor holds true in all collieries where women worked. Jane Humphries notes that "Not only was hewing a *male* job, it was reserved for *adult* males."[63] This also fits the model because boys had less strength than grown men, and would be expected to choose the less strength-intensive jobs. However, this allocation of work seems to have been based on individual characteristics rather than simply on the sex of the worker.

---

[59] Journal of John Locke for March 1, 1685. Quoted in Roberts, "Sickles and Scythes," p. 19.

[60] When interviewed by Alfred Austin, Mary Haynes was a widow. Her husband died "not long ago" and had earned 10s. per week in the summer and 9s. per week in the winter. *Women and Children in Agriculture*, p. 69.

[61] BPP 1842 (381) XVI, p. 243. Humphries interprets this quote as an attempt by the employer to shift responsibility for the treatment of child workers from himself to the adult male worker. Jane Humphries, "Protective Legislation, the Capitalist State, and Working Class Men: The Case of the 1842 Mines Regulation Act," *Feminist Review* 7 (1981), pp. 11–13. While the piece-rate payment system may not clear the employer of all responsibility, it does suggest that work groups had some freedom in how tasks were allocated among the workers in their group.

[62] Women did carry coal on their backs out of the mines, which would have required strength. I do not have measures of strength requirements for hewing as compared to carrying coal up ladders, but would note that women have a greater disadvantage in arm strength than in leg strength. At age 20 females have 64 percent as much leg strength as men, but only 46 percent as much arm strength. Lynch, "Muscle Quality."

[63] Humphries, "Protective Legislation," p. 10.

Though hewing was a male job, on rare occasions women worked as hewers, and when women did hew they earned as much as men. In 1840 one surgeon gave evidence that, "The work these women do will be generally hurrying; but sometimes women 'get,' and one I have known to do so and she earned more than her husband."[64] This woman was obviously on the high end of the female strength distribution. Her unusual abilities allowed her to do "men's work" and be paid accordingly. Similarly, the women who worked as coal carriers in south Gloucestershire, carrying coal from the pits to the city, were unusually strong women: "A few Amazons yet practice the vocation of coal carriers, on their own account, from the pits into the city or suburbs, rivaling the men in strength of sinew and vigor of lungs."[65] Women were not barred from this occupation by artificial barriers, but only a few women were strong enough to profit from it. As predicted, the distribution of occupations seems to have been based on individual ability rather than simply by gender.

3. Regional patterns

Sometimes regional differences in the gender division of labor are seen as evidence that these differences were the result of custom rather than market forces. For example, Pamela Sharpe points out that in some villages women would reap or hoe, while in other villages they did not. Sharpe is not convinced that economic models can explain these differences: "The point here is not only should we be mindful of local distinctiveness, but also that our explanations may be flawed if we assume that only economic rules held sway."[66] However, economic rules do not suggest that the gender division of labor should be the same everywhere. The gender division of labor should respond to local demand conditions. It is not a contradiction of the competitive model if we find that women did strenuous work in coal mines while in other areas men did less strenuous tasks. If individuals were completely mobile then we would expect women to migrate from regions with strength-intensive jobs, such as mining, to regions with low-strength jobs, such as cottage industry, but the fact that men and women usually live in family groups limits the extent of such migration.[67] All local labor markets will contain both men and women, and economic theory predicts that within the local market women should do the less strenuous of the local jobs.

---

[64] BPP 1842 (381) XVI, p. 248.   [65] BPP 1842 (380) XV, p. 37.
[66] Sharpe, "The Female Labor Market," p. 178.
[67] Migration did produce some gender sorting in response to relative wages. Women would earn high wages in the lace-making industry in seventeenth-century Devon, and the sex ratio of burials fell to 75 males per 100 females. Sharpe, "Literally Spinsters," pp. 49, 55.

In fact, we do observe sorting by strength within local labor markets, and changes in the gender division of labor that respond to local demand conditions. In textile areas, men wove because it was more strenuous than spinning. In mining areas, women "hurried" coal because that was less strenuous than hewing it. The work that women did depended on local opportunities. In regions with high demand for strength-intensive jobs, women engaged in heavier work. In the more labor-scarce north, women more often did "men's work." In 1833 Thomas Baker, rector of Whitburn, Durham, noted: "In the Northern Counties, the Women engage in Men's work much more than in the Southern Districts; serving the masons with mortar, bricks, &c. is not uncommonly done by Women in the Towns."[68] Women and children were not employed in mining in northern Staffordshire because they worked in the potteries instead.[69] One young woman in West Yorkshire stated that she only worked in the mines because she could not get work in textiles.[70] In Ireland, no women or girls were employed in mining, only men. The reason seem to be the excess supply of labor. A parliamentary investigator asked the Irish employers why they did not employ children and was told, "that as labor was so abundant and cheap they would not be troubled with Children."[71]

Women were less productive than men at agricultural work, so where other work requiring little or no strength was available, they did less farm work. In Eden's 1797 *State of the Poor* we find that, in areas where the pillow-lace trade flourished, women did not work in agriculture. Eden claimed that in Roade, Northamptonshire, "Women here are never employed in reaping; and it is even very rare to see them milk a cow." The reason for this was the relatively high wage available in lace-making: "lace-workers earn from 6d. to 1s. or 1s.2d. the day; but generally 8d. or 10d. a day."[72] Male agricultural laborers could earn from 1s. to 1s.6d. a day in the winter, so the best lace-makers could earn as much as a man.[73] Given their lower productivity in agriculture, the women could not have made as much in farm work as they earned making lace. Farmers who wanted to hire women had to pay them high wages to convince them to accept the work. In 1813 in Buckinghamshire female servants earned £10.10s. per year, approximately the same as male

---

[68] BPP 1834 (44) XXX, p. 169.   [69] BPP 1842 (380) XV, p. 9.

[70] Ann Eggley, 18, stated, "there was nought else for us to do. I have tried to get winding to do, but could not." *Ibid.*, p. 75.

[71] *Ibid.*, p. 106.   [72] Eden, *State of the Poor*, vol. II, p. 544.

[73] The wages of male agricultural workers are actually from the neighboring town of Yardley Gobion, where we find that the women also make lace and "do very little out of doors." *Ibid.*, vol. II, p. 548.

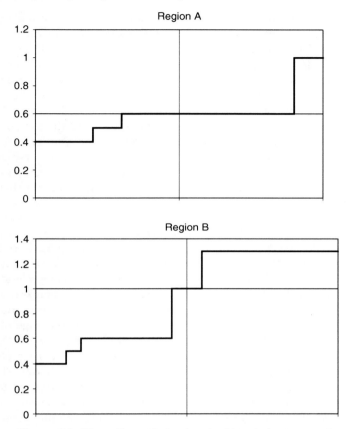

Figure 3.9 The effect of the lace-making industry on the market wage ratio

servants, who earned between £10.10s. and £12.12s per year.[74] The result was the one we would expect: no women worked in agriculture, even in the traditionally female agricultural jobs such as milking cows.

We can use Model B to understand how a high demand for female labor in cottage industry can raise the wage ratio and reduce female employment in farming. Figure 3.9 compares the r-profiles and equilibrium wage ratios in two regions. In region A, agriculture, which I have assumed to have a wage ratio of 0.6, is large, and is the marginal industry determining the market wage ratio. Other industries with higher or lower productivity ratios exist, and hire only men or only women. Region B, by

[74] Verdon, *Rural Women Workers*, p. 50.

contrast, has relatively high levels of employment in lace-making, an industry where women are more productive than men. In region B the demand for lace making is so great that it employs nearly all the women in the labor force. This makes the industry where men and women are equally productive the marginal occupation, and male and female wages are equal. Comparing regions A and B, we can see that the model predicts different incomes for employment and wages. In region A both women and men will be employed in agriculture, and the market wage ratio will be 0.6. In region B, however, no women will be employed in agriculture because the market wage ratio, 1.0, is higher than the productivity ratio. Farmers will not be willing to pay high enough wages to entice women away from lace making, and may complain that they can't hire women.

The relationship between opportunities in cottage industry and the number of women working in agriculture can be shown statistically. Even in 1841, when the demands for lace and straw-plait were lower than during the Napoleonic Wars, these industries still affected agricultural employment. In the 1841 census there is a negative relationship between the use of females in agriculture and the prevalence of either lace making or straw plaiting. The correlation between the percentage of occupied women who were in lace-making and the percentage of agricultural laborers who were female was −0.27, and the correlation between the percentage of occupied women who were in straw plaiting and the percentage of agricultural laborers who were female was −0.17.[75] Census data are not ideal because the censuses undercounted female agricultural laborers. However, using farm account books I also find that regions with more cottage industry were less likely to employ women in agriculture. Counties with higher levels of female employment in cottage industry paid women significantly higher wages and employed significantly fewer women. The impact of cottage industry employment on agricultural employment was substantial. The movement from a county with low employment in cottage industry such as Norfolk, to the county with the greatest employment in cottage industry, Bedfordshire, resulted in a decline in the employment of females from 10.1 to 2.8 percent of the agricultural labor force.[76] These statistical results support what Eden told us and what Model B predicts: opportunities for higher wages in cottage industry drew women away from agricultural employment.

---

[75] There are forty-two observations. The first correlation is statistically significant at the 10 percent level, but the second is not. Data from BPP 1844 (587) XXVII.

[76] These calculations are based on the regressions presented in Burnette, "Wages and Employment," p. 680.

Differences in work patterns might be very local. While women in general were frequently engaged in agricultural labor in Dorset, a resident of Whitchurch, Dorset, noted that "The women are much engaged in buttoning in this village: it is with difficulty they can be got out at 4s. a-week."[77] Local differences in the gender division of labor are usually interpreted as the result of local custom. This was true in 1843, when Mr. Vaughn wrote in his report to parliament:

Custom, too, which by perpetuation of other causes becomes a cause in itself, is not without its authority in determining the degree and manner in which this kind of labor is applied. In a small tract of country here spoken of, slight differences are observable, and steadily adhered to. So about Tunbridge Wells, women are rarely employed in opening the hills in the hop-grounds. At Maidstone and Farnham it is their common occupation.[78]

However, we should not necessarily accept Mr. Vaughn's claim that custom caused the variation in female employment. Tunbridge Wells was closer to London than Maidstone; if opportunities in London drew women away from agriculture, farmers in Tunbridge Wells may have hired men to open the hop-hills because fewer women were available to do agricultural work. Even if the allocation of labor seems customary to the farmers, it may still have a basis in economic incentives. In South Molton, Devon, employment for women in lace making and wool manufacturing was sufficient to make it difficult for the farmer James Huxtable to hire women: "I can't get so many women to work for me as I should like, owing to the lace-making and woolen manufactory in the neighborhood. Last spring I had to hire a man to weed corn."[79] Though this farmer thought that weeding ought to be done by women, the labor market determined who he actually hired. In other words, the work women did depended on the resources and requirements of the local labor market rather than ideology.

4.   *Responses to changes in technology and demand*
The models presented above can also accurately predict how the gender division of labor changes in response to new technology. The most dramatic change was in spinning. In the eighteenth century, spinners were generally women, and weavers were generally men. Weaving frequently requires some strength (although the strength requirement varies with the type of cloth) and hand spinning requires no strength, so this allocation was consistent with comparative advantage. Spinning eventually became a male occupation, but only when spinning began to

[77] *Women and Children in Agriculture*, p. 7.   [78] *Ibid.*, p. 133.   [79] *Ibid.*, p. 105.

require strength. The switch from female to male labor did not follow the invention of new machines, or even the movement from the home to the factory, but occurred only when strength requirements increased enough that men were more productive than women. The first machine to spin multiple threads was the spinning jenny. This machine was used in the home, and was designed for use by young women. Arkwright's water frame was the first spinning machine to use a centralized power source, and moved spinning into the factory. Spinners were still women. The mule, invented in 1779, was a combination of the jenny and the water frame and produced a better yarn. Women worked the earlier mules, and only left the occupation when mules grew so large that strength became an important factor in a spinner's productivity. A mule carriage with 336 spindles for spinning coarse yarn weighed 1400 pounds, and this had to be moved by the spinner three and a half times per minute.[80] The invention of the self-actor eventually removed this strength requirement by using the power of the steam engine to move the carriage, but by this time the male spinners had formed a union, and explicit exclusion prevented women from returning to spinning.[81] Even when women were still working as spinners, the new machines increased productivity and reduced the total number of spinners needed, so many women found themselves without employment. Many of these women moved into handloom weaving.[82] Handloom weaving, an occupation that had been almost completely male, soon had nearly as many female workers as male workers (see Table 1.3). Thus the gender allocation of labor between spinning and weaving was completely reversed in response to a change in spinning technology. The ease of this transition suggests an allocation based on the market rather than on ideology.

The entry of women into handloom weaving occurred not only in Britain, but also in France and the United States. For France, Gay Gullickson finds that, while weavers had been uniformly male in the eighteenth century, by 1850 women dominated the trade. By 1851 the canton of Auffay had three times as many female weavers as male weavers, and women dominated the weaving trade in other regions as well.[83] In New England women moved into weaving, which had been a male occupation, in the late eighteenth century, though here the circumstances

---

[80] Lazonick, "Industrial Relations and Technical Change," p. 235. A mule of 336 spindles was not particularly large. Beginning in the 1820s employers began to use "doubled" mules of 500 to 600 spindles. A mule could have as many as 1000 spindles. See Freifeld, "Technological Change and the 'Self-Acting' Mule," pp. 335–6.

[81] See Chapter 5.   [82] See Collier, *The Family Economy of the Working Classes*, p. 3.

[83] Gullickson, *Spinners and Weavers of Auffay*, p. 109, and Gullickson, "Love and Power," p. 218.

of work were different for women. While the male weavers had worked as artisans, the women worked part-time from their homes.[84] The models discussed above clearly show that a biological difference in strength, combined with a change in technology, could have caused the observed change. In this case the disappearance of an occupation requiring no strength pushed women into an occupation requiring some strength, and thus increased the gender wage gap.[85] Over the course of half a century the handloom weaving trade was transformed from a male trade to a female trade, not as a result of changing ideology, but as a predictable response to the substitution of mule-spinning for hand spinning.

I conclude that the division of labor between the sexes in much of the labor market can be explained by differences in strength. Women had less strength than men and thus a comparative advantage in tasks requiring less strength. When technology changed the strength requirements of different tasks, the gender division of labor changed to reflect the new comparative advantage. Comparative advantage also explains local variations in employment patterns. Though employers may have had expectations about what sex should be hired for certain jobs, they responded to market forces. The result was a division of labor between the sexes based on comparative advantage. The only case that seems to be an exception to this rule is laundry, which required strength but was done by women.

Usually the dictates of market efficiency matched well with socially determined gender roles. When the two did conflict, comparative advantage determined the division of labor more often than ideology. While ideology seems to have prevented men from doing laundry, there are many more cases where women did "men's work" because men were scarce. In agriculture farmers had definite ideas of what work ought to be done by women, but the labor market determined actual employment. In 1833 a farmer from Cornwall noted that "When married, [women] leave off work. Farmers in this neighborhood are obliged to employ men for what women and children should do."[86]

II. Occupational sorting and child care

Another important biological difference between men and women is the fact that women bear children and men do not. During the Industrial

---

[84] Ulrich, "Wheels, Looms and the Gender Division of Labor," pp. 12–13.
[85] For evidence that the gender wage gap increased between 1750 and 1850, see Burnette, "Wages and Employment," p. 680.
[86] BPP 1834 (44) XXX, Newlyn East, Cornwall, p. 95.

Revolution, fertility was high, and women spent a great deal of time bearing and breast feeding children. As with strength, reproductive duties led women to be concentrated in certain occupations. Work done in the home was more convenient for women with young children to care for, so women workers were concentrated in cottage industries. Brenner and Ramas suggest that women's role in child-bearing was an important determinant of the gender division of labor because of "the incompatibility of child care and work outside the home."[87] This claim, though, just leads us to the question of why women were responsible for child care. Sally Alexander points to social expectations that linked women to child-bearing:

> Women's vulnerability as wage-workers stemmed from their child-bearing capacity upon which "natural" foundation the sexual division of labor within the family was based ... a wife's responsibility for the well-being of her husband and children always came before her work in social production, and in a patriarchal culture, this was seen to follow naturally from her role in biological reproduction.[88]

Rose claims that "Although women do have special needs in pregnancy, childbirth, and nursing, nothing about these biological processes per se would cause women to work at low-paying jobs in general or homework in particular."[89] While it is true that there is no *necessary* relationship, these biological processes did influence decisions by changing relative prices, and made homework more attractive to mothers. Women's monopoly on pregnancy, birth, and breast feeding, combined with their comparative advantage in child care because of their lesser strength, resulted in women usually being responsible for child care. Given this responsibility, substantial child care costs encouraged women to concentrate more heavily in work done in the home, such as work in various cottage industries.

A.   Why mothers took responsibility for child care

It is not obvious that mothers must provide child care. Fathers are capable of most child-care tasks (with a couple of important exceptions), but mothers provided virtually all the child care during the Industrial Revolution period. This section will examine why mothers, and not fathers, were responsible for child care. There were many different possible criteria for choosing which parent would provide the child care, and all suggested the same answer – the mother.

---

[87] Brenner and Ramas, "Rethinking Women's Oppression," p. 51.
[88] Alexander, *Becoming a Woman*, p. 21.   [89] Rose, *Limited Livelihoods*, p. 98.

Table 3.3. *Age-specific marital fertility (births per 1000 woman-years)*

Time period	20–24	25–29	30–34	35–39	40–44	Source
1750–1799	411	338	283	234	118	a
1800–1850	427	361	318	261	162	b

Sources: a. E. A. Wrigley and R. S. Schofield, *The Population History of England, 1541–1871* (Cambridge: Cambridge University Press, 1981), p. 254.
b. Michael W. Flinn, *The European Demographic System, 1500–1820* (Baltimore: Johns Hopkins University Press, 1981), p. 104.

1.   Biological reasons

Certain child-care tasks can be done only by the mother. The father cannot give birth to or breast feed the child. These tasks were frequently required of a woman because fertility was high during the Industrial Revolution. Table 3.3 shows marital fertility for the late eighteenth and early nineteenth centuries. For every 1000 married women between the ages of 20 and 24, there were over 400 births in a year. A young wife could expect to give birth every two and a half years. Because of this high fertility, women spent a large portion of their time with infants. A married woman in her child-bearing years could be pregnant or nursing almost continually. Davidoff and Hall give the example of Mary Brightwen, the wife of an Essex merchant, to illustrate the possibilities. Between the ages of 26 and 45 Mary Brightwen bore ten children, so if she nursed each child for one year, she was either pregnant or breast feeding for 85 percent of the time during these years.[90] Davies described the wives of laborers as "mere nurses for ten or twelve years after marriage, being always either with child, or having a child at the breast; consequently incapable of doing much other work besides the necessary business of their families, such as baking, washing, and the like."[91] Being a mother in an era of high fertility meant many years of attention to nursing infants, and there was relatively little scope for shifting this work to others. The period of nursing could be shortened, but alternative foods for babies were much inferior. Given the low quality of alternative foods for infants, a father was a poor substitute for the mother when the child was an infant, so during the first months of a child's life the child-care duties fell to the mother.

2.   Comparative advantage in the labor market

Since child care required less strength than most market work, women had a comparative advantage in this type of work. Because strength was

---

[90] Davidoff and Hall, *Family Fortunes*, pp. 337–8.
[91] Davies, *The Case of Laborers in Husbandry*, p. 14.

valued in the market, the father could typically earn a higher wage in the market than the mother. The mother was at least as productive as the father in providing child care, and more productive in the feeding of infants, so the family could maximize its income by sending the father to work in the market and assigning child-care duties to the mother. Thus, the fact that women were assigned the responsibility of caring for children can be seen as another case of sorting by comparative advantage.

3.   *Gender roles*

While the allocation of work within the family may have been based on comparative advantage, we must not discount the power of gender roles. The expectation that a married woman would remain at home was strong. Many women stayed at home because their husbands wished it rather than because they chose to. In 1833 Jane Falp, a worker in a Scottish flax mill, gave evidence that she "has been married seven months; her husband is going to take her away to take care of his house, not to do anything else: she would rather stay and work at the mill."[92] (Note, however, that at the time of the interview she was working in the mill.) Even apart from the work done in the home, having a wife who did not work became a status good for the husband.[93] Social expectations were probably strong enough to prevent fathers from taking on the child care in all but the most desperate circumstances.

Cases where comparative advantage and gender roles conflicted would have been relatively rare. All three forces acted in one direction – to keep the mother in charge of the children. In general the question of which force determined the allocation of child-care duties is unidentified; the result cannot really be ascribed to either comparative advantage or gender roles, since both had a part, and both suggested the same outcome. Only if market incentives changed can we identify whether economic incentives or gender roles determined work patterns. Heidi Hartmann argues that the allocation of housework in modern families is determined by gender roles. The evidence she presents is that the allocation of housework to women did not change when women's market work increased.[94] If comparative advantage rather than gender ideology assigned women the household tasks, then this assignment should have changed when patterns of market work changed.

---

[92] BPP 1833 (450) XX, A2, p. 4.

[93] This was Thorstein Veblen's argument in *The Theory of the Leisure Class*, first published in 1899.

[94] Heidi Hartmann, "The Family as the Locus of Gender, Class, and Political Struggle: The Example of Housework," *Signs: Journal of Women in Culture and Society* 6 (1981), pp. 336–94.

During the Industrial Revolution, comparative advantage sometimes overruled gender roles, though only in extreme circumstances. In the few cases where men did provide the child care, they did so only because they could not find work and their wives could. In Lancashire women had good opportunities for work, and many supported an unemployed husband. As mentioned earlier, Engels tells a story of a man unable to find employment who takes on the home production tasks:

[a] working-man, being on tramp, came to St. Helens, in Lancashire, and there looked up an old friend. He found him in a miserable, damp cellar, scarcely furnished; and when my poor friend went in, there sat Jack near the fire, and what did he, think you? why he sat and mended his wife's stockings with the bodkin; as soon as he saw his old friend at the door-post, he tried to hide them. But Joe, that is my friend's name, had seen it, and said: "Jack, what the devil art thou doing? Where is the missus? Why, is that thy work?" and poor Jack was ashamed and said: "No, I know that this is not my work, but my poor missus is i' th' factory; she has to leave at half-past five and works till eight at night, and then she is so knocked up that she cannot do aught when she gets home, so I have to do everything for her what I can, for I have no work, nor had any for more nor three years ... *There is work enough for women folks and childer hereabouts, but none for men; thou mayest sooner find a hundred pound in the road than work for men* ... when I got married I had work plenty ... and Mary need not go out to work. I could work for the two of us; but now the world is upside down. Mary has to work and I have to stop at home, mind the childer, sweep and wash, bake and mend" ... And then Jack began to cry again, and he wished he had never married.[95]

Clearly the only reason that this father took care of the house and children was that he had no work opportunities. The passage suggests that the situation was ideologically unacceptable. We are told that "the world is upside down." Engels claims that in Manchester "many hundred such men could be cited, condemned to domestic occupation."[96] While market forces were obeyed in this case, a smaller difference in market opportunities may not have been enough to overcome the dictates of gender roles. It took a very large difference in market productivities to alter the gender allocation of housework. Gender roles could be overruled, but only in extreme circumstances.

B.   Why women worked in cottage industry

One reason that women were so heavily concentrated in cottage industry was the fact that such work was more convenient for women, given their

---

[95] Frederick Engels, *Condition of the Working Class in England in 1844* (London: George Allen and Unwin, 1926), pp. 145–6.
[96] *Ibid.*, p. 144.

domestic duties. Whether the allocation of housework was based on comparative advantage or gender roles, the sorting of women into cottage industries was an efficient market response to that allocation. Of course, a preference for work done in the home only reinforced the allocation of women into cottage industry, since these occupations also required little strength, and thus would have been chosen by women for that reason even without the convenient location. However, location in the home does seem to have been one of the forces encouraging women to choose cottage industry.

To see the advantage of work done in the home, imagine being a mother who is deciding whether to work, and if so where. You will choose the best option available to you, given your constraints (which are many). Your husband (if present) works in the market; as we have seen in the previous section, both ideology and comparative advantage suggest that the father will specialize in market work. If you choose to work outside the home, you must pay for child care, which is expensive.

Although young children were occasionally left home alone, this was done only rarely because the dangers were real. *The Times* reports this incident in 1819:

A shocking accident occurred at Llandidno, near Conway, on Tuesday night, during the absence of a miner and his wife, who had gone to attend a methodist meeting, and locked the house door, leaving two children within; the house by some means took fire, and was, together with the unfortunate children, consumed to ashes; the eldest only four years old![97]

Mary Hunt, a laborer from Studley, Wiltshire, seems to have worried a great deal about the safety of her children when she went out to work:

I have always left my children to themselves, and, God be praised! nothing has ever happened to them, though I have thought it dangerous. I have many a time come home, and have thought it a mercy to find nothing has happened to them. It would be much better if mothers could be at home, but they must work. Bad accidents often happen.[98]

Occasionally children who were left alone died. A farm bailiff from Wiltshire noted that "I know of two or three cases of deaths from burning of children, since I have been in the neighborhood."[99] Evidently children were left alone often enough to result in occasional deaths, but the dangers were great enough that some women did not consider it an option. Mrs. Smart from Calne, Wiltshire, reported: "Sometimes I have had my

---

[97] *The Times*, February 6, 1819.   [98] *Women and Children in Agriculture*, p. 68.
[99] Evidence of Mr. Henry Phelps, agent of the Marquis of Lansdowne, *ibid.*, p. 63.

mother, and sometimes my sister, to take care of the children, or I could not have gone out."[100] If leaving your children alone was too dangerous, another form of child care must be found.

Sometimes mothers would take their infants to work when working outside the home. A 1739 poem by Mary Collier, "The Woman's Labor," suggests that women workers carried their babies into the fields:

> Our tender Babes into the Field we bear,
> And wrap them in our Cloaths to keep them warm,
> While round about we gather up the Corn;
> ...
> When Night comes on, unto our Home we go,
> Our Corn we carry, and our Infant too.[101]

An 1835 Poor Law report found that in Sussex, "the custom of the mother of a family carrying her infant with her in its cradle into the field, rather than lose the opportunity of adding her earnings to the general stock, though partially practiced before, is becoming very much more general now."[102] This option, however, would not have been available for all mothers.

Sometimes relatives were available to provide child care. Grandmothers sometimes took care of children. Elizabeth Leadbeater, who worked for a Birmingham brass founder, worked while she was nursing and had her mother look after the infant.[103] More commonly, though, older siblings provided the child care. "Older siblings" generally meant children of 9 or 10 years old, and included boys as well as girls.[104] In a family from Presteign, Wales, containing children aged 9, 7, 5, 3, and 1, we find that "The oldest children nurse the youngest."[105] When asked what income a laborer's wife and children could earn, some respondents to the 1833 "Rural Queries" assumed that the eldest child would take care of the others, leaving the mother free to work. The returns from Bengeworth, Worcester, report that "if the Mother goes to field work, the eldest Child had need to stay at home, to tend the younger branches of the Family."[106] Ewhurst, Surrey, reported that "If the Mother were employed, the elder Children at home would probably be required to attend to the younger Children."[107] This type of child care was not free.

---

[100] *Ibid.*, p. 65.   [101] Collier, "The Woman's Labor," p. 10.
[102] BPP 1835 vol. XXIX, p. 221, quoted in Pinchbeck, *Women Workers*, p. 85.
[103] BPP 1843 (431) XIV, p. 710.
[104] Mrs. Britton of Calne, Wiltshire, left her children in the care of her eldest boy. *Women and Children in Agriculture*, p. 66.
[105] Eden, *State of the Poor*, vol. III, p. 904.   [106] BPP 1834 (44) XXX, p. 593.
[107] *Ibid.*, p. 488.

Although siblings had no direct cost, they did have an opportunity cost equal to either the market wage, or the value of the education given up. Children under 10 were employed during the Industrial Revolution, not only in factories, but also in many other industries. If nothing else, a child could be hired out to look after a neighbor's children. Only if market work was unavailable for that child would the cost be zero.

When relatives were not available, a mother could hire child care, but such care was expensive. As today, paid child care was available both inside and outside the home. If a daughter was not available to look after the younger children, someone else's daughter, or a neighbor, could be hired. In 1843 Charlotte Clark, who worked at a paper factory in Kent, claimed that "The married women who have families, if some of the children be not old enough to look after the younger, hire someone for the purpose."[108] Elizabeth Leadbeater of Birmingham claimed that "It is a common custom for infants to be fed by the hand whilst their mothers are at the shop; they are under the charge of either young girls, 7, 8, or 9 years old, or put out to some neighbors."[109] A Scottish mother sent her children to the home of another woman for 2s.6d. per week: "I used to take them to her house at 4 o'clock in the morning, out of their own beds, to put them into hers."[110]

The closest counterpart of today's day-care center was the dame school. Women often took in a number of children and formed a small school. The quality of the instruction was not high, and many considered these schools to be, in fact, child-care arrangements. Critics of dame schools who focus on how little children learned there are ignoring the other important function of these schools. Dame schools thrived because they provided day care, along with some minimal instruction. In 1840 an observer of Spitalfields noted, "In this neighborhood, where the women as well as the men are employed in the manufacture of silk, many children are sent to small schools, not for instruction, but to be taken care of whilst their mothers are at work."[111] Most likely, the dame schools served both purposes: child care and some very basic education. While they were located in homes rather than in specialized buildings, they seem to have been much like day-care centers. In areas where lace-making or straw-plaiting thrived, young children were often sent to "schools" where they learned the trade. At one straw-plaiting school in Hertfordshire:

Children commence learning the trade about seven years old: parents pay 3d. a-week for each child, and for this they are taught the trade and taught to

---

[108] BPP 1843 (431) XIV, p. 20.   [109] *Ibid.*, p. 710.
[110] BPP 1844 (592) XVI, p. 6.   [111] BPP 1840 (43) XXIII, p. 261.

read. The mistress employs about from 15 to 20 at work in a room; the parents get the profits of the children's labor.[112]

At these schools there was very little instruction; some time was devoted to teaching the children to read, but they spent most of their time working. The standard rate of 3d. per week seems to have been paid for supervision of the children rather than for the instruction.

Mothers might use a combination of different types of child care. Elizabeth Wells, who worked in a Leicester worsted factory, had five children, ages 10, 8, 6, 2, and four months. The eldest, a daughter, stayed home to tend the house and care for the infant. The second child worked, and the 6-year-old and the 2-year-old were sent to "an infant school."[113] In response to a question about shorter hours, she responded, "I should like to work less, though I made less; that is, because I have so many little children at home."[114] Mary Wright, an "over-looker" in the rag-cutting room of a Buckinghamshire paper factory, had five children. The eldest worked in the rag-cutting room with her, the youngest was cared for at home, and the middle three were sent to a school; "for taking care of an infant she pays 1s.6d. a-week, and 3d. a-week for the three others. They go to a school, where they are taken care of and taught to read."[115]

The cost of hired child care was substantial. Davies quotes the price at 1s. a week, which was about a quarter of a woman's weekly earnings in agriculture.[116] In 1843 parliamentary investigator Alfred Austin reports, "Where a girl is hired to take care of children, she is paid about 9d. a week, and has her food besides, which is a serious deduction from the wages of the woman at work."[117] Agricultural wages in the area were 8d. per day, so even without the cost of food, the cost of child care was about one-fifth of a woman's wage. One Scottish woman earned 7s. per week in a coal mine and paid 2s.6d., or 36 percent of her income, for the care of her children.[118] In 1843 Mary Wright, an "over-looker" at a Buckinghamshire paper factory, paid even more for child care; she told parliamentary investigators that "for taking care of an infant she pays 1s.6d. a-week, and 3d. a-week for three others."[119] She earned 10s.6d. per week, so her total child-care payments were 21 percent of her

---

[112] BPP 1843 (431) XIV, p. 64.   [113] BPP 1833 (450) XX, C1 p. 33.   [114] *Ibid.*, p. 369.
[115] BPP 1843 (431) XIV, p. 46.
[116] Davies, *The Case of Laborers in Husbandry*, p. 14. Agricultural wages for this time period are found in Eden, *State of the Poor.*
[117] *Women and Children in Agriculture*, p. 26.   [118] BPP 1844 (592) XVI, p. 6.
[119] BPP 1843 (431) XIV, p. 46.

wage.[120] Engels put the cost of child care at 1s. or 18d. a week.[121] Factory workers often made 7s. a week, so again these women may have paid around one-fifth of their earnings for child care. Some estimates of child care costs as a portion of the mother's earnings were even higher. The overseer of Wisbech, Cambridgeshire, suggests a higher fraction; he reports, "The earnings of the Wife we consider comparatively small, in cases where she has a large family to attend to; if she has one or two children, she has to pay half, or perhaps more of her earnings for a person to take care of them."[122] A woman hired for child care had to be paid the going wage; as Ellspee Thomson, who worked in a Scottish coal mine, claimed, "neighbors, if they keep the children, they require as much as women sometimes earn."[123] Child care in dame schools, which took older children, was less expensive. In 1840 the wife of a Gloucester weaver earned 2s. a week from running a school; she had twelve students and charged each 2d. a week.[124] In 1843 the lace-making schools of the midlands generally charged 3d. per week.[125]

If you were an Industrial Revolution mother deciding whether to work outside the home, you would have considered the high costs of child care. Working would have produced a wage, but net earnings from such work would be substantially reduced by the cost of child care. Against this lower wage must be set the value of time spent at home. More efficient household management could save money, and in the end you might have decided that working outside the home would not increase the family's welfare. Mrs. Sumbler of Calne, Wiltshire, told a parliamentary investigator that she thought the net benefit of agricultural work was very small:

I do not think a great deal is got by a mother of a family going out to work; perhaps she has to hire a girl to look after the children, and there is a great waste of victuals and spoiling of things; and then working in the fields makes people eat so much more. I know it was so with me always. I often say there is not fourpence got in the year by my working out.[126]

Having estimated the net benefit of working at only 4d., it is not surprising to hear her say that "Sometimes the children have prevented my going

[120] Assuming she paid 3d. per week for *each* of the middle three children, she paid 2s.6d. per week. I make this assumption because the going rate for schools was 3d. per week.
[121] Engels, *Condition of the Working Class in England*, p. 143.
[122] BPP 1834 (44) XXX, p. 76. Malcolmson reports a case where a woman earning 11s. paid 4s.8d. for child care (42 percent of her wage). Malcolmson, *English Laundresses*, p. 36.
[123] BPP 1842 (381) XVI, p. 450.   [124] BPP 1840 (220) XXIV, p. 419.
[125] BPP 1843 (431) XIV, pp. 46, 64, 71, 72.
[126] *Women and Children in Agriculture*, pp. 67–8.

Table 3.4. *Women's wages in cottage industry compared to wages in other industries, 1833* (*earnings per week*)

County	Cottage industry		Agriculture	Factory work		Src
Bedfordshire	Lace	1s.6d.–3s.				
Berkshire			4s.–5s.			
Buckinghamshire	Lace	2s.	4s.–5s.			
	Straw	2s.6d.				
Derbyshire	Embroidery	2s.–7s.	5s.	Cotton	6s.–7s.	a
				Silk	6s.7d.	b
				Lace	8s.3d.	b
Devonshire			3s.–4s.	Lace	5s.4d.	b
Essex	Straw	1s.–5s.	5s.–6s.			
Gloucester	Stockings	2s.–4s.	4s.		6s.–7s.	a
				Wool	5s.6d.	b
Herefordshire	Gloves	3s.–4s.	3s.–4s.			
Hertfordshire	Straw	1s.6d.–3s.6d.	4s.–6s.			
Lancashire	Handloom weaving	4s.	5s.–6s.	Cotton	8s.7d.	b
Leicestershire	Lace	3s.	4s.–5s.	Worsted	7s.8d.	c
Northamptonshire	Lace	1s.6d.–3s.6d.	3s.–4s.			
Nottinghamshire	Lace-running	2s.–4s.	4s.–6s.	Lace	8s.	c
Oxfordshire	Lace	2s.–3s.	3s.–4s.			
Somerset			4s.	Silk	2s.6d.–4s.	a
Westmoreland	Knitting	1s.	6s.–9s.			
Wiltshire	Lace	2s.–3s.	4s.			
Worcestershire	Gloves	2s.	4s.–5s.			
Yorkshire, West Riding	Handloom weaving	2s.6d.–3s.	5s.	Wool	5s.–6s.	a
				Wool	7s.2d.	b
				Flax	6s.4d.	b
				Flax	6s.4d.	c

Sources: All wages for cottage industry and agriculture are from the "Rural Queries," BPP 1834 (44) XXX. Factory wages are from various sources, as indicated in the column labeled "Src."
a. BPP 1834 (44) XXX.
b. BPP 1834 (167) XIX, pp. 291–5. Average wages of workers age 21 and older.
c. BPP 1833 (450) XX. Average wages of workers age 21 and older.

out." If work outside the home did not provide much net benefit, work that could be done in the home may have been an attractive option.

The high cost of child care helps to explain why women worked in cottage industry, even though the wages were lower than in other occupations. Table 3.4 compares women's wages in cottage industry to women's wages in agriculture and factory work, and shows that wages in cottage industry were lower than wages in either agriculture or factory work. In Devonshire, women working in lace factories averaged 5s.4d. per week, but those making lace by hand at home made only 6d. per day, or 3s. per week if they worked six days. At the same time that women were earning 3s. per week in cottage industry in Leicestershire, women were earning more than twice that sum in worsted factories. Maria Hook, 16, earned 7s.6d. per week, and Elizabeth Wells, 35, earned 10s.6d. per week as worsted spinners.[127]

In spite of the low wages, women exhibited a preference for work done in the home. Brenner and Ramas claim that "Many jobs that are 'women's work,' such as charring and dressmaking, were taken up because they could more easily be combined with family responsibilities than factory work."[128] When framework knitters worked in their homes, women most often seamed stockings, but they would also work on the knitting frames. When knitting frames moved from the home into workshops in the mid-nineteenth century, women became even more concentrated in the seaming of stockings, since this work remained in the home. Osterud found that, in both the hosiery industry and the boot and shoe industry of Leicester, women worked in their homes, while men went out to work in workshops.[129]

Why did women continue to work in cottage industry if they could earn twice as much in the factories? Pinchbeck observed the preference that women showed for cottage industry "in spite of the great and obvious disadvantages," but she interpreted this as a dislike of factory discipline, claiming that "domestic workers regarded discipline and regularity with horror."[130] This suggests that women had very strong preferences for avoiding factories. While the dislike of factory discipline is probably part of the story, I do not think it is the whole story. Women avoided factory discipline, not only because they disliked it, but also because it made child care much more difficult. Of course, many factors caused women to choose cottage industry. Cottage industries such as lace making and straw plaiting were particularly suited to women's skills; they required no strength, and they took advantage of a type of skill that women in particular developed, dexterity. Factory employment and cottage industry were available in specific locations, and women often did not have both available where they lived. In addition to these reasons, though, I suggest that women chose to work in cottage industry,

---

[127] BPP 1833 (450) pp. XX, pp. 358, 369.
[128] Brenner and Ramas, "Rethinking Women's Oppression," p. 58.
[129] Osterud, "Gender Divisions and the Organization of Work."
[130] Pinchbeck, *Women Workers*, p. 237.

in spite of the low wages they received there, because child-care costs were low.

One factor attracting women to cottage industry was the flexibility of the work, and the opportunity to work part-time. A portion of the wage gap between factory work and cottage industry likely results from a difference in the number of hours worked. Unfortunately we do not know how many hours per day, or per week, women worked in cottage industry. In 1840 women handloom weavers who worked at home averaged only 4s. per week, compared to 5s.5d. earned by women working on the same machines in weaving shops. Parliamentary investigator James Mitchell attributed this difference to the fact that women working at home spent some of their time in household production tasks: "The lower average of the wages of the women working at home is, in a considerable degree, attributable to the circumstance that many of them are married women, and their time is partly occupied by their domestic duties."[131] The fact that hours of work in cottage industry were flexible, and thus work was more easily combined with household responsibilities, may have been one of the things that attracted women to these industries, even if the hourly wages were lower. Even today women seem to be willing to accept a lower wage for the privilege of working part-time.[132]

Another factor attracting women to cottage industry, in spite of the low wages, was the location of work. Since the work was done in the home, the mother could be physically present with the children. Part of child care is simply being present to prevent accidents, the fear of which prevented most women from leaving their children home alone. Of course, this is not all there is to child care. As noted in the previous paragraph, women working at home seem to have worked fewer hours because of their household responsibilities. One method women used to increase the hours they could devote to work was to sedate their children. Mothers sometimes used laudanum, or other opiate mixtures such as Godfrey's cordial, to quiet their babies and give them time to work. Sarah Johnson of Nottingham claimed that she:

Knows it is quite a common custom for mothers to give Godfrey's and the Anodyne cordial to their infants, "it is quite too common." It is given to infants at the breast; it is not given because the child is ill, but "to compose it to rest, to

---

[131] BPP 1840 (43) XXIII, p. 157.
[132] Controlling for observable differences, British women working part-time earned 6 percent less than similar women working full-time. Heather Joshi and Pierella Paci, *Unequal Pay for Women and Men: Evidence from the British Birth Cohort Studies* (Cambridge, Mass.: MIT Press, 1998), pp. 93–4.

sleep it," so that the mother may get to work. "Has seen an infant lay asleep on its mother's lap whilst at the lace-frame for six or eight hours at a time." This has been from the effects of the cordial.[133]

This method of coping with child care, though harmful to the children, had low immediate costs for the mother. The cost of laudanum was only about 2d. per week. Mary Colton, a lace worker from Nottingham, described her use of the drug:

Was confined of an illegitimate child in November, 1839. When the child was a week old she gave it a half teaspoonful of Godfrey's twice a-day. She could not afford to pay for the nursing of the child, and so gave it Godfrey's to keep it quiet, that she might not be interrupted at the lace piece; she gradually increased the quantity by a drop or two at a time until it reached a teaspoonful; when the infant was four months old it was so "wankle" and thin that folks persuaded her to give it laudanum to bring it on, as it did other children. A halfpenny worth, which was about a teaspoonful and three-quarters, was given in two days; continued to give her this quantity since February, 1840, until this last past (1841), and then reduced the quantity. She now buys a halfpenny worth of laudanum and a halfpenny worth of Godfrey's mixed, which lasts her three days.

While aware that this method of child care was not good for her child, she used the laudanum because it was the only way that she could work the thirteen-hour days necessary to earn a living:

If it had not been for her having to sit so close to work she would never have given the child Godfrey's. She has tried to break it off many times but cannot, for if she did, she should not have anything to eat.[134]

Whatever its effects on health, laudanum was a cheap form of child care, and allowed the mother to work without paying the high cost of hiring someone else to take care of the child. Cottage industry, combined with opiates, allowed mothers to earn a (somewhat lower) market wage without paying the relatively high costs to hire child care.

The fact that women earned low wages in domestic industry does not necessarily mean they were prevented from entering other occupations. If the ability to work at home was an advantage to a woman, then the supply curve for work in the home would lie below the supply curve for work outside the home. If the demand was the same for both types of

---

[133] BPP 1843 (430) XIV, p. 613. This mother was probably not an anomaly. Robert W. Fogel, "Nutrition and the Decline in Mortality since 1700: Some Preliminary Findings," in S. Engerman and R. Gallman, eds., *Long-Term Factors in American Economic Growth* (Chicago: University of Chicago Press, 1986), p. 507, claims that, "the administration of opiates to infants also appears to have been widespread for some stretches of time."

[134] BPP 1843 (431) XIV, p. 630.

labor, then work done in the home would pay a lower wage. Thus the low wages earned in cottage industry do not necessarily indicate a segmented labor market. One of the many reasons that women were concentrated in cottage industry was the fact that this work could be more easily combined with child care than could work outside the home. Given their child-care duties, many women found that even at lower wages they could do better working in domestic industry, since they did not have to hire child care.

Conclusion

In this chapter I have presented two reasons why women and men would be sorted into different occupations even in a competitive market – strength and child-care duties – thus showing that differences in occupations by sex do not necessarily indicate the presence of labor market discrimination against women. I have also shown that sorting by comparative advantage reduced, rather than increased, the gender wage gap. The following chapter presents statistical evidence that, in the more competitive portions of the labor market such as agriculture, occupational sorting responded to labor market incentives. Readers less comfortable with statistics can skip Chapter 4 without losing the train of the argument.

4   Testing for occupational barriers in agriculture

The last chapter presented two models of occupational sorting by strength and argued that, in the more competitive portions of the labor market, the division of labor between the sexes can be explained by comparative advantage. This chapter will present statistical tests for occupational barriers in agriculture. Both discrimination and free markets would imply that men and women worked different jobs. This chapter will attempt to distinguish between those two theories by testing whether the labor market was segmented or integrated. If customary barriers kept women in certain types of work, then changes in the supply of or demand for their labor would not influence the wage or employment of male workers. However, if the division of labor was the result of the sorting models presented in the last chapter, then men and women should be substitutable, and changes in the wages of one sex should affect the labor market opportunities for the other sex.

Having established that sex differences in wages and occupations are not proof of occupational segregation constraints, I will now provide evidence that the agricultural labor market did not have discriminatory occupational constraints. The results in this chapter will show that men and women were hired in an integrated labor market; employers were willing to substitute men and women workers in response to wage changes. As we shall see in later chapters, these results do not apply to the entire labor market. The evidence provided here is for agriculture only. However, the agricultural sector was still large, employing more than a quarter of employed males and somewhere between 4 and 33 percent of employed females in 1841 (see Table 1.2). While I do not have the same data for other industries, I believe the results presented here for agriculture would apply to some other sectors where the labor market was competitive. However, the results would not apply to all sectors of the labor market. There were parts of the labor market where barriers to competition were erected, and men and women could not move freely into any occupation they wished. The portions of the labor market with occupational barriers are examined in Chapters 5 and 6.

186

The tests in this chapter provide a useful complement to the discussion of wages in Chapter 2. Two very different ways that labor market discrimination can occur are wage discrimination and occupational crowding. Wage discrimination occurs if an individual is paid a wage less than his or her marginal productivity. Occupational crowding occurs if women are prevented from moving from low-paying occupations to high-paying occupations, where they could be more productive, by discriminatory occupational barriers.[1] These forms of discrimination operate independently, and showing that women's wages were fair market wages requires showing that neither form of discrimination prevailed. In Chapter 2 I argued that women were paid market wages in the sense that their wages matched their productivity, that is, that there was no wage discrimination. However, even if women were paid wages equal to their marginal product they may still have suffered from discrimination in the form of occupational crowding. In the crowding model women are paid wages equal to their marginal product, but, because of the diminishing marginal product of labor, confining women to a small number of jobs results in "overcrowding" and reduces their marginal product. This chapter tests for discrimination in the form of occupational crowding. A gender division of labor is not sufficient evidence of crowding because, as Chapter 3 argued, a free market that sorted individuals into occupations efficiently would also have produced occupational differences. This chapter will attempt to distinguish between the two possible causes of gender differences in occupations (occupational barriers and efficient sorting) by examining whether men and women were substitutable. If there were rigid employment constraints, that would imply that men and women were not substitutable. If men and women were substitutes, this suggests a division of labor based on the models presented in Chapter 3, rather than a division of labor based on rigidly defined gender roles.

Historians of the British Industrial Revolution rely on conflicting and largely untested claims about whether men and women were substitutable. For example, Lindert and Williamson justify excluding women's wages from their wage index by claiming that women were substitutes for unskilled men, and that their wages must therefore have followed the same path.[2] Other historians, however, note the extensive differences

---

[1] The wage discrimination model was developed by Becker, and the occupational crowding model by Bergmann. Becker, *The Economics of Discrimination*; Bergmann, "The Effect on White Incomes of Discrimination" and "Occupational Segregation." See Appendix 4.1 for a mathematical description of these models.

[2] Peter Lindert and Jeffrey Williamson, "English Workers' Living Standards during the Industrial Revolution: A New Look," *Economic History Review* 36 (1983), p. 17.

between men and women in wages and occupations and conclude that the labor market was segmented by gender. According to this thesis, women were confined to occupations considered "women's work." Deborah Valenze claims generally that women were "squeezed out of mainstream industrial production and confined to low-paid, exploitative occupations."[3] For agriculture specifically, Duncan Bythell claims that among farm servants "there was a clear distinction between the work done by the two sexes, with girls generally *confined* to work in the dairy and poultry-yard, to weeding in the fields, and to household tasks" [italics added].[4] In the last chapter we saw that the allocation of labor between the sexes was consistent with comparative advantage, and thus with a non-discriminatory labor market. It remains to be shown, however, whether the unskilled labor market was characterized by occupational segregation constraints. This chapter presents statistical evidence that in the unskilled labor market women were not confined to a few occupations because of their sex.

I.   Cross-price elasticities

The first test of occupational constraints I use is the cross-price elasticity between male and female farm servants.[5] This elasticity measures the extent to which the employment of male servants responds to changes in the price of female servants, or the extent to which the employment of female servants responds to changes in the price of male servants. If men and women were substitutes, then employers would respond to an increase in the price of men by substituting women for men – hiring fewer men and more women. Employers should also respond to an increase in the price of women by hiring more men and fewer women. Both situations would produce a positive cross-price elasticity (the employment of one group increases when the price of the other group increases). Alternatively, if tasks were strictly assigned by gender, then an employer facing a higher price for male workers might economize on the use of men, but would not hire women in their place, and would not be expected to hire more women. If men and women were not substitutable, we would expect to find no relationship between the employment of one group and the price of the other group, and the cross-price

---

[3] Valenze, *The First Industrial Woman*, p. 4.

[4] Duncan Bythell, "Women in the Work Force," in Patrick O'Brien and Roland Quinault, eds., *The Industrial Revolution in British Society* (Cambridge: Cambridge University Press, 1993), p. 39.

[5] Appendix 4.2 describes this test mathematically.

elasticity would be zero. I find positive cross-price elasticities, indicating that male and female workers were substitutes. This suggests that the division of labor was not fixed by gender constraints, but responded to changes in prices. If, in addition, British women were paid their marginal product, then the agricultural labor market in Industrial Revolution Britain was not discriminatory.

While many studies of the modern labor market have examined substitutability between different types of labor, these studies have not generally been used to examine occupational constraints. Most studies have used the elasticity of complementarity, which measures how wages respond to exogenous changes in employment. The elasticity of complementarity provides an explanation of how changes in the demographic structure of the workforce have changed wages. By calculating the elasticity of complementarity, Freeman found that young men and older men were not good substitutes.[6] He thus explained a change in the male age–earning profile during the 1970s as a response to the increase in the number of younger workers. Grant and Hamermesh found that youths and white women were substitutes; the more women in a city's labor force, the lower the wages of youths.[7] They suggest that the growth of female participation has hurt the earnings of youths. Borjas examined substitutability between black, whites, and Hispanics by looking at how wages responded to changes in the percentage of each group in the labor force of the city.[8] He interpreted the lack of substitutability between blacks and Hispanics as showing that the immigration of Hispanics has not hurt blacks. While the elasticity of complementarity has been most popular because of the types of questions researchers were asking, a few studies have used the elasticity of substitution, which examines the response of employment to an exogenous change in wages.[9] Welch and Cunningham, for example, used the elasticity of substitution to examine

---

[6] Richard Freeman, "The Effect of Demographic Factors on the Age–Earnings Profiles," *Journal of Human Resources* 14 (1979), pp. 289–318.

[7] James Grant and Daniel Hamermesh, "Labour Market Competition among Youths, White Women and Others," *Review of Economics and Statistics* 63 (1981), pp. 354–60.

[8] George Borjas, "The Substitutability of Black, Hispanic, and White Labor," *Economic Inquiry* 21 (1983), pp. 93–106.

[9] Whether we expect wages to respond to employment or employment to respond to wages depends on the level of analysis. Wages are set by supply and demand in the labor market as a whole, but individual firms, if the are small enough that they do not have monopsony power, are price-takers and must pay the going wage. Studies using the elasticity of complementarity examine the response of wages in a city, state, or country to changes in labor supply. Below I will examine wages and employment at the level of an individual farm. These farms are price-takers and thus the wage is exogenous, and the number of workers hired at the farm responds to exogenous changes in the wage.

the effects of the minimum wage on youth employment.[10] One study used the elasticity of substitution to study labor market segmentation. Merrilees calculated the elasticity of substitution for four labor market groups: male and female youths and adults.[11] He found no substitutability and interpreted this as evidence of labor market segmentation. Like Merrilees, I will examine the response of employment to an exogenous change in wages and will interpret the result as a test of labor market segmentation.

In this section I will use data on English farm servants from 1768 to 1770 to test whether men and women were substitutes. Section II will show that the conclusions in this section are valid throughout the Industrial Revolution. While I test only agriculture, this industry was an important one and provides an appropriate test of the claims I have made. In keeping with the models I have outlined, agricultural work required strength, and the labor market was competitive.

A.   Data

In the late 1760s, Arthur Young set out to tour England. He believed that scientific study would improve English farming, and to that end he collected data about the farms he visited. The data for this chapter come from two of his books, both of which were based on extensive travels in England. The first, *A Six Months' Tour through the North of England* (1770), is based on travels in 1768, and the second, *A Farmer's Tour through the East of England* (1771), is based on travels in 1770. At this point in his career, Young was well known enough that he could get landlords to cooperate with his inquiries, but he was not yet so famous that he spent most of his touring time being entertained by gentlemen, as he did during his 1776 Irish tour.[12] Both *A Six Months' Tour* and *A Farmer's Tour* present information for the towns Young visited and end with his conclusions from the data he collected. Young was very careful collecting his data, and while his conclusions have not held up under further examination (his own data have been used to contradict his conclusions), his data have fared much better. Allen used Young's data on particular farms to examine how employment varied with farm size

---

[10] Finis Welch and James Cunningham, "Effects of Minimum Wages on the Level and Age Composition of Youth Employment," *Review of Economics and Statistics* 60 (1978), pp. 140–5.

[11] William Merrilees, "Labor Market Segmentation in Canada: An Econometric Approach," *Canadian Journal of Economics* 15 (1982), pp. 458–73.

[12] Robert C. Allen and Cormac O' Grada, "On the Road Again with Arthur Young: English, Irish and French Agriculture during the Industrial Revolution," *Journal of Economic History* 48 (1988), pp. 100, 106.

Table 4.1. *Descriptive statistics: Arthur Young's data*

Variable	Mean	SD	Min.	Max.	N
Farm-level data					
Acres	324.39	620.88	35	6000	222
Arable acres	153.76	261.99	0	2000	222
Percent arable	0.51	0.28	0	1	222
Rent	167.54	197.93	21	1500	220
Men	1.89	2.10	0	17	222
Boys	1.29	1.10	0	6	222
Women	1.44	1.04	0	6	222
Laborers	3.56	7.54	0	80	222
Milk cows	11.29	9.45	0	60	222
Other cattle	20.73	30.82	0	280	222
Horses	8.61	10.04	0	100	222
Sheep	241.63	651.48	0	8000	222
Town-level data					
Men's wage	8.53	1.47	6.0	12.0	68
Women's wage	3.55	0.68	2.5	5.0	68
Boys' wage	3.28	1.23	1.0	6.0	67
Laborers' wage	19.15	3.07	13.0	26.2	67
Alternative wage	3.78	3.56	0.0	12.0	20
Spinning employment	0.71	0.45	0.0	1.0	52
High-wage employment	0.10	0.30	0.0	1.0	52

Source: Young, *Northern Tour* and *Eastern Tour.*

and found that the results closely match the results from a different data set, which suggests that we can have confidence in Young's data.[13] Brunt has recently defended Young against critics, and concluded that he was a careful researcher, and that "Although the Young data-set is not perfect, its quality, quantity, and scope make it far superior to any other data source available on English agriculture in the late eighteenth and early nineteenth centuries."[14]

For a number of locations, Young presented statistical descriptions of a few farms in the area, which he labeled "particulars of farms." Table 4.1 provides descriptive statistics of some of the variables he provides. Farm employees are listed in four categories. "Men," "boys," and "maids" are servants who were hired annually and received room and board from the farmer, while "laborers" received daily wages and lived on their own. Servants were typically single, and married workers

[13] Allen, *Enclosure and the Yeoman.*
[14] Liam Brunt, "Rehabilitating Arthur Young," *Economic History Review* 56 (2003), pp. 294–5.

Table 4.2. *Distribution of farm size*

Size (acres)	Arthur Young sample		Allen's tax sample	
	N	%	%	% > 30
0–30	0	0	58.4	
30–59	26	11.7	9.9	23.8
60–99	37	16.7	8.9	21.5
100–199	62	27.9	12.6	30.3
200–299	31	14.0	5.4	12.9
300–399	19	8.6	2.4	5.7
400–499	16	7.2	1.1	2.5
500–1000	18	8.1	1.2	2.8
1000 +	13	5.9	0.2	0.5

The second column of Allen's sample reports the percentage distribution among farms greater than 30 acres.

Source: Young, *Northern Tour* and *Eastern Tour,* and Allen, *Enclosure and the Yeoman,* p. 82. Allen's sample is from tax assessments, c. 1790.

were typically laborers. My study will focus on the employment of servants because the employment of day-laborers is not well represented in this data set. The number of "laborers" given by Young probably counts only the male laborers who worked regularly through the year and thus ignores female laborers, as well as male laborers whose work was more casual and intermittent.

Although not a random sample, the farms described by Young were broadly representative of English agriculture. While advertised as "Northern" and "Eastern" tours, Young's books actually cover most of England, and Brunt finds that Young did not over-sample arable farms.[15] The farms Young recorded are larger than average, though. The average size of farms in his sample is 324 acres, while the average farm size in a sample taken by Robert Allen from 1790 tax assessments is 119 acres.[16] Table 4.2 compares the distribution of farm size in Young's farm sample with the actual distribution of farm size in 1790. The smallest farm in my sample is 35 acres, so the smallest farms are missed. The last column of the table shows that Young's sample is much closer to the actual distribution of farms greater than 30 acres, though he still over-sampled larger farms. While Young's sample omits the smallest farms, that is not a serious problem for this study, since the smallest farms would not have hired servants. Young did report on one 30-acre farm, but this was eliminated from the sample because it employed no servants.

[15] *Ibid.*, pp. 290–1.   [16] Allen, *Enclosure and the Yeoman,* p. 81.

Young included a number of farms small enough to hire only one servant, the smallest farms useful in a study of employment.

For each town, Young gave wages that indicate the prevailing wage in the local labor market. I have constructed a two-tiered data set that matches the wages for a given location with data from one or more farms in that area. In order to arrive at one wage for each employment category, I have averaged some wages together. Averaging is necessary because in most cases Young recorded annual money wages for five different categories of servants: "first man," "second man," "dairy maid," "other maid," and "boy."[17] The "first man" received a higher wage than the "second man," presumably because he had more responsibility and/or more skill. Similarly, the wages of "dairy maids" are higher than those of "other maids." The wage variables used in the regressions result from averaging together the higher and the lower wage for each sex.

B.   Results

I estimate the cross-price effect in both directions, using both women's employment and men's employment as dependent variables. I estimate each equation by both OLS and Tobit, since a number of farms have zero employment levels for either men or women (about 15 percent of farms for each). For women, I also test whether wages were exogenous. The explanatory variables include the wages of men and women servants, measures of farm size, and controls for the type of farming. Farm size is measured either in acres or in rental value, and I will present estimates using both measures of farm size. The variable "Rent" measures the total rent paid for the farm, not rent per acre, and is a measure of farm size that weights each acre by its value. Eighteenth-century farmers favored rent as a measure of farm size; they usually described farms by their rent payment rather than acres, and the poor-rate taxes were assessed as a percentage of the farm's rent.[18]

In order to control for across-task substitution and show that farmers were willing to substitute male and female workers rather than just adjusting the farm's output and thus the tasks required in response to changes in wages, I also include variables indicating the farm's labor needs.[19] These variables are the percentage of the land that is arable and the number of milk cows, other cattle, horses, and sheep on the farm. Cows were used for dairying, an occupation in which women had the

---

[17] In some cases, though, only one wage is given for men or for maids.
[18] This preference may have been due to the fact that rent was more easily observable than acres. A survey was required to measure the acreage of a farm.
[19] See Appendix 4.2 for a discussion of within-task versus across-task substitution.

Table 4.3. *OLS and Tobit estimations: specification one*

	OLS		Tobit	
	Women	Men	Women	Men
Constant	0.5727	−0.9913	0.5209	−2.2139**
	(0.4342)	(0.8308)	(0.4933)	(0.9592)
Acres	0.0158	0.1272**	0.0128	0.1422**
(in hundreds)	(0.0278)	(0.0531)	(0.0312)	(0.0587)
Acres squared	−0.0016**	−0.0056**	−0.0016**	−0.0064**
(in 10,000s)	(0.0005)	(0.0010)	(0.0006)	(0.0011)
Percent arable	−0.0622	0.4740	−0.0819	0.9875*
	(0.2347)	(0.4491)	(0.2689)	(0.5216)
Milk cows	0.0273**	0.0106	0.0294**	0.0176
	(0.0065)	(0.0125)	(0.0074)	(0.0139)
Other cattle	0.0025	−0.0075	0.0030	−0.0025
	(0.0031)	(0.0060)	(0.0036)	(0.0067)
Horses	0.0551**	0.1813**	0.0569**	0.1897**
	(0.0122)	(0.0233)	(0.0138)	(0.0258)
Sheep	0.0347	0.0641	0.0374	0.0655
(in hundreds)	(0.0225)	(0.0431)	(0.0253)	(0.0476)
Women's wage	−0.2509**	0.1424	−0.2987**	0.1723
	(0.0876)	(0.1676)	(0.0999)	(0.1896)
Men's wage	0.1034**	0.0363	0.1178**	0.0809
	(0.0392)	(0.0751)	(0.0446)	(0.0853)
N	222	222	222	222
R²	0.455	0.510		
Log-likelihood			−281.94	−385.23

Standard errors in parentheses.
* = *significantly different from zero at the 10% level*
** = *significantly different from zero at the 5% level*
Normalized coefficients are presented for the Tobit estimations.
Source: Young, *Northern Tour* and *Eastern Tour.*

comparative advantage, so this variable should increase the number of women hired. Arable agriculture, on the other hand, required more strength and was therefore better suited to male workers. Horses may be associated with plowing, which was a male task. It is less clear how cattle or sheep should affect the relative demand for men and women, so I do not expect any particular effect.

The results of OLS and Tobit estimations are presented in Tables 4.3 and 4.4. The first specification, in Table 4.3, includes acres and acres squared, allowing a non-linear relationship between employment and farm size. The second specification, in Table 4.4, divides the dependent variable and each farm stock variable by rent. Both specifications give

Table 4.4. *OLS and Tobit estimations: specification two*

	OLS		Tobit	
	Women/rent	Men/rent	Women/rent	Men/rent
Constant	0.5096	0.2140	0.4595	−0.1630
	(0.4771)	(0.5750)	(0.5434)	(0.6654)
Rent	−0.0825**	−0.0494	−0.0776**	−0.0279
(in hundreds)	(0.0330)	(0.0398)	(0.0374)	(0.0457)
Percent arable	−0.4610*	0.2442	−0.4596	0.4565
	(0.2615)	(0.3152)	(0.2991)	(0.3655)
Milk cows/rent	0.0510**	−0.0267**	0.0554**	−0.0381**
	(0.0100)	(0.0121)	(0.0115)	(0.0146)
Other cattle/rent	0.0017	0.0046	0.0038	0.0097
	(0.0055)	(0.0066)	(0.0062)	(0.0077)
Horses/rent	0.0935**	0.1412**	0.0983**	0.1500**
	(0.0201)	(0.0242)	(0.0229)	(0.0282)
Sheep/rent	−0.0147	−0.0368	0.0246	−0.0419
(in hundreds)	(0.0405)	(0.0488)	(0.0456)	(0.0565)
Women's wage	−0.2173**	0.1793	−0.2884**	0.1984
	(0.0905)	(0.1091)	(0.1046)	(0.1262)
Men's wage	0.0934**	−0.0199	0.1061**	−0.0132
	(0.0411)	(0.0496)	(0.0468)	(0.0571)
N	220	220	220	220
R^2	0.367	0.249		
Log-likelihood			−285.46	−317.96

Standard errors in parentheses.
* = *significantly different from zero at the 10% level*
** = *significantly different from zero at the 5% level*
Normalized coefficients are presented for the Tobit estimations.
Source: Young, *Northern Tour* and *Eastern Tour.*

similar results, and the Tobit estimations are similar to the OLS estimations, indicating that the results are robust.

Employment patterns followed the predictions of comparative advantage. The number of cows on the farm increases the number of women hired, but not the number of men. The percent arable land increases the number of men hired, but not the number of women. Horses increase both types of labor, perhaps because, other things being equal, more horses meant more work to be done. However, the presence of horses does have a greater effect on male employment than female employment, which would be expected if horses were associated with arable agriculture. Other cattle and sheep, for which we had no a priori expectations, have little or no effect on the employment of either men or women. These results increase our confidence in the estimation results.

The effect of a higher wage for either men or women should be to reduce the employment of that type of labor because it is more expensive. This prediction holds up well for women; the women's wage always has a significantly negative effect on women's employment. Men's employment, however, does not seem to respond to the men's wage. While I will be able to test whether the wage is exogenous in the women's equations, I do not have an instrument for the men's wage. We are left with the unsatisfactory own-wage effect in the men's equations.

The men's wage coefficients in the women's equations indicate that an increase in the male wage was associated with an increase in female employment. The cross-price effect is always significantly positive. When I control for the type of farming activity by including variables such as the number of farm animals and "percent arable," the number of women hired still responded to the price of hiring men. Even after deciding how many cows to keep and how much arable land to work, the farmer's decision about how many women to hire still responded to the price of men, suggesting he or she was willing to substitute men and women within tasks rather than, for example, always assigning dairy work to women. To assess the size of the estimated effects, Table 4.5 presents elasticities at the mean. For women's employment, the cross-wage effect has a larger elasticity than the other explanatory variables, suggesting that the substitution effect was relatively strong. The employment of women was more responsive to changes in male wages than it was to changes in the number of cows on the farm. Farm employment was not simply determined by gender roles, but responded to wages.

While the cross-price effect in the women's employment equations is significantly positive, the cross-price effect in the men's equations is not significant in the first specification and only marginally significant in the second specification. In Table 4.5 we see that the size of the response of male employment to the women's wage is smaller than the response of male employment to the number of horses on the farm. However, these relatively low elasticities are consistent with the higher elasticities for women's employment. As noted in Appendix 4.1 (see p. 344), the input with the larger factor share will have a lower cross-price elasticity. The average farm spent £16 per year on men servants, but only £5 per year on women servants. This is enough of a difference to explain the difference in elasticities.[20] Thus the smaller cross-price

---

[20] These factor shares imply that the ratio of the cross-elasticities should be 0.31. The ratio of the estimated elasticities in Table 4.5 is actually larger than this, ranging from 0.43 to 0.76.

Table 4.5. *Elasticities*

Dependent variable	Independent variable	Elasticity at the mean	
		OLS	Tobit
Specification one			
Women	Percent arable	−0.022	−0.029
	Cows	0.214*	0.230*
	Horses	0.329*	0.340*
	Women's wage	−0.619*	−0.737*
	Men's wage	0.623*	0.710*
Men	Percent arable	0.128	0.266
	Cows	0.063	0.105
	Horses	0.825*	0.863*
	Women's wage	0.268	0.324
	Men's wage	0.167	0.371
Specification two			
Women/rent	Percent arable	−0.179	−0.178
	Cows/rent	0.389*	0.423*
	Horses/rent	0.446*	0.469*
	Women's wage	−0.587*	−0.779*
	Men's wage	0.617*	0.701*
Men/rent	Percent arable	−0.019	0.171
	Cows/rent	−0.197*	−0.281*
	Horses/rent	0.652*	0.693*
	Women's wage	0.469	0.519
	Men's wage	−0.127	−0.084

Elasticities for Tobit estimations are elasticities of the index.
* = *coefficient is significant at the 5% level*
Source: Young, *Northern Tour* and *Eastern Tour.*

elasticities in the men's equations do not necessarily contradict the results from the women's equations. Since men had a larger factor share, their cross-price elasticity should be lower. In this case, the cross-price effect is low enough that it does not show up as statistically significant.

My estimates of cross-wage elasticities are valid only if the wages are exogenous, and not influenced by the farmer's employment decisions. The employment measures in this data set are for individual farms which are likely to be price-takers. The wages that Young reports are the wages prevailing in the local labor market, which were influenced by demand conditions, but if each farm was small relative to the market, the employment decisions of an individual farmer would not be enough to determine the wage rate. Fortunately, I do not have to rely on this explanation alone, but can test whether the wages in my data set are exogenous. Using wages in alternative employments such as spinning as an instrument for female agricultural wages, I find that a Hausman specification test fails to reject the null hypothesis that female wages were exogenous to the farmer's employment decisions.

If wages were not exogenous, the supply and demand equations would be a simultaneous system:

$$\text{Demand:} \quad N_f = a_1 + a_2 w_m + a_3 w_f + X'\beta + e$$
$$\text{Supply:} \quad N_f = b_1 + b_2 w_f + b_3 w_A + u$$

where N_f is female employment, w_m is the male wage, w_f is the female wage, X is the matrix of controls, and w_A is the wage in a woman's alternative employment. If I were measuring the employment of married women, then the labor supply equation would include the male wage, since a married woman's labor supply would be affected by her husband's wage. In this case, however, the dependent variable is female servants, who were overwhelmingly single, and thus the male wage does not affect women's labor supply.

If this simultaneous system is the correct specification, then I need to use instrumental variables to estimate the demand equation. Young provides an instrument for women's wages by including information on alternative wages in such statements as, "The employment of the poor women is spinning of flax: a woman can earn from 3d. to 6d. a day."[21] These statements mainly described the work of married women, but spinning was also the alternative to farm service for the single woman and thus affected her labor supply decision. In almost all cases the alternative wage that Young supplied was for spinning. In one case it was for mining, and in one case it was for lace-making. I also include towns where Young specifically noted there was no non-agricultural employment for women, assigning a wage of zero to the alternative.[22] Since the wage is only given in a few cases, I also use a dummy variable for the presence of alternative work. "Spinning" is a dummy indicating the presence of spinning work, the wage for which averaged 5d. a day. The "high wage" dummy indicates the presence of either mining or lace-making, which each paid about 1s. a day,[23] or more than twice as much

---

[21] Young, *Northern Tour*, vol. I, p. 326. Where a range of wages is given I take the mid-point, so this wage would be recorded as 4.5 pence a day.

[22] The absence of employment was indicated by such statements as, "The poor women and children in total idleness." *Ibid.*, vol. II, p. 174.

[23] Young gives one wage quote for each of these occupations. Mining paid 1s. a day in Reeth, North Riding, and lace-making paid 11d. a day in Maidenhead, Berkshire. *Ibid.*, vol. I, p. 357, and vol. III, p. 9.

as a woman could earn spinning. The omitted category is towns specifically noted to have no non-agricultural work for women. Using these dummies increases the sample size, and still provides an instrument correlated with the agricultural wage.

The wage in alternative work is a valid instrument for women's wages; it enters the supply equation but not the demand equation. Work opportunities in other industries were an important determinant of the labor supply curve facing the farmer, but should not affect his or her demand for labor. Using these instruments, I can calculate the Two-Stage Least Squares (2SLS) estimates and use a Hausman specification test to determine whether wages were exogenous.[24] Under the null hypotheses of exogenous wages, the 2SLS estimates are consistent but inefficient, while under the alternative that wages are endogenous, OLS estimates are inconsistent. Thus, I will use the Hausman test to compare OLS and 2SLS estimates. Table 4.6 presents two sets of 2SLS estimates, one using the alternative wage, and one using the dummy variables. The own-price coefficients are no longer significantly negative, and in the dummy variable specification the cross-price effect is not statistically significant, but otherwise the results are similar to the OLS and Tobit results. The Hausman tests do not reject the null, so we cannot reject the hypothesis that the wage is exogenous.[25] To test the quality of the instruments I am using, I also ran 2SLS estimations including the residuals from the first stage. The residuals are not statistically significant in either case, and including the residuals did not change the conclusion that female employment increased when male wages increased.

The results are robust; men and women farm servants were substitutes. The employment of women clearly responded to the wages of men. Men's employment responded less strongly to women's wages, but this is consistent with the relative factor shares of men and women workers. Employers were willing to hire more women if men's wages increased, indicating that they made hiring decisions based on profit maximization rather than strictly according to gender roles. In 1770 the market for farm servants was not segregated by gender; men and women were not hired in completely isolated labor markets. Bergmann's occupational segregation model is not a good description of employment in the agricultural labor market of 1770.

---

[24] J. A. Hausman, "Specification Test in Econometrics," *Econometrica* 46 (1978), pp. 1251–71.

[25] The possibility remains, however, that large standard errors may cause us to accept the null when we should not.

Table 4.6. *Two-stage least squares estimates and specification test*

	1st stage women's wage	2nd stage women	1st stage women's wage	2nd stage women
Constant	1.6258**	−0.0419	1.7770**	1.1054
	(0.3161)	(0.8945)	(0.3163)	(0.7276)
Acres	−0.0320*	0.0221	−0.0432*	0.0089
(in hundreds)	(0.0172)	(0.0363)	(0.0220)	(0.0315)
Acres squared	0.0013**	−0.0026**	0.00077*	−0.0017**
(in 10,000s)	(0.0003)	(0.0008)	(0.00040)	(0.0006)
Percent arable	0.1121	−0.0932	−0.1223	−0.0541
	(0.2037)	(0.3756)	(0.1949)	(0.2699)
Milk cows	0.0156**	0.0482**	0.0068	0.0147**
	(0.0063)	(0.0119)	(0.0055)	(0.0074)
Other cattle	0.0021	0.0002	0.0012	0.0074**
	(0.0027)	(0.0051)	(0.0026)	(0.0034)
Horses	−0.0194*	0.0890**	−0.0103	0.0539**
	(0.0109)	(0.0204)	(0.0108)	(0.0146)
Sheep	−0.0306**	0.0358	−0.0013	0.0295
(in hundreds)	(0.0128)	(0.0253)	(0.0173)	(0.0236)
Men's wage	0.1874**	0.1309*	0.1931**	0.1683**
	(0.0264)	(0.0695)	(0.0296)	(0.0536)
Predicted wage		−0.2345		−0.5288**
		(0.2887)		(0.2439)
Alternative wage	0.0892**			
	(0.0136)			
Spinning			0.3021**	
Dummy			(0.1196)	
High wage			1.1213**	
Dummy			(0.2022)	
N	81	81	184	184
R^2	0.755	0.718	0.362	0.471
Specification test		0.004		1.491
Critical value for 5% test		16.92		16.92

Standard errors in parentheses.
* = *significantly different from zero at the 10% level*
** = *significantly different from zero at the 5% level*
Source: Young, *Northern Tour* and *Eastern Tour*.

II.   Wage correlations

While the previous section used data from Arthur Young's tours to test whether men and women were substitutable in agricultural work in 1768–70, this section will use wage correlations to test for substitutability over a broader range of years. If women did not face occupational barriers, then the markets for male and female labor should be integrated, and their wages should be correlated. This test is analogous to tests of geographical integration of markets which examine price correlations. Hatton and Williamson use wage correlations to test for integration between rural and urban markets by asking whether rural wages responded to urban wages.[26] They examine the gap between urban and rural wages in the later nineteenth century and find that the urban and rural labor markets were not segregated; rural wages responded to changes in urban wages. Appendix 4.3 presents a mathematical model demonstrating how the correlation in wages indicates an integrated market; here I apply this test to ask whether men and women were hired in segregated markets.

The correlation between male and female wages has also been explored by E. H. Hunt, though for a different purpose. Hunt was trying to explain the persistence of regional wage gaps and hypothesized that a negative correlation between women's wages and men's wages would equalize family income and discourage the migration necessary to equalize male wages across regions. In his own words, "if women's and adolescents' work was unobtainable or very badly paid in areas where men's wages were high then migration was less likely."[27] He finds that the evidence does not support this conclusion. Although he does not specifically calculate a correlation, he concludes, "regional variations in the wages of women and young people failed to compensate for regional variations in men's wages. On the contrary, there was a generally positive correlation between the two variables."[28] He does not, however, draw the conclusion that the labor market was integrated by gender. On the contrary, he claims, "the differentials between the earnings of men, women, and young people were strongly influenced by custom. Women's wages were determined, in large part, by consideration of what most people believed they ought to earn and this was usually measured as a customary proportion of the male ratio."[29] I will use wage correlations to argue that, in fact, wages were set by the market, rather than by custom.

I will use wage correlations to test for occupational segregation constraints. Appendix 4.3 presents a mathematical model of this test. The model predicts observable differences that will allow us to distinguish between integrated and segregated markets. If the market for male and female labor is integrated, male and female wages will be correlated. If there are occupational constraints, wages will not be correlated

---

[26] Timothy Hatton and Jeffrey Williamson, "Integrated and Segmented Labor Markets: Thinking in Two Sectors," *Journal of Economic History* 51 (1991), pp. 413–25.
[27] Hunt, *Regional Wage Variations*, p. 106.   [28] *Ibid.*, p. 117.   [29] *Ibid.*, pp. 117–18.

because changes in the market for male labor would not translate into changes in the market for female labor and vice versa.

In order for this test to work, there must be some variation in wages that is not due to locational factors affecting all wages, such as the cost of living. Evidence on wage gaps suggests that local labor markets were indeed independent, and not part of a unified national labor market. Both Hunt and Williamson found large wage gaps that persist even after correcting wages for prices and compensating differentials.[30] Looking at the same data that I will use below, Cunningham noted that "What is striking is how localized these employment markets were."[31] While there was some labor mobility, there was not enough to equalize wages. Persistent wage gaps are not surprising in light of the discouragements to mobility. The Poor Laws played an important part in reducing labor mobility, and thus preventing the equalization of wages. The poor could only receive relief in the parish where they had a settlement, so the poor were generally tied to the parish where they were born. New settlements became difficult to get because rate-payers did everything they could to keep their poor law payments low. Before 1795, individuals could be removed (sent back to their parish of settlement) if there was any suspicion that they might collect poor relief sometime in the future. Adam Smith painted the effect of the settlement laws in extreme terms:

The very unequal price of labor which we frequently find in England in places at no great distance from one another, is probably owing to the obstruction which the law of settlements gives to a poor man who would carry his industry from one parish to another ... it is often more difficult for a poor man to pass the artificial boundary of a parish, than an arm of the sea or a ridge of high mountains.[32]

Thus I feel confident that there is some variation in real wages not due to compensating factors.

Another problem, and one I cannot correct for, is that even if men and women were always paid according to their productivity ratio, the correlation would not be perfect if the productivity ratio varied from place to place. Since different regions specialized in different industries and different types of agriculture, they should have different productivity ratios, and thus different wage ratios. If the market was truly integrated, a low correlation might still result, owing to differences in the productivity ratio. Wages in each parish would reflect the true productivity ratio, but differences among parishes would lead to a less than perfect

---

[30] *Ibid.*, and Williamson, "Did English Factor Markets Fail."
[31] Hugh Cunningham, "The Employment and Unemployment of Children in England," *Past and Present* 126 (1990), p. 136.
[32] Adam Smith, *The Wealth of Nations* (New York: Modern Library, [1776] 1965), p. 140.

correlation. For example, if the productivity ratio was one-half in parish A and one-third in parish B, and male wages were 10 in parish A and 12 in parish B, female wages could be 5 in parish A and 4 in parish B under perfect competition, which would give a negative correlation between male and female wages. Thus, the correlation of wages might be low even in an integrated market if there is variation in the productivity ratio. This problem would lend a downward bias to the wage correlation, so if we do find a strong positive correlation, we can still be confident that the markets for male and female labor were integrated.

The model presented in Appendix 4.3 implies an observable difference in the behavior of wages under the two different hypotheses and will be the basis of the test which uses the correlation of wages. If the labor market was competitive, male and female wages would be positively correlated. However, if there were occupational constraints, male and female wages would not be correlated. Thus I will examine the correlation of male and female wages to test for discriminatory constraints. Because this test is so simple, I am able to look at many different data sets and track wage correlations through time. Most of the wages in this section are for agricultural work, though the 1833 data also includes other female occupations. This section shows that, for the agricultural labor market, there is no indication that occupational segregation constraints appeared during the course of the Industrial Revolution.

A.   1768–70

In the previous section, I used data on employment and wages of farm servants provided by Arthur Young. In his books, Young also provided wages for day-laborers. Data on day wages for agricultural laborers are provided for about seventy-five towns. Fortunately, Young provides multiple wages for each location, so that I can correct for the locational fixed effect. Unfortunately, for many locations no female winter wage is reported (because women were less likely to be employed during the winter), so that correlations including winter wages will have a smaller sample size.

Table 4.7 presents the means of wages for men and women by season. The wage ratios are about one half, which matches estimates of the wage ratio presented in Chapter 2. The female–male wage ratio is 0.49 in winter, 0.47 in hay harvest, and 0.56 in harvest. The fact that the ratio is highest in harvest and lowest in hay harvest fits with what we know about the technologies used. Women were relatively effective with the sickle, which was used to harvest grain, but were not as effective with the scythe, which was used to cut the grasses for hay-making. Thus, the

Table 4.7. *Means of wages: 1770 (shillings per week)*

		Mean	SD	Min.	Max.	N
Men	Winter	6.56	1.22	4.50	11.00	75
	Hay	9.45	2.17	4.00	14.00	76
	Harvest	11.27	2.85	6.00	21.00	76
Women	Winter	3.20	0.93	2.00	5.50	47
	Hay	4.47	1.53	2.00	11.50	77
	Harvest	6.30	1.59	3.00	14.50	74

Source: Young, *Northern Tour* and *Eastern Tour.*

Table 4.8. *Correlations of men's and women's wages: 1770*

	Correlation	P-level	N
Winter	0.44**	0.002	46
Hay	0.19*	0.096	75
Harvest	0.38**	0.001	74
Harvest – hay	0.20*	0.086	73
Harvest – winter	0.42**	0.004	46
Hay – winter	–0.01	0.947	45

* = *significantly different from zero at the 10% level*
** = *significantly different from zero at the 5% level*
Source: Young, *Northern Tour* and *Eastern Tour.*

wage ratio was highest when the productivity ratio was highest, and lowest when the productivity ratio was lowest.

Table 4.8 presents the wage correlations. Correlations of male and female wages in winter and harvest are significantly different from zero at the 5 percent level, but the correlation of male and female hay-making wages is lower and is only significantly different from zero at the 10 percent level. This difference may reflect the fact that, because the scythe required so much strength that it was never used by women, hay-making offered fewer opportunities for substituting one sex for the other.[33] Because locational fixed effects may induce a spurious correlation, I also present correlations of the difference in wages across seasons. Two of these correlations are positive. The differences between hay and winter wages is the exception, showing no correlation. Table 4.9 presents log regressions, which indicate the elasticity of the response.

[33] Women never used the scythe because it required a great deal of strength. See Roberts, "Sickles and Scythes."

Table 4.9. *Log-log regressions: 1770 (dependent variable = women's wage)*

	Winter	Hay	Harvest
Constant	−0.290	0.949**	1.083**
	(0.416)	(0.323)	(0.255)
Men's wage	0.750**	0.227	0.307**
	(0.221)	(0.145)	(0.107)
R^2	0.207	0.032	0.103
N	46	76	74

Wages in logs. Standard errors in parentheses.
* = *significantly different from zero at the 10% level*
** = *significantly different from zero at the 5% level*
Source: Young, *Northern Tour* and *Eastern Tour*.

For winter wages, the male-wage elasticity of female wages is 0.75, indicating a fairly strong response. For the other seasons, however, the elasticity of the response is lower. Again, the relationship is not significant during hay-making, when the strength required to use a scythe created a more rigid gender division of labor.

We saw in the previous section that English farmers in Young's tours were willing to substitute men and women farm servants. The wage correlations just presented suggest that farmers also substituted male and female day-laborers, though less so during hay-making. As we shall see, wages from later dates show a positive correlation at least as large as these, suggesting that the substitutability found in the 1770 agricultural labor market persisted through the Industrial Revolution.

B.   1833

Wage data from the first half of the nineteenth century is provided by an 1833 survey conducted by the Poor Law Commissioners, just previous to the passage of the New Poor Law. The survey contained a wide variety of questions, and fortunately included questions on both male and female wages.[34] The survey was filled out by local poor law

---

[34] The questions on wages were: "8. Weekly wages, with and without Beer or Cyder, in Summer and Winter?" and "12. What can Women and Children under 16, earn per Week, in Summer, in Winter, and Harvest, and how employed?" Some wage information was also obtained from question 13: "What in the while might a laborer's Wife and Four Children, aged 14, 11, 8 and 5 Years respectively (the eldest a boy), expect to earn in the Year, obtaining, as in the former case, an average amount of Employment?" BPP 1834 (44) XXX. For a summary of what this survey tells us about the employment of women and children, see Nicola Verdon, "The Rural Labour Market in the Early Nineteenth

administrators at the parish level, so each observation corresponds to a parish in England or Wales. The advantages of this data source are its large size and broad coverage. The data cover all of England and Wales, and there are 809 observations with summer wages for both men and women. The data also have some disadvantages. The wages are sub-jective reports by a parish official. They do not represent actual wages paid to any individual, and the survey respondent may not have been as conscientious an observer as Arthur Young. The data are from rural areas, and most of the wages are for agricultural work. In spite of these flaws, the survey is valuable because it provides scarce data on wage rates throughout England and Wales.

In constructing this data set, I added the value of in-kind payments in the form of beer and food, which were sometimes given to workers, to the cash wages. Sometimes the survey respondent would report wages with and without beer; the difference is the correct valuation of this in-kind payment. I used these valuations to estimate the value of beer in parishes where beer was given but only the money wage was reported. Where beer was given but I do not know its value, I used an imputed value equal to the average value of beer in parishes reporting wages both with and without beer, either in parishes of the same county, or, if none of these existed, from surrounding counties. The value is usually about 1s. per week. On a few occasions, meals were also part of the wage. The value of board was estimated the same way, but not for every county, since it was used less frequently than beer. Since prices in Wales were much different, the value of board in Wales was estimated separately from England. I estimate the value of board for women by assuming it to be worth three-fourths the value for men.[35]

The wages given for men are for agricultural work. Women's wages, however, are wages for a variety of unskilled occupations. Agriculture was the most commonly cited employer of women, but some of the wages in this data set are for weaving, lace-making, straw-plaiting, and factory work. Thus, these data cover the unskilled labor market more broadly than did Young's purely agricultural data.

Women's wages in this data set are biased for a number of reasons. Wages are reported by the day, not by the hour, and since women often worked fewer hours than men, this biases female wages down. In domestic industry, women with children could work in their homes and

Century: Women's and Children's Employment, Family Income, and the 1834 Poor Law Report," *Economic History Review* 55 (2002), pp. 299–323.

[35] The value of board for a man is assumed to be 4.8 shillings in England and 3.5 shillings in Wales. I chose three-fourths as the sex ratio because adult women use about 73 percent as many calories as adult men. See Bekaert, "Caloric Consumption," p. 638.

Table 4.10. *Wages in 1833 (shillings per week)*

		Mean	SD	Min.	Max.	N
Men	Summer	11.54	2.26	5.00	21.00	866
	Winter	10.29	1.74	5.00	19.00	871
	Harvest	17.63	5.30	5.00	34.38	182
Women	Summer	4.37	1.28	1.00	9.60	563
(strict defn.)	Winter	3.78	1.21	1.00	8.50	324
	Harvest	7.87	3.28	1.50	18.00	380
Women	Summer	4.27	1.37	1.00	9.60	834
(loose defn.)	Winter	3.60	1.26	0.75	9.60	508
	Harvest	7.52	3.23	1.00	18.00	595
Boys	Summer	3.31	0.97	1.00	7.50	205
	Winter	3.22	1.01	1.00	7.50	145
	Harvest	5.08	2.01	1.00	15.00	66

Note: "Strict definition" means that only those wages specified as being for women and not children are included. "Loose definition" means that ambiguous wages are also included.
Source: BPP 1834 (44) XXX.

thus save the child-care expense that would come with work outside the home. The wage in domestic industry fails to capture this extra benefit, and may lead to a wage that differs from the market wage for unskilled women. Another important source of bias is the fact that the survey includes only one question on both female and child wages. As a result, the reply often does not distinguish between the two. I will use two different definitions of female wages. The "strict definition" female wage variable includes female wages only if the wages of women are clearly distinguished from the wages of children. The "loose definition" variable includes also the ambiguous answers. Using the looser definition will result in a downward bias in the mean, but will not bias the correlations as long as the measurement error is not correlated with the male wage. The advantage of using the looser definition is the larger sample size, which will be especially useful when I examine differences across the seasons.

Table 4.10 provides descriptive statistics for these data. Ratio of female to male wages is 0.38 in summer, 0.37 in winter, and 0.45 in harvest (using the strict definition). These ratios are lower than the ratios from the 1770 data, which is consistent with other studies that have also found a declining female–male wage ratio over this time period.[36] As in the 1770 data, the ratio is the highest in harvest. The simple correlation between male and female summer wages, using the loose definition, is

[36] See Burnette, "Wages and Employment."

Table 4.11. *Correlations of men's and women's wages: 1833*

	Summer	Winter	Harvest
A. Correlations			
Women: strict definition			
Correlation	0.433**	0.359**	0.282**
N	540	317	82
P-level	0.000	0.000	0.010
95% confidence interval	(0.36, 0.50)	(0.26, 0.45)	(0.07, 0.47)
Women: loose definition			
Correlation	0.416**	0.323**	0.379**
N	806	499	111
P-level	0.000	0.000	0.000
95% confidence interval	(0.36, 0.47)	(0.24, 0.40)	(0.21, 0.53)
B. Rank correlations			
Women: strict definition			
Correlation	0.463**	0.364**	0.258**
N	540	317	82
P-level	0.000	0.000	0.019
95% confidence interval	(0.39, 0.53)	(0.26, 0.46)	(0.03, 0.46)
Women: loose definition			
Correlation	0.442**	0.334**	0.369**
N	806	499	111
P-level	0.000	0.000	0.000
95% confidence interval	(0.38, 0.50)	(0.25, 0.41)	(0.20, 0.52)

Standard errors in parentheses.
* = *significantly different from zero at the 10% level*
** = *significantly different from zero at the 5% level*
Source: BPP 1834 (44) XXX.

0.416 and is significantly positive (see Table 4.11). The correlation using the "loose definition" is slightly lower than the correlation using the "strict definition," probably because of the greater measurement error. The size of the summer wage correlations is the same or higher than correlations from 1770 wages, which were around 0.4 in winter and harvest, but lower in haytime. Correlations for winter and harvest wages are lower than for summer wages, but all are significantly positive. To check the robustness of the correlations, I also present rank correlations, which are presented in panel B of Table 4.11. The rank correlations give slightly higher correlations during the summer and winter, and slightly lower correlations during harvest, but the differences are small.

The regressions presented in Table 4.12 indicate that the elasticity of the effect was less than one, but still quite strong. For summer and winter wages, a 10 percent increase in the male wage was associated with an increase in the female wage of about 7 percent. The low R^2's,

Table 4.12. *Log-log regressions: 1833 (dependent variable = women's wage)*

	Summer	Winter	Harvest
A. Women's wage: strict definition			
Constant	−0.226	−0.330	1.079**
	(0.155)	(0.258)	(0.497)
Men's wage	0.681**	0.696**	0.317*
	(0.064)	(0.111)	(0.175)
R^2	0.175	0.110	0.039
N	540	317	82
B. Women's wage: loose definition			
Constant	−0.269**	−0.215	0.320
	(0.136)	(0.220)	(0.400)
Men's wage	0.684**	0.620**	0.558**
	(0.056)	(0.095)	(0.142)
R^2	0.157	0.079	0.124
N	806	499	111

Standard errors in parentheses.
* = *significantly different from zero at the 10% level*
** = *significantly different from zero at the 5% level*

however, show that differences in male wages explain only a small part of the differences in female wages. To explain more of the variation in wages, I add to the regressions dummy variables indicating in which industry the women were working. Results are presented in Table 4.13. Including industry effects reduces the coefficient on male wages only slightly. The dummies have significant effects on women's wages, and the R^2 increases, though the majority of the variation remains unexplained. Women's wages in cottage industry were lower than in agriculture, while wages in washing were higher. These differences may simply reflect the fact that women tended to work fewer hours in cottage industry, and more hours in washing, or they may reflect productivity differences arising from the selection of women into those industries.

Regressions in the second and fourth columns of Table 4.13 also include regional dummies. Women's wages were higher in the north, west, and south-east than in the midlands. While adding the industry dummies does not substantially change the coefficient on the men's wage, adding regional dummies does. This result makes sense because some of the covariance between male and female wages is simply the result of different levels of demand for labor in different regions. However, the coefficient on the male wage is still significantly positive, indicating that even controlling for industry and regional effects, male and female wages moved together.

Table 4.13. *Industry regressions: 1833 (dependent variable = women's wage)*

	Summer		Winter	
Constant	−0.164	1.682**	−0.111	1.342**
	(0.125)	(0.253)	(0.206)	(0.349)
Men's wage	0.658**	0.206**	0.598**	0.204**
	(0.051)	(0.020)	(0.089)	(0.032)
Manufacture	−0.118**	−0.459**	0.020	0.022
	(0.053)	(0.230)	(0.067)	(0.245)
Washing	0.442**	2.843**	0.273	1.801**
	(0.162)	(0.641)	(0.238)	(0.780)
Straw	−0.215**	−0.229	−0.093	0.213
	(0.071)	(0.286)	(0.088)	(0.296)
Lace	−0.585**	−1.581**	−0.558**	−1.290**
	(0.046)	(0.195)	(0.058)	(0.208)
Other cottage	−0.219**	−0.526*	−0.257**	−0.566*
industry	(0.073)	(0.292)	(0.088)	(0.293)
Weaving	−0.109	−0.686**	−0.140	−0.771**
	(0.079)	(0.329)	(0.100)	(0.354)
North		0.969**		0.792**
		(0.141)		(0.183)
Industrial north		0.468**		0.552**
		(0.158)		(0.193)
West		0.395**		0.512**
		(0.193)		(0.219)
East		−0.203		−0.078
		(0.146)		(0.194)
Lincoln		0.618*		0.472
		(0.339)		(0.406)
South-east		0.442**		0.584**
		(0.131)		(0.198)
South-west		0.100		0.052
		(0.145)		(0.169)
Wales		0.224		0.677**
		(0.241)		(0.319)
R^2	0.321	0.343	0.241	0.279
N	806	806	498	498

All wages are in logs. Standard errors in parentheses.
* = *significantly different from zero at the 10% level*
** = *significantly different from zero at the 5% level*
The loose definition is used for women's wages. The omitted occupation is agriculture; the omitted region is the midlands.
Source: BPP 1834 (44) XXX.

There are reasons the correlations measured here may be spurious. The most important reason is location-specific effects that will raise or lower all wages in an area. Wage differentials that compensate for disamenities would produce such location-specific effects. Also, since all wages for one parish were reported by the same person, the measurement error may have a parish-specific component. I correct for this problem by subtracting winter from summer wages (and summer from harvest wages), to eliminate the fixed effects.[37] The question becomes: In areas where the male wage increases substantially from winter to summer, are female wages also more likely to increase? Unfortunately, using wage differences will increase the relative size of the measurement error, and thus should increase the bias due to measurement error. Since measurement error introduces a downward bias, increasing the importance of the measurement error will result in more of an underestimate.

Table 4.14 presents the correlations of wage differences. The summer–winter wage differences have a correlation of 0.28, or 0.22 using the strict definition of women's wages. As expected, the correlation of seasonal wage differences is lower than the correlations of wage levels, but there is still evidence that seasonal changes in male wages are positively associated with seasonal changes in female wages. Most likely, the original correlations contained some spurious correlation due to location-specific effects. After purging these effects, however, there is still evidence of market integration: women's wages increase where men's wages increase. Table 4.15 presents regressions of the wage differences. The elasticities are much lower for the summer–winter differences, and negative for the harvest–summer differences. Again, some of the correlation seems to have been spurious. The summer–winter differences indicate an integrated labor market. The harvest-summer differences do not, but in this case the productivity ratio probably changed because of the increased use of the scythe. The scythe required so much strength that women never used it. The resulting inability to substitute women for men in harvesting may have meant that in arable regions male wages rose substantially during harvest but female wages did not.

While male and female wages were clearly not independent, as they would be if there was complete occupational segregation, the relationship may have been weaker than it should have been in a perfectly competitive market. Women might have been at a disadvantage in their competition with men if employers favored men and used women as

---

[37] Assume that the parish-specific component of the wage is additive, and is the same in both seasons. The observed male summer wage is $W_{ms} = w_{ms} + \Delta i$, where Δi is specific to parish i. Then the difference $W_{ms} - W_{mw} = (w_{ms} + \Delta) - (w_{mw} + \Delta) = w_{ms} - w_{mw}$.

Table 4.14. *Correlation of seasonal wage differences: 1833*

	Summer–winter	Harvest–summer
A. Correlations		
Women's wage: strict definition		
Correlation	0.216**	0.229*
N	305	71
P-level	0.000	0.054
95% confidence interval	(0.11, 0.32)	(−0.005, 0.44)
Women's wage: loose definition		
Correlation	0.283**	0.296**
N	483	102
P-level	0.000	0.003
95% confidence interval	(0.20, 0.36)	(0.11, 0.46)
B. Rank correlations		
Women's wage: strict definition		
Correlation	0.259**	0.228*
N	305	71
P-level	0.000	0.056
95% confidence interval	(0.15, 0.36)	(−0.006, 0.44)
Women's wage: loose definition		
Correlation	0.337**	0.300**
N	483	102
P-level	0.000	0.002
95% confidence interval	(0.26, 0.41)	(0.11, 0.47)

Standard errors in parentheses.
* = *significantly different from zero at the 10% level*
** = *significantly different from zero at the 5% level*
Source: BPP 1834 (44) XXX.

marginal workers. Some of the survey responses suggested that women were not hired if men were unemployed. This subordination of women's employment is suggested by such statements as, "Women ... have but little other work [besides harvest], there are so many Men and Lads out of employ,"[38] and "In consequence of the number of male hands, Females are generally unemployed."[39] I look for this relationship in the data by including in the regression male unemployment, as reported in response to question 6: "Number of laborers generally out of employment, and how maintained in Summer and Winter?" The response to this question is divided by the answer to question 5 – "Number of Agricultural laborers in your parish?" – to produce an estimate of the unemployment rate. Table 4.16 presents regressions including this variable. I find that

[38] BPP 1834 (44) XXX, Bramshaw, Southampton, p. 423
[39] BPP 1834 (44) XXX, Rotherfield, Sussex, p. 529 .

Table 4.15. *Difference-of-log regressions: 1833 (dependent variable = difference of log women's wages)*

	Summer–winter	Harvest–summer
A. Women's wage: strict definition		
Constant	0.091**	0.501**
	(0.015)	(0.021)
Men's log wage difference	0.229**	−0.109
	(0.088)	(0.112)
R^2	0.037	0.003
N	305	351
B. Women's wage: loose definition		
Constant	0.107**	0.496**
	(0.014)	(0.016)
Men's log wage difference	0.437**	−0.095
	(0.079)	(0.082)
R^2	0.060	0.002
N	483	573

All wages are in logs. Standard errors in parentheses.
* = *significantly different from zero at the 10% level*
** = *significantly different from zero at the 5% level*
Source: BPP 1834 (44) XXX.

Table 4.16. *The effect of unemployment: 1833 (dependent variable = women's wage)*

	Summer	Winter
Constant	−0.131	−0.321
	(0.176)	(0.303)
Men's wage	0.642**	0.664**
	(0.071)	(0.129)
Unemployment rate	−0.769**	−0.248
	(0.159)	(0.164)
R^2	0.184	0.091
N	548	306

Standard errors in parentheses.
All wages are in logs. The loose definition is used for the women's wage.
* = *significantly different from zero at the 10% level*
** = *significantly different from zero at the 5% level*
Source: BPP 1834 (44) XXX.

Table 4.17. *Correlations with boys' wages: 1833*

	Summer	Winter	Harvest	Summer–winter	Harvest–summer
Women's wage, strict definition					
Correlation	0.303**	0.541**	0.642**	0.338**	0.477**
N	148	64	45	59	38
P-level	0.000	0.000	0.000	0.009	0.003
95% confidence interval	(0.15, 0.44)	(0.34, 0.69)	(0.43, 0.79)	(0.09, 0.55)	(0.19, 0.69)
Men's wage					
Correlation	0.295**	0.378**	0.434*	0.264**	0.579**
N	198	142	20	128	16
P-level	0.000	0.000	0.055	0.003	0.019
95% confidence interval	(0.20, 0.42)	(0.23, 0.51)	(−0.01, 0.74)	(0.09, 0.42)	(0.012, 0.84)

Standard errors in parentheses.
* = *significantly different from zero at the 10% level*
** = *significantly different from zero at the 5% level*
Source: BPP 1834 (44) XXX.

the unemployment rate reduced women's summer wages, which suggests that the demand for women workers went down when men were unemployed. Such a relationship could be the result of gender discrimination, or of incentives created by the poor law to employ male workers.[40] However, the negative effect of unemployment may also simply reflect the fact that male wages were somewhat sticky, and thus do not fully capture demand conditions in a region. If men were unemployed, that suggests that the market-clearing male wage would be lower than the prevailing market wage.[41] If the unemployment rate is an indicator of weak labor demand, then we would expect it to reduce women's wages.

This data set also includes wages of boys, which can be used for comparison. Examining correlations with boys' wages may help us determine if the correlation of men's and women's wages is large or small. Table 4.17 shows that the correlation between women's wages and boys' wages is 0.30 in the summer and 0.54 in the winter, using the strict definition of women's wages. The correlation between men's wages and boys' wage is 0.30 in the summer and 0.38 in the winter.

[40] On the incentives created by the poor law system, see George Boyer, *An Economic History of the English Poor Law, 1750–1850* (Cambridge: Cambridge University Press, 1990).

[41] Failure of male wages to fall to the market-clearing level may be explained either by the incentives of the poor law system, or by efficiency wage models. For a survey of firms' reasons for not lowering wages in a contemporary labor market, see Carl Campbell and Kunal Kamlani, "The Reasons for Wage Rigidity: Evidence from a Survey of Firms," *Quarterly Journal of Economics* 112 (1997), pp. 759–89.

Table 4.18. *Wages in England and Wales: 1860–1 (shillings per week)*

		Mean	SD	Min.	Max.	N
Men	1860:III	12.39	2.29	8.50	20.50	101
	1860:IV	11.39	1.67	8.50	15.50	101
	1861:I	11.48	1.92	6.33	18.50	100
	1861:II	11.95	2.23	6.67	20.25	101
Women	1860:III	5.38	1.76	2.25	11.25	98
	1860:IV	4.70	1.56	1.00	10.00	90
	1861:I	4.46	1.41	1.00	11.00	87
	1861:II	5.00	1.39	2.75	9.50	96
Children under 16	1860:III	4.14	1.33	2.00	8.00	94
	1860:IV	3.60	1.08	1.50	7.00	92
	1861:I	3.67	1.12	1.50	7.50	87
	1861:II	3.79	1.04	1.50	6.50	92

Source: BPP 1861 (14) L.

These correlations are similar to the correlations between men's and women's wages, and are also significantly positive. Women seem to have been substitutable with men to the same extent that boys were.

For unskilled wages in 1833, I find a significantly positive correlation between men's wages and women's wages that is robust. The simple correlations seem to contain some location-specific effects, and correcting for these reduces the strength of the correlation. However, even after correcting for fixed effects, there is still evidence that men and women competed in the same labor market. The correlations were as strong in 1833 as correlations in 1770, so I find no evidence that the unskilled labor market became more segregated between 1770 and 1833.

C.   1860

Data from the middle of the nineteenth century are provided by a wage survey contained in the 1861 parliamentary returns. This survey covers only agricultural wages and is smaller in size than the 1833 survey. Fortunately, this data set contains different wages over the season, allowing for a fixed-effect estimation. The survey also contains information on in-kind payments. As in the 1833 data, internal evidence is used to estimate the value of these in-kind payments where the money value is not specifically given.

Table 4.18 presents the descriptive statistics for this data set. Wages are given by quarter, so that "Wages for the quarter ending Michaelmas, 1860" are recorded as wages for 1860:III, and similarly for the other

Table 4.19. *Correlations of men's and women's wages: 1860–1*

	1860:III	1860:IV	1861:I	1861:II
Men & women				
Correlation	0.740**	0.508**	0.619**	0.694**
N	98	90	87	96
P-level	0.000	0.000	0.000	0.000
95% confidence interval	(0.63, 0.82)	(0.34, 0.65)	(0.47, 0.73)	(0.57, 0.79)
Men & children				
Correlation	0.503**	0.369**	0.552**	0.490**
N	94	92	87	92
P-level	0.000	0.000	0.000	0.000
95% confidence interval	(0.33, 0.64)	(0.18, 0.53)	(0.39, 0.68)	(0.32, 0.63)
Women & children				
Correlation	0.642**	0.474**	0.382**	0.551**
N	91	83	80	89
P-level	0.000	0.000	0.001	0.000
95% confidence interval	(0.50, 0.75)	(0.29, 0.64)	(0.19, 0.55)	(0.39, 0.68)

Standard errors in parentheses.
* = *significantly different from zero at the 10% level*
** = *significantly different from zero at the 5% level*
Source: BPP 1861 (14) L.

quarters. The female–male wage ratios are not surprising: 0.43 for 1860: III, 0.41 for 1860:IV, 0.39 for 1861:I, and 0.42 for 1861:II. Wages are lowest in the first and fourth quarters (winter), and highest in the third quarter, which includes harvest.

The simple correlations are presented in Table 4.19. The correlation of men's and women's wages is higher than in the previous two data sets, ranging from 0.51 to 0.74, and all the correlations are significantly positive. Correlations with children's wages are similar to the correlations of men's and women's wages, but somewhat lower. This suggests that the women were at least as good a substitute as children for men's labor. Table 4.20 shows the male wage elasticities of female wages. Women's wages appear to be very responsive to men's wages; the elasticities in Table 4.20 are higher than in previous data sets, and in three of the four quarters exceed one. Do the higher correlations result from larger location-specific effects? Table 4.21 presents correlations of wage differences, to correct for location-specific effects. The correlations drop substantially compared to the correlations in Table 4.19, suggesting that some of the correlation was due to location-specific effects. However, even correcting for fixed effects, the correlations remain generally higher

Table 4.20. *Log-log regressions: 1860–1 (dependent variable = women's wage)*

	1860:III	1860:IV	1861:I	1861:II
Constant	−1.427**	−1.562**	−1.605**	−0.691**
	(0.307)	(0.622)	(0.540)	(0.277)
Men's wage	1.222**	1.262**	1.259**	0.919**
	(0.122)	(0.257)	(0.223)	(0.112)
R^2	0.509	0.215	0.273	0.418
N	98	90	87	96

All wages in logs. Standard errors in parentheses.
* = *significantly different from zero at the 10% level*
** = *significantly different from zero at the 5% level*
Source: BPP 1861 (14) L.

Table 4.21. *Correlations of wage differences: 1860–1*

	1860:III–1860:IV	1860:III–1861:I	1860:III–1861:II	1861:II–1860:IV
Men–women				
Correlation	0.489**	0.380**	0.436**	0.273**
N	89	86	96	88
P-level	0.000	0.000	0.000	0.010
95% confidence interval	(0.31, 0.63)	(0.18, 0.55)	(0.26, 0.59)	(0.07, 0.46)
Men–children				
Correlation	0.370**	0.363**	0.184*	0.262**
N	89	84	89	87
P-level	0.000	0.001	0.084	0.014
95% confidence interval	(0.18, 0.54)	(0.16, 0.54)	(−0.03, 0.38)	(0.05, 0.45)
Women–children				
Correlation	0.532**	0.374**	0.545**	0.446**
N	79	76	86	79
P-level	0.000	0.001	0.000	0.000
95% confidence interval	(0.35, 0.70)	(0.16, 0.55)	(0.38, 0.68)	(0.25, 0.61)

Standard errors in parentheses.
* = *significantly different from zero at the 10% level*
** = *significantly different from zero at the 5% level*
Source: BPP 1861 (14) L.

than those in Table 4.8 or Table 4.11. Seasonal variation in female wages was not as responsive to seasonal variation in male wages as female wage levels were to male wage levels, but there was still a significant relationship. The elasticities in Table 4.22 are below one, ranging from 0.33 to 0.86. However, these elasticities are still relatively high

Table 4.22. *Difference-of-log regressions: 1860–1 (dependent variable = difference of the log of women's wages)*

	1860:III– 1860:IV	1860:III– 1861:I	1860:III– 1861:II	1861:II– 1860:IV
Constant	0.064*	0.127**	0.037	0.059
	(0.038)	(0.035)	(0.024)	(0.039)
Difference of	0.858**	0.586**	0.481**	0.328
men's wages	(0.234)	(0.228)	(0.152)	(0.254)
R²	0.134	0.073	0.096	0.019
N	89	86	96	88

All wages are in logs. Standard errors in parentheses.
* = *significantly different from zero at the 10% level*
** = *significantly different from zero at the 5% level*
Source: BPP 1861 (14) L.

compared to those in the 1770 and 1833 data. The relationship between male and female wages certainly did not erode over the course of the Industrial Revolution; if anything it seems to be stronger in 1860 than it was earlier. The evidence does not suggest that occupational segregation constraints appeared in the agricultural labor market during the course of the Industrial Revolution.

D.   France in 1839

I have shown that there definitely was a positive correlation between male and female agricultural wages in England. However, it is more difficult to say whether the relationship should be considered strong or weak. I have compared correlations over time, and I have compared the correlations with children's wages to those between male and female adults, to get some idea of whether the correlations were large. Another place to turn for comparison wages is another country. How did the English labor market compare to the labor market in other countries? Evidence on wages in France helps to put the English results in context.

The French wage data I will use come from a British parliamentary report. The investigator, J. C. Symons, corresponded with government officials in France, who sent him wage returns. The wages seem to be based on correspondence with employers in France.[42] Table 4.23 presents descriptive statistics for these wage data. The wage ratio is 0.65,

---

[42] Along with the list of agricultural wages, there are transcripts of letters from French employers stating wages paid. BPP 1839 (159) XLII, pp. 137–49.

Table 4.23. *Descriptive statistics: French agricultural day-laborers in 1839*

	Mean	SD	Min.	Max.	N
Male wage	0.992	0.28	0.33	1.63	63
Female wage	0.646	0.20	0.23	0.97	63

Source: BPP 1839 (159) XLII, pp. 147–9.

Table 4.24. *French agricultural day-laborers: 1839*

	Wages	Residuals§
Correlation	0.719	0.682
N	63	63
95% confidence interval	(0.573, 0.821)	(0.523, 0.795)
Regressions (dependent variable = log female wage)		
Constant	–0.447**	–0.000
	(0.029)	(0.027)
Log male wage	0.926**	1.030**
	(0.091)	(0.114)
R^2	0.629	0.571
N	63	63

Standard errors in parentheses.
§ Residuals from regressions of each wage on dummies for province.
* = *significantly different from zero at the 10% level*
** = *significantly different from zero at the 5% level*
Source: BPP 1839 (159) XLII, pp. 147–9.

higher than in any of the measured ratios in English agriculture, but still well within the range of gender wage ratios presented in Table 2.1. Table 4.24 presents wage correlations and regressions. The wage correlation is high – comparable to the correlations in the 1860 English data. Unfortunately, seasonal wages are not given, so I cannot correct for fixed effects. The best I can do is to correct for region-specific effects. The second column shows the correlation of wage residuals, after correcting for variation in wages across provinces. I first regress wages on dummies for eight provinces, and then take the correlations of the residuals. The correlation is still high, so it is possible that French agricultural labor markets were more integrated by gender than English agricultural labor markets. It remains possible, though, that the high elasticities measured in France reflect my failure to correct for location-specific effects.

Conclusion

I have presented wage correlations from a variety of data sets. The results consistently indicate a positive correlation between male and female wages, although the correlations are in many cases small. Overall, the evidence suggests that men and women did compete in the same labor market. Most importantly, the results suggest that the integrated labor market which we found in 1770 persisted throughout the whole Industrial Revolution period. The correlations in 1860 were even stronger than in 1770. French agricultural labor markets were also integrated by gender, and may have been more integrated than English labor markets.

This chapter has examined agricultural labor markets, and has shown that men and women were considered substitutable by employers, suggesting that employment was not determined by rigid gender roles. I have tested only agricultural labor markets and, while I could expect to find the same results in competitive portions of the labor market, there were some sections of the labor market where men and women were clearly not substitutable because monopolization allowed men to construct barriers preventing women from entering the occupation. Chapters 5 and 6 discuss those portions of the labor market.

The pressure of male trade unions appears to be largely responsible for that crowding of women into a comparatively few occupations, which is universally recognized as a main factor in the depression of their wages.
Edgeworth, 1922[1]

Having presented models of market-based occupational sorting, and argued that in some portions of the labor market gender differences in occupations and wages were the results of differences in strength, this chapter turns to segments of the labor market where discriminatory barriers, rather than comparative advantage, kept women out of the best-paid occupations. I begin by examining cases where the predictions of the sorting models do not hold, and then move on to examine possible causes of the discriminatory barriers. I find that barriers were erected where men could use their market power to reduce competition in order to improve their own labor market outcomes. In this case occupational sorting benefited men and made women worse off, but increased competition would have reduced occupational sorting. The conclusions of this chapter thus support my general claims that the gender division of labor was driven by economic motivations, and that women benefited from competition.

I.   Occupational sorting not based on strength

While the absence of women from some occupations can be explained by the strength requirements of the occupation, in many cases women were absent from occupations not requiring strength, suggesting that other forces must have been at work. Table 5.1 shows the prevalence of women in certain occupations in the 1841 census. Section A of Table 5.1 shows the number of men and women in lower-skill wage-labor occupations. In section B I have selected some white-collar, craft, and

---

[1] F. Y. Edgeworth, "Equal Pay to Men and Women for Equal Work," *Economic Journal* 32 (1922), p. 439.

Table 5.1. *The percentage of women in selected occupations: the 1841 census (Great Britain, persons 20 and over)*

Occupation	Men	Women	Percent women
A. Wage labor			
Agricultural laborer	874,294	41,879	4.6
Laborer	333,786	12,474	3.6
Domestic servant	144,072	562,392	79.6
Textile manufacture[a]	268,557	177,251	39.8
B. Craft and professional			
No strength required			
Accountant	4684	0	0.0
Agent, factor	5365	61	1.1
Artist	3805	277	6.8
Attorney	13,918	0	0.0
Auctioneer, appraiser	3156	37	1.2
Banker	1791	8	0.4
Broker	2869	464	13.9
Clergyman, minister	23,496	0	0.0
Clerk	46,368	152	0.3
Dressmaker, milliner	436	84,064	99.5
Civil servant	15,853	617	3.7
Musician	3223	216	6.3
Pastry cook, confectioner	4241	1808	29.9
Tailor and breeches-maker	100,030	5339	5.1
Teacher	25,207	31,557	55.6
Strength required			
Anchor-smith and chain-maker	1384	54	3.8
Blacksmith	80,543	512	0.6
Boat builder	24,149	142	0.6
Brass founder	4776	39	0.8
Brazier	5540	39	0.7
Bricklayer	36,049	107	0.3
Carpenter, joiner	141,750	452	0.3
Currier	9273	155	1.6
Engine and machine maker	5761	58	1.0
Mason, pavior	72,934	184	0.3
Saddler	12,962	309	2.3
Sawyer	27,929	20	0.1
Wheelwright	22,537	147	0.6
Total employed in Britain	4,279,004	1,246,585	22.6

a Cotton manufacturer, flax and linen manufacturer, silk manufacturer, weaver (unspecified), woollen and cloth manufacturer, and worsted manufacturer.
Note: Total employed does not match Table 1.1 because these totals include only persons over 20.
Source: BPP 1844 (587) XXVII.

Table 5.2. *Occupational sorting in skilled occupations: Manchester, 1846*

Occupation	Male	Female	Unknown	Percent female
Not requiring strength				
Accountant	36	0	7	0.0
Agent	362	1	82	0.3
Attorney	168	1	59	0.6
Auctioneer and appraiser	45	0	3	0.0
Confectioner	59	28	7	32.2
Draper, mercer	167	21	25	11.2
Grocer and tea dealer	252	21	32	7.7
Hairdresser	116	0	2	0.0
Hosier, haberdasher	180	67	28	27.1
Librarian	27	13	0	32.5
Milliner, dressmaker	12	245	18	95.3
Pawnbroker	142	23	16	13.9
Publican	496	91	42	15.5
Schoolmaster/mistress	232	181	17	43.8
Shopkeeper	776	128	4	14.2
Tailor	239	1	18	0.4
These 16 occupations	3309	821	360	19.9
Requiring strength				
Blacksmith and farrier	84	6	6	6.7
Brazier and coppersmith	116	8	33	6.5
Currier	96	8	4	7.7
Iron founder	29	0	16	0.0
Joiner and builder	187	0	33	0.0
Machine maker	117	5	33	4.1
Millwright	25	0	14	0.0
Saddler	34	1	0	2.9
Slater	14	1	0	6.7
Stone and marble mason	40	0	4	0.0
These 10 occupations	742	29	143	3.8

Source: Slater's National Commercial Directory of Ireland, 1846.

professional occupations that I think would not require strength, and some I think would require much strength. Differences in strength explain some of the occupational sorting; women were generally less likely to work in occupations requiring strength. They were more likely to work as domestic servants than as agricultural laborers. Few women worked as blacksmiths, masons, or sawyers. The same pattern can be seen in Table 5.2, which presents employment by sex from the 1846 commercial directory for Manchester. While business owners in the strength-intensive trades selected were only 4 percent female, owners in

Table 5.3 *The gender division of labor in staymaking*

Trade	Men	Women	Unknown	Percent women
Sheffield, 1774	3	0	0	0.0
Manchester, 1788	10	2	2	16.7
Coventry, 1791	5	0	0	0.0
Manchester, 1824–5	9	2	1	18.2
Coventry, 1835	3	3	0	50.0
Manchester, 1846	14	11	0	44.0
Birmingham, 1850	6	59	6	90.8
Derby, 1850	4	12	0	75.0
Coventry, 1892	0	3	0	100.0

Sources: Sketchley's Sheffield Directory, 1774; Lewis's Manchester Directory for 1788; The Universal British Directory, 1791; Pigot and Dean's Directory for Manchester, 1825; Pigot & Co.'s National Commercial Directory, 1835; Slater's National Commercial Directory of Ireland, 1846; Slater's Royal National and Commercial Directory, 1850.

the selected trades not requiring strength were 20 percent female. Gender differences in strength had some impact on what trades women were engaged in.

Changes in the amount of strength required may explain the change in the prevalence of women in staymaking. In the eighteenth century, staymakers were primarily male. Among the married couples Peter Earle reports from London in 1695 to 1725 there are five male and two female staymakers, and both the females had husbands who were staymakers.[2] In Sheffield in 1774, and in Coventry in 1791, all of the staymakers were male (see Table 5.3). Over the course of the Industrial Revolution, women became more common in the trade, and by the middle of the nineteenth century most staymakers were women. In the 1841 census 86 percent of staymakers were female.[3] This shift seems to have resulted from a change in how stays were constructed. In the first half of the eighteenth century, only men made stays because it required strength. In 1747, R. Campbell commented on the prevalence of men in staymaking:

I am surprised the Ladies have not found out a Way to employ Women Stay-Makers rather than trust our Sex with what should be kept as inviolably as Free-Masonry; But the Work is too hard for Women, it requires more Strength than they are capable of, to raise Walls of Defence about a Lady's Shape... After the Stays are stitched, and the Bone cut into thin Slices of equal Breadths and the

---

[2] Earle, "The Female Labor Market in London," pp. 348–52.

[3] BPP 1844 (587) XXVII. The summary tables for male occupations from the 1851 census do not list staymaker as a separate category.

proper Lengths, it is thrust in between the Rows of Stitching: This requires a good deal of Strength.[4]

In this passage Campbell both expresses the ideology which led to gender segregation in the garment trades and explains why staymaking was the exception. In staymaking, the strength requirement was great enough to overcome the fear of physical intimacy between the sexes, and in the eighteenth century most staymakers were men. However, in the later eighteenth century the work became easier. Lane notes that "After the mid-eighteenth century, stays were lighter, using less whalebone, and the craft came within a woman's capabilities."[5] Once staymaking no longer required the strength of a man, women took over the trade. Thus a dramatic change in the gender division of labor seems to have been the result of changes in the amount of strength required.

Strength requirements, however, are not sufficient to explain the sorting. Women did not have equal access to all occupations where strength was unnecessary. Among the occupations in Table 5.1 not requiring strength, women are clearly sorted into a few occupations. Nearly all the dress-makers and milliners were women, and about half of the teachers, but other occupations were dominated by men. Many of the occupations requiring no strength, such as accountant, attorney, and clerk, had even fewer women than occupations such as blacksmith and brass founder, which is not consistent with physical comparative advantage. The absence of women from white-collar occupations such as law cannot be explained by physical strength and must have been the result of exclusion. The clearest gender division is in the garment trades; women were dressmakers but not tailors, though the two occupations are very similar. Wages were much lower in dressmaking or millinery than in tailoring, suggesting that women were not free to choose the more lucrative trade.[6] The same occupational patterns are evident in the commercial directories. Table 5.2 shows that, while women are in general less likely to appear in occupations requiring strength, there were many occupations requiring no strength that had no women at all, or even fewer women than the blacksmith trade. Manchester had no female accountants, auctioneers, or hairdressers. Strength certainly does not explain all the occupational sorting.

Human capital, while it is clearly important in occupational choice, is not sufficient to explain the sorting either. Even when they had similar

---

[4] R. Campbell, *The London Tradesman* (New York: Augustus M. Kelley, [1747] 1969), pp. 224–5.
[5] Lane, *Apprenticeship in England*, p. 123.
[6] In 1800 journeywomen milliners earned 6s. a week in Colchester, while journeymen tailors in London earned 27s. a week. Davidoff and Hall, *Family Fortunes*, p. 302, and BPP 1840 (43) XXIII, p. 582.

levels of human capital, men and women worked in different occupations. Women often did invest in human capital, but these women generally ended up in teaching or dressmaking. Though dressmaking and tailoring required similar human capital investments, the gender segregation between the two trades was almost complete. In 1788 all the tailors in Manchester were male, and all the dressmakers were female.[7] In 1846 only one out of 240 tailors was female, and only 12 out of 257 milliners and dressmakers were male.[8] The large number of women who entered the dressmaking trades, whose apprenticeship fees were substantial,[9] is evidence that many were willing to invest in human capital. However, wages in dressmaking were low compared to wages in tailoring, suggesting that the concentration of women in dressmaking was due to exclusion rather than choice.

Choice is not a sufficient explanation for the absence of women from certain skilled trades, because some women attempted to work in skilled trades but were rebuffed by men who excluded them from the occupations. Tailors in London went on strike to prevent women from entering their trade, as did mule-spinners in Glasgow.[10] The hatters of Stockport agreed to strike against any employer who hired women.[11] The opposition of male workers to the employment of women will be examined later in this chapter. For now it is sufficient to note that women who wished to work in certain skilled trades were prevented from doing so. The women who were affected resented the constraint. In a letter to *The Pioneer* in 1834, a woman criticized the tailors' union, which was engaged in a strike to keep women out of the tailoring trade:

Surely the men might think of a better method of benefiting themselves than that of driving so many industrious women out of employment. Surely, while they loudly complain of oppression, they will not turn oppressors themselves. Surely they will not give their enemies cause to say, when a woman and her offspring are seen begging in the streets, – This is the work of union.[12]

[7] *Lewis's Manchester Directory for 1788.*
[8] These calculations ignore eighteen tailors and eighteen milliners and dressmakers whose gender could not be determined. *Slater's National Commercial Directory of Ireland*, 1846; *Slater's Royal National and Commercial Directory*, 1850.
[9] Neff, *Victorian Working Women*, p. 117, quotes premiums of £40 to £60 for dressmaking in the mid-nineteenth century, and Sally Alexander, *Women's Work in Nineteenth-Century London: A Study of the Years 1820–1850* (London: Journeyman Press, 1983), p. 34, quotes premiums of £30 to £50.
[10] Barbara Taylor, *Eve and the New Jerusalem: Socialism and Feminism in the Nineteenth Century* (New York: Pantheon Books, 1983), ch. 4, and BPP 1824 (51) V, p. 525.
[11] A. Aspinall, *The Early English Trade Unions: Documents from the Home Office Papers in the Public Record Office* (London: Batchworth Press, 1949), p. 107.
[12] *The Pioneer*, March 19, 1834, quoted in Taylor, *Eve and the New Jerusalem*, p. 108.

Women demonstrated a desire to work, but they were not allowed to enter many trades. Thus the low numbers of women in these occupations are partially due to occupational segregation constraints. In the skilled labor market, in contrast to the unskilled labor market, gender discrimination was an important part of the story.

Many factors contributed to the lower numbers of women in most of the skilled craft, white-collar, and professional occupations. First, the fact that many women workers were unrecorded means that their measured participation is lower than their actual participation. Second, women may have chosen not to invest in the human capital necessary for skilled work because they expected to spend less time in the labor force. This choice was the indirect result of the assignment of women to household tasks, which may be the result of either comparative advantage or gender discrimination within the family. Third, women in higher social classes may have felt more social pressure to stay out of the labor force, resulting in fewer women with the means to enter business willing to do so. Fourth, women may simply have been excluded from certain occupations, and not permitted entry when they tried to enter skilled occupations. While all of these factors had some influence on the relative absence of women from high-paid occupations, in this chapter I will focus mainly on the fourth, the direct method of exclusion. I do acknowledge, though, that the other factors may have played an important role. Evidence of explicit barriers is not hard to find, and in light of such evidence we can conclude that gender discrimination reduced the number of women in skilled and professional occupations.

Having established that the sorting models presented in Chapter 3 do not fully explain the gender division of labor for skilled craft, white-collar, and professional occupations, I turn to examining the possible sources of the occupational barriers that prevented women from working in occupations where they could have been productive. I divide the discussion of barriers to entry into two parts: occupational barriers for employees in skilled crafts, and occupational barriers in business and professional occupations. This chapter examines the barriers faced by employees, and the following chapter examines the barriers faced by women in self-employment.

II. Sources of occupational barriers among employees

We have seen, in Chapter 3, that in some parts of the labor market, economic forces operated freely and the division of labor between the sexes was not the result of discriminatory barriers. In other occupations, there clearly were barriers keeping women out, even women who expressed a desire to work in those occupations. What made these segments of the labor market different? This section will argue that exclusionary barriers appeared in less competitive parts of the labor market, where control of an important skill allowed the workers in that occupation to limit competition. Where work was unskilled, or the skills needed were easily learned, competitive markets ensured that workers were allocated according to their comparative advantage.

Some of the potential sources of exclusion were not, in fact, important in creating occupational segregation. I argue in this section that government regulations, guilds, and employers, while they may have occasionally contributed to the exclusion of women, were not important sources of occupational barriers. None of these factors was capable of explaining a substantial amount of occupational segregation. By contrast, the actions of employee organizations such as unions explain a great deal of occupational segregation. Male workers actively fought to exclude women from their occupations, and often won. The role of unions in limiting women's employment opportunities explains why unskilled occupations were less likely to have barriers to women's employment, and why skilled occupations were more likely to have such barriers. Women were not excluded from unskilled occupations because unions had no power in those occupations. Only in skilled occupations, where the unions had the power to enforce their desires, could the exclusionary desires of the male workers overrule the desire of employers to hire women. An important part of this explanation is the claim that unions were successful in skilled occupations, but not in unskilled occupations. To establish this fact, I will turn to the historical record and examine unions in different occupations. Once I have shown that unions were not successful in unskilled occupations, and that unions were the most important source of exclusion, I can explain why women were not excluded from unskilled occupations.

A.   Government regulation

While government regulation has been blamed for gender segregation,[13] these laws were not an important source of occupational segregation during the Industrial Revolution. Government restrictions on women's employment only appeared at the very end of the time period, and thus

---

[13] Honeyman and Goodman, "Women's Work, Gender Conflict," p. 622, claim that protective legislation "was designed to reinforce the position of women as wives and mothers" and "provided the capitalist with the opportunity to remove women from the factory into the more economical environment of the sweatshop."

are a characteristic of the Victorian era, but not of the Industrial Revolution. Even when they were in place, these laws had relatively little effect on women's employment.

Laws limiting women's work did not appear until the 1840s. The first act restricting women's employment was the Mines and Collieries Act of 1842, which prohibited women from working underground in collieries.[14] This was the only act to completely exclude women from an occupation. The first factory act to apply to adult women was the Bill of 1844, which limited their hours of work to twelve.[15] Women's hours were further limited to ten in 1847. Thus government regulation cannot be blamed for any occupational segregation that occurred before 1842.

Also, we must not assume that government regulations were always effective. To determine the effect of laws restricting women's employment we must look at their actual effect, rather than just their wording or intent. The 1842 Mines Act, which outlawed the employment of women underground, seems to have reduced the opportunities for women to work in mines, but did not completely exclude women. The 1851 census reports 2535 female coal miners, a slight increase from the 2350 reported in the 1841 census. During the same period, though, the number of male coal miners increased 58 percent, so the law seems to have slowed the growth of female employment in coal mining.[16] However, it does not seem to have completely prevented women from working in mines. The 1842 law did not prevent women from working above ground, so the 2535 female coal miners reported in 1851 may have been working legally, but there is other evidence that the law was not always well enforced. Angela John finds that women continued to work underground, some of them dressing as men.[17] In some cases, the existence of illegal women workers was revealed only when they died in mine accidents.[18] The government provided only one commissioner for the enforcement of this law, and the fine for an offense was too low to be a serious deterrent (£10 maximum).[19] In 1845 the inspector estimated that 200 women were working illegally in Wigan. One employer even

---

[14] 5 & 6 Vict. c. 99. Laws regulating child labor began earlier, in 1802.
[15] B. L. Hutchins and A. Harrison, *A History of Factory Legislation* (Westminster: P. S. King & Son, 1903), ch. 4.
[16] BPP 1844 (587) XXVII and 1852–3 (1691) LXXXVIII.
[17] Angela V. John, *By the Sweat of their Brow: Women Workers at Victorian Coal Mines* (London: Croom Helm, 1980), pp. 55–8, and "Colliery Legislation and Its Consequences: 1842 and the Women Miners of Lancashire," *Bulletin of the John Rylands Library* 61 (1978), pp. 78–114.
[18] For example, Hannah Hatharington was killed in February 1845 when a mine roof fell. *Ibid.*, p. 99.
[19] *Ibid.*, p. 79.

complained that some men refused to work for him because he would not employ their wives and daughters.[20] The 1842 law seems to have reduced the demand for female mine workers without completely eliminating their use. Petitions from workers asking parliament to repeal the prohibition suggest that the workers felt they were harmed, and at least one woman noted that she earned lower wages after the law.[21]

The factory acts limiting the hours of employment of women and children were also widely evaded. The early acts applied only to children and were not very effective. By the time women were included in the factory acts in the 1840s, enforcement had been improved somewhat. Factory inspectors were appointed in 1831. Still, the acts of 1844 and 1847, which were the first to limit women's hours of employment, were difficult to enforce. Employers worked women and children on shifts, while the men worked longer hours, and "under such a system the Ten Hours Act was completely nullified, and it was impossible for the inspectors to detect overtime employment."[22] If the factory was operated more than ten hours, it was difficult to monitor whether any women and children worked more than ten hours. One factory inspector complained that if the factories used shift work, "no practical system of inspection could prevent extensive fraudulent overworking."[23] The laws limiting women's employment were not effective until 1850, when parliament limited the number of hours the factory machinery could run.

Even when they were enforced, factory acts did not prohibit women from working, but simply limited the number of hours they could work and thus made them less useful to the employer than male workers. Employers *might* have chosen to employ only men, who could work longer hours, but they did not do so. Employers continued to employ women, and the percentage of women employed in factories even rose slightly between 1838 and 1856, from 55 to 57 percent of the workforce.[24] This increase may have been less than what would have occurred in the absence of the law, but the law clearly did not lead to reductions in female factory employment. The hours limitation may still have harmed women if it prevented them from taking the more highly paid factory jobs. Rose claims that the effect of the acts was to keep women out of certain higher-wage jobs: "although women and men both

---

[20] *Ibid.*, p. 104.
[21] This woman claimed that she earned 3s. less per week as a result of the law. *Ibid.*, p. 10.
[22] Hutchins and Harrison, *A History of Factory Legislation*, p. 102.
[23] BPP 1849, XXII, p. 135, quoted in *ibid.*, p. 102.
[24] Women over 13 were 55.2 percent of the factory labor force in 1838, 55.9 percent in 1850, and 57.0 percent in 1856. *Ibid.*, ch. 6.

worked as cotton weavers and earned equal piece rates, legally men, and men only, could clean their machines after working hours, so some men could and did earn higher weekly wages than women."[25] So it is possible that hours regulations hurt women's opportunities.

While government regulations had some marginal impact on women's employment opportunities, such effects were limited to a few industries (mining and textile factories). When in place, laws limiting women's employment did not prevent the use of women workers. More importantly, government regulations cannot have been an important source of occupational barriers during the Industrial Revolution because the regulations appeared too late. None of the laws passed before 1842 applied to adult women. We must look elsewhere for the causes of occupational segregation.

B.   Gender ideology

During the nineteenth century we see the rise of a number of different ideologies which may have influenced women's opportunities. The family wage ideal suggested that the male head should earn a wage high enough to support his whole family, without his wife or children working to contribute to the family's income.[26] This idea was new to the nineteenth century; earlier generations expected women and children to contribute.[27] By the late nineteenth century, the ideal of the family wage was strong enough that men felt a loss of status if their wives worked. The nineteenth century also saw the rise of domestic ideology, which assumed that a woman's place was in the home.[28] While households in earlier generations often included servants or apprentices, the household was increasingly restricted to the nuclear family (even apprentices no longer lived "in"), and the home was increasingly seen as a retreat from the world. The woman's role was to be the "angel of the house." The woman's sphere of influence, the home and family, was separate from the man's sphere of influence, which included the outside world.[29]

---

[25] Rose, *Limited Livelihoods*, p. 74.
[26] See Hilary Land, "The Family Wage," *Feminist Review* 6 (1980), pp. 55–77; Rose, "Gender at Work"; and Wally Seccombe, "Patriarchy Stabilized: The Construction of the Male Breadwinner Wage Norm in Nineteenth-Century Britain," *Social History* 11 (1986), pp. 53–76.
[27] Pinchbeck, *Women Workers*, pp. 1–2.
[28] See Joan Scott and Louise Tilly, "Women's Work and the Family in Nineteenth-Century Europe," *Comparative Studies in Society and History* 17 (1975), pp. 36–64.
[29] See Roberts, *Women's Work, 1840–1940*, pp. 4–5; Simonton, *European Women's Work*, pp. 87–90.

Another attitude that may have influenced women's work opportunities was concern about sexual morality. Parliamentary reports of the early nineteenth century show great concern with sexual purity and the moral results of mixing men and women. The 1843 parliamentary report on *Women and Children in Agriculture* shows that the clergy and gentry were greatly concerned with the moral effects of crowded cottages and single men and women working together. For example, parliamentary investigator Alfred Austin worried that:

The sleeping of boys and girls, and young men and young women, in the same room, in beds almost touching one another, must have the effect of breaking down the great barriers between the sexes, – the sense of modesty and decency on the part of women, and respect for the other sex on the part of the men. The consequences of the want of proper accommodation for sleeping in the cottages are seen in the early licentiousness of the rural districts.[30]

Humphries has suggested that concerns about the consequences of sexual activity led to a separation of the sexes at work.[31]

We do observe people using gender ideology to explain constraints on women's employment. In 1845 the male potters' union justified its opposition to female employment with this appeal: "To maidens, mothers, and wives, we say machinery is your deadliest enemy ... It will destroy your natural claims to home and domestic duties."[32] However, the question still remains whether the domestic ideology these men appealed to was the real cause of the barriers, or simply justification for barriers that had other causes. Other historians have noted that men may have been using the ideology as a cover for pursuing their economic interests. For example, Hilary Land, in her discussion of the concept of the family wage, a wage high enough for a man to support his family without his wife working, notes that:

It is difficult to know how far skilled and organized working-class men, that is the labor aristocracy, accepted this form of marriage relationship as an ideal or merely couched their arguments in terms which would appeal to the social reformers and some sections of the capitalist class in order to further their own ends.[33]

While gender ideology may have played a role in declining participation (see Chapter 7), I do not think it was the most important cause of occupational barriers, because it could be disregarded when more powerful economic interests were at stake. While both workers and

---

[30] *Women and Children in Agriculture*, p. 24.   [31] Humphries, "Most Free from Objection."
[32] Quoted by Barbara Drake, *Women in Trade Unions* (London: Virago Press, [1920] 1984), p. 6.
[33] Land, "The Family Wage," p. 57.

employers shared similar gender ideology, they took different sides in the battle over whether women could be hired for certain jobs. As described in the introduction, Glasgow mule spinners fought a violent battle with their employers about whether women could be hired as mule spinners. The workers fought for restrictions because such restrictions limited the supply of workers and thus allowed them to earn higher wages. Employers, on the other hand, fought for the right to hire women because the larger labor supply and lower wages would increase their profits. Gender ideology, then, was not sufficient to enforce restrictions on women's employment, which were only effective when a group with market power had an economic incentive to enforce such restrictions.

C.   Guilds

Guilds have been an important source of barriers to women's employment in certain times and places. Sheilagh Ogilvie has shown that they were a powerful force in limiting German women to a few low-paid occupations.[34] Women were allowed to work in skilled trades only as wives and widows, indicating that they could and did acquire the necessary skills, but females were not admitted to guilds as apprentices. In England, however, guilds were both less powerful and more open to females. Even if guilds did create barriers excluding women in the pre-industrial period, by the nineteenth century they had lost their monopoly power over employment and thus had lost any power they might have once had to exclude women from well-paying occupations.

Guilds were a product of the pre-industrial economic system. They organized workers into three classes: apprentices, who were bound to a master for a number of years; journeymen, who worked for wages; and masters, who set up in business for themselves. Both the employers (masters) and the employees (journeymen) were members of the same guild. Before the Industrial Revolution, journeymen could usually expect to becomes masters themselves in the space of a few years because capital requirements for setting up independent shops were low. Guilds included both masters and journeymen because there was relatively little distinction between the two. The Webbs note that "it was the prospect of economic advancement that hindered the formation of permanent combinations among the hired journeymen of the Middle Ages."[35]

---

[34] Sheilagh Ogilvie, *A Bitter Living*, and "Guilds, Efficiency, and Social Capital: Evidence from German Proto-Industry," *Economic History Review* 57 (2004), pp. 286–333.

[35] Sidney Webb and Beatrice Webb, *The History of Trade Unionism* (London: Longmans, Green, & Co, 1894), p. 7.

In other words, the masters and journeymen did not have industrial disputes because their interests coincided. Masters as well as journeymen saw new workers as potential competitors. With the Industrial Revolution, however, the economic interests of the two groups diverged. Capital requirements increased, and it became harder for journeymen to become masters. If journeymen were not able to set up as masters and had to remain wage earners their whole lives, masters no longer had an interest in limiting their numbers. Journeymen, however, wished to maintain strict limits on entry, in order to keep their wages up. When the interests of masters and journeymen began to diverge, the guild became obsolete, and journeymen organized themselves into unions whose purpose was to oppose the masters. Since unions represented a different industrial structure from guilds and had different interests, they will be investigated separately.

Guilds included both employers and employees and thus were not likely to take actions that benefited employees but hurt employers. The interests protected by the guild were those of the small master. Entry to the trade was restricted, to limit competition. The main tools the guild used to limit the supply of its product were to allow only apprenticed individuals to practice the trade, and to limit the number of apprentices. If the guild successfully enforced both of these limits, then it effectively held monopoly power over the trade and could enjoy monopoly rents. While usually justified as training, apprenticeship rules were also about restricting entry. Apprenticeships of up to seven years were required in trades that could be learned in a few months. Citing Defoe's claim that clock- and watch-making could be learned in a few weeks, Simonton suggests that "the training had less to do with expertise and rather more to do with the status carried by the trade."[36] Dunlop concludes that in sixteenth-century England apprenticeship was "a formidable weapon in the hands of the guilds" and that it "could be employed as an instrument of monopoly."[37] In England the prohibition against unapprenticed workers was supported by law; under the Elizabethan Statute of Artificers only those apprenticed to a trade could practice it. Masters could limit entry to the trade by limiting the number of apprentices they took. There was still a free rider problem, since individual masters could benefit individually from cheap labor if they took more apprentices, while all masters shared the costs of the increase in supply. For this

[36] Deborah Simonton, "Apprenticeship: Training and Gender in Eighteenth-Century England," in Maxine Berg, ed., *Markets and Manufactures in Early Industrial Europe* (London: Routledge, 1991), p. 230.
[37] O. Jocelyn Dunlop, "Some Aspects of Early English Apprenticeship," *Transactions of the Royal Historical Society* 3rd series, 5 (1911), pp. 193–208.

reason guilds usually had explicit rules about how many apprentices a master could have.

In England, these exclusionary barriers were not aimed specifically at women. Women could and did participate in guilded trades. One way that a woman could do so was as the wife or widow of a male member of the trade. The trade was carried on by the family unit, and women were an important part of that unit. Women worked as assistants to their husbands, keeping the shop or supervising the apprentices. The fact that a tradesman's wife was his partner in business is evident in the custom of admitting a widow to the guild upon the death of her husband. The widow of a guild member could enter the guild, practice the trade, and take apprentices, even if she had never been apprenticed herself. A widow had the ability to carry on the business in her own right because she had been actively involved in the trade while her husband lived.

Many English guilds, unlike continental guilds, also allowed females to be apprenticed.[38] Girls, as well as boys, could be apprenticed and could enter the guild as "freemen." Dunlop and Denman note that girls were apprenticed in the carpenters', wheelwrights', and clockmakers' trades.[39] In most guilds males had an advantage over females because the son of a master could enter the trade without a formal apprenticeship while a daughter could not, but in a number of guilds men did not even have this advantage. In London the butchers, carpenters, and drapers all allowed the daughter as well as the son of a freeman to gain her freedom (guild membership) by patrimony.[40] Not all guilds admitted female apprentices; Lane claims that girls "were rigorously excluded from apprenticeships in the building or leathers trades, and the heavy metal skills (wheelwright or blacksmith)," but these are trades that girls would not have chosen anyway because of the high strength requirement.[41]

Guild rules were frequently written in inclusionary language. In the records of the carpenters' guild we find, "If any Apprentice or Apprentices Marry or Absent themselves from their Master or Mistress during their Apprenticehood, then within one month the Master or Mistress is to Bring their Indenture to the hall to be Registered and

---

[38] German guilds admitted widows, but did not allow girls to be apprenticed. See Ogilvie, "Guilds, Efficiency, and Social Capital."

[39] O. Jocelyn Dunlop and Richard Denman, *English Apprenticeship and Child Labor: A History* (London: Unwin, 1912), p. 151.

[40] Philip Jones, *The Butchers of London* (London: Secker and Warburg, 1976), p. 21; Jupp and Pocock, *The Worshipful Company of Carpenters*, p. 544; Percival Boyd, *Roll of the Drapers' Company of London: Collected from the Company Records and Other Sources* (Croydon: J. A. Gordon, 1934).

[41] Lane, *Apprenticeship in England*, p. 39.

Entered."[42] In 1704 the Curriers' Company agreed that no "foreigners" should be allowed to work if members of the guild were unemployed. They decreed:

that ye Beadle shall goe with any ffreeman that is out of worke to any of ye places where a fforiner is at worke & acquait ye Master or Mistress that it is ordered by this Court that he or she turn away ye fforiner & sett ye freeman to worke which if they disobey ye Master and wardens are to take such ... with them as is provided against disobedient members by ye Orders of this Company.[43]

The rule suggests that women were employers and members of the company.

Women who were guild members seem to have carried on their trade in the same way as the men. We find women taking apprentices. In records of the Carpenters' Company we find "Richard Stevenson sonne of Robt. Stevenson late of Dublin in the Kingedome of Ireland Pavier bound to Anne Nicholson Widowe the Relict of Anthony Nicholson, for eight years," in April of 1686, and "Robert Harper sonne of William Harper of Notchford in the county of Chesheire, bound to Abigail Taylor for Seaven Yeares," in June of 1692.[44] Katherine Eyre, a member of the London Carpenters' Company, took three apprentices between the years of 1701 and 1707.[45] Records of the Witney Blanket Weavers' Company show that on October 24, 1733, Richard Ashfield was bound to Eliza Jefferson for seven years.[46] In 1824 a mistress shipwright from Liverpool, Mrs. Simpson, had four apprentices.[47] Simonton finds that 3 percent of those taking apprentices were women.[48]

Apprenticeship requirements did function as barriers to entry, but these barriers were not particularly aimed at females. In England, girls could be apprenticed. In 1742 the butchers of London admitted to the freedom of the company Hester Maynard, who had been apprenticed to Francis Baker.[49] In 1815 Caroline Atherton was admitted to the Drapers' Company of London by right of apprenticeship.[50] While he

---

[42] *Records of the Worshipful Company of Carpenters*, 1913, vol. I, p. vii, quoted in Clark, *Working Life of Women*, p. 173.

[43] Curriers' Company, *Fair Copy Extracts from Court Minute Books*, vol. I, fos. 216–20, quoted in C. R. Dobson, *Masters and Journeymen: A Prehistory of Industrial Relations* (London: Croom Helm, 1980), pp. 47–8.

[44] *Records of the Worshipful Company of Carpenters*, 1913, vol. I, p. 189, quoted in Clark, *Working Life of Women*, p. 174. See also Jupp and Pocock, *The Worshipful Company of Carpenters*, p. 161.

[45] Jupp and Pocock, *The Worshipful Company of Carpenters*, pp. 543–4.

[46] Alfred Plummer, *The Witney Blanket Industry: The Records of the Witney Blanket Weavers* (London: Routledge, 1934), p. 161.

[47] BPP 1824 (51) V, p. 227.   [48] Simonton, "Apprenticeship," p. 245.

[49] Jones, *The Butchers of London*, p. 21.   [50] Boyd, *Roll of the Drapers' Company*, p. 7.

Table 5.4. *The apprenticeship of girls*

Years	Town	Percent female	Source
1532–65	Bristol	4	a
1542–53	Bristol	3	b
1563–1713	Kingston upon Hull	0.4	a
1603–14	Salisbury	3.6	b
1600–45	Bristol	2.2	c
1710–31	Surrey	5.2	d
1710–52	Sussex	3.2	d
1710–60	Warwickshire	3.6	d
1710–60	Wiltshire	7.4	d
1711–20	Bedfordshire	5.0	d
1710–60	Sussex	2.9	e
1710–60	Warwickshire	3.1	e
1710–60	Wiltshire	6.9	e

Source:
a. Roberts, "Words They Are Women."
b. Wright, "Churmaids, Huswyfes and Hucksters."
c. Ben-Amos, "Women Apprentices."
d. Snell, *Annals of the Labouring Poor*, Table 6.4.
e. Lane, *Apprenticeship in England*, p. 40.

observed that it was not the general practice, Stephen Smith, a Gloucestershire weaver, claimed that girls were often apprenticed as weavers. He noted a current apprentice, Rachael Smith, who lived near him.[51] Female apprentices were taught the trade; if an apprentice was employed only in household work, the contract could be broken. From 1715 court records we learn of "Sarah Gibson discharged from her apprenticeship to Joanna Worthington of St. Andrew's Holborn widow, mantua-maker [dressmaker], upon proof that the said Sarah, instead of learning the trade of mantua-maker had been employed in common household work."[52]

However, while girls clearly *could* be apprenticed, few actually were. If we focus on private apprenticeship, as opposed to parish apprenticeship, only about 4 percent of apprentices were girls. Simonton finds that 4 percent of private apprentices were girls in the late eighteenth century,[53] and the other estimates presented in Table 5.4 suggest similar rates,

[51] BPP 1806 (268) III, p. 346.
[52] George, *London Life in the Eighteenth Century*, pp. 234, 418. See also Snell, *Annals of the Laboring Poor*.
[53] Simonton, "Apprenticeship," p. 245.

with some variation. While some guilds may have discouraged women from entering, the low number of female apprentices was probably more the result of family decisions than guild rules. Parents deciding how to invest their scarce resources were more likely to apprentice sons. Partially this reflects the expected return of this human capital investment. Daughters would bring lower returns to the investment over their lifetime because they spent less time in the labor force. Partially, however, this decision also reflects gender discrimination. To the extent that discrimination worked to lower women's opportunities here, it was discrimination that operated through the family.

More girls were bound as parish apprentices; about a third of parish apprentices were girls.[54] However, these apprenticeships did not provide a route to higher-paying occupations because fewer parish apprentices were bound to higher-paying trades. Training was not the only goal of parish apprenticeship; the system also served to provide support for children dependent on the parish.[55] Because overseers were reluctant to pay high premiums out of the poor rate to bind parish apprentices, they were rarely bound to trades with good earnings prospects. Some parishes set an upper limit on the premium that could be paid for a parish apprentice.[56] Female parish apprentices were often apprenticed to "housewifery."[57] Thus the larger percentage of girls among the parish apprenticeship does not mean that large numbers of girls were being trained in skills valued in the labor market.

Even if they wished to, guilds did not always have the power to exclude women workers. English guilds were weaker than continental guilds in the pre-industrial era. Hutton notes that in the fourteenth century, "Gild and civic regulations were not necessarily strictly obeyed ... The most one can say about such regulations is that they represent a situation which the civic and craft elite would have liked to bring into existence."[58] Ogilvie suggests that English guilds began to decline in the sixteenth century, and notes that in the West Riding of Yorkshire "rural people took up first woollen weaving, then worsted weaving, without lengthy (and often without any) apprenticeship ... when guilds did manage to secure apprenticeship legislation, it was widely ignored."[59]

---

[54] Snell finds that in the eighteenth century 34 percent of parish apprentices were female, while in the nineteenth century 31 percent were female. Snell, *Annals of the Laboring Poor*, Table 6.1. See also Hindle, "'Waste' Children?," p. 34.

[55] Hindle, "'Waste' Children?"   [56] Lane, *Apprenticeship in England*, p. 25.

[57] Hindle, "'Waste' Children?," p. 37.

[58] Diane Hutton, "Women in Fourteenth Century Shrewsbury," in Lindsay Charles and Lorna Duffin, eds., *Women and Work in Pre-Industrial England* (London: Croom Helm, 1985), p. 83–4.

[59] Ogilvie, *A Bitter Living*, p. 96, and "Guilds, Efficiency, and Social Capital," p. 303.

In 1702 only about half the weavers in Taunton had served an apprenticeship.[60]

What little power guilds did have was lost during the Industrial Revolution. Certainly by the nineteenth century English guilds had little power and apprenticeship had ceased to be an important barrier to entry into a trade. The Statute of Artificers, which forbade non-apprenticed workers, was repealed in 1814, but the institution of apprenticeship had fallen into decline before this. Where apprenticeship was not necessary to learn the skills, non-apprenticed workers often worked in the trade. In weaving, apprenticeship was not necessary; in 1803 only 13 percent of the weavers employed by a Gloucester clothier had served an apprenticeship.[61] Richard Fawcett, a Bradford manufacturer, noted of weavers "I believe nineteen out of twenty have not served regular apprenticeships."[62] In Leeds, only apprenticed clothiers were allowed to sell cloth in the two main cloth halls, but there was a third hall, known as Tom Paine Hall, where anyone could sell cloth, and many persons not apprenticed to the trade sold cloth there.[63] A Leeds clothier noted that in this third hall, "any persons who have not served an apprenticeship go and shew a coloured piece there."[64] Under the pressure of this competition, the white cloth hall agreed in 1803 to accept cloth from non-apprenticed persons.[65] One indicator of the declining power of guilds was the declining portion of youth who were apprenticed. Simonton notes that "apprentices were clearly a declining proportion from 1771, with a fairly steep drop from 1786."[66] Where apprenticeship was not truly necessary to learn the skill, guilds found themselves unable to restrict the trade to apprenticed workers.

English guilds were not an important source of occupational segregation during the Industrial Revolution. Guilds allowed girls to be apprenticed, so the fact that few girls were apprenticed reflects choices made in the family rather than discriminatory barriers within the guild system. The fact that fewer girls were apprenticed became increasingly irrelevant as the guild system disintegrated. If apprenticeship was no longer necessary for employment, girls could not be disadvantaged by their lack of apprenticeship. During the Industrial Revolution, the interests of employers and employees diverged, leading to the decline of the guild system and the rise of unions, which were important in excluding women from certain occupations.

---

[60] *Ibid.* [61] Hammond and Hammond, *The Skilled Labourer*, p. 170.
[62] BPP 1806 (268) III, p. 184.
[63] See Adrian Randall, *Before the Luddites* (Cambridge: Cambridge University Press, 1991), p. 211, and BPP 1806 (268) III.
[64] BPP 1806 (268) III, p. 10. [65] *Ibid.*, p. 201. [66] Simonton, "Apprenticeship," p. 238.

D.   Employers

While they are obvious candidates for excluding women from waged work, employers were not an important source of occupational segregation during the Industrial Revolution.[67] Their actions were generally the opposite: employers fought for the right to hire women. One mistake that could lead us to blame employers for occupational segregation is accepting the ideological statements of employers as accurate descriptions of their actions. In assessing the role of employers in excluding women, we must remember that statements of cultural ideals do not always match actions. Employers' statements that married women should not work are not proof that such women were not hired. One employer claimed to oppose the employment of married women at the same time he admitted to employing them himself:

> As to married women, in one particular department of our establishment we have forty-nine married women and we wish that the present state of things as regards married women should not be disturbed ... but we have as a rule an objection to employing married women, because we think that every man ought to maintain his wife without the necessity of her going to work.[68]

Employers seemed to have no trouble saying one thing and doing another. Struggling to survive in a competitive market, they could not afford to indulge their personal preferences.

A brief look at labor history reveals that employers were not an important source of occupational segregation. Most employers considered it their right to hire women if they could benefit by doing so, and opposed restrictions on women's employment. Employers who wished to maximize profits wanted to employ women and were willing to hire women if it meant increased profits. M'Connel and Kennedy, for instance, found its male workforce troublesome and began to hire women as mule spinners in 1810. The experiment did not work; problems with increased wastage of raw material and high turnover rates, both resulting from the fact that the women did not recruit and discipline their own assistants like the men did, meant that the shift to female workers did not increase the firm's profits, even though the women were paid lower piece-rate wages. Huberman notes that:

---

[67] An example of a historian who blames employers for occupational segregation is Jordan, "The Exclusion of Women," who claims that employers refused to hire women simply out of "androcentric blindness."

[68] Frederick Carver of Nottingham, BPP 1876, XIX, p. 258, quoted in Rose, *Limited Livelihoods*, p. 32.

The firm might have persevered with the policy if profits remained healthy for like other firms, it saw the long-term benefit of getting rid of recalcitrant male workers and replacing them with women. However, after 1820 when the fall in margins signaled a squeeze on profits, the firm was compelled to find a way to reduce costs or to raise productivity by some means other than the hiring of women.[69]

It was falling profits, not gender ideology, that caused M'Connel and Kennedy to cease hiring female mule spinners. The willingness of the employers to hire women when they thought they could benefit from doing so indicates that it was productivity rather than gender which prevented women from being spinners.

When it was in their economic interest to hire women, employers were willing to fight unions for the right to do so. Both James Dunlop and William Kelly of Glasgow attempted to hire women as mule spinners, but the women did not stay because of the violent reactions on the part of the male workers.[70] From 1810 to 1834, the journeymen and master tailors of London fought over whether women could be employed.[71] In 1861 employers attempted to hire women to work stocking frames, but the male workers went on strike.[72] Sonya Rose has studied many of these worker–employer conflicts in the later nineteenth century, and concludes that "when it was possible to do so, employers attempted to hire women in place of men."[73] As we shall see when examining unions, employers were more likely to fight for the right to hire women than to exclude them from employment.

While most theories of employer discrimination assume that gender roles motivated constraints, a somewhat different theory suggests that occupational constraints were based on the need to prevent contact between the sexes that could result in sexual misconduct. Humphries claims that concerns about sexual behavior motivated occupational segregation.[74] Concern about sexual propriety, however, seems to have motivated action in the upper classes (and particularly in parliamentary committees), more often than among the laboring or employer classes.[75] Employers showed by their actions that they were willing to mix the sexes. Men and women often worked side by side. In some regions much agricultural work was done by gangs, which included workers of

---

[69] Huberman, *Escape from the Market*, pp. 28–9.
[70] BPP 1824 (51) V, p. 525, and Aspinall, *The Early English Trade Unions*, p. 390.
[71] Taylor, *Eve and the New Jerusalem*, ch. 4.   [72] Rose, "Gender Segregation," p. 171.
[73] Rose, "Gender Antagonism," p. 195.   [74] Humphries, "Most Free from Objection."
[75] Humphries claims that upper-class concerns about morality extended down into the working classes. However, to establish this point she uses statements from workers about what they thought was proper rather than evidence of actual work patterns. If we look at work patterns, revealed preference tells us that the lower classes were willing to allow men and women to work together.

both sexes.[76] Farmers were not averse to allowing men and women to work together, as indicated by the adage advising mixed groups of workers: "One man among women, one woman among men."[77] Men and women often worked in the same location even when they were occupationally segregated. Young women were piecers but were never mule spinners; concern about morality cannot explain this occupational difference because spinners and piecers necessarily worked side by side. Even if employers had wished to separate the sexes, they could have established different factories for each sex. James Dunlop of Glasgow, for example, installed smaller mules in his factory so that he could hire women exclusively.

> Messrs. James Dunlop and Sons, some years ago, erected cotton mills in Calton of Glasgow, on which they expended upwards of 27,000l. forming their spinning machines ... of such reduced size as could easily be wrought by women. They employed women alone ... These they paid the same [piece] rate of wages, as were paid at other works to men.[78]

Even the desire for a segregated work environment would not prevent both men and women from working in the same occupation.

Economic theory tells us that discriminatory employers who refuse to hire women on ideological grounds are less efficient and can only succeed in monopolistic markets. Becker's model of discrimination predicts that in a competitive market employers who discriminate against women should fail.[79] Only monopolistic employers should be able to discriminate against women. If Becker is correct, we should observe that employers in competitive markets hire women willingly, while only employers in monopolistic markets are able to exclude women. Davidoff and Hall point to the chocolate manufacturer George Cadbury, who in the 1870s "was strongly opposed to the employment of married women and refused to have them working at Bournville."[80] George Cadbury could afford to indulge his gender ideology, and refuse to hire married women, because his brand gave him a certain amount of monopoly

---

[76] Pinchbeck, *Women Workers*, p. 86.   [77] Kussmaul, *Servants in Husbandry*, p. 47.
[78] BPP 1824 (51) V, p. 525. Men and women were paid the same piece-rate wages, so they were treated equally but may have had different earnings. Dunlop eventually stopped hiring women because of the violent attacks of the male union: "But they [the women] were waylaid and attacked, in going to, and returning from their work; the houses in which they resided, were broken open at night. The women themselves were cruelly beaten and abused; and the mother of one of them killed; in fine, the works were set on fire in the night, by combustibles thrown into them from without; and the flames were with difficulty extinguished."
[79] Becker, *The Economics of Discrimination*, ch. 3.
[80] Davidoff and Hall, *Family Fortunes*, p. 58.

power. Employers in more competitive markets may have shared Cadbury's ideology, but we observe them fighting for the right to hire women.

While employers may have been the source of discrimination in a few cases, employer discrimination cannot explain widespread occupational segregation. The importance of employers in occupational segregation has been overstated both because a few examples are taken as representative of the whole and because statements of employers are too readily accepted as statements of fact. Looking at their actions, we find that employers allowed men and women to work together and were even willing to fight for the right to hire women.

E.   Unions

The nineteenth century saw the emergence and growth of trade unions.[81] As we have seen, guilds organized both employers and employees into one trade organization. With the Industrial Revolution, however, it became harder for a journeyman to move from being a wage-earner to being a self-employed producer. As the potential threat of a new worker as a competitor became more remote, the employer lost the incentive to limit the number of wage-earners in the trade, but the wage-earners still benefited from limiting entry to the occupation, and they organized unions and threatened their employers with strikes in order to do so. Employers were not an important force in limiting women's opportunities because their economic interests conflicted with, and usually overruled, their ideas about gender roles. Because their gender ideology coincided with their economic interest, male workers became the most important force excluding women from wage-earning occupations. When unions were successful, they were able to enforce constraints on women's employment, and occupational segregation thrived because the market mechanism was overruled.

Though they were illegal until 1824, unions existed early in the Industrial Revolution. "Conspiracies in restraint of trade" were illegal under common law, and the Combination Acts of 1799 and 1800 specifically outlawed collective action. The law gave the masters more power to prosecute, but it certainly did not prevent unions from forming and acting. The law was only partially effective because employers did

---

[81] By "union" I mean any group of employees working together to promote their own interests. Women theoretically could be members of such groups, but in practice were not. Unions of the Industrial Revolution period did not have the same formal structures as unions today because the law was different; union activity was illegal until 1824.

not always find it in their interests to enforce the law, and when they did it was a slow and costly process. Unions existed and exerted influence even when they were illegal. The Combination Acts must have had some effect on reducing union activity, though, since there was a surge of union activity after they were repealed. After 1824 unions grew in number and importance. The 1830s saw two failed attempts at organizing a general union.[82] The Webbs identified three periods of union expansion: 1833–4, 1873–4, and 1889–90.[83] By the later half of the nineteenth century, union power was firmly established in Britain.

While guilds used apprenticeship rules to maintain their incomes, unions relied on other rules to limit the supply of workers and thus maintain high wages. When they were able, unions enforced closed shops. A Bradford magistrate noted in 1802 that "the shearmen will not suffer any man to work who has not got a ticket," the ticket being proof of membership in the Shearmen's Club.[84] Unions also limited the number of new workers entering the trade. The most powerful unions admitted only relatives of current members. The Lancashire mule spinners only allowed sons, brothers, or orphaned nephews of current members to enter the trade.[85] The Dublin carpenters also allowed only sons, brothers, and nephews of current members to be apprenticed.[86] In these cases unions enforced rules that were more restrictive than the guilds' apprenticeship rules had been.

Gender ideology and economic incentives played a joint role in leading unions to demand the exclusion of women from their trades.[87] Unions desired to limit access to their trades, in order to reduce labor supply and increase their wage. Gender ideology made women a natural target.[88] Without either one of these factors things would have turned out differently. Without gender ideology, women would not have been an easily identifiable group, and exclusion would have been based on

---

[82] The National Association for the Protection of Labor, and the Grand National Consolidated Trades Union. See G. D. H. Cole, *Attempts at General Union: A Study in British Trade Union History, 1818–1834* (London: Macmillan, 1953).

[83] Webb and Webb, *The History of Trade Unionism*, p. 314.

[84] Aspinall, *The Early English Trade Unions*, p. 50.

[85] Rose, *Limited Livelihoods*, p. 143.   [86] BPP 1824 (51) V, p. 430.

[87] Similarly, racist ideology and economic incentives played a joint role in creating the system of apartheid in South Africa. Frederick Johnstone, *Class, Race and Gold: A Study of Class Relations and Racial Discrimination in South Africa* (London: Routledge and Kegan Paul, 1976), emphasizes the role that white workers played in instituting the color bars that prevented non-white workers from entering skilled occupations. White workers worked to institute racial discrimination because they benefited economically.

[88] On gender ideology, see Davidoff and Hall, *Family Fortunes*; Hartmann, "Capitalism, Patriarchy, and Job Segregation"; Rose, "Gender at Work"; and Scott and Tilly, "Women's Work and the Family."

other factors such as nationality or family connection. Without an economic incentive driving the exclusion, it is doubtful that unions would have pushed hard to exclude women. Employers had the same gender ideology, but they were willing to hire women anyway because they benefited economically from doing so.

Thus, unions of the Industrial Revolution did everything they could to exclude women from employment. The Bookbinders' Trade Society excluded women in 1810.[89] Barbara Drake reports that women were initially allowed to be members of the Manchester Spinners' Union, but were excluded after 1818.[90] In 1820 the Glasgow mule spinners went on strike, demanding an end to the employment of women. One employer received an anonymous letter threatening:

I am authorized to intimate [the] jeoperdy and hazardious prediciment you stand in at the present time ... by keeping them weomen officiating in mens places as cotton spinners, and plenty of men going idle out of employ.[91]

Spitalfields silk weavers combined to restrict women to the cheaper work. In 1769 they succeeded in getting the masters to agree to a book of prices stipulating, "No woman or girl to be employed in making any kind of work except such works as are herein fixed and settled at 5d. per ell ... And no woman or girl is to be employed in making any sort of handkerchief of above the usual or settled price of 4s.6d. per dozen."[92] The Stockport Hatmakers' Society excluded women in 1808.[93] Their rules included an agreement to strike ("knock off") against women workers: "And it is unanimously agreed that all women are to be knocked off against, to knock one woman off at one shop at a time, till it is gone round the trade, and so on till they are all done away with."[94] Other historians have noted the fact that male workers fought for

---

[89] Felicity Hunt, "Opportunities Lost and Gained: Mechanization and Women's Work in the London Bookbinding and Printing Trades," in Angela John, ed., *Unequal Opportunities* (Oxford: Basil Blackwell, 1986), p. 74.

[90] "The Manchester Spinners' and the Manchester Small Ware Weavers' Societies are known to have had women members in the 18th century. During the spinners' strike of 1818, men and women drew equal strike pay; but, owing it would seem to their failure to observe trade union conditions, the women were afterwards excluded." Drake, *Women in Trade Unions*, p. 4.

[91] BPP 1824 (51) V, p. 531.

[92] *A List of Prices in those Branches of the Weaving Manufactory called the Black Branch, and the Fancy Branch* ..., 1769, quoted in George, *London Life in the Eighteenth Century*, p. 182.

[93] Maxine Berg, "Women's Work, Mechanisation and the Early Phases of Industrialisation in England," in Patrick Joyce, ed., *The Historical Meanings of Work* (Cambridge: Cambridge University Press, 1987), pp. 64–98.

[94] Aspinall, *The Early English Trade Unions*, p. 107. Rules agreed to, September 19, 1808. Here they agree to use a rolling strike, that is, to strike against only one master at a time.

restrictions on female employment that benefited them economically. Rose emphasizes the *"active role* played by skilled male workers in creating gender segregation as they attempted to preserve their own jobs."[95]

Male workers used gender ideology to argue that a woman's place was in the home, and that the male wage should be high enough to support his wife and children, that men should earn a "family wage."[96] They justified the exclusion of female workers as a method to obtain a family wage. Humphries suggests that working-class women as well as men benefited from such restrictions because they increased male wages enough to keep total family earnings constant, while women gained leisure.[97] It is theoretically possible that a removal of women from labor supply could raise wages enough to keep the wage bill constant, if the labor demand curve was unit elastic, but Humphries provides no evidence that this was so.[98] More importantly, even if family income did not decline, women lost bargaining power within the household. Concern about the gender gap arises not just because low earnings leave women poor, but also because the difference between male and female earnings ensures that men have more power than women. Even if total family income did not change, a shift in the composition of income that increased male earnings and reduced or eliminated female earnings would have increased the gender gap and made women more dependent on men. Hartmann suggests that men used occupational segregation not only to maintain their wages, but also to maintain their patriarchal power within the home.[99] Men wanted to keep their jobs, and to continue to enjoy the benefits of women's domestic labor, so they excluded women from skilled occupations.

Deborah Simonton claims that gender, not economics, was the primary reason for unions' rules against women, and she supports this claim by arguing that if their motivation had been primarily economic, then unions would have excluded other men as well.

On the one hand, it was not about women, but about protecting their craft position and independence vis-a-vis capitalists who wished to control labor

---

[95] Rose, "Gender at Work," p. 120.

[96] Seccombe, "Patriarchy Stabilized"; Land, "The Family Wage."

[97] Jane Humphries, "Class Struggle and the Persistence of the Working-Class Family," *Cambridge Journal of Economics* 1 (1977), p. 251.

[98] Humphries uses Marx's theory of wage determination and opinions of the workers themselves to support her claim that total family income would remain constant. Neither is convincing evidence that labor demand was elastic or unit elastic. Modern studies sometimes find that labor demand is elastic, but most estimates suggest inelastic demand. Daniel Hammermesh, *Labor Demand* (Princeton: Princeton University Press, 1993), pp. 78–9.

[99] Hartmann, "Capitalism, Patriarchy, and Job Segregation."

supply. On the other hand, it clearly was about gender, because the workers against whom it was aimed were women, since they perceived female labor, not unskilled male labor, as the threat.[100]

However, it is not true that exclusion was aimed only at women. While women were an identifiable group likely to be targeted, they were not the only group excluded. At the extreme, mule spinners allowed only male relatives of current workmen to enter the trade. In this case most men experienced the same exclusion as women. Alexander Erskine, a worker at a Glasgow cotton mill, gave evidence that:

he would wish to be a spinner, and earn the same high wages as they do, but he was not brought up a spinner, and the spinners would not therefore allow him to learn, for the spinners have an association to prevent this, by refusing to teach anybody to spin who has not been brought up with them.[101]

Clearly Alexander was excluded from employment as effectively as any female. Restrictions on employment prevented workers in dying trades such as handloom weaving, men as well as women, from entering other trades. In 1841 a parliamentary investigator noted:

I am perfectly convinced that the distress of the hand loom weavers is mainly and almost entirely to be ascribed to the exclusive monopoly established by the forcible conduct of the trades in all other lines, which prevents their sons getting into any other line ... every trade is fenced round by prohibitions, which render it impossible for a person to get into it, except a son or a brother, or some near relation of an already existing member.[102]

Other groups besides women were also targeted for exclusion. In 1812 the wool-combers' union agreed not to admit Irishmen.[103] The fact that women were occasionally the insiders also supports the claim that gender was not the only line dividing insiders from outsiders. In powerloom weaving in Glasgow, women operated their own exclusionary society. Mary Donald, age 11, gave evidence in 1833 that she was not a weaver, since "Her mother wants to get her into the mill, but can't afford to pay 10s.6d. to the association."[104] This girl found her employment opportunities limited, not by men, but by other women.

Not every combination sought to exclude women. On one occasion, journeymen pipe-makers argued for maintaining women's jobs. They asked the public to avoid "marked Pipes" because the new type of pipe

---

[100] Simonton, *European Women's Work*, p. 172.   [101] BPP 1833 (450) XX, A1, p. 81.
[102] BPP 1841 (296) X, p. 108.
[103] The rules agreed to in 1812 include this statement: "No Irishmen to be admitted to society, after the date of these Articles." Aspinall, *The Early English Trade Unions*, p. 135.
[104] BPP 1833 (450) XX, A2, p. 54.

resulted in unemployment for women: "a great many Women are in Want of Business that were always brought up to it; for by the aforesaid Pipes, two Women can do as much Work as would require four."[105] In this case, women were not the threat to employment; new pipes were. Since the interest of the journeymen coincided with that of women workers, they promoted the employment of women. However, when they found it in their interest to do so – when doing so would decrease competition and maintain their high wages – male unions attempted to exclude women workers.

In most cases the fierce resistance of employers to rules against hiring women suggests that these rules were binding. The presence of a strong union was important in determining whether women worked in a trade, as can be observed in a few trades where unions had differing success in different cities. After the self-acting mule was invented in 1833, strength was no longer necessary and women were able to operate mules productively.[106] In Glasgow, where the union was not effective, women sometimes worked as mule spinners.[107] In Lancashire, however, the mule spinners maintained an effective union, and no women worked mules there. Similarly, in the later nineteenth century, Edinburgh had numerous women compositors but England had few. Bradley and Black explain this by pointing to the difference in the strength of the compositors' unions:

Why are women employed so largely in Edinburgh, so little in England? Factory law is the same for the whole of Britain, so the cause must be sought elsewhere. The answer would seem to lie in the attitude adopted by men's Trade Unions. The Union in Edinburgh has never recovered from the blow dealt it in 1872–3, and is not now in a position to make any effective stand against the inroads of the army of women compositors. In London and Lancashire, on the contrary, the unions are strong.[108]

The large numbers of women compositors in Edinburgh are explained by the fact that the Edinburgh union lost a strike in 1872–3 and had not recovered the strength necessary to prevent the employment of women. Thus, the presence of an effective union does seem to be a constraining force.

We have seen that neither government regulations, guilds, nor employers explain the limits to women's employment. Government regulations

---

[105] An advertisement from 1745, quoted by Dobson, *Masters and Journeymen*, p. 41.
[106] See below.
[107] In particular, James Dunlop and Mr. Crombie employed women. BPP 1824 (51) V, pp. 615, 618.
[108] Barbara Bradley and Anne Black, "Women Compositors and the Factory Acts," *Economic Journal* 9 (1899), p. 264.

limiting female employment did not appear until the 1840s, and limits on hours do not seem to have reduced female factory employment. Unlike German guilds, which severely limited women's opportunities, English guilds did not have sufficient power to exclude women workers.[109] Employers were not an important source of occupational constraints because they were eager to hire women when they could profit from doing so. I conclude that the main source of employment barriers for wage-earning women was male unions. Male unions benefited economically from excluding women from their occupations, and did so whenever they could. In most cases gender ideology coincided with unions' economic interests, making it difficult to determine which force was driving the desire to exclude women. I believe that economic interest was the primary force because employers, who shared similar gender ideology but had opposing economic interests, chose to side with their economic interests. Gender ideology was a convenient rhetorical device for unions, but their primary motivation was economic.

If unions were the cause of the exclusion of women from certain trades, they needed not only the desire to exclude women, but also the ability to enforce this desire. Why were some unions successful while others were not? Jordan does not accept the union explanation for the exclusion of women because "only a few of the strongest craft unions had sufficient power to impose their wishes on employers."[110] She is right that we should be skeptical about the ability of a union to impose its will on the employer. Not all unions were successful in imposing employment restrictions. As we shall see in the next section, the amount of power a union possessed depended on the skill level of the job; unions in skilled trades were more successful. This difference in union power, then, provides the explanation of why we observe occupation segregation in more highly skilled trades, but not in low-skilled trades.

III.   Where unions could be successful

The previous section concluded that unions were the most important cause of occupational segregation constraints. This section will show that unions had the economic power to enforce their demands only in skilled occupations, thus providing an explanation of why there were

---

[109] On restrictions imposed by German guilds, see Ogilvie, *A Bitter Living*.
[110] Jordan, "The Exclusion of Women," p. 286. Where unions were weak, Jordan ascribes occupational segregation to employers, while I ascribe it to sorting based on strength, as described in Chapter 3.

occupational segregation constraints in skilled occupations but not in unskilled occupations. Where unions were not strong enough to erect barriers to women's employment, the division of labor was determined by comparative advantage, as described in Chapter 3.

Both contemporaries and historians have noted that in Industrial Revolution Britain there was a clear distinction between skilled and unskilled occupations in terms of union success. In 1836 Andrew Ure noted that "it is, moreover, a well established fact, that those artisans who are the worst paid seldom combine, and never with any force; but only those who enjoy the best wages, such as cotton spinners, engineering mechanics, founders ... &c."[111] More recently, Rule noted that skilled laborers had the power to win disputes, but that "this power depended upon the defense of the skill, both against deskilling innovation and as a frontier against the unskilled, including large numbers of women workers."[112] To establish that the success of unions depended on skill, I will present both a model explaining why skill should matter and examples from a number of different unions showing that skilled workers were in fact more successful.

The classic model of union bargaining was presented by Hicks in 1932.[113] Figure 5.1 shows the essence of the model. Hicks predicted that the outcome of wage bargaining would depend on the "employer's concession curve" and the "union's resistance curve," both of which map wage offers against length of strike. The employer's concession curve gives the wage the employer would be willing to pay to prevent a strike of a given length. The union's resistance curve gives the length of time the workers would be willing to strike to obtain a given wage. When bargaining, each party will foresee the outcome, and thus both will agree on w^*, the wage where the two curves meet. In this model, strikes occur only if the decision-makers incorrectly predict the curves, leading each side to different estimates of the curves and thus different estimates of w^*.

Neither the workers nor the employer can hold out forever. The workers have to eat, and when their assets and credit are exhausted they will be forced to return to work. The employer has fixed costs to pay, and cannot endure a strike indefinitely because he is constrained by the possibility of bankruptcy. Anything that allows the striking workers to hold out longer, such as a large strike fund, would shift the union's

---

[111] Andrew Ure, *The Cotton Manufacture of Great Britain* (London: Charles Knight, 1836), vol. I, p. xxv.
[112] John Rule, "The Formative Years of British Trade Unionism: An Overview," in John Rule, ed., *British Trade Unionism, 1750–1850: The Formative Years* (New York: Longman, 1988), p. 6.
[113] J. R. Hicks, *The Theory of Wages* (New York: Peter Smith, [1932] 1948), ch. 7.

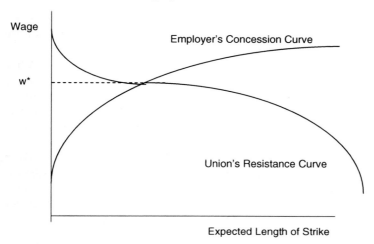

Figure 5.1 Hicks's bargaining model

resistance curve to the right and increase the wage the union can secure. A strike may not be necessary to win the higher wage, because the employer will foresee a longer strike and will be willing to give a higher wage to avoid the strike.

Hicks drew some specific conclusions about what factors would influence the position of the two curves. The union's resistance depends on its ability to support its members:

> The actual duration of resistance depends on ability as much as on willingness. Strikers' ability to hold out depends, in its turn, partly on the size of the union's accumulated funds (the amount of strike pay it can give), partly on the savings of the members (which enable them to be content with a low rate of strike pay, or to hold out when strike pay has disappeared), partly on the attitude toward the strike of parties not directly concerned (the willingness of shopkeepers to give credit, the willingness of other unions or independent well-wishers to give loans or donations to the union). The greater the extent of such resources, the stronger the union will be.[114]

In order to win a strike, a union must be able to build up a strike fund large enough to support itself. Unskilled workers, because they were so poorly paid, had difficulty building up large strike funds and lost many strikes when their funds ran out. Skilled workers had an advantage, in the form of a higher resistance curve, because they were more highly paid, and could more easily save money and build up strike funds.

---

[114] *Ibid.*, pp. 153–4.

Occasionally a strike was won on the charity of the townspeople, who offered loans to the strikers, but dependence on others could not provide the basis of consistent power.

Skilled unions also found it easier to maintain discipline. While the group as a whole benefits from maintaining the strike, an individual worker could do better by working. To win a strike, a union must prevent its members from agreeing to go back to work. As Mancur Olson points out, this is more difficult in large groups because social pressure is less effective. The larger the group, the greater the chance that free-riding will prevent any action.[115] Skilled occupations have the advantage because the number of workers is usually smaller. Also, skilled occupations can impose discipline by threatening to prevent a person from working in the trade. This was a real threat because being able to work in the skilled trade was valuable; the alternative was unskilled work, at a much lower wage.

Anything that makes the strike more costly to firm profits will shift the employer's concession curve to the left, and increase the wage that the union can secure. Hicks noted that the employer's concession curve depends on "the degree to which the union can make the strike effective in causing a stoppage of the employer's business" and on the costs of the stoppage to the firm.[116] If the business can continue to operate in spite of the strike, the employer can hold out longer. Here again skilled workers had the advantage over unskilled workers. Strikes were more costly to the firm if the business of the firm had to be suspended during the strike. Unskilled workers could be replaced, and the business could continue to operate with minimal loss of profit. Skilled workers, however, were difficult to replace, and a strike of skilled workers might stop production. The employer needed to recruit skilled workers who were not in the union or train new workers. If the work was highly skilled, training took much too long and could not be used to win a strike. A union is the strongest if all workers with a particular skill are part of the union. If the union has a monopoly on the skill and there is no good substitute for the skill, that union will be able to extract monopoly wages because the employer cannot hope to train strike-breakers at all. One of the important sources of power for these unions was the fact that they controlled training. If the union could control the skill – determining who could acquire it and who could not – it could control employment. Since the method of training for most skilled wage-earners was

---

[115] Mancur Olson, *The Logic of Collective Action* (Cambridge, Mass.: Harvard University Press, 1965).
[116] Hicks, *The Theory of Wages*, pp. 154–5.

apprenticeship with a current worker, skilled unions had effective power over who was trained and thus who would work.

Sometimes unions with insufficient economic power to win their demands tried to improve their bargaining position by using violence. This was the one important factor in which skilled trades did not have the advantage. By using violence, a union could win a strike even if it did not have economic power. James Dunlop of Glasgow let go his women spinners because the protests of the male union were so violent. His women spinners:

were waylaid and attacked, in going to, and returning from their work; the houses in which they resided, were broken open in the night. The women themselves were cruelly beaten and abused; the mother of one of them killed; in fine, the works were set on fire in the night, by combustibles thrown into them from without.[117]

In 1824 John Martineau testified before a parliamentary committee that "Last Monday, while I was at Liverpool, a man was murdered in the streets, for having refused to join a combination."[118] Violence could be very important in determining the outcome in a particular situation. Thus, predictions of success based on whether the trade was skilled will predict the outcome only with a certain amount of error.

Violence, however, was rarely a source of consistent power, and its use was generally the sign of a weak union. The most successful unions did not resort to violence. If the union could obtain its demands using economic pressure only, there was no need for violence. The unskilled trades, on the other hand, had little economic power and were most likely to turn to violence since it was the most effective method available to them. Agricultural laborers, for instance, rarely bothered to attempt a strike, but sometimes turned directly to violence to win their demands, as during the Swing riots.[119] The main weakness of using violence to obtain higher wages was that the effects were not likely to be long-lasting. Unskilled trades, although sometimes able to win concessions in a strike, benefited little because these concessions disappeared soon after the strike was over.

Overall, skilled workers were in a stronger position than unskilled workers. They could hold out longer in the event of a strike, and employers found it difficult to find substitutes. While violence could be used to replace market power, in general the skill of the occupation was a

---

[117] BPP 1824 (51) V, p. 525.   [118] *Ibid.*, p. 13.
[119] See E. J. Hobsbawm and George Rudé, *Captain Swing* (London: Lawrence and Wishart, 1969).

deciding factor in determining whether the union could exclude women. The importance of skill is best seen in the fact that unions lost their power when their occupations were deskilled due to technological change. An example is the house-painters. The Painters-Stainers' Company was strong until 1749, when it ceased to have control over the trade. The cause of this change in fortunes was that "new methods of mixing paint had eliminated much of the skill."[120] Once skill was no longer needed, the company ceased to have power because workers were easily replaced. Thus, the skill required for the work was an important determinant of whether a union could successfully obtain its demands.

A.   Unions among low-skilled workers

The importance of skill for union success can be seen by observing examples of different trades. This section will examine a number of low-skilled occupations and show that attempts at unionization were not successful here. The next section will examine unions in skilled occupations, which had a very different experience.

In Industrial Revolution Britain, low-skilled workers did not organize to exclude women workers because they were not able to. These workers were not able to form effective unions. Indeed, low-skilled occupations are notable for their lack of collectivization. The Webbs noted that "it is not among the farm servants, miners, or general laborers, ill-paid and ill-treated as these often were, that the early Trade Unions arose."[121] Unskilled workers, when they did combine, had little success in gaining their demands, and when they did win, the gains were short-lived. Since they lacked power, unskilled workers generally failed to exclude women from their trades. Men in these occupations had to compete with women workers in the open market.

1.   Handloom weavers

Handloom weaving was not a skilled trade.[122] While the amount of skill necessary varied with the type of cloth, in general handloom weaving was easily learned. Frances Collier noted that the trade was easily learned and easily entered: "If a man had a room and could rent a loom, or had 40s. with which to buy one, he could become a weaver; and because of the facility with which newcomers acquired the necessary skill to weave

---

[120] Dobson, *Masters and Journeymen*, p. 51.
[121] Webb and Webb, *The History of Trade Unionism*, p. 37.
[122] Bythell, *The Handloom Weavers*, p. 270, claimed that "The Hammonds were never more misleading than when they consigned their account of the weavers' political and industrial agitations to a volume entitled *The Skilled Laborer*."

the staple cloths, people who came to the cotton centers drifted into an occupation in which it was easy to eke out a living."[123] The Irish entered weaving in large numbers because it was so easy to learn. The parliamentary investigator Richard Muggeridge noted in 1840, "I have had abundant testimony, as well as direct personal proof, that a young person of either sex ... will, with a few weeks' practice, acquire the requisite skill, to weave an ordinary cotton fabric."[124] While he noted that certain types of cloth required skill, Mr. Symons found that skill was less important than strength in weaving: "The requisite strength I always found a more powerful ingredient in the value of wages than that of skill."[125] Parliamentary investigator H. S. Chapman concluded that the excess supply of weavers was due to the "great facility of acquiring the art of weaving."[126]

Handloom weavers were not successful in using collective action to maintain their wages. They only rarely went on strike. Bythell relates the lack of collective action to the poverty of the workers, which prevented them from amassing strike funds, and to the fact that they "could do little to inconvenience their masters by withholding their labor."[127] The employers had no factories to stand idle, so their fixed costs were low, and strikes were not very costly to them. The weavers were not unified, and the strikers had to steal shuttles in order to prevent others from continuing to work.[128] Weavers' unions were not able to enforce strikes, and there were many strike-breakers. An 1816 report to the Home Office stated that the Lancashire cotton weavers "have never been able for any considerable length of time and in any considerable numbers to *turn out* (or strike) from their employ, so as materially thereby to affect the interest of their masters."[129] With workers unable to support themselves while on strike and employers who suffered little, it is no wonder that handloom weavers were not able to maintain their wages by collective action.

The history of collective action among handloom weavers is one of failure. Handloom weavers held a number of strikes, but these produced temporary successes at best. Any wage increase that might be granted after a long strike was removed within a few months. In 1782 Manchester weavers tried to enforce the seven-year apprenticeship (which was still required by law), but they failed.[130] In 1812 a strike of Scottish weavers

---

[123] Collier, *The Family Economy of the Working Classes*, p. 6.
[124] BPP 1840 (220) XXIV, p. 601.   [125] *Ibid.*, p. 616.
[126] BPP 1840 (43) XXIII, p. 582.   [127] Bythell, *The Handloom Weavers*, p. 17.
[128] "In the year 1808, at the general turn-out of the weavers, a number of families were brought into distress by having their shuttles, &c. took from them." Aspinall, *The Early English Trade Unions*, p. 215.
[129] *Ibid.*, p. 214.   [130] Bythell, *The Handloom Weavers*, p. 52.

was a complete failure; some of the leaders were arrested and the strike ended without any wage gain at all.[131] Lancashire weavers struck in 1808 and 1818. The weavers were able to draw on the funds of friendly societies to support themselves, which helped their efforts.[132] These strikers obtained some wage gains, but the gains were only temporary. The level of wages was determined by the state of the trade. The gains of the 1808 strike persisted because the trade recovery of 1809–10 bolstered the demand for weaving.[133] The gains of the 1818 strike, however, disappeared immediately as the trade entered a depression.[134] Strikes had no more than a slight, temporary effect on weavers' wages. In 1819 a strike of Leeds weavers was "entirely unsuccessful."[135] In Lanark, a union of weavers was successful and "a table of prices was agreed to by the manufacturers, dated December 2, 1833. This table was adhered to for some time, but, eventually, some of the weavers took lower wages."[136] Parliamentary investigator J. Symons found that, in Ireland, "Combinations of hand loom weavers have had the effect of raising their wages hitherto only for a very limited time, and to a small extent, in comparison with the influence of combinations in other trades."[137]

The linen weavers of Knaresborough found that, although they could get their wages increased by a strike, this increase only lasted for a few months, so that collective action had almost no effect on the downward trend of their wages. In 1815 the weavers went on strike to resist wage reductions. The strike lasted thirteen months and was successful. In only a few months, however, the masters implemented a reduction of wages, and the weavers, having exhausted their resources, found that "we were under the necessity of submitting to it."[138] The same thing happened in 1816. The weavers went on strike to resist another reduction in wages and were successful, but "again in a very short time, probably two months after, they reduced us 1s. more; they saw our helpless situation and took advantage and reduced us."[139] A later strike, in 1823, lasted twenty-eight weeks and failed completely.

Anthony Austin, in his parliamentary report on handloom weavers, discusses strikes only briefly:

Combinations and strikes have not been frequent in this district [Somerset, Wiltshire, Devon, and Dorset], nor has their effect been very important on the state of trade. The weavers have rarely gained their object; but, on the contrary, have spent the little money which they had previously saved. The following

---

[131] *Ibid.*, pp. 196–7.   [132] *Ibid.*, p. 182.   [133] *Ibid.*, p. 191.
[134] *Ibid.*, p. 196. See also E. P. Thompson, *The Making of the English Working Class* (New York: Vintage Books, 1966), p. 279.
[135] Cole, *Attempts at General Union*, p. 48.   [136] BPP 1839 (159) XLII, p. 27.
[137] *Ibid.*, p. 65.   [138] BPP 1824 (51) V, p. 540.   [139] *Ibid.*, p. 541.

quotations from the evidence of different manufacturers are not out of place here: – ... "Eight, nine, or ten years ago the manufacturers proposed to lower the wages; the weavers struck, and combined together to support each other, and then were obliged to come in on worse terms than those originally proposed." ... In another manufacturing town, viz., Bradford, it is stated that "there has been no combination which has affected that state or condition of the weavers." Again, "The combination which was made against us two or three years ago has in no way affected the trade."

The only instance of successful combination which has come under my observation has been noticed in my Report, when mentioning that state of the serge trade at Cullompton.[140]

In his four-county territory, Austin could find only one example of a successful union of weavers, and that one was no longer operative at the time of the report, having collapsed in 1825.[141] His conclusion seems warranted: unions of handloom weavers were not successful.

The weakness of the unions seems to have made a difference for women's opportunities. Anthony Austin, while concluding that weavers' unions are unsuccessful, notes one exception: Cullompton. As long as the union maintained its strength, "it was forbidden to any female of their families to learn the art of weaving" and Cullompton women did not weave.[142] When the union lost its strength, in about 1825, women began to weave alongside the men.

The result of the general weakness of weavers' unions was that male workers could not prevent anyone from entering the trade. In 1840 parliamentary investigator H. S. Chapman noted that "whilst all, or nearly all, other trades have regulations to protect themselves from an undue increase of numbers from external causes, handloom weaving has been open to all comers."[143] In particular, women were able to enter the weaving trade. When hand-spinning employment disappeared, women moved rapidly into handloom weaving. By 1840, nearly half of the weavers for some types of cloth were women (see Table 1.3).

2.   Framework knitters

Framework knitting was not a skilled trade, and its workers did not successfully combine. The stocking frame was not difficult to learn, and "A youth of ten or twelve soon learns to work it."[144] The workers were first incorporated into a company of framework knitters in 1657. The guild, however, was weak and often could not enforce its rules on apprentices.[145] Felkin tells us, "The trade still labored under the

---

[140] BPP 1840 (43) XXIII, p. 459.   [141] *Ibid.*, p. 410.   [142] *Ibid.*, p. 410.
[143] *Ibid.*, p. 581.   [144] Felkin, *A History of the Machine-Wrought Hosiery*, p. 49.
[145] *Ibid.*, pp. 63, 73.

constant influx of too many apprenticed boys and girls and non-freed workmen. This led in 1776–7 to the formation in the midland counties of a Stockingmakers' Association for Mutual Protection."[146] The guild could not enforce its limits on employment because the trade was simply too easily learned.

Later we find that the framework knitters had little success in their strikes for wages. Numerous strikes were unable to prevent the fall of wages over the first half of the nineteenth century. In 1813 the Leicester framework knitters went on strike for higher wages. They were unsuccessful, and were prosecuted under the Combination Acts.[147] The Nottingham knitters went on strike in 1814 and were able to support themselves only because of contributions from sympathizers. When two leaders were convicted under the Combination Acts, the union collapsed and the strike ended in failure.[148] The year 1819 saw a massive strike of framework knitters, supported by a sympathetic public. The Leicester knitters obtained a wage increase that lasted a few years. Framework knitters in Derby did not win their strike.[149] The Nottingham workers won a wage gain, but the gain was partial and temporary. The Hammonds note that, while the employers agreed to a wage increase:

Unfortunately, however, there was no method of compelling all masters to adhere to this; in Nottingham sixty-seven agreed to the prices, twenty-three refused. Funds in Nottingham were getting low, and the men had to go back to work, even at the houses who refused to give the statement prices. The other employers kept to the statement for six or eight months, and then wages fell as low as ever.[150]

The same pattern was seen in the strikes of 1821 and 1824: the workers went on strike for higher wages, the masters agreed and paid the higher wages for a few months, but soon wages fell again.[151] The framework knitters' attempts to raise their wages by collective action, though admirable attempts at cooperation, were futile.

Little wonder, then, that the framework knitters have gone down in history for their attempts to gain their demands through violence. In one of England's famous episodes of Luddism, the knitters of Nottingham turned to frame-breaking in 1811–12. The knitting frames of employers paying too low a price were targeted and destroyed. The use of violence is an indication that the workers did not have sufficient economic strength to gain their demands through peaceful means. Frame-breaking seems to have occurred when more peaceful means proved unfruitful, as

---

[146] *Ibid.*, p. 115.   [147] BPP 1824 (51) V, p. 262.
[148] Hammond and Hammond, *The Skilled Laborer*, p. 234.
[149] BPP 1824 (51) V, pp. 266, 279.
[150] Hammond and Hammond, *The Skilled Laborer*, p. 252.   [151] *Ibid.*, p. 252.

in 1814 when the failure of the Nottingham strike led to a recurrence of frame-breaking.[152] The Luddism of 1811–12 resulted in a wage increase, but since the workers had no real economic power, the increase was only temporary.[153]

Male framework knitters probably wished to exclude women from their trade, but they were not able to do so. Women worked in this occupation on the same terms as men. In 1845 the parliamentary committee on framework knitters found that "vast numbers of women and children are working side by side with men, often employed in the same description of frames, making the same fabrics, at the same rate of wages, the only advantage over them which the man possesses being his superior strength."[154]

3.   Miners

Coal miners provide an intermediate case. They seem to have had more power than handloom weavers or framework knitters, but ultimately the employers had the upper hand. Colliers did have skill, but not enough skill to give them effective power in dictating the conditions of their work. There is some evidence of collective action in the eighteenth century, but the use of violence suggests that the miners had little economic power.[155] After the repeal of the Combination Acts, unions sprang up throughout Britain, and had some success for about a decade, but then became ineffective.

Colliers of northern England won a few strikes in the late 1820s and early 1830s, but ultimately failed because their skill was not scarce enough, and they could be replaced with other miners. In 1829 a colliery manager noted that, in spite of the fall in the price of coal, he could not lower the wages of the miners "without great disturbance and perhaps not succeeding in the end."[156] In 1831 the colliers went on strike to correct various grievances, the chief of which was irregularity of work. No coal was produced during the strike, and after a couple of months the employers agreed to the demands of the miners. The next strike, though, did not end so successfully. In 1832 the colliers went on strike for the right to unionize, and this time employers imported lead miners from neighboring districts to work in their place. Since they did not have to stop production, employers could now outlast the workers. The strike lasted half a year, and ultimately the union was defeated.[157]

---

[152] Ibid., p. 234.   [153] Ibid., p. 266.   [154] BPP 1845 (609) XV, p. 101.
[155] Raymond Turner, "English Coal Industry in the Seventeenth and Eighteenth Centuries," American Historical Review, 27 (1921), pp. 13–14.
[156] Hammond and Hammond, The Skilled Laborer, p. 26.   [157] Ibid., ch. 3.

Similarly, colliers' unions in Scotland had little power because employers frequently replaced strikers with unskilled laborers. The Scottish
colliers formed a union immediately after the repeal of the Combination
Act in 1824. They had some initial success in raising wages, but soon the
employers brought in replacement workers, and the union failed. George
Taylor, a mine owner in Ayrshire, broke an 1824 strike in the same way
he had broken a strike in 1817, by employing laborers to replace the
striking miners.[158] In Stirlingshire, when the striking workers used violence to keep the blacklegs from working, the Duke of Hamilton
employed guards to protect the blacklegs, and the strike failed.[159] In
1825, "Lord Belhaven dismissed the entire workforce of his collieries
and recruited new men."[160] The miners did not have enough skill to be
successful in their strikes because replacement workers could be taught
what they needed to know fairly easily.

A national union, the Miners' Association of Great Britain and Ireland,
was formed in 1842, but was unable to give the miners power over
employers. The Association's income did not cover its expenses, so it was
unable to build up a strike fund. It was also unsuccessful in eliminating
strike-breaking. An 1844 strike in north-east England ended in failure; the
striking workers were replaced, and evicted from their cottages.[161]

Since the miners' union did not have enough power to prevent wages
from falling, it also did not have enough power to exclude women. In
1836, colliers in Scotland banned women workers, but this attempt to
exclude women did not succeed, because "the temptation to employ
them proved too strong, and they found their way back again."[162] Once
more we see that unions without effective power were not able to prevent
the employment of women. Women were not excluded until 1842, when
an act of parliament forbade women to work underground. As we have
seen, however, even this law was not completely effective in preventing
women from working in mines.

4.   Agriculture

Agricultural laborers, among the poorest of all workers, had no success
in combining to raise their wages. These laborers were too poor to build
up an adequate strike fund, and, because their work was relatively

---

[158] Alan Campbell, "The Scots Colliers' Strikes of 1824–1826," in John Rule, ed., *British
Trade Unionism, 1750–1850: The Formative Years* (New York: Longman, 1988),
pp. 151–2.
[159] *Ibid.*, pp. 152–3.   [160] *Ibid.*, p. 156.
[161] A. J. Taylor, "The Miners' Association of Great Britain and Ireland, 1842–48: A
Study in the Problem of Integration," *Economica*, 22 (1955), pp. 45–60.
[162] Pinchbeck, *Women Workers*, p. 265. See also John, "Colliery Legislation," p. 91.

unskilled, other workers were easily hired to replace them.[163] Since they had no monopoly power, male agricultural workers could not enforce artificial constraints on female employment, and agricultural labor markets functioned competitively.

There are some instances of agricultural laborers striking. In 1763 the haymakers of Islington successfully went on strike for higher wages. They picked an opportune time; the price of hay was high, and the hay was ready to harvest. Employers' concession curves were high, because the potential lost profits were high, so they gave in to the strikers' demands. However, the 1763 strike was an unusual situation, and the haymakers could not maintain their power. They tried another strike in 1766, when conditions were less favorable, and they lost.[164] In 1800 some laborers from Essex were tried for conspiracy because "they had prevailed upon several laborers to leave their work, and join their party."[165] They had intended to strike in order to prevent plowing, but the attempt never got that far. In 1835, following the new Poor Law, a union of agricultural laborers, called the United Brothers, formed in the south-east. They had hoped to strike during the harvest of 1835, when farmers needed them the most, but the farmers pre-empted them with a lock-out in the spring and summer. Unity was broken as many left the union in order to work. The union's funds were quickly exhausted, and the union ended in complete failure.[166]

As was the case in other trades unable to form effective unions, agricultural laborers sometimes resorted to violence. In the Swing riots of 1830, laborers demanded higher wages by means of intimidation; they burned farms and broke threshing machines.[167] While the violence may have gained them higher wages in the short run, it had no lasting effect. We can see the effect of the Swing riots on wages in the farm accounts of Thomas Estcourt's farm in Shipton Moyne, Gloucestershire. Letters to Estcourt from his brother Edmund, and his bailiff Thomas Marshall, suggest that the Tetbury riot reached as far as Shipton Moyne, and that laborers there were demanding higher wages. On November 26, 1830, Edmund Estcourt wrote:

My dear Brother,
The Morning was ushered in with demonstrations of a most determined spirit on the part of our Laborers. They being all assembled in a body at Palmer's corner

---

[163] Evidence from wage profiles suggests that agricultural laborers acquired some skill, but had less skill than factory workers. Burnette, "How Skilled."
[164] Dobson, *Masters and Journeymen*, p. 23.   [165] *The Times*, August 9, 1800.
[166] Roger Wells, "Tolpuddle in the Context of English Agrarian Labor History," in John Rule, ed., *British Trade Unionism, 1750–1850: The Formative Years* (New York: Longman, 1988), p. 124.
[167] Hobsbawm and Rudé, *Captain Swing*.

about 9 o-clock in pursuance of the resolution they formed yesterday evening to proceed to each Farmer & demand an increase of wages to the amount of 2s. a day instead of 8 [shillings per week]. Earl and I joined them yesterday evening and found them bent upon this, notwithstanding any suggestions we could offer. They were joined by numbers from Tetbury and we began much to fear how it would end – when most happily some of the Tetbury folk had tonight a Travelling Threshing Machine which they seized on its route through the Town, up into the Turnpike Road near Sam Poole's and there made it a bonfire.[168]

Two days later Thomas Marshall reported that the farmers paid their laborers 2s. per day for one week, but then settled on 10s. per week, or half the wage increase requested by the laborers:

As to the disturbance in this Parish the Farmers through fear acceded to the demand of the laborers (2s. per day) for one week or until your arrival, considering they have done wrong in complying with the terms of a combination of Laborers & which is contrary to your advice in the printed papers I have therefore advised the Farmers to call a Vestry tomorrow morning to consider what is best to be done, our proposition is to give 10s. per week to the able bodied men & all those that will not comply to be discharged[169]

Though Marshall claims that the men he employed on Estcourt's farm did not participate in the riot, they also received an increase in wage to 20d. per day. Figure 5.2 shows the median male wage paid on Estcourt's farm, in summer and winter, from 1822 to 1840. Before the riots Estcourt's laborers were earning 18d. per day in the summer and 16d. per day in the winter, but after the riot they received a raise to 20d. per day throughout the year. Figure 5.3 shows that the wage increase occurred in December 1830, immediately after the riots. John Rickards earned a wage of 18d. per day between June 12 and November 27, 1830. On the next payday, December 24, 1830, John Rickards was paid 20d. per day for twenty days of work. Boys working at the farm also received a wage increase, though the men who were already earning 20d. or more did not receive a raise.[170] The wage increase, though, was not permanent. After three years at 20d. the summer wage fell to 18d. in 1834 and 17d. in 1835. In this case violence was successful in winning the laborers higher wages, but these wages only lasted three years.

The industrial weakness of the agricultural laborers continued through the nineteenth century. They formed a union in 1872, under the direction of Joseph Arch. Boyer and Hatton find that, while the union had some success in raising their wages, this success was short-lived. The union did raise the wages of agricultural laborers between

---

[168] Gloucestershire Record Office D1571 X62.   [169] *Ibid.*
[170] Gloucestershire Record Office D1571 vol. A41.

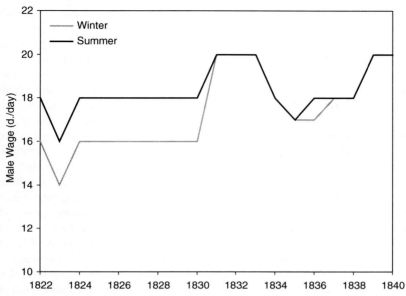

Figure 5.2 Male wages at the Estcourt Farm in Shipton Moyne, Gloucestershire
Source: Gloucestershire Record Office D1571 vol. A37–A48.

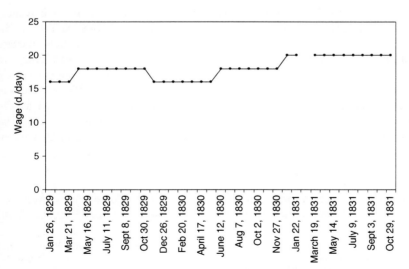

Figure 5.3 Daily wage of John Rickards at the Estcourt farm
Source: Gloucestershire Record Office D1571 vol. 41.

1872 and 1874, but in 1874 the fortunes of the union changed. Employers organized a lock-out and the union ran out of funds for strike pay. After this point, union membership declined and the wage gains were lost. By 1880 the wage gains attributable to the union had disappeared.[171] The agricultural laborers did not have enough power to raise their wages for more than a few years. Agricultural laborers were relatively unskilled and thus could not successfully unionize to control their employment or wages. The result was a competitive labor market where men and women competed for employment. Men were stronger than women and thus earned more, but, as we have seen in Chapter 4, employers considered male and female farm workers substitutable.

The history of unions in low-skilled occupations thus is one of valiant efforts in the face of constant failure. Unions were unsuccessful, not for lack of effort, but because they simply did not have enough market power to enforce their demands. Because unions were so weak in these low-skilled trades, there was no force excluding women, and women entered these trades freely. The gender division of labor in these occupations was determined by comparative advantage, as described in Chapter 3. However, the models in Chapter 3 do not apply to the more highly skilled trades because there unions were able to enforce barriers to women's employment.

B.   Unions among highly skilled workers

While the unskilled trades fought losing battles to maintain their wages, employers complained that they were being ruled by their skilled workmen. The Scottish calico printers, for example, "reduced their masters almost to a state of dependence upon them."[172] The Yorkshire croppers were called "the tyrants of the county"[173] because they "were constantly able to exert effective limitation of entry to their trade."[174] Skilled workers had bargaining power and thus were able to enforce rules such as the exclusion of women workers. The importance of the skilled nature of the work in producing union power is demonstrated by the fact that when trades became deskilled, the unions in those trades lost their power.

1.   Mule spinners
Many factors combined to make mule-spinning a male trade, but in the end it was limited access to the skill which excluded women from

---

[171] George Boyer and Timothy Hatton, "Did Joseph Arch Raise Agricultural Wages? Rural Trade Unions and the Labour Market in Late Nineteenth-Century England," *Economic History Review* 47 (1994), pp. 310–34.
[172] Aspinall, *The Early English Trade Unions*, p. 191.   [173] *Ibid.*, p. 64.
[174] Randall, *Before the Luddites*, p. 33.

employment. Between 1795 and 1830, the mule was only partially mechanized. The steam engine moved the carriage out, but the spinner provided the motive power to move the carriage back. A mule carriage with 336 spindles for spinning coarse yarn weighed 1400 pounds, and this had to be moved by the spinner three and a half times per minute.[175] All mules required some strength, and larger mules required a great deal of strength. Of course, firms could choose to install smaller mules and hire women, though the strength required for mule spinning would still affect the output and earnings of female spinners, just as it affected the output and earnings of male spinners as they aged. Wage profiles of males in the Lancashire cotton industry peak at age 30–35.[176] One mule spinner, who was 34 in 1833, noted that he had already seen a fall in his wage.

Alexander Pitcairn, aged thirty-four, solemnly sworn, depones, that he is a mule spinner at this work, and at present makes about 25s. a week; that his wheels contain five hundred and twenty-eight spindles; that seven or eight years ago, he, at this work, made from 28s. to 30s. per week, but at wheels containing seven hundred and twelve spindles.[177]

This quote makes clear the reason why Alexander's earnings had fallen. While he previously worked a mule of 712 spindles, in 1833 he worked a mule with only 528 spindles. Since the trend in the industry was toward larger mules, this reduction must have been the result of waning strength. Thus strength affected male earnings as well as female earnings. Men were also more productive as mule spinners because they more effectively disciplined their assistants.[178] M'Connel and Kennedy tried hiring female mule spinners between 1810 and 1818, but found its profits falling. The lower labor costs resulting from hiring women were off-set by increased wastage of raw material and higher turnover costs because the women did not hire and discipline their assistants.[179]

The self-actor, introduced in 1830, eliminated the need for strength, and employers thought that they would be able to employ women in place of the more expensive men spinners. Elsewhere women worked the self-actor effectively. In 1856 there were only a few self-acting mules in Barcelona, but women worked 80 percent of these machines.[180] The

---

[175] Lazonick, "Industrial Relations and Technical Change," p. 235.
[176] BPP 1834 (167) XIX.   [177] BPP 1833 (450) XX, A1, p. 112.
[178] Lazonick, "Industrial Relations and Technical Change."
[179] Huberman, *Escape from the Market*, ch. 2.
[180] Natalia Mora-Sitja, "Labor Supply and Wage Differentials in an Industrialising Economy: Catalonia in the Long Nineteenth Century," unpublished PhD thesis, University of Oxford, 2006, p. 155.

self-actor, however, still required skill, a skill on which the male union had a monopoly. Freifeld demonstrates that the self-actor required the attendance of a skilled spinner, who knew how to correctly adjust the machine.[181] Women, who had been eliminated from spinning by the strength requirements, did not have the necessary skills, and they could not acquire these skills because the male union guarded them tightly. The Manchester mule spinners excluded women from their union in 1829, and refused to teach women the skills.[182] This union was very restrictive, and allowed its members to teach the trade only to "the son, brother, or orphan nephew of spinners, and the poor relations of the proprietors of the mills."[183] In Lancashire, this policy was effective because the union had a monopoly on the skill. Since they and not their employers controlled the skills, they could effectively prevent women from being employed as mule spinners by refusing to teach them the skills.

In Scotland, however, the male monopoly was not complete, and some women worked the mules. In 1810 the Glasgow spinners "combined to prevent the masters from employing or excluding from employment any workmen, except those whom the operatives themselves thought should be employed or excluded."[184] Like the Lancashire union, the Glasgow union attempted to exclude women. One employer claimed, "In general they did not allow women or boys to work as spinners; nor will they now allow a man from a neighboring county to enter a Glasgow mill."[185] The Glasgow union, however, was unable to maintain control over employment. By 1837 there were as many female as male spinners in Glasgow.[186] Since the Scottish union did not have complete control over the necessary skill, it was not successful in preventing the employment of women. Thus the main factor in determining whether women operated the self-acting mules was the strength of the male spinners' union.

2.   Tailors

The tailors are often cited as an example of an occupation which increased its wages by combination. In 1840 a parliamentary investigator blamed the tailors' union for the fact that women were more likely to be weavers than tailors:

Where the men have opposed the employment of women and children, by not permitting their own family to work, or where the work is of such a nature that neither women nor children can perform it, their own wages have kept up to a

---

[181] Freifeld, "Technological Change and the 'Self-Acting' Mule."
[182] Kirby and Musson, *The Voice of the People*, p. 94.   [183] *Ibid.*, p. 93.
[184] Evidence of Henry Houldsworth, BPP 1824 (51) V, p. 476.   [185] *Ibid.*, p. 479.
[186] Wood, *History of Wages in the Cotton Trade*, p. 103.

point equal to the maintenance of a family. The tailors of London have in this way not merely *kept up*, but have *forced up* their wages, though it is an occupation better adapted to women than weaving, where women are employed in some branches of the trade, and wherein the tendency to employ them is therefore much more difficult, indeed impossible wholly to resist.[187]

He was correct in noting that, compared to weaving, women had a comparative advantage in sewing, which did not require strength. However, in this case the actions of male tailors prevented women from pursuing their comparative advantage. A union of journeymen tailors was formed in London as early as 1721.[188] In 1824 Francis Place claimed that "The journeymen tailors have a perfect and perpetual combination among them."[189] In 1810 and 1814, employers attempted to introduce women workers in the tailoring shops, and the journeymen tailors successfully went on strike to prevent this. Place noted that from 1795 to 1813 the journeymen's weekly wages rose from 25s. to 36s., and "Not a single shilling was obtained at any one of these periods but by compulsion."[190] In 1831 Gravenor Henson noted that the tailors were "with few exceptions, victorious."[191] These strikes had the effect of confining the women workers to certain types of needlework and reserving the more lucrative tailoring work for the male tailors. The restrictions created occupational crowding, and meant that tailors and dressmakers did essentially the same work for different wages.

The tailors were successful until 1833. In 1800 their employers complained that the journeymen, though many in number (15,000 to 18,000 as an estimate), were well organized. Each tailor belonged to one of the "houses of call," and these smaller groups communicated effectively, allowing them to act in unison. The tailors were thus able to enforce a closed shop. We find that "in all parts of the metropolis these houses are established and every journeyman is compelled to belong and resort to a Society there formed."[192]

Tailors were successful because they were hard to replace. Masters were not able to break the strike because replacements had to be skilled workers, and sufficient numbers of replacements could not be obtained. Masters tried bringing in tailors from outside of London: in 1764 they

[187] BPP 1840 (43) XXIII, pp. 383–4.
[188] Jenny Morris, "The Characteristics of Sweating: The Late-Nineteenth-Century London and Leeds Tailoring Trade," in Angela John, ed., *Unequal Opportunities* (Oxford: Basil Blackwell, 1986), p. 102.
[189] BPP 1824 (51) V, p. 45.
[190] Quoted in Thompson, *The Making of the English Working Class*, p. 255.
[191] Gravenor Henson, *History of the Framework Knitters* (New York: Augustus Kelley, [1831] 1970), p. 380.
[192] Aspinall, *The Early English Trade Unions*, p. 34.

managed to employ 800 tailors from the country and 230 foreigners. However, this number was not sufficient to break the strike. The masters needed more men than they could attract from elsewhere.[193] The strike that occasioned this complaint was settled by arbitration in 1801, and the journeymen received two-fifths of the raise they requested.

The tailors' union lost its power when the work was deskilled. During the Napoleonic Wars, a system of "slop" work was developed for making army and navy clothing. This work was done by piece-rate in the worker's own home, rather than by time-rate wages in the master's workshop. The finer division of labor reduced the amount of skill necessary. The slop system of the "dishonorable" section of the trade proved competitive and eroded the power of the tailors' union. The "honorable" workers, called "Flints," refused to work on a piece-rate basis, and this refusal distinguished them from the "Dungs" who worked in the "dishonorable" section of the trade. Over time the size of the "dishonorable" section of the trade grew. In 1824 there were four "Flints" for every "Dung," but by 1849 there were only three "Flints" to every twenty "Dungs."[194] Tailors' strikes were no longer successful because the mass of workers in the slop trade provided strike-breakers. The London tailors went on strike in 1827, 1830, and 1834; none of these strikes was successful. During the 1834 strike, many women were used as strike-breakers, and some were attacked by strikers.[195] That the strikes were essential to maintaining the gender division of labor can be seen in what happened when the tailors finally lost a strike in 1834; following this loss, "large numbers of women were introduced into the striking workshops."[196] After 1834 the well-paid tailors lost ground to the women slop-workers. The market maintained continual pressure and the unionized men fought a losing battle to maintain their excess wages. As the trade was deskilled, the tailors lost their union power and their high wages.

3.   Wool-combers

Wool-combing was highest paid of the occupations in the worsted industry.[197] The Hammonds described the wool-combers thus:

The wool-combers may be called the aristocracy of the worsted workers. An ancient, skilled, select, and well-organized body whose insubordinate conduct

[193] Dobson, *Masters and Journeymen*, p. 71.   [194] Taylor, *Eve and the New Jerusalem*, p. 104.
[195] *Ibid.*, p. 115.   [196] Rose, *Limited Livelihoods*, p. 144.
[197] James Burnley, *The History of Wool and Woolcombing* (London: Sampson Low, Marston, Searle and Rivington, 1889), p. 160.

gave much trouble to their employers, they form an example of a trade that was long able by combination to keep up its wages."[198]

The combing process did require strength, but how much is not clear. It did not require enough strength to prevent women from doing it in every case. Wives of wool-combers often assisted their husbands, indicating that some women found the work to be profitable. In the middle ages women commonly combed wool.[199] While these women found it profitable to be wool-combers, the occupation was in most cases strictly limited to men, indicating that wool-combers succeeded in controlling access to the trade.

Early wool-combers' strikes were generally successful. In 1726 in Norwich, wool-combers won a strike against the employment of a man who had not been apprenticed.[200] A 1741 pamphlet notes that the wool-combers:

For a number of years past erected themselves into a sort of a corporation ... and when they became a little formidable they gave laws to their masters, as also to themselves – viz., That no man should comb wool under 2s. per dozen; that no master should employ any comber that was not of their club; if he did they agreed one and all not to work for him.[201]

In the eighteenth century, "No wool-comber was permitted to take an apprentice except his eldest son, and they not only dictated their own rate of wages, but sought to prescribe the prices which the masters should ask for the products of their labor."[202] Evidently the wool-combers had a great deal of power and were able to enforce whatever rules they desired. In 1776 Adam Smith located the power of the wool-combers in their ability to stop the whole manufacture: "Half a dozen wool-combers, perhaps, are necessary to keep a thousand spinners and weavers at work." Their ability to create a bottleneck increased the cost of a strike to the employer, which increased their bargaining power. Thus wool-combers are able to "reduce the whole manufacture into a sort of slavery to themselves, and raise the price of their labor above what is due to the nature of their work."[203]

It is not surprising, then, that we find wool-combing to be an exclusively male trade. In the 1830s, Robert Clough of Keighley employed no

---

[198] Hammond and Hammond, *The Skilled Laborer*, p. 195.
[199] Eileen Power, *Medieval Women*, ed. M. M. Postan (Cambridge: Cambridge University Press, 1975), p. 67.
[200] Hammond and Hammond, *The Skilled Laborer*, p. 196.
[201] *A Short Essay upon Trade in General*, 1741, quoted in Webb and Webb, *The History of Trade Unionism*, p. 31.
[202] Burnley, *The History of Wool and Woolcombing*, p. 164.
[203] Smith, *The Wealth of Nations*, p. 126.

female wool-combers.[204] His handloom weavers were about a quarter female, and his powerloom weavers almost exclusively female, but no female wool-combers appear in the wage books. Women may well have worked at wool-combing with their husbands; we only know that no women brought in the finished wool. We do know, however, that the men were able to keep the occupation under their control. The wool-combers were able to keep out all outsiders, allowing only their own sons to enter the trade.

By the mid-nineteenth century, wool-combers had lost their power. This was due mainly to the advent of workable combing machines, which gave employers a viable alternative to the hand-combers. Once the combers lost their monopoly power, they began to lose strikes. In 1825 the Bradford combers lost a long strike. After this failure, the trade was inundated with new workers, indicating that the union had constrained employment before this point.[205] By the 1840s, wool-combers' wages had sunk to starvation levels.[206] In 1846 those employed by Robert Clough of Grove Mill, Keighley, went on strike for a wage increase. They were not successful, and many of those who went on strike were not re-employed.[207] Until there was a substitute for their skill, the wool-combers remained powerful and maintained control over employment. They lost this power, however, when the combing machine provided an alternative source of combed wool.

Unions of skilled workers were successful because their skills gave them market power. As long as a union maintained a monopoly on its skill, it could do whatever it wished to increase its wages, including excluding women. In trades where the work was deskilled, unions lost their power, and rules excluding women became ineffective. The most important source of occupational segregation among wage-earners was the desire of union members to increase their wages by excluding competitors, coupled with the market power to enforce this desire.

Later in the nineteenth century, unskilled unions seem to have had some success in raising their wage above the wages of non-unionized workers, but this success was short-lived. Hatton, Boyer, and Bailey report that among unskilled industrial workers union membership increased wages by about 16 percent in 1889–90.[208] They interpret this

[204] Wage books of Robert Clough, University of Leeds Archives, Clough 61.
[205] Thompson, *The Making of the English Working Class*, p. 282.
[206] Maurice G. Smith, "Robert Clough, Grove Mill, Keighley: A Study in Technological Redundancy, 1835–65," MA thesis, University of Leeds, 1982, p. 73.
[207] *Ibid.*, pp. 75–7.
[208] T. J. Hatton, G. R. Boyer, and R. E. Bailey, "The Union Wage Effect in Late Nineteenth-Century Britain," *Economica* 61 (1994), p. 447.

as the "impact effect" of the sudden increase in the membership in new
unions that occurred at this time. They note that, while unions of low-
skilled workers reached a membership of 350,000 in 1890, "their success could not be maintained, and a counter-attack by employers
combined with worsening economic conditions caused membership in
the new unions to fall to under 200,000 in 1892 and further to about
150,000 in 1896," and this decline "suggests that they may not have
been able to hold the wage gains."[209] They do not find higher union
wage effects among workers studied, but their study does not include
any workers in craft unions, which would have had more control over
skill and which do seem to have been successful without resorting to
strikes.[210]

My claim that the more skilled occupations had more successful
unions does not seem to fit the twentieth-century USA, where the wage
gap between union and non-union workers is larger for blue-collar
workers than for white-collar workers, and the wage gap falls with
education.[211] These facts suggest that, unlike the unions of Industrial
Revolution Britain, US unions are currently more successful in raising
wages for less-skilled occupations. What accounts for the difference?
One important difference between modern unions and unions of
Industrial Revolution Britain is structure, i.e., how workers band
together into unions. In the USA, the National Labor Relations Board
(NLRB) runs union elections for what it considers to be the appropriate
bargaining unit. While the bargaining unit is sometimes the craft, frequently it is an employer or a plant. When the NLRB began its work,
there were bitter struggles between the AFL, which advocated a craft
structure, and the CIO, which advocated the employer, plant, or
industry bargaining unit. The NLRB accepted both types of units but
made it difficult for a craft unit to break away from a functioning
employer unit.[212] The result of the historical process was a union
structure very different from that of Industrial Revolution Britain.
Unions are today likely to be groups of workers in different occupations
who work at the same location, rather than organizations of workers who
share the same occupation. By contrast, unions of the Industrial Revolution were organized by craft rather than employer. In an Industrial
Revolution cotton factory, the mule spinners had their union, and the
weavers had their own separate union. Since unions tend to compress

---

[209] *Ibid.*, pp. 437, 439.   [210] *Ibid.*, p. 438.
[211] Richard Freeman and James Medoff, *What Do Unions Do?* (New York: Basic Books,
1984), pp. 49–50.
[212] Frank McCulloch and Tim Bornstein, *The National Labor Relations Board* (New York:
Praeger, 1974), p. 132.

the wage structure of the workers within the union, the modern structure leads to a compression of wages across occupational levels and thus produces smaller wage gaps for the better educated.

Also important is the difference between white-collar and blue-collar skilled jobs. While white-collar occupations generally require more education, they are not the types of occupations that provide monopoly power. Skilled workers of Industrial Revolution Britain had power because they had a monopoly on the skill used in their occupation. They trained all new workers themselves and thus had perfect control over who could learn the trade. The skills were specific to a narrowly defined occupation, and the entire occupation was unionized. Only a limited number of people knew how to operate a spinning mule well. White-collar skills are more general and are often learned in schools, making it hard for the union to exert much influence over who learns the skill. White-collar skills are more easily transferred from one industry to another. An accountant can work for retailing as well as manufacturing. The pool of potential competitors is large, so that striking workers are easily replaced. Thus the fact that white-collar workers have less success in raising wages is consistent with the model I outlined above.

One characteristic of unions has persisted: women benefit less than men from unionization. While many unskilled workers have managed to gain from unionization, women have not achieved equal representation. In the modern USA, women are concentrated in less-unionized sectors and thus have lower rates of unionization.[213] In 1977, 27 percent of male employees, but only 11 percent of female employees, were unionized.[214] This difference does not reflect a lower desire for unionization among women. Among unrepresented workers, 41 percent of women but only 27 percent of men said they would vote for a union.[215] Women are not only less likely to be in unions, but those who are members gain less than men from the union. In 1979 the union wage gap was 19 percent for men but only 15 percent for women.[216] Even today, unions help men more than they help women.

Conclusion

Among wage-earners, the most important mechanism excluding women from the best jobs was the union. Employers and government regulations had only a small impact. Unions enforced the exclusion of women because they had not only the ability, but also the economic incentive.

---

[213] Freeman and Medoff, *What Do Unions Do?*, p. 28.   [214] *Ibid.*, p. 27.   [215] *Ibid.*, p. 29.
[216] *Ibid.*, p. 49.

Unlike employers, they benefited from constraints on women's employment. Where unions had market power, and where it was in their interest to restrict employment, they excluded women from employment. The skill level of the occupation was important in determining whether workers could enforce their demands. The outcome in any given industry was not fully determined; how much power a union had depended not only on the skill content of the job, but also on the use of violence, on the organization of the union itself, and, to a certain degree, on luck. However, the relationship between skill and union power is strong enough to explain why women were excluded from highly skilled occupations but not from low-skilled occupations. The fact that unions were more successful in skilled occupations explains why women competed freely with men in the unskilled labor market, but not in the skilled labor market.

The power of labor unions grew over the course of the nineteenth century. Since unions were such an important force in limiting opportunities for women workers, this suggests that women saw their opportunities further restricted as the nineteenth century progressed. Mancur Olson points to the gradual accumulation of "distributional coalitions" as the cause of Britain's slower rate of growth in the later nineteenth and twentieth centuries.[217] These distributional coalitions were also the cause of increasing constraints on women's occupational opportunities. Unions were not the only distributional coalitions limiting women's opportunities; in the next chapter we will see that professional organizations were also effective in excluding women.

[217] Olson, *The Rise and Decline of Nations.*

6 Occupational barriers in self-employment

The previous chapter examined the mechanisms that excluded women from skilled wage-earning jobs and concluded that unions with some monopoly power were the main exclusionary force. This chapter asks how women were excluded from self-employment. The occupations studied here include the professions, retailing, and entrepreneurship in general. Because the labor market was not perfectly competitive, there was room for gender discrimination. In these occupations, the causes of discriminatory constraints were the family, consumer discrimination, and professional groups organized to circumvent the market.

Economic theory suggests that gender discrimination can only persist where it is protected from competitive forces. The family, because it is not subject to competitive forces, is an important source of discrimination. In this chapter we shall see that women's economic opportunities were limited by family decisions such as investment in human capital and inheritance of capital. Competitive markets protected women against discrimination; only employers who were protected from the discipline of the market, specifically those with some monopoly power, could discriminate against women and survive. Consumer discrimination, however, will not be eliminated by competition. Thus, women are more vulnerable to gender discrimination if consumers care about the gender of the individual making the good or delivering the service. Also, professional organizations made the market less competitive; they took control of employment away from the market, so that they could limit entry to their professions. As in the last chapter, we will see that, of the many factors that have been blamed for occupational segregation, the most important were those which removed employment decisions from the competitive market.

I   Consumer discrimination

One way that gender ideology may have had an effect on women's opportunities was through the preferences of customers for one gender

274

over the other. If customers have a taste for discrimination, they receive less utility from a service provided by an individual of a particular race or gender, and thus will only patronize women if the price of the service is lower. Consumer discrimination may explain why blacks are less likely to be self-employed than whites.[1] Consumer discrimination is similar to taste discrimination among employers, where employers will not hire women workers unless their price is lower. However, unlike employer discrimination, consumer discrimination will not be eliminated by competition.[2] Unlike employers, customers who have a taste for discrimination do not go bankrupt. Thus competition did not protect women from this type of discrimination, and even in competitive markets women might find their opportunities limited by gender ideology.

Consumer discrimination may have been important in keeping women out of certain occupations. While there is no obvious reason why women could not be hairdressers, women were rare in this occupation. Perhaps men preferred to have their hair dressed by other men, or considered it improper to have a female hairdresser. With the exception of staymaking, the garment trades did not require strength, and yet there was stark occupational segregation by gender. Table 6.1 shows sorting within the garment trades. We see a clear gender division of labor, with work segregated according to which gender wore the garments. Even outside of tailoring, where a powerful combination of male workers prevented the employment of women, men generally made clothes for men, and women made clothes for women.[3] There were eight male and only one female breeches-makers (the female was a widow). Mantua-makers and dressmakers were overwhelmingly female.[4] The intimacy required for fitting clothes may have encouraged customers to seek individuals of the same gender to make their clothes. Millinery seems to have had less gender segregation than dressmaking or tailoring (half of Coventry milliners were male in 1791), perhaps because hats were a less

---

[1] George Borjas and Stephen Bronars, "Consumer Discrimination and Self-Employment," *Journal of Political Economy* 97 (1989), pp. 581–605.

[2] See Lawrence Kahn, "Customer Discrimination and Affirmative Action," *Economic Inquiry* 29 (1991), pp. 555–71.

[3] The neutral case is horse millinery (making decorations for horses). Note that this is a mixed trade.

[4] Alison Kay notes that "Millinery and dressmaking, catering to an all-female clientele, were the main exceptions to the male dominance of the higher reaches of retailing." Kay, "Retailing, Respectability and the Independent Woman in Nineteenth-Century London," in Robert Beachy, Beatrice Craig, and Alastair Owens, eds., *Women, Business and Finance in Nineteenth-Century Europe: Rethinking Separate Spheres* (Oxford: Berg, 2006), p. 159.

Table 6.1. *Sorting in the garment trades*

Trade		Men	Women	Unknown	Percent women
Sheffield, 1774	Breeches maker	2	0	0	0.0
	Milliner	1	2	0	66.7
	Staymaker	3	0	0	0.0
	Tailor	5	0	0	0.0
Manchester, 1788	Breeches maker	6	0	0	0.0
	Horse milliner	3	1	0	25.0
	Mantua-maker	0	10	2	100.0
	Milliner and dressmaker	0	24	0	100.0
	Sempstress	0	3	0	100.0
	Staymaker	10	2	2	16.7
	Tailor	59	0	1	0.0
Coventry, 1791	Horse milliner	1	0	1	0.0
	Leather breeches maker	0	1	1	100.0
	Mantua-maker	0	2	0	100.0
	Milliner	4	4	0	50.0
	Staymaker	5	0	0	0.0
	Tailor	7	0	0	0.0
Manchester, 1824-5	Milliner	0	20	14	100.0
	Staymaker	9	2	1	18.2
	Tailor and habit maker	61	1	14	1.6
Coventry, 1835	Milliner and dressmaker	0	19	0	100.0
	Staymaker	3	3	0	50.0
	Tailor	28	0	1	0.0
Manchester, 1846	Milliner and dressmaker	12	245	18	95.3
	Staymaker	14	11	0	44.0
	Tailor	239	1	18	0.4
Birmingham, 1850	Milliner and dressmaker	11	489	16	97.8
	Staymaker	6	59	6	90.8
	Tailor	382	7	7	1.8
Derby, 1850	Milliner and dressmaker	0	97	4	100.0
	Staymaker	4	12	0	75.0
	Tailor	116	1	0	0.9

Sources: Sketchley's Sheffield Directory, 1774; Lewis's Manchester Directory for 1788; The Universal British Directory, 1791; Pigot and Dean's Directory for Manchester, 1835; Slater's National Commercial Directory of Ireland, 1846; Slater's Royal National and Commercial Directory of Ireland, 1850.

intimate item of dress. As noted in Chapter 5, staymaking was an exception to the rule that women made clothing for women because the work required strength. Over the course of the Industrial Revolution, staymaking gradually became a female trade. Lane suggests that this shift was a response to changes in fashion that reduced the staymaker's need for strength, but may also have been the result of changing customer preferences, as in the nineteenth century "it was no longer thought suitable for a man to measure and fit a woman for so personal a garment as stays."[5] If nineteenth-century customers did worry about the gender of the individual fitting their clothes, then women were more likely to be dressmakers and staymakers, but less likely to be tailors, because of customer discrimination.

The gender of the customer, though, is at best a weak predictor of the gender of the tradesman. Lane reports that drapers and mercers did essentially the same tasks, "but the draper dealt chiefly with male customers ... while the mercer 'traficks most with the Ladies'."[6] However, there is no evidence that mercers were more likely to be female than drapers. In Manchester women were more likely to be mercers than drapers in 1824–5, when 29 percent of mercers and none of the drapers were female, but in 1788 a greater percentage of drapers were female, and in 1846 women were equally represented in both occupations.[7] Customer discrimination probably had some effect on the occupations open to women, but it does not seem to be the dominant determinant of the gender division of labor.

II.   Married women and the law

The law treated men and women differently, and thus was a source of discrimination. The law did not prevent women from going into business, and sometimes it even protected women's business interests. The ability of women to protect their commercial interests is illustrated by one London law suit. In 1819, *The Times* reported on the law suit *Lazenby* v. *Hallett and Hardy*:

This is an action brought by Mrs. Elizabeth Lazenby, the proprietor of an anchovy sauce, generally denominated "Harvey's Fish Sauce," to recover damages of Messrs. Hallett and Hardy, wholesale druggists, for vending a certain spurious sauce of their making, under the same name, to the manifest injury of her, the said Elizabeth Lazenby, who was the only person acquainted with the secret by which the said sauce was made.[8]

---

[5] Lane, *Apprenticeship in England*, p. 123.   [6] *Ibid.*, p. 124.
[7] In 1788, 10 percent of mercers and 28 percent of drapers were female. In 1846, 5 percent of both occupations were female. *Lewis's Manchester Directory for 1788; Pigot and Dean's Directory*, 1825; *Slater's National Commercial Directory of Ireland*, 1846.
[8] *The Times*, January 7, 1819.

The court upheld Mrs. Lazenby's property rights and fined the defendants. It is not clear whether Mrs. Lazenby was a widow or a married woman, but she was able to use the legal system to protect her trademark. However, the unequal treatment that women received in the law led to some limits on their economic opportunities.

Marriage was the crucial factor affecting a woman's legal status. A single woman was relatively autonomous; she was a *feme sole*, and had most of the legal rights a man had. In some towns female heads of household could vote.[9] A married woman, however, was a *feme covert* and had no legal existence. Her legal identity was subsumed within her husband's. She could not testify in court; she owned no property and could not be sued for debts. Blackstone described the position of the married woman thus:

By marriage, the husband and wife are one person in the law: that is, the very being or legal existence of a woman is suspended during marriage, or at least incorporated and consolidated into that of the husband: under whose wing, protection and *cover*, she performs everything; and is therefore called in our law-french a *feme covert*.[10]

Nicola Phillips, however, warns against taking this statement of women's legal status at face value, suggesting that "Legal commentaries should not be taken as literal statements of women's legal status."[11] While one would expect that laws denying married women a legal existence would have a large impact on their ability to act in the business world, we find married women engaging in trade in spite of this law. In 1707 the wife of Alexander Brown went to London to buy goods, while her husband remained in Edinburgh. She was able to buy goods without her husband in spite of the fact that "what goods she bought cannot be said to be hers but her husband's, although she was the buyer."[12] There is evidence, though, that couverture did affect women's opportunities, at least in the USA. Zorina Khan used patent records to show that couverture laws limited women's commercial activity in the USA. In the late nineteenth century, states that had passed laws giving married women ownership of their earnings and wealth had substantially more patents granted to women than states where married women's rights remained restricted.[13]

---

[9] For example, Preston. See Lilian Lewis Shiman, *Women and Leadership in Nineteenth-Century England* (New York: St. Martin's Press, 1992), p. 38. The Reform Act of 1832 "introduced the first specific gender restriction on the franchise" (p. 40).

[10] William Blackstone, *Commentaries on the Laws of England* (Oxford: Clarendon Press, 1765), vol. I, p. 430.

[11] Phillips, *Women in Business*, p. 46.   [12] Sanderson, *Women and Work*, p. 24.

[13] B. Zorina Khan, "Married Women's Property Laws and Female Commercial Activity: Evidence from United States Patent Records, 1790–1895', *Journal of Economic History* 56 (1996), pp. 356–88.

While no similar study exists for Britain, the impact of *couverture* on women's business opportunities may have been smaller in Britain because exceptions were made for married women in business. London allowed married women to carry on their trades as if they were *feme sole*, with full rights to make contracts and assume debts. The custom of London was that:

> where a *Feme Covert* useth any Craft in the City on her sole Account, whereof the Husband meddleth nothing; such a Woman shall be charged as a *Feme Sole*, concerning every thing, that toucheth her said Craft; and, if the Husband and Wife shall be impleaded in such a Case; the Wife shall plead as a *Feme Sole* in a Court of Record, and shall have her Law and other Advantages, by way of Plea, as a *Feme Sole*; and, if she is condemned, she shall be committed to Prison, until she has made satisfaction, and the Husband and his Goods shall not be charged or impeached.[14]

Blackstone notes the exception briefly: "But a feme covert in London, being a sole trader according to the custom, is liable to a commission of bankrupt."[15] Abram claims that in London the privilege of trading as a *feme sole* was first given only to the wives of freemen, but was extended to other married women in the sixteenth century.[16] Other towns also followed this custom. Lacey documents that both Lincoln and York followed the custom of London in this regard, and Merry Wiesner reports that the practice was widespread among English cities.[17] D'Cruze finds that women business owners in eighteenth-century Colchester "made out bills in their own names even when married."[18]

A married woman trading as a *feme sole* was responsible for her own debts and could be sued. The designation of *feme sole* allowed a married woman to legally enter a partnership.[19] Though a husband generally

---

[14] William Blackstone, *Reports of Cases Determined in the Several Courts of Westminster-Hall from 1746 to 1779* (London: His Majesty's Law Printers, 1781), p. 570.

[15] Blackstone, *Commentaries on the Laws of England*, vol. II, p. 477.

[16] A. Abram, "Women Traders in Medieval London," *Economic Journal* 26 (1916), p. 280.

[17] Kay E. Lacey, "Women and Work in the Fourteenth and Fifteenth Century in London," in Lindsay Charles and Lorna Duffin, eds., *Women and Work in Pre-Industrial England* (London: Croom Helm, 1985), pp. 44–5. Lacey generalizes these examples to claim, "in many towns a married woman could register as a trader with the town authorities, and be treated as a *femme sole* in relation to her occupation" (p. 42). Wiesner, *Women and Gender in Early Modern Europe*, p. 37.

[18] D'Cruze, "To Acquaint the Ladies," p. 159.

[19] "A *feme covert* cannot sustain the character of partner, because she is legally incapable of entering into the contract of partnership ... But it should seem, that, by the custom of London, a *feme covert* trading separately from her husband may be a partner ... where the law allows the wife to act as a *feme sole*, there may be just ground to presume, that, as she is thereby generally restored to her rights as a *feme sole*, she may enter into a partnership in trade." John Collyer, *A Practical Treatise on the Law of Partnership* (Boston, Mass.: Charles C. Little and James Brown, 1848), pp. 11–12.

owned his wife's property, the husband did not own the goods of a wife trading as a *feme sole*, as can be seen by the following court case. In 1764, James Cox and his wife Jane were operating separate businesses, and both went bankrupt within the space of two months. Jane's creditors sued James's creditors for the recovery of five fans, goods from her millinery shop which had been taken for James's debts. The court ruled that, since Jane was trading as a *feme sole*, her husband did not own the goods in her shop, and thus James's creditors had no right to seize them.[20] Married women had no legal rights in other areas, but in the sphere of economic activity the law of *feme covert* was circumvented.

Prior claims that the right of a married woman to operate as a *feme sole* gradually disappeared: "By the nineteenth century it only held in London."[21] Phillips agrees that the courts were less likely to uphold *feme sole* status after 1788, when Kenyon replaced Mansfield as Chief Justice of King's Bench, but suggests that this change did not have a big impact on women's opportunities.[22] Even if *feme sole* status was not available, women could still trade on their own account using the separate property provisions available in courts of equity.[23] In fact, Phillips finds that businesswomen were able to use variation in the laws to their own advantage, claiming *couverture* or *feme sole* status depending on which was most advantageous, and seeking to move cases from common law courts to courts of equity when they found it in their interest to do so.

Another exception to the law of *couverture* applied to women whose husbands were at sea. A sailor's wife had power of attorney to conduct business on behalf of her husband. According to Sharpe, this power allowed female relatives of men at sea "to collect all or part of their male relatives' wages, to receive money on bills, transact in property, appear in court on their husbands' or male relatives' behalf and carry out business in their name."[24]

While the exceptions described above limited the impact of *couverture* on women's economic opportunities, the law was still a factor in reducing women's opportunities. The law did not prevent a married woman from engaging in trade if her husband was agreeable, but a wife whose husband opposed such work was effectively prevented from trading because she had no legal independence from her husband. Any property

---

[20] Blackstone, *Reports of Cases*, pp. 570–5. The case was "LaVie and another Assignees *against* Philips and another Assignees," 1765.

[21] Mary Prior, *Women in English Society, 1500–1800* (London: Methuen, 1985), p. 103.

[22] Phillips, *Women in Business*, p. 49.   [23] *Ibid.*, pp. 49, 86.

[24] Pamela Sharpe, "Gender at Sea: Women and the East India Company in Seventeenth-Century London," in P. Lane, N. Raven, and K. D. M. Snell, eds., *Women, Work and Wages in England, 1600–1850* (Woodbridge: Boydell Press, 2004), p. 56.

that a woman owned became the property of her husband upon marriage, so a married woman could not launch a business without the consent of her husband. Married businesswomen were vulnerable to arbitrary demands from their husbands. For example, a woman from Essex operated the family business after her husband fled the country to avoid arrest on charges of homosexuality. When her husband returned and demanded money from his wife, she had no legal basis for refusing him.[25] In this case an effective constraint on women's opportunities operated through the family, an arena where the state recognized the husband's absolute authority.

The law of *couverture* probably had the greatest effect on women's opportunities indirectly, through its effect on inheritance. While the aristocracy used primogeniture, the middle classes favored partible inheritances, with daughters and sons receiving equal amounts. Daughters and sons, however, did not receive their inheritances in the same form. While sons had complete control over their inheritances, daughters usually received only the income from their inheritances, the capital being held in trust.[26] Morris suggests that the reason for this different treatment was the law of *couverture*, which would give the daughter's current or future husband complete control over her assets. Leaving the money in trust was the only way to protect the capital from a profligate or unlucky husband.[27] Though trusts were designed to protect women by keeping their capital intact, they also prevented women from using their inheritances as business capital. This protection was only necessary because the law gave husbands complete control over their wives' assets. The middle class wrote wills to circumvent this, but unfortunately the solution also left women without capital they could invest in business. Thus the greatest effect of the law of *couverture* was probably in limiting women's access to capital.

III.   Capital

Access to capital was an important restriction on the ability to start a business, for men as well as for women. Those who could not obtain enough capital to set up as masters would remain journeymen their whole lives. Table 6.2 shows some estimates of capital required to start a business in certain trades. Most businesses required at least £100 of capital, and some required substantially more. Since even a skilled

[25] Davidoff and Hall, "The Hidden Investment," p. 245.
[26] Davidoff and Hall, *Family Fortunes*, p. 206. R. J. Morris, *Men, Women, and Property in England, 1780–1870* (Cambridge: Cambridge University Press, 2005), p. 113.
[27] Morris, *Men, Women, and Property*, p. 113.

Table 6.2. *Capital requirements: Campbell's estimates compared to others*

Occupation	Campbell's estimates of capital requirements, 1747	Comparison Capital	Date	Src
Apothecary	£50–200	£100	1825	a
Baker	£100–500			
Bookseller	£500–5000			
Butcher	£20–100			
Chemist	£500–1000	£300	1825	a
Engine maker	£500–2000	£500	1817	b
Grocer	£500–1000			
Haberdasher	£100–2000	£500	1819	c
Lace-man	£1000–10,000			
Milliner	£100–1000	£100		d
Shoemaker	£100–500			
Weaver	£100–500	£300	1750	e
		£500	1850	e

Sources: Campbell, *The London Tradesman.*
a. *The Book of English Trades and Library of the Useful Arts* (London: G.B. Whittaker, 1825).
b. Crouzet, *The First Industrialists.*
c. *The Times*, February 8, 1819.
d. *Davidoff and Hall, Family Fortunes.*
e. *J. de L. Mann, The Cloth Industry in the West of England* (Oxford: Clarendon Press, 1971).

workman was not likely to earn more than a pound a week, it was difficult for a worker to save enough to go into business for himself. If women found it more difficult to obtain capital because of gender discrimination, then the access to capital was one method whereby gender roles constrained women's work opportunities.

During the Industrial Revolution, many entrepreneurs found it difficult to obtain capital. The capital on which the Industrial Revolution was based came mainly from profits, which owners plowed back into their firms.[28] Initial set-up capital generally came from personal wealth or partnerships. Loans were so hard to obtain that some hopefuls were reduced to advertising in *The Times*:

Any Gentleman or Lady who can immediately advance from £1500 to £2000 may join the Advertiser (and not wanted to take an active part) in an INVENTION much required by government and public work, and will be certain in a few years to produce a very large fortune.[29]

[28] François Crouzet, *Capital Formation in the Industrial Revolution* (London: Methuen, 1972), p. 172.
[29] *The Times*, January 14, 1819.

Capital was difficult to obtain, not because savings were inadequate, but because the capital market did not adequately channel those savings to industry. Postan described the capital market of the Industrial Revolution thus:

The insufficiency of capital was local rather than general, social rather than material ... The reservoirs of savings were full enough, but conduits to connect them with the wheels of industry were few and meagre.[30]

The imperfect capital market constrained both men and women.

The question related to women's work opportunities is not whether capital requirements were a constraint on those wishing to start their own business, but whether gender discrimination caused women to have greater difficulty obtaining capital than men. Since the capital market worked on a personal level, gender discrimination was unconstrained by competitive forces and could prevent women from having equal access to capital. Family decisions also reduced women's access to capital, through the types of money they inherited. A more institutional and competitive capital market would have benefited women as well as benefiting economic growth.

The personal nature of the capital market allowed gender discrimination to operate. During the Industrial Revolution, capital was raised mainly through two methods – personal wealth and informal credit markets. Formal credit markets were less well developed and lent conservatively. Banks preferred to lend short-term trade credit rather than long-term capital.[31] Even for short-term credit, the "very personal nature of private banking" may have resulted in discrimination against women.[32] Informal borrowing required a wide range of personal acquaintances and may have been hampered by personal discrimination. If loans were personal decisions based on subjective judgments, gender discrimination could easily have prevented women from having the same access as men.[33]

---

[30] M. M. Postan, "Recent Trends in the Accumulation of Capital," in François Crouzet, ed., *Capital Formation in the Industrial Revolution* (London: Methuen, 1972), p. 71.

[31] L. S. Pressnall, *Country Banking in the Industrial Revolution* (Oxford: Clarendon Press, 1956), pp. 304, 326, 335.

[32] *Ibid.*, p. 296.

[33] Female entrepreneurs experienced credit discrimination in the US in the 1970s. In a survey of female entrepreneurs, Schwartz found that "the initial and major barrier experienced was felt to be credit discrimination during the capital formation stage. Many of the responding female entrepreneurs said credit was denied just because they were women." Eleanor Brantley Schwartz, "Entrepreneurship: A New Female Frontier," *Journal of Contemporary Business* 5 (1976), pp. 47–76. Unfortunately, her title is misleading; female entrepreneurs are not new.

Women did not enter partnerships with men and generally lent business capital rather than borrowing it.[34]

An important constraint on married women was the fact that, when they married, all their wealth became the property of their husbands. While a married woman could operate as *feme sole* and contract debts, her ability to use her capital to start or expand her own business depended on the consent of her husband. Thus, a married woman was vulnerable to gender discrimination because she depended completely on the will of her husband. A husband who did not want his wife to engage in trade could prevent her from doing so by withholding capital. Gender discrimination could thrive in the family, which was not subject to competitive forces. Even trusts, which were often set up to keep the husband from gaining access to the wife's money, did not help because this method of protecting the wife's money did not allow her to use it as capital.[35] The differential treatment of real and personal property encouraged women to hold more of their wealth as real property, which was less useful than personal property as business capital. Combs has shown that women married after the Married Women's Property Act of 1870 held a substantially higher fraction of their wealth in personal property rather than real property.[36] This shift was a response to provisions of the act that increased women's ownership rights over personal property. Before 1870, then, the law encouraged women to hold their property in forms less useful for entrepreneurship. To the extent that married women were disadvantaged in their access to capital, it was because of limitations arising in the law and in the family rather than in the market.

Widows and single women were not under *couverture*; they could own property and dispose of it as they wished. The question is then whether they *did* own property. Unmarried women sometimes owned substantial amounts of property, but women still owned less property than men. An 1846 list of the eleven chief landowners of Denton, Lancashire, includes two women. With over 312 acres, Miss Mary Woodiwiss was the second largest landowner in the parish. Mrs. Mary Cooke owned much less,

---

[34] Davidoff and Hall, *Family Fortunes*, ch. 4.

[35] See Joan Perkin, *Women and Marriage in Nineteenth-Century England* (London: Routledge, 1989).

[36] Women married before 1870 held 56 percent of their wealth as real property, while women married after 1870 held only 25 percent of their wealth as real property. Mary Beth Combs, "'A Measure of Legal Independence': The 1870 Married Women's Property Act and the Portfolio Allocations of British Wives," *Journal of Economic History* 65 (2005), pp. 1028–57.

only twenty-one acres.[37] Larger samples, however, suggest a smaller percentage of women landowners. In the mid-nineteenth century, only 4 percent of Suffolk landowners were women.[38] Also, it is not clear whether these women held this property in trust. If women were given property in trust, they received the income from it, but they were not free to use it to start a business.

The most important source of capital was inheritance. Here widows had the advantage, since they usually inherited their husbands' businesses. Widows were common among the ranks of businesswomen, often heading the businesses they inherited from their husbands. Of the thirty-nine women listed in a 1791 business directory for Coventry, nineteen were specifically designated as widows.[39] Single women also frequently inherited capital, but as we have seen they usually received their capital in trust. The trust protected the capital from future husbands, but also prevented the woman from using the capital in a business venture. Thus, single women were handicapped by the kinds of property they inherited. Again, this type of gender discrimination operated through the family rather than through the market.

To examine whether capital requirements were a factor in determining which occupations women followed, we might ask whether women were less likely to appear in trades requiring more capital. For an estimate of capital requirements, I turn to Campbell's *The London Tradesman*, originally published in 1747.[40] Because of the date of this book, the capital estimates may not accurately reflect capital requirements in the later Industrial Revolution. However, comparisons of Campbell's capital estimates with other estimates presented in Table 6.2 suggest that Campbell's numbers are reasonable. Comparing Campbell's estimates to insurance records from the late eighteenth century, Schwarz concludes that "they compare quite well, but suggest that Campbell's own figures were on the high side."[41] If Campbell did systematically overestimate capital requirements, that would not necessarily mean the relative rankings were incorrect, and it is the relative rankings of the trades that are of interest.

---

[37] John Booker, "A History of the Ancient Chapel of Denton," *Remains Historical and Literary connected with the Palatine Counties of Lancaster and Chester*, The Chetham Society, vol. 37, 1861.

[38] Davidoff and Hall, *Family Fortunes*, p. 276.

[39] *The Universal British Directory*, 1791. Of the remaining twenty women, six had the title "Miss," four had the title "Mrs." and ten had no title.

[40] Campbell, *The London Tradesman*.

[41] L. D. Schwarz, *London in the Age of Industrialisation: Entrepreneurs, Labor Force and Living Conditions, 1700–1850* (Cambridge: Cambridge University Press, 1992), p. 65.

In Table 6.3 I examine whether women were less likely to own businesses in high-capital trades. Since we want to examine business ownership, I use percent-female figures from commercial directories. Retail trades with high turnover required the least amount of capital. Retail trades with valuable goods or low turnover required more. Wholesale trade or large manufacturing enterprises required still more capital. Women were least likely to own businesses in industries requiring large amounts of capital, such as manufacturing or brewing, suggesting that capital may have been a constraint. Note, however, that women are not completely shut out of even the most capital-intensive occupations; a relatively high portion of silk mercers women were. In Manchester in 1824 and 1846, women were more likely to own china shops than earthenware shops, though the former required more capital. If access to capital was an important force excluding women from trade, then the correlation should be negative. Correlations between the capital requirements of a trade and the percentage of business owners who were female (presented in Table 6.4) are generally negative, but are not statistically significantly different from zero. While the availability of capital may have had some effect on female employment, the relationship is not strong or simple enough to produce a strong correlation.

Access to capital, however, may have been important in a few cases. Limited access to capital contributed to the disappearance of women brewers. In the middle ages, women were often brewers. The "alewife" commonly brewed beer on a small scale from her home. Brewing seems to have been a common female trade. Lacey notes that in early London, "One father left his daughter the lease of brewhouse for eight years, at the end of which she was to keep five quarters of malt to set herself up in business to support herself."[42] In the town of Abingdon, many widows were able to support themselves by making malt.[43] By the Industrial Revolution, however, brewing was a male trade. Manchester had no female brewers in 1788 or 1824, and only five in 1846. In the 1841 census, only 2 percent of brewers were female.[44] One factor contributing to this was a change in the scale of brewing operations. What had been a relatively small-scale operation became a large-scale, capital-intensive industry. In the eighteenth century, a technological innovation, the "porter revolution," increased the size of breweries. In the mid-eighteenth

---

[42] Lacey, "Women and Work," p. 51.
[43] Barbara Todd, "The Remarrying Widow: A Stereotype Reconsidered," in Mary Prior, ed., *Women in English Society, 1500–1800* (London: Methuen, 1985), p. 78.
[44] BPP 1844 (587) XXVII.

Table 6.3. *Percent female compared to capital requirements*

	Capital requirement	Manchester			Birm. 1850	Derby 1850
		1788	1824	1846		
Large capital						
Merchant	Unlimited	1.7	0.0	0.4	0.0	0.0
Cloth manufacturer		1.5	0.2	1.1	–	0.0
Brewer	£2000–10,000	0.0	0.0	6.0	0.0	0.0
Coal factor	£1000–10,000	0.0	0.0	0.0	0.0	1.9
Lace-man	£1000–10,000	0.0	0.0	3.6	–	–
Silk mercer	£1000–10,000	11.8	28.6	4.8	–	–
Wool stapler	£1000–10,000	0.0	0.0	11.1	0.0	–
Medium-high capital						
Linen draper	£1000–5000	35.1	8.4	13.0	7.2	0.0
Timber merchant	£1000–5000	6.7	3.6	0.0	0.0	0.0
Woollen draper	£1000–5000	11.8	0.0	4.8	0.0	0.0
Medium capital						
Hosier	£500–5000	17.6	5.9	19.6	30.8	12.5
Chemist/druggist	£500–2000	12.5	2.0	2.8	2.1	3.8
Grocer	£500–2000	5.6	8.7	3.7	5.1	3.2
Ironmonger	£500–2000	12.5	9.5	4.9	1.8	0.0
Pawnbroker	£500–2000	0.0	22.1	13.9	20.7	25.0
China shop	£300–2000	25.0	22.2	12.0	12.5	5.3
Tea shop	£300–1000	22.2	23.5	22.8	13.0	66.7
Bookseller/stationer	£100–5000	0.0	8.3	6.7	4.7	0.0
Tobacconist	£100–5000	33.3	5.9	17.3	4.4	0.0
Haberdasher	£100–2000	0.0	16.7	8.0	31.7	12.5
Hatter	£100–1000	6.3	6.3	3.6	0.0	6.7
Milliner	£100–1000	100.0	100.0	95.3	97.8	100.0
Small capital						
Baker	£100–500	7.7	9.6	6.1	7.0	8.5
Dyer	£100–500	6.4	4.1	5.4	57.1	5.6
Confectioner	£100–300	37.5	35.7	32.2	18.5	25.0
Earthenware shop	£100–300	–	11.8	9.3	26.7	5.3
Fruiterer	£50–500	20.0	22.2	12.8	8.4	10.4
Music shop	£50–500	0.0	0.0	14.3	4.3	–
Calenderer	£50–100	11.4	7.4	9.8	–	33.3
Last maker*	£50–100	0.0	0.0	0.0	0.0	0.0
Butcher	£20–100	2.9	–	8.5	3.7	1.7
Summary						
Large capital		2.0	0.5	1.5	0.0	1.1
Medium-high capital		23.2	5.8	9.5	4.5	0.0
Medium capital		21.4	16.0	25.0	43.6	38.5
Small capital		9.0	10.6	10.0	9.1	6.7

* A last is a wooden form used for making shoes.
Sources: Campbell, *The London Tradesman; Lewis's Manchester Directory for 1788; Pigot and Dean's Directory for Manchester,* 1846; *Slater's Royal, National and Commercial Directory,* 1850.

Table 6.4. *Correlation of minimum capital requirements with the percentage of business owners who were women*

Location and date	Rank correlation	N	P-level
Manchester, 1788	0.038	93	0.715
Manchester, 1824-5	−0.034	92	0.744
Manchester, 1846	−0.051	105	0.604
Birmingham, 1850	−0.071	72	0.551
Derby, 1850	−0.002	109	0.981

Sources: Campbell, *The London Tradesman; Lewis's Manchester Directory for 1788; Pigot and Dean's Directory for Manchester,* 1825; *Slater's National Commercial Directory of Ireland,* 1846; *Slater's Royal, National and Commercial Directory,* 1850.

century, the leading London houses brewed 55,000 to 60,000 barrels each.[45] While women commonly owned small shops, they rarely owned large, capital-intensive businesses, so women ceased to be brewers.

While capital requirements most likely played some role in limiting women's opportunities, they do not seem to be a major determinant of the gender division of labor because capital requirements cannot explain the pattern of occupational sorting. To the extent that women were shut out by their lack of capital, this constraint arose from discriminatory inheritance practices within the family and discriminatory lending in the informal credit market. The personal nature of the institution sheltered gender discrimination which a more impersonal market would not have allowed. Women were vulnerable to gender discrimination because they were not protected by the competitive market.

IV.   Education

Women were also handicapped by their lack of education. As noted in Chapter 2, girls did not have the same access as boys to schooling. As a result, women trailed behind men at all levels of education. Women were less likely than men to be literate, or to have learned mathematics or Latin. Women were not admitted to universities, and women who acquired advanced education were either taught by tutors or relatives or, occasionally, were self-taught. Catherine Macaulay, an eighteenth-century historian who wrote *History of England from the Accession of James I to the Elevation of the House of Hanover,* a popular history text in dissenting academies, was "privately and largely self-educated."[46] She seems to

[45] Crouzet, *The First Industrialists,* p. 27.   [46] Hill and Hill, "Catherine Macaulay," p. 382.

have acquired much of her education by reading books from her father's library. Such women, however, were rare.

To some extent, women's lack of human capital was a rational investment choice. Since they would spend less time in the labor force, girls would receive lower returns from education than boys. To some extent, however, women's low human capital levels reflect discrimination in families and in schools themselves. Families may have made their investment decisions based on gender roles rather than the expected returns of the investment. Also, many schools discriminated against women by not admitting them. Even those women who wanted to could not attend grammar schools or universities. Some women found alternatives, but many did not.

Lower levels of education prevented women from entering some occupations. To some extent this lack of education reflects differences in productivity. Women could not be employed as teachers in grammar schools if they had no training in the classics. However, to a large extent this barrier was artificial. Independent of its effect on human capital, lack of formal education handicapped women by preventing them from gaining an important prerequisite for many professions. Even if they could acquire knowledge and skills, women did not have the right credentials for professional employment. A liberal education at one of the best grammar schools and at a university was a sign of social standing and was used as an entry requirement even though it provided little or no practical training. The requirement of a liberal education indirectly excluded women, since women were excluded from the schools which provided that liberal education. To a large extent, university education was an artificial constraint imposed by professional organizations to limit entry. A degree from Oxford or Cambridge was a requirement for entry into the professional elite. The Royal College of Physicians, for example, admitted only graduates of one of these two universities.[47] Women, of course, could not attend them. This method of exclusion affected other groups besides just women; Catholics and dissenters were also excluded from Oxford and Cambridge. Limited access to education, then, was a tool used by professional organizations to limit access to their professions. Here again we see the importance of the economic motivation in erecting barriers to women's employment opportunities.

V.   Professionalization

Professionalization is the organization of an occupation to increase its status and income. It works mainly through excluding those practitioners

---

[47] Reader, *Professional Men*, p. 16.

deemed inadequate. Since exclusion is a central part of professional-ization and the profession itself decides who may enter, this process is an ideal opportunity for gender discrimination. Like unions, professional organizations found it to their advantage to exclude potential competi-tors. The process by which professionals increase their incomes is described by Perkin:

> When a professional occupation has, by active persuasion of the public and the state, acquired sufficient control of the market in a particular service, it creates an artificial scarcity in the supply which has the effect of yielding a rent, in the strict Ricardian sense of a payment for the use of a scarce resource.[48]

By limiting the supply of its service, a profession can obtain a monopoly rent. As noted in the previous discussion of trade unions, gender ideology made women a natural target for exclusion.

Though similar to unions in their motives for the exclusion of women, the professions used different methods. Because professionals were less likely to work for an employer, their exclusion operated through training and certification requirements rather than through rules imposed on employers. Professionals convinced consumers that only those certified by the professional organization could provide adequate services. This gave the profession control over entry to the occupation, through cer-tification. If a license was required in order to practice, exclusion of women was very simple. They were simply not given licenses. Women could also be effectively barred from the profession if a university edu-cation was required, since they were not allowed into the universities. Professionals, like unions and unlike employers, gained from limiting the labor supply. Thus, professional organizations had both the desire and the opportunity to exclude women.

Unlike the trades, professional employment was an individual rather than a family activity. While the wife of a tradesman could help her husband with his business, the wife of a lawyer could not. Thus, one important avenue for female participation was cut off. Women did not work beside their husbands, and widows did not carry on the family business. This was probably an important reason why the professions were able to exclude women completely while few trades were able to do so.

Professional groups could exclude women from membership in the profession, but they could not always prevent women from offering the same services. Where women practiced the professions, it was because they could compete with the elite, not because they were accepted as

---

[48] Harold Perkin, *The Rise of Professional Society* (London: Routledge, 1989), p. 7.

part of the elite. This was particularly true in medicine, where physicians were exclusively male but still faced competition from females. To protect their monopoly, physicians had to convince their patients that only those accepted by the profession were capable. Organized churches also faced a competitive fringe which included women preachers. Though professional groups could bar women from membership in their profession, they did not automatically have a monopoly; they had to convince the consumer that those sanctioned by the profession offered a superior product. If people believed that physicians educated at universities were superior to those without such education, then the opportunity for competing providers was limited. When the official professionals could convince their customers to hire only from the elite sanctioned by the professional organization, women were excluded.

The Industrial Revolution period was an important time for the professions. They formed their identities and consolidated their power. The upper tiers, the barristers and physicians, had held effective power for some time. For the lower tiers of the professions, such as the attorneys and the apothecaries, the early nineteenth century was a time of gathering professional power. The lower tiers organized to improve their standing, setting up hurdles to keep out undesirable elements, including women. As with unions, limits on labor market competition explain the success of gender discrimination.

A.   Law

Lawyers maintained a tight professional organization and effectively prevented women from joining them. There were two types of lawyers, barristers and attorneys. Barristers were the more elite group, with firmly established professional power. Attorneys were less strongly professionalized in the eighteenth century, but they consolidated their power over the course of the Industrial Revolution.

Barristers had the most exclusive professional organization. They had a monopoly on the right to plead in court. They were organized into four private clubs in London, the Inns of Court. The Inns of Court had complete control over whom they admitted and thus who could plead. They had so much power that they could exclude attorneys from the Inns of Court and thus maintain a strict division between the two types of lawyers. The exclusionary power of the barristers was firmly established by the eighteenth century and remained so thereafter.

Attorneys were one rung down the ladder from barristers. They organized over the course of the eighteenth and nineteenth centuries and became a more exclusive group. In the early eighteenth century, the attorneys' professional organization was weak; an officer of King's Bench "admitted that a great many practised as attorneys who had never been sworn, but maintained that there was no power to prevent them."[49] The government helped them limit their numbers by the Act of 1729, which laid down apprenticeship and examination requirements for attorneys. An apprenticeship of five years and an examination before a judge were required before someone could practice as an attorney.[50] Entry was limited by the restriction that no attorney could have more than two clerks at once.[51] Throughout the eighteenth century, the professional societies of attorneys were local. The Society of Gentlemen Practisers operated in London, and a few provincial centers such as Bristol and Yorkshire had their own law societies. These began to exercise some control over who was allowed to practice. In 1725 the Society of Gentlemen Practisers succeeded in preventing William Wreathock, who had been convicted of highway robbery, from practicing as an attorney.[52] The society also defended the attorneys' right to practice from a challenge by the law scriveners.[53] In the early nineteenth century, attorneys organized on a national scale; the Law Society was formed in 1825. The Law Society furthered the professionalization of the profession. In 1836 it convinced the judges to make the entry examinations more than perfunctory. For the first time, a candidate had to show knowledge of the law in order to be admitted as an attorney.[54] In 1843 parliament gave the Law Society the duty of registering attorneys (now called solicitors).[55]

Since entry to the profession required the consent of the professional organizations, women were effectively excluded. Table 6.5 shows that no women were listed as barristers or attorneys in either the 1841 or the 1851 census. The only evidence I have found of a woman practicing law is in the 1846 commercial directory for Manchester, which lists Sarah Clarke as an attorney.[56] Most likely Sarah managed to practice in spite of the profession, and not with its blessing. Barristers could prevent unrecognized people from pleading in court, but since attorneys worked

---

[49] Robert Robson, *The Attorney in Eighteenth-Century England* (Cambridge: Cambridge University Press, 1959), p. 11.

[50] *Ibid.*, p. 12.

[51] E. B. V. Christian, *A Short History of Solicitors* (London: Reeves and Turner, 1896), p. 111.

[52] Robson, *The Attorney in Eighteenth-Century England*, p. 23.

[53] Reader, *Professional Men*, p. 30.   [54] Christian, *A Short History of Solicitors*, p. 181.

[55] *Ibid.*, p. 217.

[56] *Slater's National Commercial Directory of Ireland*, 1846. There were 215 attorneys and 13 barristers in the town. The fact that Sarah was not counted as an attorney in either the 1841 or the 1851 census may be due to the fact that she practiced only a short time, or may be due to the inaccuracy of the censuses.

Table 6.5. *Professional employment in the censuses*

	1841		1851		1871	
Occupation	M	F	M	F	M	F
Attorney, solicitor	14,657	0	13,013	0	13,854	0
Barrister	2,373	0	2,816	0	3,580	0
Midwife	0	1,384	0	2,024	0	2,215
Physician	1,476	0	1,771	0		
Surgeon, apothecary	18,658	0	17,419	0	19,198*	0
Clergyman	14,613	0	17,320	0	20,694	0
Minister	8,930	0	6,405	0	9,264	0
Missionary					2076	1,185
Schoolmaster/mistress	22,384	32,403	19,329	39,619	19,378	38,774
Governess			0	20,058		
Other teachers	3,970	988	8,640	7,232	13,523	55,465

* Physicians and surgeons.
Sources: BPP 1852–3 (1691) LXXXVIII; 1873 (872) LXXI.

as advisors, they found it harder to shut down the unlicensed practitioner. I have found no other exceptions; law was a completely male profession. Both medicine and the church had a larger group of people operating outside the professional organization and thus more women. Attorneys were able to keep such tight control over their profession because they maintained effective barriers to entry.

B.   Medicine

Before the Industrial Revolution, women practiced medicine both as midwives and as surgeons or apothecaries. In the sixteenth century women were allowed to join the Barber-Surgeons' Company.[57] In the late sixteenth century ten of the seventy-three medical practitioners in Norwich were women.[58] As medicine became more professionalized, though, women found their opportunities for medical practice limited. They had always provided medical care, but as medicine became a formalized profession they were excluded. Women continued to practice medicine, but unofficially, and at a much lower level of status and earnings.

[57] Margaret Pelling and Charles Webster, "Medical Practitioners," in C. Webster, ed., *Health, Medicine, and Mortality in the Sixteenth Century* (Cambridge: Cambridge University Press, 1979), p. 174. See also Abram, "Women Traders in Medieval London," p. 278.
[58] Pelling and Webster, "Medical Practitioners," pp. 222–3.

Physicians, technically members of the Royal College of Physicians, were the most elite group of medical men. They were university educated rather than apprenticed, and only graduates of Oxford and Cambridge were admitted to the Royal College. This effectively excluded women, who were not admitted to Oxford or Cambridge. The Royal College of Physicians kept such tight control over entry that there were relatively few physicians; most medical practitioners were surgeons or apothecaries rather than physicians. The lower tiers, however, also formed their own organizations to limit entry and increased their power during the Industrial Revolution period. Surgeons and apothecaries entered their trade through apprenticeship rather than through a university. Their organizations were the Company of Surgeons (which became the Royal College of Surgeons in 1800) and the Society of Apothecaries. Both organizations were livery companies of London, organized as guilds.[59]

Over the course of the Industrial Revolution, the surgeons and apothecaries consolidated their professional power by gaining control over who could practice. The most important event was the Apothecaries Act of 1815, whereby the government recognized the authority of the Society of Apothecaries to grant licenses, including the power to prevent unauthorized persons from calling themselves apothecaries.[60] A license to practice as an apothecary required a five-year apprenticeship, plus coursework and an examination.[61] Another important step came later in the century with the Medical Act of 1858, which established a single national register for all practitioners considered qualified.[62] The tightening of licensing requirements made it easier to exclude women, either simply for being female, or because they did not have the "proper" education.

One aspect of the increasing professionalization of medicine was the growing importance of formal training. Knowledge gained through practical experience was not considered as valuable as knowledge gained from a formal education. In 1819 the Apothecaries' Company took a man to court for practicing the trade without authorization. The arguments in court emphasized his lack of book-learning. We learn from *The Times*:

At Stafford Assizes a cause was brought on at the suit of the Apothecaries' Company against the son of a man who had been originally a gardener, but who had long exercised the business of a *cow-leech* and *quack-doctor*; the son claiming

---

[59] Reader, *Professional Men*, p. 32.   [60] *Ibid.*, p. 51.   [61] Digby, *Making a Medical Living*.
[62] Magali Sarfatti Larson, *The Rise of Professionalism* (Berkeley: University of California Press, 1977), p. 95.

a right of following the profession of an apothecary, through having studied under his renowned father. In the cross-examination of the father by Mr. Dauncey, he was asked if he had always been a surgeon? The witness ... at last said, "I am a *Surgent*." Mr. Dauncey asked him to spell this word, which he did several times, viz. "*Syurgent*," "*Surgend*," "*Surgunt*," "*Sergund*." Mr. Dauncey said, "I am afraid Sir, you do not often take so much time to study the cases which come before you as you do to answer my question" ... Witness said, he never employed himself as a gardener, but was a farmer till he learnt his present business. Mr. Dauncey said, "Who did you learn it of?" – "I learnt it of Mr. Holme, my brother-in-law; he practiced the same as the Whitworth doctors, and they were regular physicians" ... "Do you bleed from the vein or from the artery?" "From the vein." "There is an artery somewhere about the temples; what is the name of that artery?" "I do not pretend to have so much learning as some have" ... The Jury almost instantly returned a verdict for the plaintiffs.[63]

Those who had learned medicine from practical experience but were not associated with the professional organizations, and thus did not know the correct names of the arteries, were deemed incapable of practicing medicine. Women generally fell into the category of those who received little formal training and got their knowledge through experience. A woman usually learned midwifery from another midwife, much like the Stafford man had learned the apothecary's trade from his brother-in-law. Since women were not admitted to the universities, this emphasis on formal training prevented women from gaining professional status in medicine.

The professionalization of medicine allowed men to enter and dominate the traditionally female specialty of midwifery. For centuries, midwives were highly skilled, highly respected women who received good wages. The profession was once exclusively female; Lacey notes that in the middle ages "the profession of midwife was barred to men, as men were not allowed to be present when a child was born."[64] In the seventeenth century, men had entered the profession, but midwives could still find clients who could pay well. In 1613 Robert Loder hired a midwife. He was a farmer, and could afford to pay the midwife 20s., five times the usual weekly wage of one of his farm laborers.[65] At this time male doctors did not necessarily have higher status than midwives. In 1680 the wife of Sir John Foulis was attended by both a doctor and a midwife for her lying-in, but the doctor was paid only two-thirds what the midwife was paid.[66]

---

[63] *The Times*, April 6, 1819.   [64] Lacey, "Women and Work," p. 49.
[65] Fussel, *Robert Loder's Farm Accounts*, p. 89. However, Loder was a successful farmer, and the midwife was no doubt paid much less by her poorer customers.
[66] Clark, *Working Life of Women*, p. 280.

Men could easily deny women the title of physician, but it was somewhat harder to convince women giving birth to hire a higher-paid male physician in preference to a female midwife. Beginning in the seventeenth century, however, the male medical profession began to eliminate midwives by taking over their work. Improvements in the use of the forceps, which men used and women did not, gave men a perceived technological advantage, even though forceps were often used when not needed.[67] Men also emphasized their superior education. Alice Clark notes that "the policy of doctors, with some exceptions, was to withhold instruction from the midwives on whom the poor depended, lest their skill should enable them to compete with themselves in practice among the wealthy."[68] The medical profession also attacked women directly, with the same vigor that they attacked the "uneducated." Women were said to be too delicate for the duties of a doctor. By some inexplicable twist of logic The Lancet, the major publication of the profession, claimed that only a man could "brave ... the revolting scenes of childbirth."[69] Such denunciations were not reasoned argument, but part of a territorial dispute over whether women would be allowed into the solidifying medical profession.

By the early nineteenth century, men had gained the better-off customers, leaving only the poor for the women. Female midwives generally served only the poorer classes and thus were less well paid. Eden notes that in the 1790s poor families paid 5s. for a midwife.[70] This price was about half the weekly wage of an agricultural laborer, and much less than the 20s. that Robert Loder paid his midwife in 1613.[71] It is difficult to say how much of this price difference was due to the social status of the client, and how much represented a change over time. By the Industrial Revolution the midwife had not disappeared, though she may have suffered a loss of status and pay, as those who could afford to pay more often chose male doctors instead.

The transformation of the profession is illustrated by the change in terminology. In the eighteenth century, a man was called a "man-midwife," a term which suggests that female practitioners were still the norm. By this time, however, female midwives were relatively rare. The 1788 directory for Manchester includes only one female midwife, and

---

[67] Digby, *Making a Medical Living*, pp. 261–2.
[68] Clark, *Working Life of Women*, p. 285.
[69] *The Lancet*, August 3, 1868, p. 117, quoted in F. B. Smith, *The People's Health, 1830–1910* (New York: Holmes and Meier, 1979), p. 380.
[70] Eden, *State of the Poor*, vol. II, pp. 74, 234.
[71] Fussel, *Robert Loder's Farm Accounts*, p. 89. Twenty shillings was about five times what Robert Loder paid his agricultural laborers.

eight "man-midwives." Later the occupational title man-midwife disappeared, in favor of surgeon and physician. Male practitioners were no longer men practicing as midwives, but surgeons or physicians practicing their own trades. Midwives also disappear from the commercial directories; they still existed, but their status was so low that they were not recognized as professionals.[72] Midwives did the same work as doctors, but by the nineteenth century they ended up serving only the poorer classes, for lower pay. This transformation illustrates how men could define a profession in their own terms and successfully exclude women.

Although their number was diminishing, women still practiced various forms of medicine in the late eighteenth century. They were found, however, in the lower-paid branches. The physicians, who had the tightest professional control, prevented women from entering at all. A few women did practice as surgeons or apothecaries, though not with the approval of the professional organizations. Margaret Gorman is listed as an apothecary in an 1846 commercial directory of Glasgow,[73] but the first woman admitted to the Apothecaries Society, Elizabeth Garrett, was admitted in 1865.[74] Even then, however, the license was granted grudgingly. Women continued to provide medical services, though, outside the formal medical organizations. They could still provide medical care if they could compete against the male professionals in the open market. Wyman gives examples of payments made to women for cures in the eighteenth century, but notes that "during the eighteenth century, the status and importance of surgeonesses steadily declined."[75] To the extent that opportunities were based on the market rather than formal organizations, women could enter these occupations. However, the male professionals directed much of their effort to convincing the customers that medical practitioners not approved by the profession were quacks and not capable of providing medical services. Women could practice if they could circumvent the professional organizations and operate in the open market. However, if practice was limited to those accepted by the profession, women were excluded.

As with other types of work, we must question whether cultural statements actually reflect employment. The distinction between male and female practitioners was more related to status than to what work was performed. Table 6.5 shows that in the censuses of 1841 and 1851 the medical profession is completely segregated; men were physicians

[72] In the 1851 census, midwives were grouped in the same class as domestic servants, nurses, and charwomen. BPP 1852–3 (1691) LXXXVIII.
[73] *Slater's National Commercial Directory of Ireland*, 1846.
[74] Reader, *Professional Men*, p. 175. [75] Wyman, "The Surgeoness," pp. 37–8.

and surgeons, women were midwives. The difference in status is clear; in the 1851 census, midwives are grouped with domestic servants, rather than with professionals. However, these cultural categories hid the fact that some of the men were doing the same work as the midwives. Both men and women delivered babies. However, the men were called physicians or surgeons and were given high status and high pay, while the women were called midwives and were given low status and low pay. While women continued to work as midwives, they became invisible because their status declined. In the 1824–5 directory of Manchester, no midwives are listed in the directory of tradesmen, but the description of the Lying-In Hospital lists twenty-four midwives working alongside seven men-midwives, one physician, and one apothecary.[76] There were female midwives in Manchester, but their status was too low for these women to be listed in the commercial directory.

Women's opportunities to practice medicine were clearly limited by barriers erected by the professional organizations. As in other cases, men found that they could benefit economically from limiting entry to their occupation. To the extent that women did continue to practice medicine, it was because they could compete for customers in the open market.

C.   The church

The more institutionalized a church, and the more professionalized its clergy, the less likely it was to allow women leaders. At one extreme was the Church of England, the most conservative, which ordained its first female priests in 1994.[77] At the other extreme were the Quakers, who have no formal paid clergy and were always at the forefront of allowing women to lead. The Quakers had a number of well-known women preachers, such as Susanna Green and Sara Grubb.[78] Even here, though, when the Quakers began to keep lists of their preachers, the use of women decreased.

In the early days of puritanism, women, though not officially recognized by the church, preached, founded churches, and wrote pamphlets.[79] As the new sects were officially organized into churches, however, women were no longer given the freedom to carry on these activities. Davidoff and Hall note that, while women were important in many revival movements, "where such movements outgrew their enthusiastic

---

[76] *Pigot and Dean's Directory for Manchester*, 1825, p. 277.
[77] *Chicago Tribune*, March 13, 1994, sec. 1, p. 3.
[78] Davidoff and Hall, *Family Fortunes*, p. 138.   [79] Shiman, *Women and Leadership*, p. 15.

origins and became more bureaucratic, the women were usually pushed to the margins."[80] Professionalization of the clergy squeezed out women.

This progression can be observed in the Methodist Church, which during the Industrial Revolution was the main opposition to the established Church of England. When the movement was new, female preachers were relatively common. John Wesley was not in favor of women preaching, but when Mary Bosanquet and Sarah Crosley, important leaders in the movement, insisted on preaching, he reluctantly allowed it. In a 1771 letter to Sarah Crosley, Wesley wrote:

> I think the strength of our Case rests there in your Having an *Extraordinary* Call. So I am persuaded has every one of our Lay-preachers; otherwise I could not countenance his preaching at all ... Therefore I do not wonder, if several things occur therein which do not fall under ordinary Rules of Discipline; St. Paul's ordinary rule was "I permit not a woman to speak in the Congregation": yet in Extraordinary Cases, he made a few exceptions: at Corinth in particular.[81]

In 1787 a conference of Methodists accepted the principle of women preaching. As long as the Methodists remained a lay movement within the Church of England, women preachers were allowed. When the Methodist Church was created in 1794, however, it created its own official clergy, and women were soon excluded. While women could be tolerated as lay preachers, they were not allowed into the professional clergy and soon their preaching was silenced. In 1803 a conference in Manchester decreed that a woman could only preach if she had an "extraordinary calling," and then only to women's groups. Eventually, the Methodists rejected all lay preachers, and the clergy was completely professionalized. One sign of the professionalization of Methodist ministers was the adoption of the title "Reverend" in 1818. Perhaps more tellingly, they also asked for higher salaries.[82] As a result of the move to a professional clergy, the Methodists ceased to have female preachers.

A few splinter groups refused to join the official Methodist Church, and these groups continued to have women preachers. The major sects to break off from the Methodist movement were the Independent Methodists (1796), the Methodist New Connexion (1797), the Primitive Methodists (1812), and the Bible Christians (1815).[83] In 1818 one-fifth of the

---

[80] Davidoff and Hall, *Family Fortunes*, p. 107.   [81] Shiman, *Women and Leadership*, p. 22.
[82] Deborah Valenze, *Prophetic Sons and Daughters: Female Preaching and Popular Religion in Industrial England* (Princeton: Princeton University Press, 1985), p. 20.
[83] *Ibid.*, p. 21.

Primitive Methodist preachers were women.[84] In his memoirs James Hopkinson recalls:

Of my early religeous impressions I may say I was not more than 5 or 6 years old [c. 1825] when a Lady preachess came to a primitive Methodist chapel near to where I lived. And as a great favor my Mother let me go to the service. *That night young* as I *was* the spirit of God was *stiring* in me.[85]

Women continued to preach, and continued to move their listeners, but only in the marginal sects.

As in medicine, the few women who worked in this profession were not acknowledged by society and thus remain largely hidden from the historian. An example is Mary Barritt, later Mrs. Zachariah Taft. A charismatic preacher, she played an important part in the Yorkshire revival of the 1790s. However, her obituary in the 1851 *Methodist Magazine* made no mention of her preaching. The obituary only noted that she was the "widow of the late Rev. Zachariah Taft" and that "For many years she had been 'a mother of Israel'."[86] The church that she had helped to build did not acknowledge her contribution. As in the other professions, the women who fought the barriers set up against them remained largely invisible.

D.   Teaching

Teaching is the exception that proves the rule. During the Industrial Revolution teaching was not organized as a profession, and did not have licenses or formal entry requirements. Because there were few barriers to entry, many women were teachers. While teaching in higher education was closed to women, much of the teaching profession was open to them. The grammar schools and universities that did not accept girls as students did not hire women as teachers.[87] Other schools, however, hired women, and many women opened their own schools. While other professions were characterized by entry restrictions, teaching at the primary level was characterized by free competition. Since anyone could open her own school, teaching remained open to women, and even became one of the few occupations in which women outnumbered men (see Table 6.5). In an occupation which was governed only by the

---

[84] Shiman, *Women and Leadership*, p. 28. Some examples are Elizabeth Moore, Elizabeth Gorse Gaunt, and Hannah Howe; see Valenze, *Prophetic Sons and Daughters*, pp. 22, 38, 40.

[85] Hopkinson, *Victorian Cabinet Maker*, p. 6. Emphasis his.

[86] Valenze, *Prophetic Sons and Daughters*, p. 64.

[87] See Davidoff and Hall, "The Hidden Investment," p. 264.

competition, women could thrive. Thus the one profession that did not have the professional organization to limit entry was flooded with women.

Teachers can be divided into two groups, those who were hired by an institution and those who were self-employed. Women were prominent in both groups. Charity schools and national schools hired teachers, and upper-class families hired governesses. When women were hired as salaried teachers, they received lower salaries than men. To some extent the difference in salaries was justified by men's greater skills, since women usually did not teach mathematics, bookkeeping, or the classics, but some portion of the wage gap may also have been due to wage discrimination.[88]

Many teachers, however, were self-employed. Small private schools were often located in the teacher's house. Private schools covered a wide social range, from the cheapest working-class schools to the most elite boarding schools. The incomes of the self-employed teachers varied with the social class of their students. The women who ran working-class private schools, sometimes called "dame schools," were not well paid. For example, the wife of a Gloucester weaver earned 2s. a week from running a school; she had twelve students and charged each 2d. a week.[89] Schools for wealthier students had higher fees and produced larger incomes for the schoolmaster or mistress. Enrollment at a girls' boarding school might cost as much as £100 a year.[90] One Warwickshire girls' boarding school charged £26.5s. per half-year, but payments for extra subjects such as dancing and French could triple this amount.[91]

During the Industrial Revolution period, teaching had no legal barriers to entry. In earlier centuries there had been some restrictions. During the reigns of Elizabeth I, James I, and Charles I, the government tried to keep dissenters out of teaching by requiring all teachers to be licensed.[92] Even then, many teachers succeeded in evading the requirement. In the early seventeenth century, the Catholic Margaret Ford was arrested three times for teaching children, and the high rate of recidivism implies the restrictions were not very effective.[93] By the Industrial Revolution, however, there were no legal restrictions on entry into the profession. Easy entry into the field made teaching an attractive temporary employment and many treated it as such rather than as a lifetime profession. Men trained for the clergy who could not immediately

---

[88] *Ibid.*, p. 265.   [89] BPP 1840 (220) XXIV, p. 419.
[90] Reader, *Professional Men*, p. 170.   [91] Roach, *A History of Secondary Education*, p. 117.
[92] O'Day, *Education and Society*, p. 27.   [93] *Ibid.*, p. 170.

find a position in their chosen profession would commonly take up teaching while they waited.[94]

The market for primary schooling was competitive, with free entry and exit. It was easy to enter the occupation by simply opening a small school. Janet Bathgate, who was born in Sunderland, Scotland, about 1806, had very little formal education, and experience only as an agricultural worker and a nurserymaid. After her husband died she worked as a sempstress but was unable to earn enough to live on, so a friend suggested that she open a school. Janet protested that "I never was six weeks at a regular school at one time, and I feel that it would be the very height of presumption for me to pretend or attempt to teach any one."[95] She was convinced to try, though, and succeeded. The first week she had nine students, but on Monday of the second week, "It is ten o'clock, the school door is opened; and to her surprise, instead of nine, she had eighteen scholars, including two little boys, each carrying a little stool and twopence for school wages."[96] Janet Bathgate was at the bottom end of the schooling market, but she did much better as a schoolteacher than as a sempstress.

Self-employed teachers were subject only to market constraints, and the success of a schoolmaster or mistress depended on whether he or she could attract students. Though often looked down on for being mere babysitters, the schoolmistresses in "dame schools" survived only because they provided the services their customers demanded. Publicly funded charity schools competed with dame schools, but many parents preferred private dame schools to the public schools because the private schools, placing less emphasis on religion and morals, taught literacy better. Parents were known to move their children out of public schools and into dame schools in order to improve their education. In 1861 a parliamentary investigator reported that:

It is almost the universal opinion of parents that children are taught to read quicker and better in the dames' schools than in the lower classes, (particularly if left to the charge of monitors,) of the public schools. I continually found in the private schools young children who had been removed from the public schools, because, as the dames informed me, "they learnt nothing" there.[97]

Parliamentary investigator Josiah Wilkinson reports that one London schoolmistress "had children frequently returned to her from public schools on the alleged ground of expense and bad teaching."[98] Another

---

[94] Ibid., p. 169.
[95] Janet Bathgate, *Aunt Janet's Legacy to Her Nieces: Recollections of Humble Life in Yarrow in the Beginning of the Century* (Selkirk: George Lewis and Son, 1894), p. 186.
[96] Ibid., p. 188.   [97] BPP 1861 (2794) XXI, Pt 2, p. 36.   [98] Ibid., Pt 3, p. 376.

schoolmistress "told me very gravely that she had several scholars from the National schools, because their parents said they learnt nothing there but clapping hands and singing."[99] Schoolmistresses had to please parents in order to stay in business, and doing so usually meant ensuring their pupils' rapid progress in reading skills.

Teachers who could not compete lost their students and went out of business, and schoolmasters had no advantage over schoolmistresses in this regard. In his autobiography, Christopher Thomson notes that, "anybody could make a schoolmaster ... to be a school master is one of the few comfortable trades which require no previous training."[100] However, while Christopher found entry into the occupation easy, entry did not guarantee success. He soon found that "my school was soon at a discount; I struggled on for a time, but the school returns were insufficient for my family."[101] He blamed his failure on complaints from the parents that he refused to beat the boys, and taught them poetry instead of the Bible. His failure may also have been due to his limited skills: "I could read a little, write a decent hand, and figure simples and a few compounds."[102] While entry to the occupation was open, success was not guaranteed. Some private teachers thrived, and some failed, and success seems to have been determined by ability, not by gender.

Professionalization of teaching did not begin until the middle of the nineteenth century. In 1846 the government established a certification process for teachers.[103] However, since certification was not required, the market remained open and those without certificates could still teach. The first national professional organization, the General Associated Body of Church Schoolmasters in England and Wales, was formed in 1853.[104] Private schoolmasters and mistresses competed successfully with public institutions until the 1870s, when the government made attendance at an officially sanctioned "efficient" school necessary for obtaining permission to work at the age of ten.[105] Until the government gave specific monopoly privileges to public institutions, independent teachers thrived and entry into the teaching profession remained open. Teaching is different from the other professions because increasing professional restrictions did not reduce the percentage of women in teaching.

While primary teaching was competitive, women faced barriers to employment in higher education; women could not teach at schools for

---

[99] *Ibid.*, Pt 3, p. 375.
[100] Christopher Thomson, *The Autobiography of an Artisan* (London: Chapman, 1847), p. 207.
[101] *Ibid.*, p. 208.   [102] *Ibid.*, p. 207.   [103] Tropp, *The School Teachers*, p. 19.
[104] *Ibid.*, p. 51.   [105] Gardner, *The Lost Elementary Schools*, p. 204.

older boys, and were limited to schools for younger children or for girls. This restriction did not prevent female teachers from outnumbering male teachers (see Table 6.5), but it did prevent women from entering the most highly paid segment of the market.

During the Industrial Revolution, higher education for boys was closed to women, but the bulk of the teaching market remained competitive, open for all who wished to take up the employment. Success depended on teaching ability, not on gender. Parents sent their children to the schools where they received the best education, and women could successfully compete with men. Since teaching was the only profession open to women, some women entered it even though they would have preferred to be elsewhere. Because teaching was open and competitive, while law, medicine, and the church were closed to women, women flocked to teaching, driving down the wages there relative to wages in other professions. Still, the fact that the teaching profession remained open ensured that these women could support themselves without turning to unskilled labor.

Conclusion

This chapter supports two basic claims: that gender discrimination was strongest when competition was weakest, and that economic motivations were a more important cause of these barriers than gender ideology.

While neither seems to have been the primary determinant of the gender division of labor, customer discrimination and the law both allowed gender ideology to have some impact on women's opportunities. The legal invisibility of married women had a direct effect on their ability to conduct business and, probably more importantly, had an indirect effect on the type of property women inherited, since fathers sought to protect their daughters' inheritances from the bad judgment or bad luck of current or future husbands by giving daughters their inheritances in the form of trusts. Customer preferences may have created barriers to women's employment where customers preferred to be served by males. No women were hairdressers. To the extent that these factors limited women's opportunities, they did so because the competitive mechanism was blocked. Since households and governments do not go bankrupt when they discriminate against women, competition cannot eliminate discrimination in consumer preferences or in the law.

The degree of competition was also important in determining where women would face barriers to employment within the professions. Women were more widely employed in professions where the market was most competitive. At one extreme, the market for primary teachers was highly competitive, and women out numbered men. At the other extreme, lawyers were able to effectively prevent competition from unapproved practitioners, and women were shut out. Both medicine and the clergy faced a competitive fringe, but were able to keep the bulk of the market, with the highest status and pay, for approved professionals.

In this chapter we also see the importance of economic motivations in erecting restrictions on women's employment. While men may have appealed to gender ideology to justify their restrictions, this ideology was easily cast aside when it conflicted with their economic incentives. If gender ideology was the real motivation, then people should have applied it more consistently. Instead we observe that where gender ideology conflicted with the economic interests of a powerful group, gender ideology took a back seat. One of the most intimate of all occupations, midwifery, went from gender segregated (female midwives and female clients) to mixed (male physicians and female clients). Mary Wollstonecraft noticed this contradiction in 1792:

Women might certainly study the art of healing, and be physicians as well as nurses. And midwifery, decency seems to allot to them, though I am afraid the word midwife in our dictionaries will soon give place to *accoucheur*, and one proof of the former delicacy of the sex be affaced from the language.[106]

Though some men expressed concern about the moral implications, these issues were easily swept aside in order to advance the male profession. In the most intimate of professions, concerns about the mixing of the sexes were easily set aside when they conflicted with the economic interests of a powerful group.

[106] Wollstonecraft, *A Vindication of the Rights of Woman*, pp. 221–2.

7   Women's labor force participation

Much has been written on the question of whether the Industrial Revolution increased or decreased women's employment opportunities.[1] Friedrich Engels suggested that industrialization emancipated women by providing them with an independent income: "since large-scale industry has transferred the woman from the house to the labor market and the factory, and makes her, often enough, the bread winner of the family, the last remnants of male domination in the proletarian home have lost all foundation."[2] Engels, however, probably focused too much on factory employment, ignoring employment opportunities that were lost due to industrialization. Eric Richards suggests the opposite, that women's participation in paid work was high in the early eighteenth century and fell substantially with industrialization.[3] More recent literature favors Richards. Davidoff and Hall, for example, emphasize the withdrawal of middle-class women from active involvement in the family business during the first half of the nineteenth century.[4] Andrew August suggests that working-class women in the later nineteenth century did not accept the middle-class notion of separate spheres, and paid work continued to be an accepted part of their lives even when married.[5]

Unfortunately it is difficult to address questions about aggregated employment without reliable aggregate data. Census data are available for the later part of the nineteenth century, and suggest a decline in the participation rate of married women from 25 percent in 1851 to 10 percent in 1901.[6] Andrew August finds that in the 1881 census 23 percent of married women were employed (27 percent if we count wives in

---

[1] For one review, see Janet Thomas, "Women and Capitalism: Oppression or Emancipation? A Review Article," *Comparative Studies in Society and History* 30 (1988), pp. 534–49.
[2] Frederick Engels, "Origin of the Family, Private Property and the State," in Karl Marx and Frederick Engels, *Selected Works* (New York: International Publishers, 1986), p. 508.
[3] Eric Richards, "Women and the British Economy since about 1700: An Interpretation," *History* 59 (1974), pp. 337–57.
[4] Davidoff and Hall, *Family Fortunes*.   [5] August, "How Separate a Sphere?"
[6] Land, "The Family Wage," p. 61.

Table 7.1. *Married women's labor force participation from census totals*

	Wives	Occupied wives	Excluded	Employed wives Corrected	LFP	Corrected LFP
1851	3,461,524	830,141	371,959	458,182	24.0	13.2
1861	3,488,952	838,856	318,643	520,213	24.0	14.9
1911	6,630,284	680,191	0	680,191	10.2	10.2

The "Excluded" category contains women whose occupation was listed as innkeeper's wife, shoemaker's wife, shopkeeper's wife, farmer's wife, butcher's wife, or licensed victualler's wife. These women are included in the category "occupied wives," but not counted as employed for the corrected figures.
Source: McKay, "Married Women and Work."

families who took in boarders or lodgers as employed).[7] Hatton and Bailey have used other sources to confirm the accuracy of the female participation rates in the early twentieth-century censuses, so we can accept the figure of 10 percent as accurate for the beginning of the twentieth century.[8] John McKay has suggested that the participation rate for 1851 is actually too high, and that married women's labor force participation did not fall during the second half of the nineteenth century. He claims that a woman listed as the wife of a tradesman (farmer's wife, shoemaker's wife, butcher's wife, etc.) should not be counted as employed in 1851, since these categories were not included as occupations in the twentieth-century censuses.[9] Table 7.1 shows the labor force participation rates for married women with and without these calculations. McKay concludes that participation did not decline during the second half of the nineteenth century. However, I believe that a woman listed as "shoemaker's wife" was so listed because she was participating in her husband's business, and should be counted as employed, so I prefer the uncorrected participation rates. For the first half of the nineteenth century we cannot rely on census data because they are not available until 1841. Unfortunately this means that evidence on female participation for the first half of the nineteenth century is not comprehensive, and refers only to certain segments of the population.

Evidence on female participation before the Industrial Revolution suggest higher rates of labor force participation than either the 1851 or the 1901 census. Using information on witnesses found in early

[7] August, "How Separate a Sphere?," pp. 298, 306.
[8] Hatton and Bailey, "Women's Work in Census and Survey".
[9] John McKay, "Married Women and Work in Nineteenth-Century Lancashire: The Evidence of the 1851 and 1861 Census Reports," *Local Population Studies* 61 (1998), pp. 25–37.

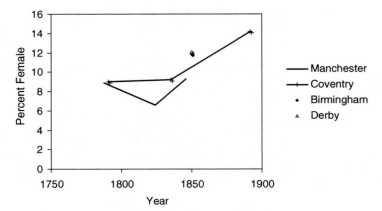

Figure 7.1   Changes over time in the prevalence of women in commercial
directories
Sources: Table 1.5 and Kelly's Directory, 1892.

eighteenth-century court records, Peter Earle finds that one-third of
married women answered the question of how they were maintained by
mentioning paid employment, and another 27 percent mentioned paid
employment as well as other sources of support, such as the husband's
income. A minority of married women, 40 percent, did not report any
paid employment. Single women and widows had higher participation
rates; overall only 28 percent of women reported no paid employment.[10]

The best statistical evidence on women's participation rates in the first
half of the nineteenth century is from family budgets collected by Sara
Horrell and Jane Humphries.[11] Because the family budgets were originally collected by contemporaries concerned with poverty, they refer
mainly to the poorest classes. These budgets suggest that the participation rate of working-class married women was 66 percent at the
beginning of the nineteenth century, and 45 percent at the middle of the
century. Even after controlling for wages, family size, and other household income, the labor force participation of married women declined
during the first half of the nineteenth century.

This decline, however, does not appear to be a universal female
experience. Commercial directories show no evidence of declining
numbers of female business owners. Figure 7.1 plots the percentage of

[10] Earle, "The Female Labour Market in London," p. 337.
[11] Sara Horrell and Jane Humphries, "Women's labour force participation and the
transition to the male-breadwinner family, 1790–1865," Economic History Review 48
(1995), pp. 89–117.

business owners in commercial directories who were female from Table 1.5. To see if there was a downward trend that began after 1850, I also calculated the prevalence of female business owners in an 1892 directory for Coventry. There is no evidence of a downward trend during the nineteenth century; if anything the trend is upwards.

There may still have been a decline in participation among tradeswomen if it occurred among wives, whose participation was not recorded in commercial directories if they assisted their husbands rather than carrying on a separate trade. Davidoff and Hall claim that this was the case. They provide the example of two generations of the Cadbury family. In 1800 Richard Cadbury, a draper, and his wife Elizabeth moved to Birmingham. The family lived in the same house as the shop, and Elizabeth assisted in the shop. In the next generation, however, Elizabeth's daughter-in-law Candia had no contact with John Cadbury's cocoa business; Candia and her family lived in the suburb of Edgbaston.[12] However, it is impossible to tell whether this case of reduced female participation was due to general social trends or to the improving fortunes of the family, or even if it was representative of other middle-class women. Amanda Vickery notes that:

it could be argued that a female withdrawal from active enterprise was essentially a function of increasing wealth. Therefore *any* study of an expanding business, be it in fourteenth-century York, seventeenth-century London, or nineteenth-century Birmingham, would be likely to show a reduction over three generations in the formal participation of female members of the owning family.[13]

The Cadburys' experience was certainly not universal. The autobiography of a cabinetmaker named James Hopkinson suggests no change over time in wives' participation. When he was born in 1819, James's mother assisted in the family grocers shop. James once drank too much elderberry wine while his mother was waiting on a customer.[14] Later in the century James's wife was also active in his business; James notes that "I found I had got a good and suitable companion one with whom I could take sweet council and whose love and affection was only equall'd by her ability as a business woman."[15] Were the Cadburys or the Hopkinsons more representative of their generation? More convincing evidence is provided by trade tokens; Davidoff and Hall note that: "in the late seventeenth century, for example, trade tokens used by local shopkeepers and small masters carried the initials of the man and woman's first name and the couple's surname, but by the late eighteenth

---

[12] Davidoff and Hall, *Family Fortunes* pp. 52–7.
[13] Vickery, "Golden Age to Separate Spheres?" p. 409.
[14] Hopkinson, *Victorian Cabinet Maker*, p. 9.   [15] *Ibid.*, p. 96.

century only the initials of the man were retained."[16] This suggests that by the late eighteenth century wives were no longer active business partners with their husbands.

If we accept the claim that married women's labor force participation declined during the nineteenth century, the next question is what caused that decline. This chapter examines five possible causes: market demand, barriers to employment in certain occupations, rising household income, information about germs, and gender ideology. Some of these causes can be seen as economic, and some as ideological. Some reduced participation by increasing women's choices, making them better off, and some reduced participation by decreasing women's choices, making them worse off. All these factors seem to have had some role in reducing female participation, though the timing and extent of each factor varied.

I.   Demand

In some occupations there was a decline in demand for female services. A decline in demand will result in lower total employment unless labor supply is unresponsive to the wage. One important shock to the demand for female labor was the disappearance of the occupation of hand spinning. Before the Industrial Revolution, hand spinning had been a nearly universal occupation for women, but by 1850 it had completely disappeared (see Chapter 1 for a discussion of the decline of spinning). Other cottage industries, such as straw-plaiting and lace-making, appeared, but these industries were never as ubiquitous as spinning, and could at best only partially compensate for its loss.

Data on wages and employment of agricultural laborers suggest that there must have been a decline in the demand for female workers in agriculture as well. Figure 7.2 shows the change over time in the female–male wage ratio among agricultural day-laborers, based on a sample of farm accounts from eighty-four farms.[17] The wage ratio is clearly lower in 1850 than it was in 1750, and the decline seems to have occurred before 1800. The summer wage ratio fell from 0.61 in 1741–5 to 0.37 in 1796–1800, and during the same time period the winter wage ratio fell from 0.54 to 0.31. Was this decline in relative female wages caused by the disappearance of spinning employment, which would have increased the supply of women available to farmers? If this decline in relative female wages had been caused by an increase in the supply of women available to farmers following the disappearance of spinning

[16] Davidoff and Hall, *Family Fortunes*, p. 272.   [17] Burnette, "Wages and Employment."

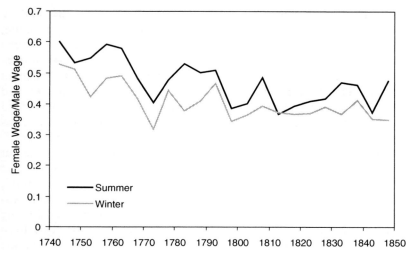

Figure 7.2 Female–male wage ratio in agriculture
Source: Burnette, "Wages and Employment."

employment, then we would expect to see an increase in relative female employment in agriculture. In fact we observe the opposite. The percentage of day-laborers who were female declined between 1750 and 1850. Based on a sample of wage accounts from sixty-five farms, I estimated that, among agricultural day-laborers, the percentage of days worked by females fell from 13.6 percent in 1751 to 10.6 percent in 1851. The fact that both relative female wages and relative female employment fell suggests that there was also a decline in the demand for female labor in agriculture.

What could have caused this decline in demand for female agricultural laborers? Snell suggested that in the southeast it was due to increased specialization in arable agriculture, combined with the replacement of the sickle by the scythe, which reduced women's role in harvest.[18] As discussed in Chapter 3, women did not use the scythe because it required too much strength. Both women and men used the sickle, and when the sickle was used to cut grain women had an active part in harvest. The increased use of the scythe caused a decrease in the demand for female labor during harvest. This raises the question of why the scythe replaced the sickle.

The scythe had been used for centuries to mow grass or harvest less valuable grains, but its use expanded to more valuable grains at the

[18] Snell, *Annals of the Laboring Poor,* ch. 1

beginning of the nineteenth century. Pamela Sharpe suggests that the move from the sickle to the scythe cannot explain the declining employment of women in agriculture because the sickle and the scythe co-existed.[19] However, the fact that two technologies can co-exist does not contradict the claim that economic forces caused the changes observed. The sickle and the scythe each had their own advantages, and it was changes in relative prices that determined which technology would be used, and thus the demand for male and female labor. The scythe was not a new technology, and had been used since the Roman era.[20] However, various properties of the tool limited its use. The scythe cut the grain closer to the ground, and in an open-fields system, where the stubble was common property, the use of the scythe was sometimes forbidden.[21] Grain could be cut faster with a scythe, but the sickle was neater, and spilled less grain on the ground,[22] so a farmer considering using the scythe would have to trade the savings in labor costs from using the scythe against the loss of grain that would result. The scythe was a grain-using and labor-saving technology, while the sickle was a grain-saving and labor-using technology. This difference explains why the scythe was first used for the cheaper grains, and applied to wheat last. It also explains why high-wage areas were more likely to use the scythe. In 1769 Young found the scythe being used for wheat near Hull, though cutting wheat with a scythe was unusual at that time. The reason for the region's deviation from normal practice is clear; Young notes that "The prices of labor are most of them extremely high."[23]

The tendency for the wage of male laborers to rise relative to the price of grain caused the scythe to replace the sickle. In the eighteenth century the scythe was used to cut grass, and sometimes cheaper grains. It was used for oats, barley, peas, and beans in early modern England, but was not used for wheat until the nineteenth century.[24] Its application to the wheat harvest began in the south during the Napoleonic Wars and then spread north. Overton claims that 90 percent of the wheat harvest was cut with a sickle in 1790, and only 20 percent in 1870.[25] The cause of the shift from the sickle to the scythe was not technological change, since the scythe was not a new tool, but a shift in prices that induced farmers to choose a different harvest technology.

---

[19] Sharpe, *Adapting to Capitalism*, p. 75. "This straightforward economic reason for the growing demarcation of labor can then be dispelled immediately."
[20] Roberts, "Sickles and Scythes," p. 4.   [21] *Ibid.*, p. 14.
[22] *Ibid.*, p. 16, and Roberts, "Sickles and Scythes Revisited," p. 92.
[23] Young, *Northern Tour*, vol. I, p. 113.   [24] Roberts, "Sickles and Scythes," p. 15.
[25] Overton, *Agricultural Revolution in England*, p. 124.

The change in harvest technologies is probably not the only reason for decreasing demand for female agricultural laborers. Even farms which were primarily pastoral, such as that of the Oakes family in Norton, experienced a decline in demand for female agricultural laborers.[26] Another possible explanation for the declining demand for women is institutional rather than technological. The early nineteenth century saw a large increase in poor law payments, and farmers began to be more concerned about the amount of money spent on the poor. Since poor rates were paid locally, farmers, especially large farmers, were concerned about the level of the rates, and were willing to adjust their hiring patterns to minimize the rates.[27] Farmers would have preferred hiring men if male unemployment increased poor law payments but female employment did not. If a woman's husband was already employed and not receiving poor relief, employing the woman would not further reduce poor law payments. A preference for hiring males may have been a method of spreading the work out among the greatest possible number of families, in order to minimize poor relief payments.

Declining demand most likely reduced female labor force participation as the market wage fell below some women's reservations wages. The value of the woman's contribution to the household was high enough that low wages barely covered the opportunity cost of working. Austin estimates: "Where a girl is hired to take care of children, she is paid about 9d. a-week, and has her food besides, which is a serious deduction from the wages of the woman at work."[28] If the cost of food doubled the cost of hiring child care, a working woman would have to pay about a third of her earnings for child care. Mrs. Sumbler, sometimes an agricultural laborer from Wiltshire, told parliamentary investigator Alfred Austin that she did not think working outside the home increased the family's net income:

I do not think a great deal is got by a mother of a family going out to work; perhaps she has to hire a girl to look after the children, and there is a great waste of victuals and spoiling of things; and then working in the fields makes people eat so much more. I know it was so with me always. I often say there is not fourpence got in the year by my working out.[29]

If the net benefit of work was so small, even a small decrease in the wage could cause a woman to drop out of the labor force.

---

[26] Burnette, "Labourers at the Oakes."
[27] For a model that incorporates poor law payments in the farmer's maximization problem, see Boyer, *Economic History of the English Poor Law*, ch. 3.
[28] *Women and Children in Agriculture*, p. 26.
[29] *Women and Children in Agriculture*, pp. 67–8.

II.   Barriers to employment

Decline in the demand for female labor decreased the options available to women and thus made them worse off. Barriers preventing women from entering certain occupations also decreased the women's options. One possible cause of declining female participation was increased barriers that pushed women out of various occupations. If they were pushed out of many occupations, women may not have been able to find alternative employment, and may have dropped out of the labor force. In some cases we have direct evidence of such barriers. Commercial directories show no tendency toward increased occupational segregation over the nineteenth century, but census data do indicate increased segregation between 1851 and 1871.

We know that there were barriers preventing women from being employed in certain occupations because we hear women complain about not being able to work where they chose. One tailoress responded to news of a tailors' strike against women's employment by writing this to *The Pioneer*: "surely the men might think of a better method of benefiting themselves than that of driving so many industrious women out of employment. Surely, while they loudly complain of oppression, they will not turn oppressors themselves."[30] Women were pushed out of mule-spinning. Women who tried to work as mule spinners at James Dunlop's mill in Glasgow were "waylaid and attacked, in going to, and returning from their work" and "beaten and abused" by male mule spinners.[31] Chapters 5 and 6 contain numerous examples of occupations which set up barriers to women's employment, including mule-spinning, wool-combing, law, medicine, and the church. The occupations from which women were excluded were those where male workers had enough economic power to monopolize an industry and exclude women. Many of these barriers were new during the Industrial Revolution. Women had been mule spinners and midwives, but were pushed out of these occupations.

To investigate whether a general increase in occupational barriers may have contributed to declining female participation, I examined occupational segregation in commercial directories and the censuses. The usual method for measuring occupational segregation is to calculate the index of segregation, or the Duncan index. The index is:

$$\frac{\sum_i |m_i - f_i|}{2}$$

---

[30] The Pioneer, March 19, 1834, quoted in Taylor, *Eve and the New Jerusalem*, p. 108.
[31] BPP 1824 (51) V, p. 525.

where m_i is the percentage of males in occupation i, and f_i is the percentage of females in occupation i. For example, if there are 200 women listed in the town's directory, and 40 of them are milliners, then the f_i for the occupation milliner is 20 percent. If men and women have exactly the same occupational distribution, so that the female percentage in each occupation is equal to the percentage of women in the workforce as a whole, then the index will equal zero. If occupations are completely segregated, so that women never work in male occupations and men never work in female occupations, then the index is equal to 100.

Humphries used census data to calculate the index of occupational segregation for each county in 1851 and 1871, and found that the index "rose for all counties between 1851 and 1871."[32] The smallest increase was in Northamptonshire, where the index rose from 65.1 to 65.4, and the largest increase was in Cumberland, where the index rose from 50.8 to 69.3. The average increase in the index was 7.1 points. We have seen that the nineteenth-century censuses were not very accurate measures of women's employment (see Chapter 1). Here, however, we are interested in trends rather than levels, and if the extent of measurement error is constant over time it will not affect the trend. Thus there does seem to have been an increase in occupational segregation between 1851 and 1871.

Unfortunately it is not possible to use the census to examine whether occupational segregation was increasing during the first half of the eighteenth century because individual-level occupational data are not available before 1841. The most comprehensive measure of occupations available for the Industrial Revolution period is the commercial directories, and these record only business owners in manufacturing and trade. We can, however, examine whether there was increasing occupational segregation among this group.

The index of segregation is very sensitive to the definition of occupational categories, so I have adjusted the occupational categories in the directories to make them as similar as possible. Because the index is so sensitive in this respect, these indexes cannot be meaningfully compared to other indexes from other studies. The indexes of segregation are presented in Table 7.2. While the highest level of segregation seems to be in Derby in 1850, within towns there is no evidence of increasing segregation over time. The index of segregation for Manchester is slightly lower in 1846 than in either 1788 or 1824–5. The index of segregation for Coventry also falls over time. Overall there is no evidence of an upward trend in occupational segregation in commercial directories.

---

[32] Humphries, "Most Free from Objection," p. 932.

Table 7.2. *Indexes of occupational segregation from commercial directories*

Date	Town	Index of segregation	Percent female
1788	Manchester	0.593	8.9
1791	Coventry	0.658	9.0
1824–5	Manchester	0.606	6.6
1835	Coventry	0.589	9.2
1846	Manchester	0.577	9.3
1850	Birmingham	0.645	11.8
1850	Derby	0.685	12.1
1892	Coventry	0.568	14.2

Notes: Occupational categories were made as similar as possible. Persons of undetermined sex were assigned a sex based on the sex ratio within the occupation.
Sources: Lewis's Manchester Directory for 1788; Universal British Directory, 1791; Pigot and Dean's Directory for Manchester, 1825; Pigot & Co.'s National Commercial Directory, 1835; Slater's National Commercial Directory of Ireland, 1846; Slater's Royal National and Commercial Directory, 1850; Kelly's Directory, 1892.

Table 7.3 shows the progression over the years in the percentage of tradeswomen in some of the larger occupational categories, for Manchester and Coventry. This table tells the same story as the indexes; there is no clear downward trend in the participation of women. In Manchester the relative number of women drapers decreased, but the proportion of women butchers increased. Between 1788 and 1846, the proportion of women increased in eight occupations and decreased in seven. Most of these changes were very small. Taken together, shopkeepers and grocers were 14 percent female in 1788, 12 percent in 1824, and 13 percent in 1846. Dyers were 6 percent female in 1788, 4 percent in 1824, and 5 percent in 1846. Part B of Table 7.3, which examines Coventry, shows that the same pattern also holds during the second half of the nineteenth century. Between 1791 and 1835, the portion of women increased in eight occupations and decreased in four, while between 1835 and 1892 the portion of women increased in eight occupations and decreased in five. While women drapers seem to have been disappearing in Manchester, they were on the rise in Coventry. Overall there is no evidence of increasing occupational segregation in the commercial directories. In fact, this table shows surprising stability over time.

Evidence from commercial directories, then, leads to a different conclusion than evidence from the census. The difference must be due to the fact that the directories measure only a limited segment of the workforce. The segment of the labor force that appeared in commercial directories, business owners in trade and manufacturing, did not

Table 7.3. *Trends in female participation in some of the largest occupations (percentage of business owners who were female)*

A. Manchester	1788	1824–5	1846
Agent	0.0	0.0	0.3
Attorney	0.0	0.0	0.6
Baker and flour dealer	7.7	9.6	6.1
Boot and shoe maker	0.0	6.5	2.1
Butcher	2.9		8.5
Calico printer	0.0	0.0	0.0
Cotton spinner	5.3	0.0	0.0
Draper, mercer	24.6	7.8	11.2
Dyer	6.4	4.1	5.4
Manufacturer of cloth	1.9	0.2	1.1
Merchant	1.7	0.0	0.6
Publican	9.4	15.2	15.5
Schoolmaster/mistress	35.7	48.6	43.8
Shopkeeper, grocer	13.9	12.1	12.7
Tailor	0.0	1.6	0.4
Warehouseman	0.0	5.3	7.3
B. Coventry	**1791**	**1835**	**1892**
Agent		0.0	0.0
Attorney	0.0	0.0	0.0
Baker and flour dealer	11.1	6.7	18.8
Boot and shoe maker	0.0	8.8	4.0
Butcher	6.3	1.4	2.4
Cloth manufacturer	0.0	20.0	0.0
Cycle manufacturer			0.0
Draper, mercer	0.0	13.3	21.4
Dressmaker	100.0	100.0	100.0
Dyer	1.7	0.0	40.0
Maltster	0.0	5.6	0.0
Physician and surgeon	0.0	0.0	0.0
Publican	14.7	7.3	13.4
Ribbon manufacturer	2.3	2.7	4.9
Schoolmaster/mistress	40.0	55.9	50.0
Shopkeeper, grocer	6.3	12.5	22.2
Tailor	0.0	0.0	7.2
Watch and clock maker	0.0	6.7	0.4

Notes: I took the ten largest occupations in each year (except "fustian cutter," which appears only in 1788). Butchers are missing from the 1824–5 directory. For 1791 the "Shopkeeper, grocer" category includes "Grocers, victuallers, and hucksters."
Sources: Lewis's Manchester Directory for 1788; Pigot and Dean's Directory for Manchester, 1825; Slater's National Commercial Directory of Ireland, 1846. The Universal British Directory, 1791; Pigot & Co.'s National Commercial Directory, 1835; Kelly's Directory, 1892.

experience increasing occupational segregation. However, there was increasing occupational segregation in the labor force as a whole between 1851 and 1871. Thus the increasing segregation seems to have occurred among workers who were employees.

III.   Increased household incomes

Some of the decline in female labor force participation can be explained by an increase in incomes. If market goods were inferior, then an increase in income would increase the demand for home-produced goods. For example, if purchased child care is inferior, an increase in income may lead a family to use the labor of the wife for child care, even if it is more expensive to do so. An increase in household income would encourage the mother to spend more time at home. This may provide an explanation of the withdrawal of women from the labor market over the course of the nineteenth century; as incomes increased, women were better able to afford the consumption good of raising their own children.

Numerous studies have found that women's time out of the labor force is a normal good, in the sense that increases in family income will increase the consumption of this good.[33] There are many possible reasons why households may value women's time out of the labor force. They may value the goods and services produced in the household, or higher social status, or women's leisure, or all of these. If time out of the labor force is a normal good, then we would expect it to go up, and women's labor force participation to go down, when male incomes rise.

For the first half of the nineteenth century, rising income cannot be an important cause of the general decline in female labor force participation simply because incomes were not rising. There is an extensive and lively literature on the course of real wages over the early nineteenth century. Optimists argue that the Industrial Revolution led to increases in the real wage, and pessimists argue that real wages did not rise during the Industrial Revolution. The argument, though, is mainly about the timing of real wage increases. Lindert and Williamson suggest that real male wages began to grow after 1820, and more than doubled between 1819 and 1851.[34] Feinstein, using more accurate measures of the cost of living, finds much smaller increases before 1851. All sides of the debate, though, agree that real wages rose during the second half of the nineteenth

---

[33] See, for example, Horrell and Humphries, "Women's Labour Force Participation," and James Smith and Michael Ward, "Time-Series Growth in the Female Labor Force," *Journal of Labor Economics* 3 (1985), S59–S90.

[34] Lindert and Williamson, "English Workers' Living Standards."

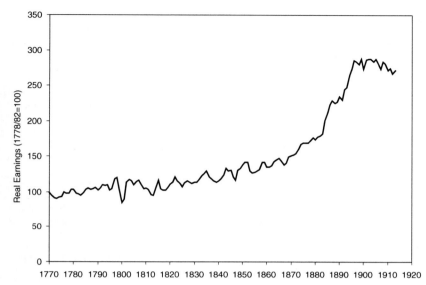

Figure 7.3 Feinstein's estimates of real earnings
Source: Feinstein, "Pessimism Perpetuated"; Feinstein, "New Estimates of Average Earnings." The price index used is the Board of Trade Wholesale Price Index from Mitchell, *Abstract of British Historical Statistics*, p. 476.

century. Figure 7.3 graphs Feinstein's 1998 estimates of average full-employment real earnings for 1770 to 1882, combined with his 1990 estimates of average money earnings for 1880 to 1913, corrected for inflation using wholesale prices.[35] Most of the nineteenth-century increase in real wages took place during the last three decades of the century. Real wages rose only 17 percent between 1770 and 1840, but rose 80 percent between 1870 and 1900. Thus it is not surprising that Horrell and Humphries find that, even after controlling for income, there is still a downward trend in female participation during the first half of the nineteenth century.[36] Given the pattern of real wages, it is likely that increases in income had the largest impact on female labor force participation in the second half of the nineteenth century.

---

[35] Charles Feinstein, "Pessimism Perpetuated: Real Wages and the Standard of Living in Britain during and after the Industrial Revolution," *Journal of Economic History* 58 (1998), pp. 625–58; Charles Feinstein, "New Estimates of Average Earnings in the United Kingdom, 1880–1913," *Economic History Review* 43 (1990), pp. 595–632. The price index used is the Board of Trade Wholesale Price Index from B. R. Mitchell, *Abstract of British Historical Statistics* (Cambridge: Cambridge University Press, 1962), p. 476.
[36] Horrell and Humphries, "Women's Labour Force Participation," p. 112.

Table 7.4. *The predicted effect of changes in real earnings on married women's labor force participation*

	1801–41	1841–61	1861–1901
Percent change in real earnings	31.2	14.4	111.9
Predicted effect on married women's LFP			
Upper bound	−12.5	−5.8	−44.8
Lower bound	−0.5	−0.2	−1.7
Actual change in married women's LFP	−12.5	−21.2	−58.4
Percent predicted by income change			
Upper bound	100.0	27.1	76.7
Lower bound	3.8	1.0	2.9

Sources: **Real Earnings**; Feinstein, "Pessimism Perpetuated"; Feinstein, "New Estimates of Average Earnings"; Mitchell, *Abstract of British Historical Statistics*, p. 476. **Elasticities for calculating the predicted effect**: Horrell and Humphries, "Women's Labour Force Participation," p. 112; Goldin, "The Changing Economic Role of Women," p. 568. **Actual changes in LFP, 1801–41 and 1841–61**: Horrell and Humphries, "Women's Labour Force Participation," p. 98. **Actual Changes in LFP, 1861–1901**: Land, "The Family Wage," p. 61; McKay, "Married Women and Work."

To estimate the effect of changing income on female labor force participation, I combine Feinstein's real earnings estimates with the income elasticity of female participation. Based on their sample of working-class household budgets, Horrell and Humphries estimate that the elasticity of married women's participation with respect to real male earnings is −0.4.[37] If the participation of poor women was more responsive to male earnings than that of non-poor women, this elasticity may overstate the response for the population as a whole. Claudia Goldin finds a much smaller elasticity, of −0.015, for US women in the twentieth century.[38] The elasticity of the participation response for all married women in nineteenth-century Britain was probably somewhere between these two elasticities. I use these two elasticities, combined with wages changes from Figure 7.3, to calculate the upper- and lower-bound estimates of what effect changes in income had on female participation (see Table 7.4). Because the elasticity of the response is so low, the lower-bound estimates suggest that change in income had little effect on female participation in the nineteenth century. The upper-bound estimates suggest a greater role for rising incomes. During the 1801–41 period, the upper-bound estimate can explain the entire

[37] *Ibid.*
[38] Claudia Goldin, "The Changing Economic Role of Women: A Quantitative Approach," in Robert Whalpes and Dianne Betts, eds., *Historical Perspectives on the American Economy* (Cambridge: Cambridge University Press, 1995), p. 568.

12 percent decline in married women's labor force participation. For the shorter period of 1841 to 1861, participation declines at a faster rate, and rising real incomes explain only 27 percent of the decline. For the end of the nineteenth century, the decline in participation is very large, 58 percent, but because incomes increased so rapidly, rising income can explain 77 percent of the decline if we use the upper-bound estimate. While the actual contribution of rising incomes was probably smaller than the upper-bound estimates, these calculations suggest that rising incomes may have been a significant factor in causing the decline in the labor force participation rate of married women during the nineteenth century.

IV.   Value of home production

Jan DeVries explains the declining female participation of the later nineteenth century as the result of increased preferences for home-produced goods and services, which he terms "Z goods":

As real earnings rose in the second half of the nineteenth century (the timing varies by social class and country), a new set of Z goods, associated with the health and training of children and the achievement of new standards of domesticity in the home, came to appear superior to the available range of market-provided goods and services. To acquire these Z goods the labor of wives and children was withdrawn from the labor force as the incomes of adult male workers rose.[39]

This process was the exact opposite of the "industrious revolution," which had drawn women and children into the workforce as a result of an increased demand for market-provided goods and services.

Mokyr suggests a possible explanation for this shift in preferences toward home-produced goods and services: new scientific knowledge about germs.[40] While the idea of germs had been proposed by others, Pasteur was finally able to demonstrate that germ theory was true in the 1860s.[41] Mokyr calls the discovery of germs "one of the most significant technological breakthroughs in history."[42] Suddenly, new techniques for avoiding disease were available. Households had always valued health, and with new information about the relationship between cleanliness and health, households placed greater value on cleanliness, not only for

---

[39] Jan DeVries, "Between Purchasing Power and the World of Goods: Understanding the Household Economy in Early Modern Europe," in Pamela Sharpe, ed., *Women's Work: The English Experience, 1650–1914* (London: Arnold, 1998), p. 229.

[40] Joel Mokyr, *The Gifts of Athena: Historical Origins of the Knowledge Economy* (Princeton: Princeton University Press, 2002), p. 200.

[41] *Ibid.*, p. 184.   [42] *Ibid.*, p. 185.

itself, but also for the better health that it provided. The result was an increase in the demand for home-produced goods and services.

However, the increased demand for cleanliness caused by the discovery of germs probably did not affect female labor force participation until late in the nineteenth century, and thus could explain only the last few decades of the decline. Even after Pasteur demonstrated the existence of germs, this new knowledge still had to be transmitted to the public. Housewives had to be convinced that germ theory was true, and that it had implications for the health of their families. Organizations such as the British Ladies' National Association for the Diffusion of Sanitary Knowledge helped to convince women of the value of cleanliness.[43] Their message was reinforced by advertisements for soap, and soon women were made to feel guilty if their homes were not spotless. By the early twentieth century, women had been persuaded of the importance of eliminating dirt from their homes, and their labor force participation had reached a low point. By 1901 married women's labor force participation had already reached its nadir of about 10 percent, where it stayed until it began to rise in the 1930s.[44]

V.   Gender ideology and changes in preferences

When they observe a change, economists generally seek to explain that change as a response to the constraints faced by decision-makers. It is possible, however, that changes in preferences may explain the change in behavior. There is evidence that women's preferences for work changed over the course of the nineteenth century and contributed to the decline of labor force participation.

The nineteenth century saw the creation of the idea that a married woman should not need to work and her husband should be able to support the family. Previously it was expected that women would contribute to the family income. An eighteenth-century pamphlet warns women that "you cannot expect to marry in such a manner as neither of you shall have occasion to work, and none but a fool will take a wife whose bread must be earned solely by his labor and who will contribute nothing toward it herself."[45] By the nineteenth century this attitude had changed, and middle-class families were ashamed if the wife had to work.[46] Men

---

[43] *Ibid.*, p. 189.   [44] Hatton and Bailey, "Women's Work in Census and Survey," Figure 1.
[45] *A Present for a Servant Maid*, 1743, quoted in George, *London Life in the Eighteenth Century*, pp. 168–9.
[46] Rose, "Gender Antagonism," p. 205.

commonly expressed concern that married women who were working would neglect their domestic duties. Seeing to the domestic comforts of the home, even if it was a small cottage, came to be seen as important work that paid employment would detract from. In the 1843 report on *Women and Children in Agriculture* we see men expressing concern about the families of women who worked in the fields. Revd Howman from Bexwell, Norfolk, did not approve of women being employed in outdoor agricultural work because:

It produces also a bad moral effect on the men. Observation shows that women employed in field-work are not so careful and clean as others; consequently, the home to which the man returns, after his day's work, is not so comfortable as it ought to be, and he is driven to the ale-house and beer-shop to avoid the discomforts, and to seek for that comfort which he ought to find at home.[47]

Somewhat later, in 1865, the managers of a Scottish paper mill report that "with a view to prevent the neglect of children in their homes, we do not employ the mothers of young children in our works."[48] For women of the upper classes, the avoidance of paid work was particularly important. In 1839 Mrs. Ellis wrote that:

It is a curious anomaly in the structure of modern society, that gentlemen may employ their hours of business in almost any degrading occupation and, if they but have the means of supporting a respectable establishment at home, may be gentlemen still; while, if a lady but touch any article, no matter how delicate, in the way of trade, she loses caste, and ceases to be a lady.[49]

Veblen explains this enforced leisure for women as a form of conspicuous consumption demonstrating the household's high status. While middle-class husbands could not afford to refrain from work, "the middle-class wife still carries on the business of vicarious leisure, for the good name of the household and its master."[50] This ideology probably encouraged many women to stay out of the labor market.

Certainly nineteenth-century individuals thought about themselves in gendered ways. This may have affected women's employment opportunities in various ways. Craft and professional organizations used gender ideology to support their restrictions on female employment. Gender ideology worked through customer preferences, by reducing the

---

[47] *Women and Children in Agriculture*, p. 244.
[48] Quoted in Simonton, *European Women's Work*, p. 141.
[49] Mrs. Ellis, *The Women of England and their Social Duties and Domestic Habits*, 2nd edn (London: Fisher, Son, and Co., 1839), pp. 344–5.
[50] Thorstein Veblen, *The Theory of the Leisure Class* (Boston: Houghton Mifflin [1899] 1973), p. 68.

demand for the services of females in certain occupations. Gender ideology also created a social cost to female employment. Families that did not follow the male-breadwinner norm lost social status. As incomes rose in the later nineteenth century, more families could afford to purchase the higher social status that came with a wife who did not work outside the home. Gender ideology may also have changed women's preferences; even if they could have found employment, women may have preferred to remain out of the labor force. Even Ivy Pinchbeck, an educated and accomplished woman, voiced this preference. She noted that, in spite of the fact that "the majority of married women lost their economic independence,"

the industrial revolution marked a real advance, since it led to the assumption that men's wages should be paid on a family basis, and prepared the way for the more modern conception that in the rearing of children and in home-making, the married woman makes an adequate economic contribution.[51]

In valuing the opportunity to remain out of the labor force above economic independence, Pinchbeck demonstrated that her preferences were different from those of many women today, who would prefer economic independence. There is no basis for saying which set of preferences is better, but the difference in preferences surely had implications for labor force participation.

However, the fact that the culture increasingly associated women with the household at a time when women's labor market participation fell does not necessarily mean that the changing ideology *caused* the change in participation. Correlation is not causation. Unfortunately, this is difficult to determine because both economic incentives and gender ideology were changing at the same time, and both implied declining female participation. It is not clear whether the change in gender ideology was independent of economic changes, or was itself driven by those economic changes. Perhaps participation declined because of changes in economic incentives, and only then did ideology change.[52]

---

[51] Pinchbeck, *Women Workers and the Industrial Revolution*, pp. 312–13.

[52] Snell argues that changes in women's agricultural employment came before changes in attitudes: "The historical determinant of women's economic and domestic roles would appear to be located primarily in seemingly autonomous changes in the structure of the economy, rather than in shifts of social attitudes. Moral sentiments antagonistic to female labor in the nineteenth century may have reinforced the pattern of change described here, and contributed to the process begun in the mid-eighteenth century. But insofar as they cannot readily be dated from before 1800, at the very earliest, their significance seems heavily undercut by the evidence that the major sexual division of labor began at least fifty years before such 'middle-class' attitudes toward the roles of women can have had influence." Snell, *Annals of the Laboring Poor*, p. 66.

Perhaps gender ideology was created as a marketing tool to convince people to accept the restrictions on female employment that benefited particular groups of male workers.

Nor should we assume that the ideological statements we hear from Victorians were accurate descriptions of reality. To a large extent female domesticity was an aspiration rather than a description of reality. Vickery criticizes the literature on separate spheres for failing to ask important questions about the primary sources used: "Did men and women actually conform to prescribed models of authority? ... Did women deploy the rhetoric of submission selectively, with irony, or quite cynically?"[53] After reviewing some of the evidence, Vickery suggests that "doubts now circulate within women's history about the conceptual usefulness of the separate spheres framework."[54] The power of gender ideology to direct women's activities should not be overstated.

Conclusion

The explanations for declining participation presented here suggest that before 1850 it had different causes and consequences than it had after 1850. Before 1850, declining participation was caused mainly by declining demand for female labor, which made women worse off. After 1850, declining participation resulted from the expansion of women's choice set as well as from its contraction. Census data suggest increasing occupational segregation after 1851, so part of the declining participation of the later nineteenth century may have been due to mounting occupational barriers, which made women worse off. Some of the decline, though, was also due to increasing family income, combined with new information about health that increased the demand for home-produced goods and services. Both of these changes made women better off.

Gender ideology also contributed to declining female participation by changing women's preferences for home versus market work. Did these changes make women worse off or better off? There is no basis for answering this question because we would have to chose one value system over the other in order to rank the outcomes. Declines in female participation rates are seen by some historians as part of a patriarchal system that ensured men continued to enjoy the services of women.[55] They made women worse off in the sense that they made them more dependent on men. The women's movement of the twentieth century included a rejection of this model of the family, largely because of the

---

[53] Vickery, "Golden Age to Separate Spheres?" p. 385.   [54] *Ibid.*, p. 393.
[55] Hartmann, "Capitalism, Patriarchy, and Job Segregation."

differences in power that it implied. The women at the time, however, did not experience the change as a bad thing. Withdrawal from market work is not necessarily bad. We consider retirement a good thing, and as Benjamin and Brandt note:

> We cannot attach a welfare interpretation to female labor force participation ... If the household was sufficiently wealthy, the women could stay at home, consuming "leisure," assuming leisure is a normal good. Put another way, just because draft animals do a lot of farm work does not mean they enjoy a high position in society or that they are better off than animals grazing in the fields.[56]

There is no basis for concluding that Pinchbeck or her contemporaries were wrong to favor home production over market production.

Declining female participation during the later nineteenth century did not necessarily represent declines in women's welfare. To the extent that it was caused by increasing employment barriers, it made women worse off, but to the extent that it was caused by increasing household incomes and new information about health, it improved women's lives. During the first half of the century, however, the decline in female participation resulted from declining demand for female labor, and thus does seem to indicate a decline in women's welfare.

---

[56] Benjamin and Brandt, "Markets, Discrimination, and the Economic Contribution of Women," p. 67.

8   Conclusion

Competition is the great, the only, the all-prevailing evil.

– a male tailor and unionist, 1834[1]

During the Industrial Revolution, women earned lower wages than men, and worked in different occupations. This book has analyzed the reasons for these differences. In competitive portions of the labor market, women were disadvantaged by their lesser strength, since strength was important in most jobs. Women's wages were on average lower than men's wages because women were on average less productive than men. Occupational segregation was not the cause of the wage gap, but a method of minimizing it. If men and women had worked in the same occupations, the wage gap would have been even larger. Occupational segregation minimized the wage gap by directing women to occupations where wages were least sensitive to strength. While individuals used gender ideology to interpret the wage differences they saw, that does not necessarily mean that gender ideology was the *cause* of those differences; people often create myths to explain things they do not understand, or to justify institutions that benefit them economically. In competitive portions of the labor market the gender division of labor was determined by comparative advantage. Women worked in jobs requiring less strength, except for a few exceptional women who were strong enough to do jobs such as hewing coal. Comparative advantage also directed women to child-care tasks, so women preferred work in cottage industry, which could more easily be combined with child care.

In less competitive portions of the labor market, male workers were able to raise their own wages by limiting the supply of labor, and usually this involved barriers to female employment. Where men worked as skilled employees, unions were the most important source of gender constraints during the Industrial Revolution. Guilds had become ineffective, and employers sought to hire women because they could profit

---

[1] *The Pioneer*, May 9, 1834, quoted in Taylor, *Eve and the New Jerusalem*, p. 115.

from doing so. Only workers with scarce skills, and thus some monopoly power, were successful in excluding women. Unskilled workers faced competition from other unskilled workers; unskilled workers tried to erect such barriers, but were unsuccessful. While men often used gender ideology to justify the exclusion of women, the real cause of their actions was economic. While employers shared the same gender ideology, they fought for the right to hire women because they could profit from doing so. When economic incentives and gender ideology conflicted, men were willing to abandon the ideology.

Professional organizations acted much like unions in seeking to limit female employment. Male physicians edged out female midwives by convincing the public that formal education made physicians more skilled. Strict limits on who could enter an occupation, such as examinations for apothecaries, also allowed professions to limit entry. Lawyers, doctors, and the clergy were all successful in erecting barriers to women's employment, severely limiting women's opportunities for high-paid work. Teaching at the primary level, which was not yet professionalized, remained open to women, and success was determined by the competitive market.

A woman's ability to go into business herself was limited by a wider range of factors, all of which were immune to competition. Customers did not compete with each other, and in certain occupations customers preferred to patronize men, limiting women's opportunities. How else can we explain the absence of women from hair dressing? Women's opportunities were also limited by the law. Married women had no legal existence, and their husbands controlled all their assets. While the *feme sole* exception allowed married women to conduct their own businesses, the law of *couverture* led to women having more limited access to capital. Daughters received their inheritances in trust, which protected the money from loss by current or future husbands, but also prevented women from using the money for a business venture. None of these factors, however, was as important in determining the gender division of labor as either strength or barriers erected by powerful groups of male workers.

Historians of women workers tend to think that free-market forces were detrimental to women. Perhaps they have been influenced by the trade union movement, which (rightly) saw competition as a threat to its power. I believe, however, that competition was beneficial to women, and that English women would have been worse off if there had been less competition in the economy. In fact, competition was a woman's strongest and most consistent ally in the struggle for economic opportunity. Institutions such as the law and the family were more likely to be swayed by gender ideology, but competition was blind.

While competition hurt organized male workers by eroding their market power, it helped women. Where there were no barriers to female employment, competitive markets guided women to the occupations where strength was least important, minimizing the wage penalty caused by women's lesser strength. Where women faced barriers to employment, competition was the most powerful force in breaking down those barriers. The powerful tailors' union was eventually defeated by competition, and the trade was opened to women. Weavers were never able to erect barriers to female employment because the trade was too easily learned, and thus too competitive. It was competition that convinced employers to hire women, even though their ideology opposed it. Only where monopoly power limited competition could barriers to female employment be maintained. The advantage of competition can also be seen in the fact that women in the British economy fared better than women in other less competitive economies; in Germany guilds had more power than in England, and the number of trades which were monopolized by men was much greater.

Competition was not the source of women's lower wages. Competition led to occupational sorting in competitive markets, but in this case occupational sorting actually increased women's wages, by directing them to the occupations where the penalty for their lesser strength was the smallest. The only places where occupational segregation reduced the wages that women could earn were places where entry to those occupations was non-competitive. Where men monopolized an occupation and did not allow women to enter, women lost, and their wages suffered. Many of the highest-paying occupations were so monopolized, severely limiting opportunities for the most educated women. The cause of these limited opportunities, though, was insufficient competition.

British women faced fewer economic constraints than German women because British markets were more competitive. Ogilvie notes that in Germany guilds were strong and were able to exclude outsiders. Only males could be apprenticed, and apprenticeship was required in "most economic activities in both towns and villages. The only exceptions were farming, laboring, spinning, and housework".[2] Most unmarried women had limited occupational opportunities; most worked in either agriculture or spinning.[3] Wages and occupations were not determined by individual ability because markets were not competitive.[4] British women, by contrast, faced fewer constraints, and participated in a wider range of occupations. They were less likely to do heavy jobs for which

---

[2] Ogilvie, *A Bitter Living*, p. 96.   [3] *Ibid.*, pp. 272–3.   [4] *Ibid.*, p. 324.

they were ill-suited, such as plowing, and participated in a wide range of commercial activity. Competitive markets benefited women economically.

In identifying the desire for economic gain as the main motive behind barriers to female employment, and in identifying competition as the most powerful defender of women's opportunities, I am suggesting that economic motives, rather than gender ideology, determined the division of labor. While I do not dispute the fact that individuals used gender ideology to make sense of their experiences, that does not mean that ideology was really the driving force behind those experiences. Gender ideology was an important part of the life experiences of men and women of Industrial Revolution Britain. It played an important role in how the British understood their world, and it could be decisive in areas where competition was weak, such as family decisions about how to educate children, or university admission decisions. When male workers sought to limit the supply of labor to their occupations, gender ideology guided them to target women. But gender ideology was not itself exogenous to the market, and was formed in response to needs created by the market. In some cases, gender ideology was used to explain the otherwise inexplicable, such as women's lower wages. In some cases, it was a tool used to persuade the broader society that women should be excluded from certain occupations.

In learning about the British labor market two hundred years ago, we have learned some useful lessons. We have learned that competition can be beneficial to women. This should not be taken to imply that laissez-faire benefits women. Competition is not the absence of government involvement. In fact, government intervention is often required to allow competition to survive. While competition tends to protect women from discrimination, this certainly does not mean that capitalist societies are free from discrimination because capitalist societies do not always, or even usually, produce competitive markets. Competition is a frail plant that, without constant tending by the gardener, will be strangled by the weeds of distributional coalitions. Accepting the conclusion that competition helps women does not imply that we should favor inactive government. It does imply, though, that we should try to use the power of competition to benefit women, writing policies that reduce monopoly power and thus help the market to function well, rather than trying to overrule the market.

We have also learned that equal opportunity does not guarantee equal outcomes. In situations requiring strength, men and women are not equally capable. In certain cases, equal outcomes can only be obtained from unequal opportunities. One example is firearms tests at the FBI. In

1995 two women complained that a test requiring new agents to pull the trigger of a handgun 29 times in 30 seconds was used to discriminate against women.[5] Another example is a debate over whether the military should set different standards for men and women combat pilots. The problem is that:

If women are expected to carry 150-pound water pumps and take the same G forces as men, a truly gender-neutral assignment policy could well lead to an across-the-board reduction in opportunities for women in the armed forces because many of them lack the strength and endurance to qualify.[6]

We must choose whether we want equal opportunities or equal outcomes, rather than pretending that we can always have both. Current military policy is something of a compromise. Physical standards for women are set lower than those for men, but the difference in requirements is less than the difference in the average abilities of the sexes, so that women still find it more difficult to meet the standard.[7]

Today the gender gaps are smaller, but women's wages and occupations still do not look identical to men's. The ratio of women's to men's median hourly earnings rose from 63 percent in 1972 to 79 percent in 1991.[8] The gender gap is now smaller than that reported in Table 2.1. The labor force participation rates of married women have increased from 10 percent at the beginning of the twentieth century to over 60 percent in 1991.[9] Women have greater opportunities than they once did for well-paid work, and have entered professions in medicine, the law, and the church. The extent of occupational segregation has decreased, but it has not disappeared.

One reason that women's opportunities in the labor market have changed is that the law has changed. Married women gained control of their earnings and wealth in the second half of the nineteenth century, eliminating the disadvantages discussed in Chapter 7. In Britain, the Married Women's Property Act of 1870 gave married women control of

---

[5] "Female FBI Trainees: Gun Test Discriminates", *Chicago Tribune*, October 5, 1995.

[6] David Evans, "Women in Combat: Raised Expectations, Lowered Standards?" *Chicago Tribune*, May 7, 1993, sec. 1, p. 23.

[7] Bernadette M. Marriott and Judith Grumstrup-Scott, "Introduction and Background", in Marriott and Grumstrup-Scott, eds., *Body Composition and Physical Performance* (Washington, DC: National Academy Press, 1992), p. 19.

[8] Jane Waldfogel, "The Price of Motherhood: Family Status and Women's Pay in a Young British Cohort", *Oxford Economic Papers* 47 (1995), p. 584. Blau and Kahn report, for the 1990s, ratios of 0.75 in the UK and 0.76 in the US. Francine Blau and Lawrence Kahn, "Gender Differences in Pay", *Journal of Economic Perspectives* 14 (2000), p. 92.

[9] Data for England and Wales. Hatton and Bailey, "Women's Work in Census and Survey", p. 88.

their personal property and the right to their own earnings. Further acts in 1882 and 1893 gave women full control of all property they brought to the marriage or acquired after marriage. In the US, Maine was the first state to grant married women ownership of their property, in 1844, and of their own earnings, in 1857. Other states followed during the second half of the century, and by 1895, forty-four states had passed some type of law expanding the ownership rights of married women.[10] Women had to wait until the 1960s for laws against employment discrimination. In the US, the Equal Pay Act of 1963 and Title VII of the 1964 Civil Rights Act forbade discrimination against women in hiring and pay.[11] In Britain gender discrimination was outlawed by the Equal Pay Act of 1970 and the Sex Discrimination Act of 1975.[12] Instead of denying married women a legal voice, the law now enforces equal opportunity in employment.

In 1825 William Thompson identified two causes of women's lower wages: their lesser strength, and child-bearing. Over the past two centuries strength has become much less important in determining women's labor market opportunities. It still plays a role in some occupations; those that require high levels of strength are overwhelmingly male. However, in most occupations strength is not a factor. Table 8.1 shows the gender division of labor in jobs of different strength intensity in the US labor force. The *Dictionary of Occupational Titles* categorizes the strength required for each of the jobs it lists as sedentary, light, medium, heavy, or very heavy. Table 8.1 shows that the percentage of women in an occupation decreases monotonically as the strength requirement of the job increases. While 55 percent of the workers in sedentary jobs are female, only 12 percent of workers in heavy jobs, and only 6 percent of workers in very heavy jobs, are female. However, strength is much less important for determining wages than it was two hundred years ago because only 12 percent of all workers are employed in occupations whose strength requirements are heavy or very heavy. Strength, then, is not in such high demand, so it does not command the wage premium that it once did. It can no longer explain the overall wage gap because there are enough jobs where strength is unnecessary to employ all the women in the labor force. Strength, though, can still explain why women are rare in certain occupations, such as fire-fighting and construction.

---

[10] Khan, "Married Women's Property Laws", pp. 363–4.
[11] Kermit Hall, ed., *The Oxford Companion to American Law* (Oxford: Oxford University Press, 2002), p. 219.
[12] David Walker, *The Oxford Companion to Law* (Oxford: Clarendon Press, 1980), p. 1137.

Table 8.1. *Gender division of labor by strength category of occupation*

Strength category	Number of workers in April, 1971 (1000s)		Percent female	Percent of all workers	Cumulative percent
	Males	Female			
Sedentary	8,172	9,926	54.8	21.4	21.4
Light	17,405	16,120	48.1	39.7	61.1
Medium	16,236	6,238	27.8	26.6	87.7
Heavy	7,585	1,038	12.0	10.2	97.9
Very Heavy	1,578	102	6.0	2.0	100.0
Total	50,976	33,423	39.6		

Note: The number of workers in each category is the total in the US labor force estimated from the April 1971 CPS sample, using the CPS weights.
Source: National Academy of Sciences, Committee on Occupational Classification and Analysis, *Dictionary of Occupational Titles (DOT): Part I – Current Population Survey, April 1971, Augmented with DOT Characteristics*, [Computer file]. ICPSR version. Washington, DC: US Department of Commerce, Bureau of the Census [producer], 1981. Ann Arbor, MI: Inter-university Consortium for Political and Social Research [distributor], 2001.

While strength has become irrelevant in most occupations, child-bearing still has important effects on women's labor market outcomes. The gender wage gap is smaller for women without children than it is for mothers. Waldfogel finds that, for British women who were 33 in 1991, mothers earned 64 percent as much as men, while women with no children earned 84 percent as much as men. Single women earn 83 percent as much as single men, but married women earn only 56 percent as much as married men.[13] Marriage and family have different effects on men's and women's earnings. The presence of children decreases female wages but increases male wages. Marriage increases wages for both men and women, but the effect is more than twice as large for men as it is for women.[14] A substantial part of the wage gap is actually a "family gap"; the labor market penalizes women, but not men, for having families.

The family gap may result from the fact that women still do most of the household labor. Table 8.2 shows the gender gap in hours spent in household work. While there has been remarkable convergence in most countries, women still do most of the household labor. Even women who work full-time do more housework than men who work full-time.

[13] Jane Waldfogel, "Understanding the 'Family Gap' in Pay for Women with Children", *Journal of Economic Perspectives* 12 (1998), p. 142.
[14] *Ibid.*, p. 146.

Table 8.2. *Men's hours of housework as a percentage of women's hours of housework*

	Denmark	Norway	Japan	USSR	US	US Full-time workers
1964	12.3					
1965	35.0		8.9	31.1	27.5	
1971		37.3				
1980		50.9				
1981					45.2	
1985			11.3	44.1		
1987	55.4					
2003					57.6	67.4

Sources: 2003 data from Daniel Hammermesh, Harley Frazis, and Jay Stewart, "Data Watch: The American Time Use Survey", *Journal of Economic Perspectives*, 19 (2005), p. 224. All other data from F. Thomas Juster and Frank P. Stafford, "The Allocation of Time: Empirical Findings, Behavioral Models, and Problems of Measurement", *Journal of Economic Literature*, 29 (1991), p. 477.

This gender division of labor in household work is currently one of the major obstacles to gender equality in the labor market. Joshi and Paci find that, while the wage penalty for being female declined between 1972 and 1991, the penalty for motherhood did not decline.[15] Men and women will not reach equality in the labor market until there is equality within the family.

Fortunately there are signs that behavior is changing. The convergence of housework time evident in Table 8.2 is encouraging, as is the increase in the number of teenage girls who expect to be in the labor market as adults. While in 1968 only 30 to 35 percent of teenage girls in the US expected to be working at age 35, by 1980 between 80 and 85 percent expected to be working at age 35. This change in expectations contributed to women's increasing college enrollment rates, and today female college students outnumber male college students.[16] Technology also seems to be helping women to reduce the conflict between child bearing and market work. Martha Bailey finds that the release of the pill in the US did not change total fertility, but it did lead to an increase in the number of female professionals because it allowed women to change the timing of births: "By providing a low-cost means

[15] Joshi and Paci, *Unequal Pay for Women and Men*, p. 124.
[16] Claudia Goldin, Lawrence Katz, and Ilyana Kuziemko, "The Homecoming of American College Women: The Reversal of the College Gender Gap", *Journal of Economic Perspectives* 20 (2006), pp. 133–56.

of delaying childbearing, oral contraception allowed women to remain in school, pursue longer-term careers, and work more in the paid labor force during ages historically associated with childrearing".[17] While the occupations and wages of men and women may never be identical, labor markets are clearly moving in that direction. Women of the twenty-first century may not have occupations and wages identical to men's, but they will face less occupational segregation and smaller wage gaps than women of the Industrial Revolution.

---

[17] Martha Bailey, "More Power to the Pill: The Impact of Contraceptive Freedom on Women's Life Cycle Labor Supply", *Quarterly Journal of Economics* 121 (2006), p. 295.

Appendix to Chapter 3

This appendix presents more mathematical versions of the sorting models presented in Chapter 3. All of these models assume that individuals do not differ by skill, but only in their strength endowment.

Model A

Here I expand Model A to allow the possibility that the distributions may overlap. Individuals get strength endowments that are random draws from normal distributions. Males and females draw their strength endowments from different distributions, and the male distribution has a higher mean. In general individuals can freely choose among T occupations. In occupation i individual j will produce $q_{ij} = a_i + b_i S_j$ units of output and will have earnings of $p_i q_{ij}$, where p_i is the piece-rate. An individual will choose the occupation in which he or she has the highest earnings. Since earnings functions are linear, each occupation will have at most one interval of possible S values over which it is the best occupational choice. (It is possible that an occupation will attract no workers if its earnings are always below those of another occupation.)

What will happen if we take the income functions from Figures 3.2 and 3.5, but allow the strength endowments to overlap? Suppose that females have strength endowments that are normally distributed with a mean of 25 and a standard deviation of 15. Males have strength endowments that are normally distributed with a mean of 75 and a standard deviation of 15. With these assumptions the male mean is $3\frac{1}{3}$ standard deviations above the female mean, which approximately matches the distance between the means in maximum lift capacity presented in Table 2.4.

In Figure 3.2, individuals with strength between 0 and 25 will choose occupation A. Since 25 is the mean female strength score, half of the women will choose occupation A and half will choose occupation B. A strength score of 25 is $3\frac{1}{3}$ standard deviations below the mean on the male distribution, so the probability of observing a man in occupation A is less than one-tenth of 1 percent. The outcome is essentially the same as above, except for the possibility of finding a very unusual man in occupation A.

Given the opportunities described in Figure 3.5, individuals with a strength score below 20 will choose occupation A, those between 20 and 60 will choose occupation B, and those above 60 will choose occupation C. We would expect that 20 percent of women will choose occupation A, 79 percent occupation B, and 1 percent occupation C, while 84 percent of men will choose occupation C, and 16 percent of men will choose occupation B. Clearly, occupations A and B are "women's work" and occupation C is "men's work," but the gender division of labor is not perfect. If there are equal numbers of male and female workers, we would expect to observe that about 1 percent of workers in occupation C are female, and 17 percent of workers in occupation B are male. It could even happen that we observe men in occupation A, though that would be a rare occurrence.

If we allow the male and female strength distributions to overlap, the general pattern remains, with one gender dominating most occupations, but the division of labor by gender is not as strict, and we could observe more than one occupation hiring members of both genders.

Model B

In this model I assume that employers can observe the worker's gender but not the worker's strength score. The employer will treat all women the same, acting as if each female worker has a strength score of:

$$S_f = E \ (S_j \mid j \text{ is female})$$

Similarly, the employer will treat all men the same, acting as if each male worker has a strength score of:

$$S_m = E \ (S_j \mid j \text{ is male})$$

Since men are stronger than women, $S_m > S_f$.

The labor power provided by an individual is a function of that individual's strength:

$$L_{ij} = a_i + b_i S_j$$

The relationship between labor power and strength can be different at different firms. At some firms strength may not matter ($b_i = 0$), in which case the firm will not prefer men. If strength does matter ($b_i > 0$), then the average man provides more labor power than the average woman.

The firm cannot observe an individual's level of strength, but does observe gender. Given gender, the firm forms a conditional expectation of strength. The firm thus expects different amounts of labor power from each gender:

$$L_{if} = E(L_{ij} \mid j \text{ is female}) = a_i + b_i S_f$$
$$L_{im} = E(L_{ij} \mid j \text{ is male}) = a_i + b_i S_m$$

Since $S_m > S_f$, then $L_{im} > L_{if}$ if $b_i > 0$. We could also write the labor power provided by a male as:

$$L_{im} = L_{if} + b_i(S_m - S_f)$$

This suggests that we can think of the labor power provided by an individual as a base level of labor power, plus a strength upgrade if the worker is male. We can normalize labor power so that the base level of labor power is one:

$$\tilde{L}_{ij} = 1 \qquad \text{if } j \text{ is female}$$
$$= 1 + \frac{b_i(S_m - S_f)}{L_{if}} \qquad \text{if } j \text{ is male}$$

If we sum this up over all the workers that the firm hires, then the total amount of (normalized) labor power hired by the firm is:

$$N + \rho_i M$$

where N is the total number of male and female workers hired by the firm ($N = F + M$) and M is the number of male workers hired. The parameter ρ_i is the value of the strength upgrade to firm i.

Including this equation for labor power in a Cobb-Douglass production function we get:

$$Q = A(N + \rho M)^{\alpha} K^{\beta}$$

The marginal product of a female worker is:

$$\frac{dQ}{dF} = A\alpha(N + \rho M)^{\alpha-1} K^{\beta} = \frac{\alpha Q}{N + \rho M}$$

and the marginal product of a male worker is:

$$\frac{dQ}{dM} = A\alpha(N + \rho M)^{\alpha-1} K^{\beta}(1 + \rho) = \frac{\alpha Q(1 + \rho)}{N + \rho M}$$

The firm's r_i, which I have defined as the ratio of the female marginal product to the male marginal product is simply:

$$r = \frac{dQ/dF}{dQ/dM} = \frac{1}{(1+\rho)}$$

The firm will choose to hire men if $(1 + \rho_i) > w_m/w_f$ (or $\rho_i > (w_m - w_f)/w_f$, or $r_i < w_f/w_m$) and to hire women if $(1+\rho_i) < w_m/w_f$ (or $\rho_i < (w_m - w_f)/w_f$, or $r_i > w_f/w_m$). This is the same thing as saying that the firm will buy the strength upgrade if the value of the upgrade is greater than its price.

In general each firm's demand for workers will depend on the price of the firm's output and the level of wages. Wages will adjust so that the demand for each type of worker is equal to the supply. If we assume that the number of workers each firm will hire is fixed, then the wage ratio can be easily determined in a simple graph. In Figure 3.6, the length of the x-axis is the total amount of labor supplied and demanded in the economy. There are OX females and XL males. Firms are ordered by r_i, and the "r-profile" is constructed by giving each firm a line segment whose height is r_i and whose length is proportional to the number of workers it hires. The wage ratio is then determined by the point at which the vertical line originating at point X intersects the r-profile. The marginal firm may hire both males and females, but all other firms will hire only one gender. Changes in the number of workers hired by a firm, or the entry and exit of new firms, will change the r-profile and, if substantial enough, will shift the market wage ratio.

Model C: the learning model

This model provides an intermediate case between Model A and Model B. Model A assumes that the employer can perfectly observe the individual worker's output, and Model B assumes that the employer has no information about the individual worker's output, and must use gender to estimate the worker's productivity. In this model the employer receives a noisy signal of the worker's output. At first the employer has little information, and pays the worker according to gender as in Model B. Over time the employer learns about the workers and pays a wage more closely matched to the individual's productivity, and the model evolves into one more like Model A. As in the two previous models, I assume that productivity differs only because of strength, so that an individual's productivity can be completely described by the strength score S.

We might expect that when an employer first hires a worker he or she does not know that individual's strength score (S_j), but that over time

the employer learns and can adjust the wage to reward actual productivity. I assume that in each industry there is a function that relates an
individual's output, q_j, to his or her strength score, S_j:

$$q_j = f(S_j)$$

The employer pays each worker his or her expected productivity, which
varies over time as the employer receives more information. Thus:

$$w_{tj} = E_t\, q_j$$

When first hired, each worker receives a wage equal to the average
productivity of that worker's sex:

$$w_{tj} = \mu_j \quad \text{where} \quad \mu_j = \mu_f = f(S_f) \quad \text{if } j = f$$
$$= \mu_m = f(S_m) \quad \text{if } j = m$$

Each period the employer receives a signal, s_{tj}, of productivity that will
allow him or her to update the estimate of the worker's productivity. The
employer observes:

$$s_{tj} = q_j + e_{tj}$$

where e_{tj} is a random error that is normally distributed with mean zero
and variance σ_e^2. Since q_j is the individual's true productivity, it is
not stochastic, so the signal s_{tj} is normally distributed with mean q_j
and variance σ_e^2.

In the second period, one signal has been observed. The expected
value of the individual's productivity is a weighted average of the
observed signal and the mean productivity of the worker's sex:

$$w_{2j} = E_2 q_j = \frac{\sigma_e^2}{\sigma_i^2 + \sigma_e^2}\mu_i + \frac{\sigma_i^2}{\sigma_i^2 + \sigma_e^2}s_{1j}$$

where μ_i and σ_i^2 (i = m, f) are the mean and variance of the true
productivity of individuals in the worker's sex. This equation can
also be written:

$$w_{2j} = \frac{\frac{1}{\sigma_i^2}\mu_i + \frac{1}{\sigma_e^2}s_{1j}}{\frac{1}{\sigma_i^2} + \frac{1}{\sigma_e^2}}$$

In the third period, the expected value of the worker's productivity will
be a weighted average of $E_2 q_j$ and s_{2j}, which reduces to:

$$w_{3j} = \frac{\frac{1}{\sigma_i^2}\mu_i + \frac{1}{\sigma_e^2}\left(s_{1j} + s_{2j}\right)}{\frac{1}{\sigma_i^2} + 2\frac{1}{\sigma_e^2}}$$

The wage in subsequent periods is updated according to observed values of s:

$$w_{tj} = \frac{\frac{1}{\sigma_i^2}\mu_i + \frac{1}{\sigma_e^2}\sum_{k=1}^{t} s_{kj}}{\frac{1}{\sigma_i^2} + t\frac{1}{\sigma_e^2}}$$

As t gets large, this approaches an average of the s_{tj}'s, and thus will converge to the true productivity, q_j. In the first period of employment, the individual is paid the average productivity of his or her sex, as in Model A. In the limit, though, the employer learns the true productivity of the worker, as in Model B.

In some cases, however, this process may fail to achieve the correct allocation of labor according to individual ability. Correct sorting may never occur for women with high strength scores. In order to learn the true productivity of a worker, the employer must first be willing to hire that individual. An unfamiliar employer may not be willing to hire a woman for any positive wage. For example, if the productivity of a worker at a firm is:

$$q_j = S^2 - 900$$

and the average female strength score is less than 30, then the expected productivity of a woman is negative, and the employer will be unwilling to hire women. A woman whose strength score was 40 could be productive in this occupation, but the employer will not discover that because he will never hire her in the first place.

Appendix to Chapter 4

4.1   Models of discrimination

In Chapter 4 I test one economic model of labor market discrimination, the occupational segregation model, formalized by Bergmann.[1] Bergmann's model assumes constraints on which workers can be hired for which jobs. Suppose there is a production function,

$$Y = f(E_1, E_2, K)$$

where E_1 and E_2 are two different jobs. Occupational segregation occurs in the form of constraints. If M is the number of male workers and F is the number of female workers, the constraints are:

$$E_1 = M \quad E_2 = F$$

Females cannot be hired for the male job and males cannot be hired for the female job. The occupational segregation model has implications for wages if women are confined to a small number of jobs. Because of the diminishing marginal product of labor, confining women to a small number of jobs results in "overcrowding" and reduces their marginal product. I test for the presence of discrimination in this form by examining whether employers were willing to substitute men and women workers. If there were rigid employment constraints, that would imply that men and women were not substitutable. If employers did in fact substitute men for women, and vice versa, such a practice implies that they were not completely limited by occupational segregation constraints.

Discrimination may also exist in the form of wage discrimination; in this case employers are willing to hire women but pay them less than their marginal product. Because wage discrimination and occupational segregation can operate independently, showing that the labor market

---

[1] Bergmann, "The Effect on White Incomes of Discrimination," pp. 294–313. Bergmann described occupational segregation between blacks and whites; I have applied the same model to segregation between men and women.

was perfectly competitive requires showing that neither form of discrimination prevailed. The labor market may be characterized by one form and not the other. Women may be allowed to enter any occupation but be paid less than their marginal product, so that the market is characterized by wage discrimination but not occupational segregation. Alternatively, women may be paid their marginal product but be confined to certain occupations.

The wage discrimination model, also called taste discrimination, was set forth by Gary Becker.[2] In Becker's employer-discrimination model, the employer has a taste for discrimination in his or her utility function, which leads the employer to offer a lower wage to the group discriminated against. The employer's utility function might look like this:

$$U = \pi(M, F) - dF$$

where M is the number of men hired, F is the number of women, π is the firm's profit, and d is the taste for discrimination against women. Utility maximization implies:

$$\pi_2 - d = w_f,$$

or the wage of a woman worker will equal her marginal product less the employer's taste for discrimination. The employer will only hire a woman if he is compensated for the disutility of doing so by a sufficiently low wage. Under Becker's wage discrimination model, the employer is willing to substitute men and women. Thus a test for substitution between men and women cannot detect the presence of wage discrimination.

Tests of wage discrimination suggest that women were paid their marginal product. For example, Cox and Nye find that women's wages were equal to their marginal productivity in French industry.[3] Such a test, however, cannot detect occupational segregation constraints. Occupational segregation lowers women's wages precisely by lowering their marginal product. The statistical test described in the next section adds to our knowledge of discrimination by testing for occupational segregation.

4.2   Cross-price elasticity as a test for gender segregation

While we can easily observe that men and women worked in different occupations, the reason that they did so is more difficult to determine.

[2] Becker, *The Economics of Discrimination*.
[3] See Chapter 2 for a more detailed discussion of the evidence on relative productivity.

Noting that men and women worked at different jobs will not tell us whether the market was characterized by occupational segregation. We need a test that can distinguish whether men and women were hired in two segregated labor markets, or whether there was one unified labor market in which men and women competed against each other. One method to distinguish between segregated and competitive markets is to test whether men and women were substitutes. If the labor market was truly segregated by gender, then the wage of one sex would not affect the employment of the other sex. If the results indicate that men and women were substitutes, then this implies that they competed against each other in a single labor market.

Substitutability would be indicated by a positive cross-price elasticity, or:

$$\frac{dx_f}{dw_m} \frac{w_m}{x_f} > 0$$

which tells us that the employment of women increased in response to an increase in the wages of men, and, similarly,

$$\frac{dx_m}{dw_f} \frac{w_f}{x_m} > 0.$$

While both elasticities must have the same sign, they will in general have different magnitudes, depending on the relative factor shares. In a two-factor model, the cross-price elasticity can be expressed as:

$$\frac{dx_1}{dw_2} \frac{w_2}{x_1} = \frac{w_2 x_2}{(w_1 x_1 + w_2 x_2)} (\sigma - \eta)$$

where σ is the elasticity of substitution and η is the elasticity of demand for the output.[4] Since σ and η are the same for both cross-price elasticities, the input that has the larger factor share will have the smaller cross-price elasticity.

Within-task versus across-task substitution

To establish that gender constraints on occupations were not present, I need to show that men and women were substitutable within tasks rather than merely across tasks. Within-task substitution exists if employers are willing to hire either men or women for any job, i.e., there are no

---

[4] R. G. D. Allen, *Mathematical Analysis for Economists* (New York: St. Martin's Press, [1938] 1964), p. 373. However, since male and female labor were clearly not the only factors, this is only an approximation.

constraints on which sex can be hired for any task. Across-task substitution exists if "women's jobs" and "men's jobs" are substitutable in production, and may or may not be coupled with gender constraints on occupations. For example, if a farmer was willing to increase the size of his or her dairy herd when women's wages were lower, but was not willing to hire women for any job except dairying, then women and men were substitutable across task but not within task. Across-task substitution means that women's wages will respond to men's wages, but does not imply equality of opportunity.

A specific model will help to make the issues clearer. Suppose there are two jobs on the farm, and employment levels in these jobs are designated L_1 and L_2. The farmer can hire two factors, M (male labor) and F (female labor). The production function is nested, with

$$y = f(L_1, L_2)$$

and

$$L_i = M_i + \varphi_i F_i.$$

The parameter φ measures the relative productivity of female workers. If $\varphi = 0.5$, then each female worker can do half as much work as a male worker, and if $\varphi = 1$ the sexes are equally productive.

I will define occupational segregation to be the constraints that assign each sex to one of the tasks, i.e., the constraints $M_1 = 0$ and $F_2 = 0$. In the absence of these constraints, the production function is:

$$y = f(M_1 + \varphi_1 F_1, M_2 + \varphi_2 F_2),$$

and men and women are substitutable within task. If the constraints hold, however, the production function reduces to

$$y = f(\varphi_1 F_1, M_2),$$

and no within-task substitution is possible. Across-task substitution is independent of the constraints, and exists if L_1 and L_2 are substitutes.

Across-task substitution is not sufficient to establish an unsegregated market. Suppose the occupational constraints hold but men's and women's jobs are perfectly substitutable. The employment of women will expand in response to a decrease in the ratio w_f/w_m, but women can still be hurt by the constraints, since they could be confined to less productive tasks. The production function in this case is:

$$y = a \varphi_1 F_1 + b M_2$$

where a and b are constants indicating the relative productivity of each task. If in addition to $\varphi_1 < 1$ we also have $a < b$, then female marginal productivity will be lower due to the constraint, as well as due to their natural disadvantages. In order to establish a non-discriminatory market, I need to establish that men and women were substitutable within tasks rather than merely across tasks.

Unfortunately, across-task substitution can potentially mask within-task constraints. If the occupational constraints hold, we have:

$$y = f(\varphi_1 F_1, M_2)$$

while if there are no constraints:

$$y = f(M_1 + \varphi_1 F_1, M_2 + \varphi_2 F_2).$$

If L_1 and L_2 are substitutable, men and women will be substitutes even if the constraint is binding. Only if L_1 and L_2 are not substitutes can we be confident that a positive cross-price elasticity indicates the absence of occupational constraints. For example, farmers might respond to an increase in the male wage by switching from grain to dairy production, and thus hiring more women because of a change in farm tasks. I want to know whether farmers were willing to hire women instead of men for grain production when male wages rose. To address this question, I need to control for changes in the production tasks. For a given level of L_1 and L_2, the cross-wage effects will be zero if the constraints hold and positive if they do not. Controlling for across-task substitution, then, allows us to use the cross-price elasticity to test for within-task substitution. If I can control for the tasks done on the farm and still find that men and women are substitutable, I can be confident that the substitution is within-task rather than across-task substitution.

Unfortunately, I cannot directly control for the levels of each production task. In the regressions in Chapter 4, I use farm animals, which are correlated with different types of output, to control for farm output. While these controls will not eliminate all variation in tasks, they will account for most of the variation. Dairy agriculture was quite different from arable agriculture but, given the type of output, the production tasks required were relatively fixed. An eighteenth-century farmer could choose between different types of output, perhaps producing less butter and more grain, and such a change would alter the production tasks required. Given the choice of product, however, there was little scope for substituting one task for another. More planting could not substitute for less harvesting. Thus, controlling for the type of output will control for most of the variation in production tasks. The remaining substitution between men and women workers will be within-task substitution.

4.3 Wage correlation as a test for gender segregation

The model presented here will generate a testable conclusion that can, under certain assumptions, distinguish between a segmented and a unified labor market. I will model the hypothesis of discrimination in the form of occupational segregation as a constraint in the employer's maximization problem that does not allow him or her to hire women for certain jobs. I will assume the constraint, when imposed, is exogenous to the employer's problem, so that the employer simply maximizes profits. Note that this differs from the taste discrimination model, which adds a discriminatory taste factor to the employer's utility function. If the no-women constraint is not binding, no decisions are distorted, and wages are the same as what they would be under perfect competition. If the no-women constraint is binding, women's jobs may become crowded, causing their wages to be below those that would prevail under perfect competition.

I assume that employers cannot accurately measure individual productivity strength and that they use sex as a signal. Individuals of the same sex cannot be distinguished. While individuals may differ in productivity, the employer cannot observe individual levels of productivity. In tasks that require strength, women are less productive than men. I also assume that the work is unskilled, so that individuals do not differ with respect to human capital.

Assume that there are two firms, each of which hires workers for a single task. One of the tasks requires strength, and the other does not. At firm A women are less productive than men, but at firm B men and women are equally productive. Firm A maximizes

$$\pi = P_A a \ln(M_A + \varphi F_A) - w_m M_A - w_f F_A,$$

where φ reflects the fact that male and female workers have different productivities, and is known by the employer but not by the researcher. Since, as I have shown in Chapter 2, strength was an important component of productivity in unskilled labor, I will assume that $\varphi < 1$. Firm B maximizes

$$\pi = P_B b \ln(M_B + F_B) - w_m M_B - w_f F_B.$$

Men and women are equally productive at firm B, reflecting the fact that some jobs in the economy did not require strength.

If there is gender discrimination in the form of occupational segregation, additional constraints are added:

$$F_A = 0, \ M_B = 0,$$

i.e., there is some arbitrary standard assigning men and women to certain jobs. These constraints represent the claim that social forces rather than profit maximization determined employment.

Women have a comparative advantage in working at firm B, so we would expect to find women specializing in that task. Given the production functions above, perfect competition without discrimination will result in segregation of workers by sex. The firms, taking wages as exogenous, will set

$$
\begin{aligned}
M_B = 0 \quad & \text{if} \quad \frac{w_f}{w_m} < 1 \\[2mm]
M_A = 0 \quad & \text{if} \quad \frac{w_f}{w_m} > \varphi \\[2mm]
F_B = 0 \quad & \text{if} \quad \frac{w_f}{w_m} > 1 \\[2mm]
F_A = 0 \quad & \text{if} \quad \frac{w_f}{w_m} > \varphi.
\end{aligned}
$$

Note that if $F_A > 0$ and $M_B > 0$, then one of the firms is not maximizing, since $\varphi < 1$. In equilibrium, one or both of the firms will hire only one sex. Occupational sorting results from differences in strength, and thus is not necessarily an indication of an exclusionary constraint. The model also implies that if strength is a scarce factor in the sense that $F_A > 0$, then female wages will be less than male wages whether or not there is an occupational constraint. Neither evidence of occupational sorting nor evidence of lower female wages will tell us whether there is a constraint on female employment.

I can combine these firm maximization problems with labor supply functions and solve for the market wage. If strength is a scarce factor in the sense that a competitive market would have an equilibrium with $F_A > 0$, then we can detect the presence of the exclusionary constraint by examining whether male and female wages are correlated. Male and female wages will be correlated only in the absence of the constraint.

Let the labor supply functions be:

$$
\begin{aligned}
M_A + M_B &= c_0 + c_1 w_m \\
F_A + F_B &= d_0 + d_1 w_f.
\end{aligned}
$$

Take the case where strength is scarce, so that $M_B = 0$.[5] In equilibrium:

$$w_m = \frac{-(c_0 + \varphi d_0) + \sqrt{(c_0 + \varphi d_0)^2 + 4(c_1 + \varphi^2 d_1)(P_B b + P_A a)}}{2(c_1 + \varphi^2 d_1)}$$

$$w_f = \varphi w_m.$$

This gives:

$$\frac{\delta w_m}{\delta P_A} > 0 \qquad \frac{\delta w_f}{\delta P_A} > 0 \qquad \frac{\partial w_f}{\partial P_A} = \varphi \frac{\partial w_m}{\partial P_A}$$

$$\frac{\delta w_m}{\delta P_B} > 0 \qquad \frac{\delta w_f}{\delta P_B} > 0 \qquad \frac{\partial w_f}{\partial P_B} = \varphi \frac{\partial w_m}{\partial P_B}$$

$$\frac{\partial w_m}{\partial d_o} < 0 \qquad \frac{\partial w_f}{\partial d_o} < 0 \qquad \frac{\delta w_f}{\delta d_o} = \varphi \frac{\delta w_m}{\delta d_o}.$$

As long as firm A finds it profitable to hire positive amounts of female workers, the wage ratio must equal the productivity ratio. A shock to the demand for either firm's product (a change in P_A or P_B), or a shock to either of the labor supply functions (such as a change in d_0), will move both male and female wages in the same direction, so male and female wages will be correlated.[6]

However, if firm A is constrained to hire only males, male and female wages will not be correlated. The male wage will solve

$$P_A a \frac{1}{M_A} = w_m$$

$$M_A = c_0 + c_1 w_m,$$

so

$$w_m = \frac{-c_0 + \sqrt{c_0^2 + 4c_1 P_A a}}{2c_1}.$$

---

[5] This requires that a, firm A's production function shifter, be large. An example of an equilibrium with $M_B = 0$ is: $a = 170$, $b = 30$, $\varphi = \frac{1}{2}$, $M_A = 5 + w_m$, $F_A + F_B = 2w_f$. Then $w_m = 10$, $w_f = 5$, $M_A = 15$, $M_B = 0$, $F_A = 4$, $F_B = 6$.

[6] The model also implies a test for time-series data:

$$\frac{dw_f}{dw_m} = \varphi = \frac{w_f}{w_m}.$$

Such a test, however, would require the assumption that the technology did not change over time, which would not be an appropriate assumption for the time period.

Similarly,

$$w_f = \frac{-d_o + \sqrt{d_o^2 + 4d_1 P_B b}}{2d_1}.$$

In this case male and female wages will not be correlated:

$$\frac{\delta w_m}{\delta P_A} > 0 \qquad \frac{\delta w_f}{\delta P_A} = 0$$

$$\frac{\delta w_m}{\delta P_B} = 0 \qquad \frac{\delta w_f}{\delta P_B} > 0$$

$$\frac{\delta w_m}{\delta d_o} = 0 \qquad \frac{\delta w_f}{\delta d_o} > 0.$$

In other words, if the constraint binds, a shock to the system will alter either the male wage or the female wage, but not both. If shocks are random, wages will be uncorrelated. The difference in the predicted outcome here, as opposed to the non-discriminatory case, allows me to test for constraints by examining whether male and female wages are correlated.

There is, however, a potential problem with this method. If shocks (for example, P_A and P_B) are positively correlated, then the wage correlation will be positive whether or not there is an occupational segregation constraint. Only if the shocks are uncorrelated can the wage correlation be used to distinguish between the two situations. This limitation is potentially a serious problem and might prevent using wage correlations as evidence of an integrated market if I could not correct for location-specific effects. Fortunately, I can correct for this problem whenever I have multiple wages for the same location. In a cross-sectional sample, wages at the same location may be correlated simply because of price level or any other location-specific effect. When I have seasonal wages, I can difference the wages across the seasons to correct for these fixed effects. I can then examine the correlation of changes in wages across the seasons. In other words, I will measure whether female wages are likely to rise more at harvest time in locations where male wages rise more. Unfortunately, differencing wages increases the attenuation effect of measurement error, which may bias my results. However, since the bias is downward, I can be confident about the results if I find a strong positive correlation.

Bibliography

PRIMARY

BRITISH PARLIAMENTARY PAPERS (BPP)

1806 (268) III, *Report from the Committee on the Woollen Manufacture of England*
1808 (177) II, *Report from the Committee on Petitions of Several Cotton Manufacturers and Journeymen Cotton Weavers*
1816 (397) III, *Select Committee on the State of the Children Employed in the Manufactories of the United Kingdom*
1818 (398 & 134) IX, *First Report from the Select Committee on the Petition of Ribbon Weavers*
1821 (668) IX, *Report from the Select Committee to Whom the Several Petitions Complaining of the Depressed State of Agriculture of the United Kingdom Were Referred*
1824 (392) VI, *Report from the Select Committee on Labourers' Wages*
1824 (51) V, *Fifth Report from the Select Committee on Artisans and Machinery*
1833 (450) XX, *First Report of the Central Board of His Majesty's Commissioners for Inquiring into the Employment of Children in Factories, with Minutes of Evidence*
1834 (167) XIX, *Supplementary Report of His Majesty's Commissioners on the Employment of Children in Factories*
1834 (44) XXX to XXXIV, *"Rural Queries." Report of His Majesty's Commissioners for Inquiry into the Administration and Practical Operation of the Poor Law*, Appendix B
1839 (159) XLII, *Reports from Assistant Hand-Loom Weavers' Commissioners*
1840 (43) XXIII, *Reports from Assistant Hand-Loom Weavers' Commissioners*
1840 (217 & 220) XXIV, *Reports from Assistant Hand-Loom Weavers' Commissioners*
1841 (296) X, *Handloom Weavers: Report of the Commissioners*
1842 (380) XV, *Children's Employment Commission: First Report of the Commissioners (Mines)*
1842 (381) XVI, *Appendix to the First Report of Commissioners (Mines)*
1843 (510) XII, *Reports of Special Assistant Poor Law Commissioners on the Employment of Women and Children in Agriculture*, reprinted by W. Clowes (London: W. Clowes, For Her Majesty's Stationery Office, 1843)
1843 (430) XIII, *Children's Employment Commission: Second Report of the Commissioners (Trades and Manufactures)*
1843 (431) XIV, *Children's Employment Commission: Appendix to the Second Report of the Commissioners (Trades and Manufactures)*

1844 (587) XXVII, *Occupational Abstract*, 1841 Census
1845 (609) XV, *Report of the Commissioner Appointed to Inquire into the Condition of the Framework Knitters*
1852–3 (1691) LXXXVIII, *Census of Great Britain*, 1851: Population Tables
1856 (2134) XXXI, *Census of Ireland*, 1851
1861 (2794) XXI, *The State of Popular Education in England*
1861 (14) L, *A Return of the Weekly Earnings of Agricultural Labourers in the Unions of England and Wales*
1873 (872) LXXI, *Census of England and Wales*, 1871: Population Abstracts

OTHER PRIMARY MATERIAL

Aiken, J., *A Description of the Country from Thirty to Forty Miles round Manchester* (London: John Stockdale, 1795)
Aspinall, A., *The Early English Trade Unions: Documents from the Home Office Papers in the Public Record Office* (London: Batchworth Press, 1949)
Bathgate, Janet, *Aunt Janet's Legacy to Her Nieces: Recollections of Humble Life in Yarrow in the Beginning of the Century* (Selkirk: George Lewis & Son, 1894)
Best, Henry, *Rural Economy in Yorkshire in 1641*, Surtees Society, vol. 33 (Durham: George Andrews, 1857)
Blackstone, William, *Commentaries on the Laws of England* (Oxford: Clarendon Press, 1765)
  Reports of Cases Determined in the Several Courts of Westminster-Hall from 1746 to 1779 (London: His Majesty's Law Printers, 1781)
Board of Agriculture, *General Report on Enclosures* (London: B. McMillan, 1808)
The Book of English Trades and Library of the Useful Arts (London: G. B. Whittaker, 1825)
Campbell, R., *The London Tradesman* (New York: Augustus M. Kelley, [1747] 1969)
Collier, Mary, *"The Woman's Labour"* (London: Roberts, 1739; reprinted by the Augustan Reprint Society, no. 230, 1985)
Collyer, John, *A Practical Treatise on the Law of Partnership* (Boston: Charles C. Little and James Brown, 1848)
Davies, David, *The Case of Labourers in Husbandry Stated and Considered* (London: Robinson, 1795)
Defoe, Daniel, *A Tour through the Whole Island of Great Britain*, abridged and edited by Pat Rogers (Harmondsworth: Penguin, [1724] 1986)
Duck, Stephen, *Poems on Several Occasions* (London, 1936)
Eden, F. M., *State of the Poor*, 2 vols. (London: Davis, 1797)
Ellis, S., *The Women of England and their Social Duties and Domestic Habits*, 2nd edn (London: Fisher, Son, and Co., 1839)
Engels, Frederick, *Condition of the Working Class in England in 1844* (London: George Allen & Unwin, [1845] 1926)
  "Origin of the Family, Private Property and the State," in Karl Marx and Frederick Engels, *Selected Works* (New York: International Publishers, 1986)
Fussel, G. E., ed., *Robert Loder's Farm Accounts, 1610–1620*, Camden Society, Third Series, vol. 53 (London: Royal Historical Society, 1936)

Glover, Stephen, *The Directory of the County of Derby* (Derby: Henry Mozley and Son, 1829)

Hardy, Mary, *Mary Hardy's Diary* (London: Norfolk Record Society, 1968)

Henson, Gravenor, *History of the Framework Knitters* (New York: Augustus Kelley, [1831] 1970)

Hopkinson, James, *Victorian Cabinet Maker: The Memoirs of James Hopkinson, 1819–1894*, ed. Jocelyne Baty Goodman (London: Routledge and Kegan Paul, 1968)

Kelly, E. R., ed., *The Post Office Directory of Warwickshire* (London: Kelly, 1892)

Lewis's Manchester Directory for 1788 (Manchester: Neil Richardson, [1788] 1984)

Marshall, William, *The Rural Economy of Gloucestershire*, 2nd edn (London: G. Nicol, 1796)

Mayhew, Henry, *London Labour and the London Poor*, 4 vols. (London: Griffin, Bohn, and Co., 1861)

Pigot & Co.'s National Commercial Directory (London: J. Pigot, 1835)

Pigot and Dean's Directory for Manchester, Salford, &c. for 1824–5 (Manchester: J. Pigot and W. Dean, 1825)

A Political Enquiry into the Consequences of Enclosing Waste Lands (London: L. Davis, 1785)

Priest, St. John, *General View of the Agriculture of Buckinghamshire* (London: Sherwood, Neely, and Jones, for the Board of Agriculture, 1813)

Pringle, Andrew, *General View of the Agriculture of the County of Westmoreland* (Edinburgh: Chapman and Co., for the Board of Agriculture, 1794)

Sketchley's Sheffield Directory (Bristol: Samuel Sketchley, 1774)

Slater's National Commercial Directory of Ireland (Manchester: Isaac Slater, 1846)

Slater's Royal, National and Commercial Directory and Topography of the Counties of Derbyshire, Herefordshire, Leicestershire, Lincolnshire, Monmouthshire, Northamptonshire, Nottinghamshire, Rutlandshire, Shropshire, Staffordshire, Warwickshire, and Worcestershire (Manchester: Isaac Slater, 1850)

Smith, Adam, *The Wealth of Nations* (New York: Modern Library, [1776] 1965)

Stephens, Henry, *The Book of the Farm*, 2nd edn (Edinburgh and London: William Blackwood and Sons, 1845)

Thompson, William, *Appeal of One Half of the Human Race, Women, against the Pretensions of the Other Half, Men, To Retain them in Political and thence in Civil and Domestic Slavery* (New York: Source Book Press, [1825] 1970)

Thomson, Christopher, *The Autobiography of an Artisan* (London: Chapman, 1847)

A Topographical Survey of the Counties of Stafford, Chester, and Lancaster (Nantwich: E. Snelson, 1787; reprinted by Neil Richardson, Manchester, 1982)

The Universal British Directory of Trade, Commerce and Manufacture (London: Chapman and Withrow, 1791)

Ure, Andrew, *The Cotton Manufacture of Great Britain*, 2 vols. (London: Charles Knight, 1836)

Wollstonecraft, Mary, *A Vindication of the Rights of Woman* (New York: Norton, [1792] 1967)

Young, Arthur, *A Six Weeks' Tour through the Southern Counties of England and Wales* (London: W. Nicoll, 1768)

A Six Months' Tour through the North of England, 3 vols. (Dublin: P. Wilson, 1770)

The Farmer's Tour through the East of England, 4 vols. (London: W. Straham, 1771)

General View of the Agriculture of Oxfordshire (Newton Abbot: David and Charles, [1813] 1969)

SECONDARY SOURCES

Abram, A., "Women Traders in Medieval London," *Economic Journal* 26 (1916), 276–85

Alexander, Sally, *Women's Work in Nineteenth-Century London: A Study of the Years 1820–1850* (London: Journeyman Press, 1983)

  Becoming a Woman and Other Essays in 19th and 20th Century Feminist History (New York: New York University Press, 1995)

Allen, Robert C., *Enclosure and the Yeoman: The Agricultural Development of the South Midlands 1450–1850* (Oxford: Clarendon Press, 1992)

Allen, Robert C. and O Gráda, Cormac, "On the Road Again with Arthur Young: English, Irish and French Agriculture during the Industrial Revolution," *Journal of Economic History* 48 (1988), 93–116

Allen, R. G. D., *Mathematical Analysis for Economists* (New York: St. Martin's Press, [1938] 1964)

Anderson, Michael, "Mis-Specification of Servants' Occupations in the 1851 Census: A Problem Revisited," *Local Population Studies* 60 (1998), 58–64

Atack, Jeremy, Bateman, Fred, and Margo, Robert, "Productivity in Manufacturing and the Length of the Working Day: Evidence from the 1880 Census of Manufactures," *Explorations in Economic History* 40 (2003), 170–94

August, Andrew, "How Separate a Sphere? Poor Women and Paid Work in Late-Victorian London," *Journal of Family History* 19 (1994), 285–309

Bailey, Martha, "More Power to the Pill: The Impact of Contraceptive Freedom on Women's Life Cycle Labor Supply," *Quarterly Journal of Economics* 121 (2006), 289–320

Bardsley, Sandy, "Women's Work Reconsidered: Gender and Wage Differentiation in Late Medieval England," *Past and Present* 165 (1999), 3–29

Becker, Gary, *The Economics of Discrimination* (Chicago: University of Chicago Press, 1957)

Bekaert, Geert, "Caloric Consumption in Industrializing Belgium," *Journal of Economic History* 51 (1991), 633–55

Ben-Amos, Ilana Krausman, "Women Apprentices in the Trades and Crafts of Early Modern Brisol," *Continuity and Change* 6 (1991), 227–52

Benjamin, Dwayne and Brandt, Loren, "Markets, Discrimination, and the Economic Contribution of Women in China: Historical Evidence," *Economic Development and Cultural Change* 44 (1995), 63–104

Berg, Maxine, *The Age of Manufactures, 1700–1820* (Oxford: Oxford University Press, 1986)

  "Women's Work, Mechanisation and the Early Phases of Industrialisation in England," in Patrick Joyce, ed., *The Historical Meanings of Work* (Cambridge: Cambridge University Press, 1987)

"What Difference Did Women's Work Make to the Industrial Revolution?" *History Workshop Journal* 35 (1993), 22–44

Bergmann, Barbara, "The Effect on White Incomes of Discrimination on Employment," *Journal of Political Economy* 79 (1971), 294–313

"Occupational Segregation, Wages and Profits when Employers Discriminate by Race or Sex," *Eastern Economic Journal* 1 (1974), 103–10

Blau, Francine and Kahn, Lawrence, "Gender Differences in Pay," *Journal of Economic Perspectives* 14 (2000), 75–99

Booker, John, "A History of the Ancient Chapel of Denton," *Remains Historical and Literary connected with the Palatine Counties of Lancaster and Chester*, The Chetham Society, vol. 37 (1861)

Borjas, George, "The Substitutability of Black, Hispanic, and White Labor," *Economic Inquiry* 21 (1983), 93–106

Borjas, George and Bronars, Stephen, "Consumer Discrimination and Self-Employment," *Journal of Political Economy* 97 (1989), 581–605

Boserup, Ester, *Women's Role in Economic Development* (New York: St. Martin's Press, 1970)

Boyd, Percival, *Roll of the Drapers' Company of London: Collected from the Company Records and Other Sources* (Croydon: J. A. Gordon, 1934)

Boyer, George, *An Economic History of the English Poor Law, 1750–1850* (Cambridge: Cambridge University Press, 1990)

Boyer, George and Hatton, Timothy, "Did Joseph Arch Raise Agricultural Wages? Rural Trade Unions and the Labour Market in Late Nineteenth-Century England," *Economic History Review* 47 (1994), 310–34

Bradley, L. Barbara and Black, Anne, "Women Compositors and the Factory Acts," *Economic Journal* 9 (1899), 261–6

Brenner, Johanna and Ramas, Maria, "Rethinking Women's Oppression," *New Left Review* 144 (1984), 33–71

Broad, John, "Regional Perspectives and Variations in English Dairying, 1650–1850," in R. Hoyle, ed., *People, Landscape and Alternative Agriculture* (Exeter: British Agricultural History Society, 2004)

Brooke, Christopher, *A History of the University of Cambridge*, vol. IV (Cambridge: Cambridge University Press, 1993)

Brooks, George and Fahey, Thomas, *Exercise Physiology* (New York: John Wiley, 1984)

Browne, Kingsley, *Divided Labours: An Evolutionary View of Women at Work* (New Haven: Yale University Press, 1999)

Brunt, Liam, "Rehabilitating Arthur Young," *Economic History Review* 56 (2003), 265–99

Burchardt, Jeremy, *The Allotment Movement in England, 1793–1873* (Woodbridge: Boydell and Brewer, 2002)

Burke, Gill, "The Decline of the Independent Bâl Maiden: The Impact of Change in the Cornish Mining Industry," in Angela John, ed., *Unequal Opportunities* (Oxford: Basil Blackwell, 1986)

Burnette, Joyce, "'Laborers at the Oakes': Changes in the Demand for Female Day-Laborers at a Farm near Sheffield during the Agricultural Revolution," *Journal of Economic History* 59 (1999), 41–67

"The wages and employment of female day-labourers in English agriculture, 1740–1850," *Economic History Review* 57 (2004), 664–90

"How Skilled Were English Agricultural Labourers in the Early Nineteenth Century?" *Economic History Review* 59 (2006), 688–716

"Married with Children: The Family Status of Female Day-Labourers at Two South-Western Farms," *Agricultural History Review* 55 (2007), 75–94

Burnley, James, *The History of Wool and Woolcombing* (London: Sampson Low, Marston, Searle and Rivington, 1889)

Bythell, Duncan, *The Handloom Weavers* (Cambridge: Cambridge University Press, 1969).

The Sweated Trades (New York: St. Martin's Press, 1978)

"Women in the Work Force," in Patrick O'Brien and Roland Quinault, eds., *The Industrial Revolution in British Society* (Cambridge: Cambridge University Press, 1993)

Campbell, Alan, "The Scots Colliers' Strikes of 1824–1826," in John Rule, ed., *British Trade Unionism, 1750–1850: The Formative Years* (New York: Longman, 1988)

Campbell, Carl and Kamlani, Kunal, "The Reasons for Wage Rigidity: Evidence from a Survey of Firms," *Quarterly Journal of Economics* 112 (1997), 759–89

Card, David and Krueger, Alan, *Myth and Measurement: The New Economics of the Minimum Wage* (Princeton: Princeton University Press, 1995)

Chartres, John, "English Landed Society and the Servants Tax of 1777," in Negley Harte and Roland Quinault, eds., *Land and Society in Britain, 1700–1914* (Manchester: Manchester University Press, 1996)

Christian, E. B. V., *A Short History of Solicitors* (London: Reeves and Turner, 1896)

Clark, Alice, *Working Life of Women in the Seventeenth Century* (London: Routledge, 1919)

Clark, Gregory, "Agriculture and the Industrial Revolution, 1700–1850," in Joel Mokyr, ed., *The British Industrial Revolution: An Economic Perspective* (Boulder: Westview Press, 1993)

Cockburn, Cynthia, *Brothers: Male Dominance and Technological Change*, 2nd edn (London: Pluto Press, 1991)

Cohen, Jacob, *Statistical Power Analysis for the Behavioral Sciences*, 2nd edn (Hillsdale, NJ: Lawrence Erlbaum Associates, 1988)

Cole, G. D. H., *Attempts at General Union: A Study in British Trade Union History, 1818–1834* (London: Macmillan, 1953)

Collier, Frances, *The Family Economy of the Working Classes in the Cotton Industry* (Manchester: Manchester University Press, 1964)

Collins, E. J. T., "Harvest Technology and Labour Supply in Britain, 1790–1870," *Economic History Review* 22 (1969), 453–73

Combs, Mary Beth, "'A Measure of Legal Independence': The 1870 Married Women's Property Act and the Portfolio Allocations of British Wives," *Journal of Economic History* 65 (2005), 1028–57

Cooper, John, Adrian, Marlene, and Glassow, Ruth, *Kinesiology* (St. Louis: C. V. Mosby, 1982)

Cowan, Ruth Schwartz, *More Work for Mother: The Ironies of Household Technology from the Open Hearth to the Microwave* (New York: Basic Books, 1983)

Cox, Donald and Nye, John Vincent, "Male–Female Wage Discrimination in Nineteenth-Century France," *Journal of Economic History* 49 (1989), 903–20

Craig, Lee A. and Field-Hendrey, Elizabeth, "Industrialization and the Earnings Gap: Regional and Sectoral Tests of the Goldin-Sokoloff Hypothesis," *Explorations in Economic History* 30 (1993), 60–80

Crouzet, François, ed., *Capital Formation in the Industrial Revolution* (London: Methuen, 1972)

The First Industrialists (Cambridge: Cambridge University Press, 1985)

Cunningham, Hugh, "The Employment and Unemployment of Children in England," *Past and Present* 126 (1990), 115–50

David, Paul, *Technical Choice, Innovation and Economic Growth* (Cambridge: Cambridge University Press, 1975)

Davidoff, Leonore, "The Role of Gender in the 'First Industrial Nation': Agriculture in England 1780–1850," in Rosemary Crompton and Michael Mann, eds.,*Gender and Stratification* (Cambridge: Polity Press, 1986)

Davidoff, Leonore and Hall, Catherine, *Family Fortunes: Men and Women of the English Middle Class, 1780–1850* (Chicago: University of Chicago Press, 1987)

" 'The Hidden Investment': Women and the Enterprise," in P. Sharpe, ed., *Women's Work: The English Experience, 1650–1914* (London: Arnold, 1998)

D'Cruze, Shani, "'To Acquaint the Ladies': Women Traders in Colchester c. 1750 – c. 1800," *The Local Historian* 17 (1986), 158–61

DeVries, Jan, "Between Purchasing Power and the World of Goods: Understanding the Household Economy in Early Modern Europe," in Pamela Sharpe, ed., *Women's Work: The English Experience, 1650–1914* (London: Arnold, 1998)

Digby, Anne, *Making a Medical Living: Doctors and Patients in the English Market for Medicine, 1720–1911* (Cambridge: Cambridge University Press, 1994)

Dobson, C. R., *Masters and Journeymen: A Prehistory of Industrial Relations* (London: Croom Helm, 1980)

Donnison, Jean, *Midwives and Medical Men* (London: Historical Publications, 1988)

Doraszelski, Ulrich, "Measuring Returns to Scale in Nineteenth-Century French Industry," *Explorations in Economic History* 41 (2004), 256–81

Drake, Barbara, *Women in Trade Unions* (London: Virago Press, [1920] 1984)

Duncan, O. D. and Duncan, B., "A Methodological Analysis of Segregation Indexes," *American Sociological Review* 20 (1955), 210–17

Dunlop, O. Jocelyn, "Some Aspects of Early English Apprenticeship," *Transactions of the Royal Historical Society*, 3rd series, 5 (1911), 193–208

English Apprenticeship and Child Labor (New York: Macmillan, 1912)

Dunlop, O. Jocelyn and Denman, Richard, *English Apprenticeship and Child Labour: A History* (London: Unwin, 1912)

Earle, Peter, "The Female Labour Market in London in the Late Seventeenth and Early Nineteenth Centuries," *Economic History Review* 42 (1980), 328–53

Edgeworth, F. Y., "Equal Pay to Men and Women for Equal Work," *Economic Journal* 32 (1922), 431–57

Feinstein, Charles, "New Estimates of Average Earnings in the United Kingdom, 1880–1913," *Economic History Review* 43 (1990), 595–632
  "Pessimism Perpetuated: Real Wages and the Standard of Living in Britain during and after the Industrial Revolution," *Journal of Economic History* 58 (1998), 625–58
Felkin, William, *A History of the Machine-Wrought Hosiery and Lace Manufactures* (London: Longmans, Green, and Co., 1867)
Fogel, Robert W., "Nutrition and the Decline in Mortality since 1700: Some Preliminary Findings," in S. Engerman and R. Gallman, eds., *Long-Term Factors in American Economic Growth* (Chicago: University of Chicago Press, 1986)
Freeman, Richard, "The Effect of Demographic Factors on the Age–Earnings Profiles," *Journal of Human Resources* 14 (1979), 289–318
Freeman, Richard and Medoff, James, *What Do Unions Do?* (New York: Basic Books, 1984)
Freifeld, Mary, "Technological Change and the 'Self-Acting' Mule: A Study of Skill and the Sexual Division of Labour," *Social History* 2 (1986), 319–43
Frohse, Franz, Brodel, Max, and Schlossberg, Leon, *Atlas of Anatomy* (New York: Barnes and Noble, 1961)
Gardner, Phil, *The Lost Elementary Schools of Victorian England* (London: Croom Helm, 1984)
Garner, S. Paul, *Evolution of Cost Accounting* (University of Alabama Press, 1954)
George, Dorothy, *London Life in the Eighteenth Century* (London: Kegan Paul, Trench, Trubner & Co., 1925)
  "The Combination Laws," *Economic History Review* 6 (1936), 172–8
Gielgud, Judy, "Nineteenth Century Farm Women in Northumberland and Cumbria: The Neglected Workforce," unpublished PhD thesis, University of Sussex, 1992
Gilboy, Elizabeth Waterman, "Labour at Thornborough: An Eighteenth Century Estate," *Economic History Review* 3 (1932), 388–98
Goldin, Claudia, *Understanding the Gender Gap: An Economic History of American Women* (Oxford: Oxford University Press, 1990)
  "The Changing Economic Role of Women: A Quantitative Approach," in Robert Whalpes and Dianne Betts, eds., *Historical Perspectives on the American Economy* (Cambridge: Cambridge University Press, 1995)
Goldin, Claudia, Katz, Lawrence, and Kuziemko, Ilyana, "The Homecoming of American College Women: The Reversal of the College Gender Gap," *Journal of Economic Perspectives* 20 (2006), 133–56
Goldin, Claudia and Sokoloff, Kenneth, "The Relative Productivity Hypothesis of Industrialization: The American Case, 1820 to 1850," *Quarterly Journal of Economics* 99 (1984), 461–87
Grant, James and Hamermesh, Daniel, "Labour Market Competition among Youths, White Women and Others," *Review of Economics and Statistics* 63 (1981), 354–60
Grier, L., "Women's Education at Oxford," *Handbook of the University of Oxford* (Oxford: Oxford University Press, 1969)

Gross, Edward, "Plus Ça Change ... ? The Sexual Structure of Occupations over Time," *Social Problems* 16 (1968), 198–208

Gullickson, Gay, *Spinners and Weavers of Auffay: Rural Industry and the Sexual Division of Labor in a French Village, 1750–1850* (Cambridge: Cambridge University Press, 1986)

"Love and Power in the Proto-Industrial Family," in Maxine Berg., ed., *Markets and Manufacture in Early Industrial Europe* (London: Routledge, 1991)

Haegeland, Torbjorn and Klette, Tor Jakob, "Do Higher Wages Reflect Higher Productivity? Education, Gender and Experience Premiums in a Matched Plant-Worker Data Set," in J. Haltwanger, J. Lane, J. R. Spletzer, J. Theeuwes, and K. Troske, eds., *The Creation and Analysis of Employer–Employee Matched Data* (Amsterdam: Elsevier, 1999)

Hall, Catherine, *White, Male and Middle-Class: Explorations in Feminism and History* (New York: Routledge, 1992)

Hall, Kermit, ed., *The Oxford Companion to American Law* (Oxford: Oxford University Press, 2002)

Hamermesh, Daniel, *Labor Demand* (Princeton: Princeton University Press, 1993)

Hamermesh, Daniel, Frazis, Harley, and Stewart, Jay, "Data Watch: The American Time Use Survey," *Journal of Economic Perspectives* 19 (2005), 221–32

Hammond, J. L. and Hammond, B., *The Skilled Labourer, 1760–1832* (London: Longmans, Green, & Co., 1920)

Hanks, Patrick and Hodges, Flavia, *A Dictionary of First Names* (Oxford: Oxford University Press, 1990)

Harrison, Brian, "Class and Gender in Modern British Labour History," *Past and Present* 124 (1989), 121–58

Hartmann, Heidi, "Capitalism, Patriarchy, and Job Segregation by Sex," *Signs: Journal of Women in Culture and Society* 1 (1976), 137–69

"The Family as the Locus of Gender, Class, and Political Struggle: The Example of Housework," *Signs: Journal of Women in Culture and Society* 6 (1981), 336–94

Hatton, Timothy and Bailey, Roy, "Women's Work in Census and Survey, 1911–1931," *Economic History Review* 54 (2001), 87–107

Hatton, T. J., Boyer, G. R., and Bailey, R. E., "The Union Wage Effect in Late Nineteenth-Century Britain," *Economica* 61 (1994), 435–56

Hatton, Timothy and Williamson, Jeffrey, "Integrated and Segmented Labor Markets: Thinking in Two Sectors," *Journal of Economic History* 51 (1991), 413–25

Hausman, J. A., "Specification Test in Econometrics," *Econometrica* 46 (1978), 1251–71

Heaton, H., "Benjamin Gott and the Industrial Revolution in Yorkshire," *Economic History Review* 3 (1931), 45–66

Hellerstein, Judith, Neumark, David, and Troske, Kenneth, "Wages, Productivity, and Worker Characteristics: Evidence from Plant-Level Production Functions and Wage Equations," *Journal of Labor Economics* 17 (1999), 409–46

Hicks, J. R., *The Theory of Wages* (New York: Peter Smith, [1932] 1948)

Higgs, Edward, "Domestic Service and Household Production," in Angela John, ed., *Unequal Opportunities* (Oxford: Basil Blackwell, 1986)

"Women, Occupations and Work in the Nineteenth Century Censuses," *History Workshop Journal* 23 (1987), 59–80

Making Sense of the Census: The Manuscript Returns for England and Wales, 1801–1901 (London: HMSO, 1989)

Hill, Bridget, *Women, Work and Sexual Politics in Eighteenth-Century England* (Oxford: Basil Blackwell, 1989)

"Women, Work and the Census: A Problem for Historians of Women," *History Workshop Journal* 35 (1993), 78–94

Hill, Bridget and Hill, Christopher, "Catherine Macaulay and the Seventeenth Century," *Welsh History Review* 3 (1967), 381–402

Hindle, Steve, "'Waste' Children? Pauper Apprenticeship under the Elizabethan Poor Laws, c. 1598–1697," in P. Lane, N. Raven, and K. D. M. Snell, eds., *Women, Work and Wages in England, 1600–1850* (Woodbridge: Boydell Press, 2004)

Hobsbawm, E. J. and Rudé, George, *Captain Swing* (London: Lawrence and Wishart, 1969)

Honeyman, Katrina, *Women, Gender and Industrialisation in England, 1700–1870* (New York: St. Martin's Press, 2000)

Honeyman, Katrina and Goodman, Jordan, "Women's Work, Gender Conflict, and Labour Markets in Europe, 1500–1900," *Economic History Review* 44 (1991), 608–28

Horn, Pamela, "The Dorset Dairy System," *Agricultural History Review* 26 (1978), 100–7

Horrell, Sara and Humphries, Jane, "Women's Labour Force Participation and the Transition to the Male-Breadwinner Family, 1790–1865," *Economic History Review* 48 (1995), 89–117

Howe, Ellic, *A List of London Bookbinders* (London: The Bibliographical Society, 1950)

Huberman, Michael, *Escape from the Market: Negotiating Work in Lancashire* (Cambridge: Cambridge University Press, 1996)

Hudson, Pat and Lee, W. R., "Women's Work and the Family Economy in Historical Perspective," in P. Hudson and W. R. Lee, eds., *Women's Work and the Family Economy in Historical Perspective* (Manchester: Manchester University Press, 1990)

Humphries, Jane, "Class Struggle and the Persistence of the Working-Class Family," *Cambridge Journal of Economics* 1 (1977), 241–58

"Protective Legislation, the Capitalist State, and Working Class Men: The Case of the 1842 Mines Regulation Act," *Feminist Review* 7 (1981), 1–33

"'... The Most Free from Objection ...' The Sexual Division of Labor and Women's Work in Nineteenth-Century England," *Journal of Economic History* 47 (1987), 929–50

"Enclosures, Common Rights, and Women: The Proletarianization of Families in the Late Eighteenth and Early Nineteenth Centuries," *Journal of Economic History* 50 (1990), 17–42

Hunt, E. H., *Regional Wage Variations in Britain, 1850–1914* (Oxford: Clarendon Press, 1973)

Hunt, Felicity, "Opportunities Lost and Gained: Mechanization and Women's Work in the London Bookbinding and Printing Trades," in Angela John, ed., *Unequal Opportunities* (Oxford: Basil Blackwell, 1986)

Hutchins, B. L. and Harrison, A., *A History of Factory Legislation* (Westminster: P. S. King & Son, Orchard House, 1903)

Hutton, Diane, "Women in Fourteenth Century Shrewsbury," in Lindsey Charles and Lorna Duffin, eds., *Women and Work in Pre-Industrial England* (London: Croom Helm, 1985)

Jacoby, Hanan, "Productivity of Men and Women and the Sexual Division of Labor in Peasant Agriculture of the Peruvian Sierra," *Journal of Development Economics* 37 (1992), 265–87

John, Angela V., "Colliery Legislation and Its Consequences: 1842 and the Women Miners of Lancashire," *Bulletin of the John Rylands Library* 61 (1978), 78–114

  By the Sweat of their Brow: Women Workers at Victorian Coal Mines (London: Croom Helm, 1980)

Johnson, Paul, "Age, Gender and the Wage in Britain, 1830–1930," in Peter Scholliers and Leonard Schwarz, eds., *Experiencing Wages: Social and Cultural Aspects of Wage Forms in Europe since 1500* (New York: Berghahn Books, 2003)

Johnstone, Frederick, *Class, Race and Gold: A Study of Class Relations and Racial Discrimination in South Africa* (London: Routledge and Kegan Paul, 1976)

Jones, Bruce, Bovee, Matthew, and Knapik, Joseph "Associations among Body Composition, Physical Fitness, and Injury in Men and Women Army Trainees," in B. Marriott and J. Gumstrup-Scott, eds., *Body Composition and Physical Performance* (Washington, DC: National Academy Press, 1992)

Jones, Philip E., *The Butchers of London* (London: Secker and Warburg, 1976)

Jordan, Ellen, "The Exclusion of Women from Industry in Nineteenth-Century Britain," *Comparative Studies in Society and History* 31 (1989), 273–96

Joshi, Heather and Paci, Pierella, *Unequal Pay for Women and Men: Evidence from the British Birth Cohort Studies* (Cambridge, Mass.: MIT Press, 1998)

Jupp, Edward Basil and Pocock, William Willmer, *An Historical Account of the Worshipful Company of Carpenters of the City of London* (London: Pickering and Chatto, 1887)

Juster, F. Thomas and Stafford, Frank P., "The Allocation of Time: Empirical Findings, Behavioral Models, and Problems of Measurement," *Journal of Economic Literature* 29 (1991), 471–522

Kahn, Lawrence, "Customer Discrimination and Affirmative Action," *Economic Inquiry* 29 (1991), 555–71

Kay, Alison, "Retailing, Respectability and the Independent Woman in Nineteenth-Century London," in Robert Beachy, Beatrice Craig, and Alastair Owens, eds., *Women, Business and Finance in Nineteenth-Century Europe: Rethinking Separate Spheres* (Oxford: Berg, 2006)

Kelsall, Keith, "Wage Regulations under the Statute of Artificers," reprinted in W. E. Minchinton, ed., *Wage Regulation in Pre-Industrial England* (Newton Abbot: David and Charles, [1938] 1972)

Kendrick, W., "Cast Iron Hollow-ware, Tinned and Enamelled, and Cast Ironmongery," in Samuel Timmins, ed., *The Resources, Products, and Industrial History of Birmingham and the Midland Hardware District* (London: Robert Hardwicke, 1866)

Khan, B. Zorina, "Married Women's Property Laws and Female Commercial Activity: Evidence from United States Patent Records, 1790–1895," *Journal of Economic History* 56 (1996), 356–88

King, Peter, "Customary Rights and Women's Earnings: The Importance of Gleaning to the Rural Labouring Poor, 1750–1850," *Economic History Review* 44 (1991), 461–76

King, Steven, "'Meer pennies for my baskitt will be enough': Women, Work and Welfare, 1700–1830," in P. Lane, N. Raven, and K. D. M. Snell, eds., *Women, Work and Wages in England, 1600–1850* (Woodbridge: Boydell, 2004)

Kirby, Peter, *Child Labour in Britain, 1750–1870* (Basingstoke: Palgrave, 2003)

Kirby, R. G. and Musson, A. E., *The Voice of the People: John Doherty, 1798–1854, Trade Unionist, Radical and Factory Reformer* (Manchester: Manchester University Press, 1975)

Kotlikoff, Laurence, "Quantitative Description of the New Orleans Slave Market, 1804 to 1862," in R. W. Fogel and S. L. Engerman, eds., *Without Consent or Contract: The Rise and Fall of American Slavery, Markets and Production: Technical Papers*, vol. I (New York: Norton, 1989)

Kussmaul, Ann, *Servants in Husbandry in Early Modern England* (Cambridge: Cambridge University Press, 1981)

Lacey, Kay E., "Women and Work in the Fourteenth and Fifteenth Century in London," in Lindsay Charles and Lorna Duffin, eds., *Women and Work in Pre-Industrial England* (London: Croom Helm, 1985)

Land, Hilary, "The Family Wage," *Feminist Review* 6 (1980), 55–77

Lane, Joan, *Apprenticeship in England, 1600–1914* (Boulder: Westview Press, 1996)

Lane, Penelope, "A Customary or Market Wage? Women and Work in the East Midlands, c. 1700–1840," in P. Lane, N. Raven, and K. D. M. Snell, eds., *Women, Work and Wages in England, 1600–1850* (Woodbridge: Boydell Press, 2004)

Larson, Magali Sarfatti, *The Rise of Professionalism* (Berkeley: University of California Press, 1977)

Lazonick, William, "Industrial Relations and Technical Change: The Case of the Self-Acting Mule," *Cambridge Journal of Economics* 3 (1979), 231–62

Levitt, Ian and Smout, Christopher, "Farm Workers' Incomes in 1843," in T. M. Devine, ed., *Farm Servants and Labour in Lowland Scotland, 1770–1914* (Edinburgh: John Donald, 1984)

Lewenhak, Sheila, *Women and Trade Unions* (New York: St. Martin's Press, 1977)

Lindert, Peter and Williamson, Jeffrey, "English Workers' Living Standards during the Industrial Revolution: A New Look," *Economic History Review* 36 (1983), 1–25

Lindle, R. S., et al., "Age and Gender Comparisons of Muscle Strength in 654 Women and Men aged 20–93," *Journal of Applied Physiology* 83 (1997), 1581–7

Lynch, N. A., et al., "Muscle Quality. I. Age-associated Differences between Arm and Leg Muscle Groups," *Journal of Applied Physiology* 86 (1999), 188–94

Lyon, John, "Family Response to Economic Decline: Handloom Weavers in Early Ninteenth-Century Lancashire," in R. Ransom, ed., *Research in Economic History*, vol. XII (London: JAI Press, 1989)

Madoc-Jones, Beryl, "Patterns of Attendance and Their Social Significance: Mitcham National School, 1830–39," in Phillip McCann, ed., *Popular Education and Socialization in the Nineteenth Century* (London: Methuen, 1977)

Malcolmson, Patricia, *English Laundresses: A Social History, 1850–1930* (Urbana: University of Illinois Press, 1986)

Mann, Julia de Lacy, *The Cloth Industry in the West of England from 1640 to 1880* (Oxford: Clarendon Press, 1971)

Marriott, Bernadette and Grumstrop-Scott, Judith, "Introduction and Background," in Bernadette Marriott and Judith Grumstrup-Scott, eds., *Body Composition and Physical Performance* (Washington, DC: National Academy Press, 1992)

Marvel, Howard P., "Factory Regulation: A Reinterpretation of Early English Experience," *Journal of Law and Economics* 20 (1977), 379–403

McCann, Phillip, "Popular Education, Socialization, and Social Control: Spitalfields 1812–1824," in Phillip McCann, ed., *Popular Education and Socialization in the Nineteenth Century* (London: Methuen, 1977)

McCulloch, Frank and Bornstein, Tim, *The National Labor Relations Board* (New York: Praeger Publishers, 1974)

McKay, John, "Married Women and Work in Nineteenth-Century Lancashire: The Evidence of the 1851 and 1861 Census Reports," *Local Population Studies* 61 (1998), 25–37

McKendrick, Neil, "Home Demand and Economic Growth: A New View of the Role of Women and Children in the Industrial Revolution," in Neil McKendrick, ed., *Historical Perspectives: Studies in English Thought and Society* (London: Europa, 1974)

McMurry, Sally, "Women's Work in Agriculture: Divergent Trends in England and America, 1800 to 1930," *Comparative Studies in Society and History* 34 (1992), 248–70

Merrilees, William, "Labor Market Segmentation in Canada: An Econometric Approach," *Canadian Journal of Economics* 15 (1982), 458–73

Middleton, Christopher, "The Familiar Fate of the Famulae: Gender Divisions in the History of Wage Labour," in R. E. Pahl, ed., *On Work* (Oxford: Basil Blackwell, 1988)

Miller, C., "The Hidden Workforce: Female Fieldworkers in Gloucestershire, 1870–1901," *Southern History* 6 (1984), 139–61

Minchinton, W. E., ed., *Wage Regulation in Pre-Industrial England* (Newton Abbot: David and Charles, 1972)

Mitch, David, *The Rise of Popular Literacy in Victorian England: The Influence of Private Choice and Public Policy* (Philadelphia: University of Philadelphia Press, 1992)

Mitchell, B. R., *Abstract of British Historical Statistics* (Cambridge: Cambridge University Press, 1962)

Mokyr, Joel, *The Lever of Riches: Technological Creativity and Economic Progress* (Oxford: Oxford University Press, 1990)

"Editor's Introduction: The New Economic History and the Industrial Revolution," in J. Mokyr, ed., *The British Industrial Revolution: An Economic Perspective* (Boulder: Westview Press, 1993)

The Gifts of Athena: Historical Origins of the Knowledge Economy (Princeton: Princeton University Press, 2002)

Montoye, Henry and Lamphiear, Donald, "Grip and Arm Strength in Males and Females, Age 10 to 69," *Research Quarterly* 48 (1977), 109–20

Mora-Sitja, Natalia, "Labour Supply and Wage Differentials in an Industrialising Economy: Catalonia in the Long Nineteenth Century," unpublished PhD thesis, Nuffield College, University of Oxford, 2006

Morgan, Carol, "Work for Girls? The Small Metal Industries in England, 1840–1915," in Mary Jo Maynes, Birgitte Soland, and Christina Benninghaus, eds., *Secret Gardens, Satanic Mills: Placing Girls in European History, 1750–1960* (Bloomington: Indiana University Press, 2005)

Morris, Jenny, "The Characteristics of Sweating: The Late-Nineteenth-Century London and Leeds Tailoring Trade," in Angela John, ed., *Unequal Opportunities* (Oxford: Basil Blackwell, 1986)

Morris, R. J., *Men, Women, and Property in England, 1780–1870* (Cambridge: Cambridge University Press, 2005)

Neff, Wanda Fraiken, *Victorian Working Women: An Historical and Literary Study of Women in British Industries and Professions, 1832–1850* (London: George Allen and Unwin, 1929)

Nicholson, John, *Men and Women: How Different Are They?* (Oxford: Oxford University Press, 1984)

O'Day, Rosemary, *Education and Society, 1500–1800* (New York: Longman, 1982)

Ogilvie, Sheilagh, *A Bitter Living: Women, Markets, and Social Capital in Early Modern Germany* (Oxford: Oxford University Press, 2003)

"Guilds, Efficiency, and Social Capital: Evidence from German Proto-Industry," *Economic History Review* 57 (2004), 286–333

Olmstead, Alan and Rhode, Paul, "'Wait a Cotton Pickin' Minute!' A New View of Slave Productivity," presented at the Economic History Association Annual Meeting in Pittsburgh, September 17, 2006

Olson, Mancur, *The Logic of Collective Action: Public Goods and the Theory of Groups* (Cambridge, Mass.: Harvard University Press, 1965)

The Rise and Decline of Nations: Economic Growth, Stagflation, and Social Rigidities (New Haven: Yale University Press, 1982)

Osterud, Nancy Grey, "Gender Divisions and the Organization of Work in the Leicester Hosiery Industry," in Angela John, ed., *Unequal Opportunities* (Oxford: Basil Blackwell, 1986)

Overton, Mark, *Agricultural Revolution in England: The Transformation of the Agrarian Economy 1500–1850* (Cambridge: Cambridge University Press, 1996)

Pelling, Margaret and Webster, Charles, "Medical Practitioners," in C. Webster, ed., *Health, Medicine, and Mortality in the Sixteenth Century* (Cambridge: Cambridge University Press, 1979)

Perkin, Harold, *The Origins of Modern English Society, 1780–1880* (London: Routledge and Kegan Paul, 1969)
   The Rise of Professional Society (London: Routledge, 1989)
Perkin, Joan, *Women and Marriage in Nineteenth-Century England* (London: Routledge, 1989)
Phillips, Nicola, *Women in Business, 1700–1850* (Woodbridge: Boydell Press, 2006)
Pinchbeck, Ivy, *Women Workers and the Industrial Revolution 1750–1850* (London: Routledge, 1930)
Pinker, Steven, *The Blank Slate: The Modern Denial of Human Nature* (New York: Penguin Books, 2003)
Plummer, Alfred, *The Witney Blanket Industry: The Records of the Witney Blanket Weavers* (London: Routledge, 1934)
Postan, M. M., "Recent Trends in the Accumulation of Capital," in François Crouzet, ed., *Capital Formation in the Industrial Revolution* (London: Methuen, 1972)
Power, Eileen, *Medieval Women*, ed. M. M. Postan (Cambridge: Cambridge University Press, 1975)
Pressnell, L. S., *Country Banking in the Industrial Revolution* (Oxford: Clarendon Press, 1956)
Prior, Mary, *Women in English Society, 1500–1800* (London: Methuen, 1985)
Randall, Adrian, *Before the Luddites* (Cambridge: Cambridge University Press, 1991)
Reader, W. J., *Professional Men: The Rise of the Professional Classes in Nineteenth-Century England* (London: Weidenfeld and Nicolson, 1966)
Rendall, Jane, *Women in an Industrializing Society: England 1750–1880* (Oxford: Basil Blackwell, 1990)
Richards, Eric, "Women and the British Economy since about 1700: An Interpretation," *History* 59 (1974), 337–57
Roach, John, *A History of Secondary Education in England, 1800–1870* (London: Longman, 1986)
Roberts, Elizabeth, *Women's Work, 1840–1940* (Cambridge: Cambridge University Press, [1988] 1995)
Roberts, Michael, "Sickles and Scythes: Women's Work and Men's Work at Harvest Time," *History Workshop* 7 (1979), 3–28
   "'Words They Are Women, and Deeds They Are Men': Images of Work and Gender in Early Modern England', in Lindsay Charles and Lorna Duffin, eds., *Women and Work in Pre-Industrial England* (London: Croom Helm, 1985)
   "Sickles and Scythes Revisited: Harvest Work, Wages and Symbolic Meanings," in P. Lane, N. Raven, and K. D. M. Snell, eds., *Women, Work and Wages in England, 1600–1850* (Woodbridge: Boydell Press, 2004)
Robson, Robert, *The Attorney in Eighteenth-Century England* (Cambridge: Cambridge University Press, 1959)
Rose, Sonya, "'Gender at Work': Sex, Class and Industrial Capitalism," *History Workshop Journal* 21 (1986), 113–31
   "Gender Segregation in the Transition to the Factory: The English Hosiery Industry, 1850–1910," *Feminist Studies* 13 (1987), 163–84

"Gender Antagonism and Class Conflict: Exclusionary Strategies of Male Trade Unionists in Nineteenth-Century Britain," *Social History* 13 (1988), 191–208

Limited Livelihoods: Gender and Class in Nineteenth-Century England (Berkeley: University of California Press, 1992)

Roy, A. D., "Some Thoughts on the Distribution of Earnings," *Oxford Economic Papers* 3 (1951), 135–46

Rule, John, *The Experience of Labour in Eighteenth-Century English Industry* (New York: St. Martin's Press, 1981)

The Labouring Classes in Early Industrial England (London: Longman, 1986)

"The Formative Years of British Trade Unionism: An Overview," in John Rule, ed., *British Trade Unionism, 1750–1850: The Formative Years* (New York: Longman, 1988)

Samuel, Raphael, "Workshop of the World: Steam Power and Hand Technology in Mid-Victorian Britain," *History Workshop* 3 (1977), 6–72

"Mechanization and Hand Labour in Industrializing Britain," in Lenard R. Berlanstein, ed., *The Industrial Revolution and Work in Nineteenth-Century Europe* (London: Routledge, 1992)

Sanderson, Elizabeth, *Women and Work in Eighteenth-Century Edinburgh* (New York: St. Martin's Press, 1996)

Sattinger, Michael, "Comparative Advantage and the Distributions of Earnings and Abilities," *Econometrica* 43 (1975), 455–68

"Assignment Models of the Distribution of Earnings," *Journal of Economic Literature* 31 (1993), 831–80

Sax, Leonard, *Why Gender Matters: What Parents and Teachers Need To Know about the Emerging Science of Sex Differences* (New York: Broadway Books, 2005)

Schofield, R. S., "Dimensions of Illiteracy, 1750–1850," *Explorations in Economic History* 10 (1973), 437–54

Scholliers, Peter and Schwarz, Leonard, "The Wage in Europe since the Sixteenth Century," in P. Scholliers and L. Schwarz, eds., *Experiencing Wages: Social and Cultural Aspects of Wage Forms in Europe since 1500* (New York: Berghahn, 2003)

Schwartz, Eleanor Brantley, "Entrepreneurship: A New Female Frontier," *Journal of Contemporary Business* 5 (1976), 47–76

Schwarz, L. D., *London in the Age of Industrialisation: Entrepreneurs, Labour Force and Living Conditions, 1700–1850* (Cambridge: Cambridge University Press, 1992)

Scott, Joan and Tilly, Louise, "Women's Work and the Family in Nineteenth-Century Europe," *Comparative Studies in Society and History* 17 (1975), 36–64

Seccombe, Wally, "Patriarchy Stabilized: The Construction of the Male Breadwinner Wage Norm in Nineteenth-Century Britain," *Social History* 11 (1986), 53–76

Sharpe, Pamela, "Literally Spinsters: A New Interpretation of Local Economy and Demography in Colyton in the Seventeenth and Eighteenth Centuries," *Economic History Review* 44 (1991), 46–65

"Time and Wages of West Country Workfolks in the Seventeenth and Eighteenth Centuries," *Local Population Studies* 55 (1995), 66–8

Adapting to Capitalism: Working Women in the English Economy, 1700–1850 (London: Macmillan, 1996)

"'The bowels of compation': A Labouring Family and the Law, c. 1790–1834," in Tim Hitchcock and Peter King, eds., *Chronicling Poverty: The Voices and Strategies of the English Poor, 1640–1840* (New York: St. Martin's Press, 1997)

"Commentary," in P. Sharpe, ed., *Women's Work: The English Experience 1650–1914* (London: Arnold, 1998)

"The Female Labour Market in English Agriculture during the Industrial Revolution: Expansion or Contraction?" *Agricultural History Review* 47 (1999), 161–81

"Gender at Sea: Women and the East India Company in Seventeeth-Century London," in P. Lane, N. Raven, and K. D. M. Snell, eds., *Women, Work and Wages in England, 1600–1850* (Woodbridge: Boydell Press, 2004)

Shaw-Taylor, Leigh, "Diverse Experience: The Geography of Adult Female Employment in England and the 1851 Census," in Nigel Goose, ed., *Women's Work in Industrial England: Regional and Local Perspectives* (Hatfield: Local Population Studies, 2007)

Shephard, Roy, *Physical Activity and Growth* (Chicago: Year Book Medical Publishers, 1982)

Shiman, Lilian Lewis, *Women and Leadership in Nineteenth-Century England* (New York: St. Martin's Press, 1992)

Shorter, Edward, "Women's Work: What Difference Did Capitalism Make?" *Theory and Society* 3 (1976), 513–27

Simonton, Deborah, "Apprenticeship: Training and Gender in Eighteenth-Century England," in Maxine Berg, ed., *Markets and Manufactures in Early Industrial Europe* (London: Routledge, 1991)

A History of European Women's Work: 1700 to the Present (London: Routledge, 1998)

Smith, F. B., *The People's Health, 1830–1910* (New York: Holmes and Meier, 1979)

Smith, James, and Ward, Michael, "Time-Series Growth in the Female Labor Force," *Journal of Labor Economics* 3 (1985), S59–S90

Smith, Maurice G., "Robert Clough, Grove Mill, Keighley: A Study in Technological Redundancy, 1835–65," MA thesis, University of Leeds, 1982

Snell, K. D. M., *Annals of the Labouring Poor: Social Change and Agrarian England, 1660–1900* (Cambridge: Cambridge University Press, 1985)

Sokoloff, Kenneth, "Productivity Growth in Manufacturing during Early Industrialization: Evidence from the American Northeast, 1820–1860," in Stanley Engerman and Robert Gallman, eds., *Long-Term Factors in American Economic Growth* (Chicago: University of Chicago Press, 1986)

Souden, David, "Migrants and the Population Structure of Later Seventeenth-Century Provincial Cities and Market Towns," in Peter Clark, ed., *The Transformation of English Provincial Towns, 1600–1800* (London: Hutchinson, 1984)

Speechley, Helen, "Female and Child Agricultural Day Labourers in Somerset, c. 1685–1870," unpublished PhD thesis, University of Exeter, 1999

Spenceley, G. F. R., "The English Pillow Lace Industry 1840–80: A Rural Industry in Competition with Machinery," *Business History* 19 (1977), 68–87

Tawney, R. H., "The Assessment of Wages in England by the Justices of the Peace," reprinted in W. E. Minchinton, ed., *Wage Regulation in Pre-Industrial England* (Newton Abbot: David and Charles, 1972)

Taylor, A. J., " 'The Miners' Association of Great Britain and Ireland, 1842–48: A Study in the Problem of Integration," *Economica* 22 (1955), 45–60

Taylor, Barbara, *Eve and the New Jerusalem: Socialism and Feminism in the Nineteenth Century* (New York: Pantheon Books, 1983)

Thale, Mary, ed., *The Autobiography of Francis Place* (Cambridge: Cambridge University Press, 1972)

Thomas, Janet, "Women and Capitalism: Oppression or Emancipation? A Review Article," *Comparative Studies in Society and History* 30 (1988), 534–49

Thompson, E. P., *The Making of the English Working Class* (New York: Vintage Books, 1966)

Todd, Barbara, "The Remarrying Widow: A Stereotype Reconsidered," in Mary Prior, ed., *Women in English Society, 1500–1800* (London: Methuen, 1985)

Toman, J. T., "The Gang System and Comparative Advantage," *Explorations in Economic History* 42 (2005), 310–23

Tropp, Asher, *The School Teachers: The Growth of the Teaching Profession in England and Wales from 1800 to the Present Day* (London: William Heinemann, 1957)

Turner, Raymond, "English Coal Industry in the Seventeenth and Eighteenth Centuries," *American Historical Review* 27 (1921), 1–23

Ulrich, Laurel Thatcher, "Wheels, Looms and the Gender Division of Labor in Eighteenth-Century New England," *William and Mary Quarterly* 55 (1998), 3–38

Valenze, Deborah, *Prophetic Sons and Daughters: Female Preaching and Popular Religion in Industrial England* (Princeton: Princeton University Press, 1985)

"The Art of Women and the Business of Men: Women's Work and the Dairy Industry, c 1740–1840," *Past and Present* 139 (1991), 142–69

The First Industrial Woman (Oxford: Oxford University Press, 1995)

Veblen, Thorstein, *The Theory of the Leisure Class* (Boston: Houghton Mifflin [1899] 1973)

Verdon, Nicola, *Rural Women Workers in Nineteenth-Century England: Gender, Work and Wages* (Woodbridge: Boydell Press, 2002)

"The Rural Labour Market in the Early Nineteenth Century: Women's and Children's Employment, Family Income, and the 1834 Poor Law Report," *Economic History Review* 55 (2002), 299–323

" ' ... subjects deserving of the highest praise': Farmers' Wives and the Farm Economy in England, c. 1700–1850," *Agricultural History Review* 51 (2003), 23–39

Vickery, Amanda, "Golden Age to Separate Spheres? A Review of the Categories and Chronology of English Women's History," *Historical Journal* 36 (1993), 383–414

Vogel, James and Friedl, Karl, "Army Data: Body Composition and Physical Capacity," in Bernadette Marriot and Judith Grumstrup-Scott, eds., *Body Composition and Physical Performance* (Washington, DC: National Academy Press, 1992)

Waldfogel, Jane, "The Price of Motherhood: Family Status and Women's Pay in a Young British Cohort," *Oxford Economic Papers* 47 (1995), 584–610

"Understanding the 'Family Gap' in Pay for Women with Children," *Journal of Economic Perspectives* 12 (1998), 137–56

Walker, Andrew, "'Pleasurable Homes'? Victorian Model Miners" Wives and the Family Wage in a South Yorkshire Colliery District," *Women's History Review* 6 (1997), 317–36

Webb, Sidney, "The Alleged Differences in the Wages Paid to Men and to Women for Similar Work," *Economic Journal* 1 (1891), 635–62

Webb, Sidney and Webb, Beatrice, *The History of Trade Unionism* (London: Longmans, Green, & Co., 1894)

Welch, Finis and Cunningham, James, "Effects of Minimum Wages on the Level and Age Composition of Youth Employment," *Review of Economics and Statistics* 60 (1978), 140–5

Wells, Roger, "Tolpuddle in the Context of English Agrarian Labour History," in John Rule, ed., *British Trade Unionism, 1750–1850: The Formative Years* (New York: Longman, 1988)

Wiesner, Merry, *Women and Gender in Early Modern Europe*, 2nd edn (Cambridge: Cambridge University Press, 2000)

Williams, Samantha, "Caring for the Sick Poor: Poor Law Nurses in Bedfordshire, c. 1700–1834," in P. Lane, N. Raven, and K. D. M. Snell, eds., *Women, Work and Wages in England, 1600–1850* (Woodbridge: Boydell Press, 2004)

Williamson, Jeffrey, "Did English Factor Markets Fail during the Industrial Revolution?" *Oxford Economic Papers* 3 (1987), 641–78

Wood, George Henry, *The History of Wages in the Cotton Trade during the Past Hundred Years* (London: Sherratt and Hughes, 1910)

Woodward, Donald, "The Determination of Wage Rates in the Early Modern North of England," *Economic History Review* 47 (1994), 22–43

Wright, Sue, "'Churmaids, Huswyfes and Hucksters': The Employment of Women in Tudor and Stuart Salisbury," in Lindsay Charles and Lorna Duffin, eds., *Women and Work in Pre-Industrial England* (London: Croom Helm, 1985)

Wrigley, E. A., *People, Cities, and Wealth* (Oxford: Blackwell, 1987)

Wrigley, E. A. and Schofield, R. S., *The Population History of England, 1541–1871* (Cambridge: Cambridge University Press, 1981)

Wyman, A. L., "The Surgeoness: The Female Practitioner of Surgery 1400–1800," *Medical History* 28 (1984), 22–41

Index

Lightning Source UK Ltd.
Milton Keynes UK
UKOW031538030312

188309UK00001B/110/P